Health 11/12

Thirty-Second Edition

EDITOR

Eileen L. Daniel
SUNY at Brockport

Eileen Daniel, a registered dietitian and licensed nutritionist, is a Professor in the Department of Health Science and Associate Vice Provost for Academic Affairs at the State University of New York at Brockport. She received a BS in Nutrition and Dietetics from the Rochester Institute of Technology in 1977, an MS in Community Health Education from SUNY at Brockport in 1987, and a PhD in Health Education from the University of Oregon in 1986. A member of the American Dietetics Association and other professional and community organizations, Dr. Daniel has published more than 40 journal articles on issues of health, nutrition, and health education. She is also the editor of *Taking Sides: Clashing Views on Controversial Issues in Health and Society,* ninth edition (McGraw-Hill/Contemporary Learning Series, 2010).

ANNUAL EDITIONS: HEALTH, THIRTY-SECOND EDITION

Published by McGraw-Hill, a business unit of The McGraw-Hill Companies, Inc., 1221 Avenue
of the Americas, New York, NY 10020. Copyright © 2011 by The McGraw-Hill Companies, Inc.
All rights reserved. Previous editions © 2010, 2009, and 2008. No part of this publication may be
reproduced or distributed in any form or by any means, or stored in a database or retrieval system,
without the prior written consent of The McGraw-Hill Companies, Inc., including, but not limited
to, in any network or other electronic storage or transmission, or broadcast for distance learning.

Some ancillaries, including electronic and print components, may not be available to customers
outside the United States.

Annual Editions® is a registered trademark of The McGraw-Hill Companies, Inc.

Annual Editions is published by the **Contemporary Learning Series** group within the
McGraw-Hill Higher Education division.

1 2 3 4 5 6 7 8 9 0 QDB/QDB 1 0 9 8 7 6 5 4 3 2 1 0

ISBN 978–0–07–805080–0
MHID 0–07–805080–4
ISSN 0278–4653

Managing Editor: *Larry Loeppke*
Developmental Editor II: *Debra A. Henricks*
Permissions Coordinator: *DeAnna Dausener*
Marketing Specialist: *Alice Link*
Project Manager: *Robin A. Reed*
Design Coordinator: *Margarite Reynolds*
Buyer: *Laura Fuller*
Media Project Manager: *Sridevi Palani*

Compositor: Laserwords Private Limited
Cover Images: © Brand X/Getty Images (inset); Nancy R. Cohen/Getty Images (background)

Library in Congress Cataloging-in-Publication Data
Main entry under title: Annual Editions: Health. 2011/2012.
  1. Health—Periodicals. I. Daniel, Eileen L., *comp.* II. Title: Health.
658'.05

www.mhhe.com

Editors/Academic Advisory Board

Members of the Academic Advisory Board are instrumental in the final selection of articles for each edition of ANNUAL EDITIONS. Their review of articles for content, level, and appropriateness provides critical direction to the editors and staff. We think that you will find their careful consideration well reflected in this volume.

ANNUAL EDITIONS: Health 11/12
32nd Edition

EDITOR

Eileen L. Daniel
SUNY at Brockport

Preface

In publishing ANNUAL EDITIONS we recognize the enormous role played by the magazines, newspapers, and journals of the public press in providing current, first-rate educational information in a broad spectrum of interest areas. Many of these articles are appropriate for students, researchers, and professionals seeking accurate, current material to help bridge the gap between principles and theories and the real world. These articles, however, become more useful for study when those of lasting value are carefully collected, organized, indexed, and reproduced in a low-cost format, which provides easy and permanent access when the material is needed. That is the role played by ANNUAL EDITIONS.

America is in the midst of a revolution that is changing the way millions of Americans view their health. Traditionally, most people delegated responsibility for their health to their physicians and hoped that medical science would be able to cure whatever ailed them. This approach to health care emphasized the role of medical technology and funneled billions of dollars into medical research. The net result of all this spending is the most technically advanced and expensive health care system in the world. In an attempt to rein in health care costs, the health care delivery system moved from privatized health care coverage to what is termed "managed care." While managed care has turned the tide regarding the rising cost of health care, it has done so by limiting reimbursement for many cutting edge technologies. Unfortunately, many people also feel that it has lowered the overall quality of care that is being given. Perhaps the saving grace is that we live at a time in which chronic illnesses rather than acute illnesses are our number one health threat, and many of these illnesses can be prevented or controlled by our lifestyle choices. The net result of these changes has prompted millions of individuals to assume more personal responsibility for safeguarding their own health. Evidence of this change in attitude can be seen in the growing interest in nutrition, physical fitness, dietary supplements, and stress management.

If we as a nation are to capitalize on this new health consciousness, we must devote more time and energy to educate Americans in the health sciences, so that they will be better able to make informed choices about their health. Health is a complex and dynamic subject, and it is practically impossible for anyone to stay abreast of all the current research findings. In the past, most of us have relied on books, newspapers, magazines, and television as our primary sources for medical/health information, but today, with the widespread use of personal computers connected to the World Wide Web, it is possible to access a vast amount of health information, any time of the day, without even leaving one's home. Unfortunately, quantity and availability does not necessarily translate into quality, and this is particularly true in the area of medical/ health information. Just as the Internet is a great source for reliable and timely information, it is also a vehicle for the dissemination of misleading and fraudulent information. Currently there are no standards or regulations regarding the posting of health content on the Internet, and this has led to a plethora of misinformation and quackery in the medical/health arena. Given this vast amount of health information, our task as health educators is twofold: (1) To provide our students with the most up-to-date and accurate information available on major health issues of our time and (2) to teach our students the skills that will enable them to sort out facts from fiction, in order to become informed consumers. *Annual Editions: Health 11/12* was designed to aid in this task. It offers a sampling of quality articles that represent the latest thinking on a variety of health issues, and it also serves as a tool for developing critical thinking skills.

The articles in this volume were carefully chosen on the basis of their quality and timeliness. Because this book is revised and updated annually, it contains information that is not generally available in any standard textbook. As such, it serves as a valuable resource for both teachers and students. This edition of *Annual Editions: Health* has been updated to reflect the latest thinking on a variety of contemporary health issues. We hope that you find this edition to be a helpful learning tool with a user-friendly presentation. The 10 topical areas presented in this edition mirror those that are normally covered in introductory health courses: Promoting Healthy Behavior Change, Stress and Mental Health, Nutritional Health, Exercise and Weight Management, Drugs and Health, Sexuality and Relationships, Preventing and Fighting Disease, Health Care and the Health Care System, Consumer Health, and Contemporary Health Hazards. Because of the interdependence of the various elements that constitute health, the articles selected were written by authors with diverse educational backgrounds and expertise including: naturalists, environmentalists, psychologists, economists, sociologists, nutritionists, consumer advocates, and traditional health practitioners.

Annual Editions: Health 11/12 was designed to be one of the most useful and up-to-date publications currently available in the area of health. Please let us know what you think of it by filling out and returning the postage paid *Article Rating Form* on the last page of this book. Any anthology can be improved. This one will be—annually.

Eileen L. Daniel
Editor

Contents

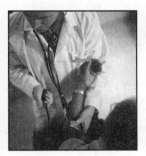

UNIT 1
Promoting Healthy Behavior Change

UNIT 2
Stress and Mental Health

The concepts in bold italics are developed in the article. For further expansion, please refer to the Topic Guide.

UNIT 3
Nutritional Health

The concepts in bold italics are developed in the article. For further expansion, please refer to the Topic Guide.

UNIT 4
Exercise and Weight Management

UNIT 5
Drugs and Health

The concepts in bold italics are developed in the article. For further expansion, please refer to the Topic Guide.

UNIT 6
Sexuality and Relationships

The concepts in bold italics are developed in the article. For further expansion, please refer to the Topic Guide.

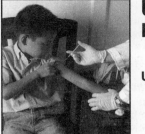

UNIT 7
Preventing and Fighting Disease

UNIT 8
Health Care and the Health Care System

The concepts in bold italics are developed in the article. For further expansion, please refer to the Topic Guide.

UNIT 9
Consumer Health

The concepts in bold italics are developed in the article. For further expansion, please refer to the Topic Guide.

UNIT 10
Contemporary Health Hazards

The concepts in bold italics are developed in the article. For further expansion, please refer to the Topic Guide.

The concepts in bold italics are developed in the article. For further expansion, please refer to the Topic Guide.

Correlation Guide

The *Annual Editions* series provides students with convenient, inexpensive access to current, carefully selected articles from the public press. **Annual Editions: Health 11/12** is an easy-to-use reader that presents articles on important topics such as *consumer health, exercise, nutrition,* and many more. For more information on *Annual Editions* and other *McGraw-Hill Contemporary Learning Series* titles, visit www.mhhe.com/cls.

This convenient guide matches the units in **Annual Editions: Health 11/12** with the corresponding chapters in two of our best-selling McGraw-Hill Health textbooks by Hahn et al. and Payne et al.

Annual Editions: Health 11/12	**Focus on Health, 10/e by Hahn et al.**	**Understanding Your Health, 11/e by Payne et al.**
Unit 1: Promoting Healthy Behavior Change	**Chapter 1:** Shaping Your Health	**Chapter 1:** Shaping Your Health
Unit 2: Stress and Mental Health	**Chapter 2:** Achieving Psychological Health **Chapter 3:** Managing Stress	**Chapter 2:** Achieving Psychological Health **Chapter 3:** Managing Stress
Unit 3: Nutritional Health	**Chapter 5:** Understanding Nutrition and Your Diet	**Chapter 5:** Understanding Nutrition and Your Diet
Unit 4: Exercise and Weight Management	**Chapter 4:** Becoming Physically Fit **Chapter 6:** Maintaining a Healthy Weight	**Chapter 4:** Becoming Physically Fit **Chapter 6:** Maintaining a Healthy Weight
Unit 5: Drugs and Health	**Chapter 7:** Making Decisions about Drug and Alcohol Use **Chapter 8:** Rejecting Tobacco Use	**Chapter 7:** Making Decisions about Drug Use **Chapter 8:** Taking Control of Alcohol Use **Chapter 9:** Rejecting Tobacco Use
Unit 6: Sexuality and Relationships	**Chapter 12:** Understanding Sexuality **Chapter 13:** Managing Your Fertility	**Chapter 14:** Exploring the Origins of Sexuality **Chapter 15:** Understanding Sexual Behavior and Relationships **Chapter 16:** Managing Your Fertility **Chapter 17:** Becoming a Parent
Unit 7: Preventing and Fighting Disease	**Chapter 9:** Reducing Your Risk of Cardiovascular Disease **Chapter 10:** Living with Cancer and Chronic Conditions **Chapter 11:** Preventing Infectious Diseases	**Chapter 10:** Enhancing Your Cardiovascular Health **Chapter 11:** Living with Cancer **Chapter 12:** Managing Chronic Conditions **Chapter 13:** Preventing Infectious Diseases
Unit 8: Health Care and the Health Care System	**Chapter 14:** Becoming an Informed Health Care Consumer	**Chapter 18:** Becoming an Informed Health Care Consumer
Unit 9: Consumer Health	**Chapter 15:** Protecting Your Safety	**Chapter 19:** Protecting Your Safety
Unit 10: Contemporary Health Hazards	**Chapter 16:** The Environment and Your Health	**Chapter 20:** The Environment and Your Health

Topic Guide

This topic guide suggests how the selections in this book relate to the subjects covered in your course. You may want to use the topics listed on these pages to search the web more easily.

On the following pages a number of websites have been gathered specifically for this book. They are arranged to reflect the units of this Annual Editions reader. You can link to these sites by going to www.mhhe.com/cls

All the articles that relate to each topic are listed below the bold-faced term.

Internet References

The following Internet sites have been selected to support the articles found in this reader. These sites were available at the time of publication. However, because websites often change their structure and content, the information listed may no longer be available. We invite you to visit www.mhhe.com/cls for easy access to these sites.

Annual Editions: Health 11/12

General Sources

National Institute on Aging (NIA)
www.nia.nih.gov

The NIA, one of the institutes of the U.S. National Institutes of Health, presents this home page to lead you to a variety of resources on health and lifestyle issues on aging.

U.S. Department of Agriculture (USDA)/Food and Nutrition Information Center (FNIC)
www.nal.usda.gov/fnic

Use this site to find nutrition information provided by various USDA agencies, to find links to food and nutrition resources on the Internet, and to access FNIC publications and databases.

U.S. Department of Health and Human Services
www.os.dhhs.gov

This site has extensive links to information on such topics as the health benefits of exercise, weight control, and prudent lifestyle choices.

U.S. National Institutes of Health (NIH)
www.nih.gov

Consult this site for links to extensive health information and scientific resources. Comprising 24 separate institutes, centers, and divisions, the NIH is one of eight health agencies of the Public Health Service, which, in turn, is part of the U.S. Department of Health and Human Services.

U.S. National Library of Medicine
www.nlm.nih.gov

This huge site permits a search of a number of databases and electronic information sources such as MEDLINE. You can learn about research projects and programs and peruse the national network of medical libraries here.

World Health Organization
www.who.int/en

This home page of the World Health Organization will provide links to a wealth of statistical and analytical information about health around the world.

UNIT 1: Promoting Healthy Behavior Change

Columbia University's Go Ask Alice!
www.goaskalice.columbia.edu/index.html

This interactive site provides discussion and insight into a number of personal issues of interest to college-age people and often those younger and older. Many questions about physical and emotional health and well-being are answered.

The Society of Behavioral Medicine
www.sbm.org

This site provides listings of major, general health institutes and organizations as well as discipline-specific links and resources in medicine, psychology, and public health.

UNIT 2: Stress and Mental Health

The American Institute of Stress
www.stress.org

This site provides comprehensive information on stress: its dangers, the beliefs that build helpful techniques for overcoming stress, and so on. This easy-to-navigate site has good links to information on anxiety and related topics.

National Mental Health Association (NMHA)
www.nmha.org/index.html

The NMHA is a citizen volunteer advocacy organization that works to improve the mental health of all individuals. The site provides access to guidelines that individuals can use to reduce stress and improve their lives in small, yet tangible, ways.

Self-Help Magazine
www.selfhelpmagazine.com/index.html

Reach lots of links to self-help resources on the Net at this site, including resources on stress, anxiety, fears, and more.

UNIT 3: Nutritional Health

The American Dietetic Association
www.eatright.org

This organization, along with its National Center of Nutrition and Dietetics, promotes optimal nutrition, health, and well-being. This easy-to-navigate site presents FAQs about nutrition and dieting, nutrition resources, and career and member information.

Center for Science in the Public Interest (CSPI)
www.cspinet.org

CSPI is a nonprofit education and advocacy organization that focuses on improving the safety and nutritional quality of our food supply and on reducing the health problems caused by alcohol. This agency also evaluates the nutritional composition of fast foods, movie popcorn, and chain restaurants. There are also good links to related sites.

Food and Nutrition Information Center
www.nalusda.gov/fnic/index.html

This is an official Agriculture Network Information Center website. The FNIC is one of several information centers at the National Agriculture Library, the Agricultural Research Service, and the U.S. Department of Agriculture. The website has information on nutrition-related publications, an index of food and nutrition related Internet resources, and an online catalog of materials.

UNIT 4: Exercise and Weight Management

American Society of Exercise Physiologists (ASEP)
www.asep.org

The ASEP is devoted to promoting people's health and physical fitness. This extensive site provides links to publications related to exercise and career opportunities in exercise physiology.

Internet References

Cyberdiet
www.cyberdiet.com

This site, maintained by a registered dietician, offers Cyberdiet's interactive nutritional profile, food facts, menus and meal plans, and exercise and food-related sites.

Shape Up America!
www.shapeup.org

At the Shape Up America! website you will find the latest information about safe weight management, healthy eating, and physical fitness.

UNIT 5: Drugs and Health

Food and Drug Administration (FDA)
www.fda.gov

This site includes FDA news, information on drugs, and drug toxicology facts.

National Institute on Drug Abuse (NIDA)
www.nida.nih.gov

Use this site index for access to NIDA publications and communications, information on drugs of abuse, and links to other related websites.

UNIT 6: Sexuality and Relationships

Planned Parenthood
www.plannedparenthood.org

This home page provides links to information on contraceptives (including outercourse and abstinence) and to discussions of other topics related to sexual health.

Sexuality Information and Education Council of the United States (SIECUS)
www.siecus.org

SIECUS is a nonprofit, private advocacy group that affirms that sexuality is a natural and healthy part of living. This home page offers publications, what's new, descriptions of programs, and a listing of international sexuality education initiatives.

UNIT 7: Preventing and Fighting Disease

American Cancer Society
www.cancer.org

Open this site and its various links to learn the concerns and lifestyle advice of the American Cancer Society. It provides information on tobacco and alternative cancer therapies.

American Diabetes Association Home Page
www.diabetes.org

This site offers information on diabetes including treatment, diet, and insulin therapy.

American Heart Association
www.amhrt.org

This award-winning, comprehensive site of the American Heart Association offers information on heart disease, prevention, patient facts, eating plans, what's new, nutrition, smoking cessation, and FAQs.

National Institute of Allergy and Infectious Diseases (NIAID)
www3.niaid.nih.gov

Open this site and its various links to learn the concerns and lifestyle advice of the National Institute of Allergy and Infectious Diseases.

UNIT 8: Health Care and the Health Care System

American Medical Association (AMA)
www.ama-assn.org

The AMA offers this site to find up-to-date medical information, peer-review resources, discussions of such topics as HIV/AIDS and women's health, examination of issues related to managed care, and important publications.

MedScape: The Online Resource for Better Patient Care
www.medscape.com

For health professionals and interested consumers, this site offers peer-reviewed articles, self-assessment features, medical news, and annotated links to Internet resources. It also contains the Morbidity & Mortality Weekly Report, which is a publication of the Centers for Disease Control and Prevention.

UNIT 9: Consumer Health

FDA Consumer Magazine
www.fda.gov/fdac

This site offers articles and information that appears in the FDA Consumer Magazine.

Global Vaccine Awareness League
www.gval.com

This site addresses side effects related to vaccination. Its many links are geared to provide copious information.

National Sleep Foundation
www.sleepfoundation.org

The goal of this site is to improve public health and safety through an understanding of sleep and sleep disorders, and through the support of sleep-related education, research, and advocacy.

UNIT 10: Contemporary Health Hazards

Centers for Disease Control: Flu
www.cdc.gov/flu

This CDC site provides updates, information, key facts, questions and answers, and ways to prevent influenza (the flu). Updated regularly during the flu season.

Environmental Protection Agency
www.epa.gov

Use this site to find environmental health information provided by various EPA agencies.

World Health Organization
www.who.org

This site offers information on health issues throughout the world. For data specific to Haiti, click www.who.int/countries/hti/en

UNIT 1

Promoting Healthy Behavior Change

Unit Selections

1. **Are Bad Times Healthy?,** Tara Parker-Pope
2. **The Perils of Higher Education,** Steven Kotler
3. **Mars vs. Venus: The Gender Gap in Health,** *Harvard Men's Health Watch*
4. **Carrots, Sticks, and Health Care Reform—Problems with Wellness Incentives,** Harald Schmidt, Kristin Voigt, and Daniel Wikler

Learning Outcomes

After reading this unit, you should be able to:

- Explain why many people practice healthier behaviors during economic downturns.

- Describe why people continue to engage in behaviors that negatively affect their health even when they know about the ill effects these behaviors have on their well-being.

- Discuss the negative health behaviors practiced by many college students.

- Explain how the negative behaviors practiced by college students contribute to academic difficulties.

- Explain why there is a gender gap in health behaviors.

- Describe the relationship between health care reform and positive health behaviors.

- Describe the factors that contribute to a successful lifestyle change.

Student Website

www.mhhe.com/cls

Internet References

Columbia University's Go Ask Alice!
www.goaskalice.columbia.edu/index.html
The Society of Behavioral Medicine
www.sbm.org

"**T**hose of us who protect our health daily and those of us who put our health in constant jeopardy have exactly the same mortality: 100 percent. The difference, of course, is the timing." This quotation from Elizabeth M. Whelan, ScD, MPH, reminds us that we must all face the fact that we are going to die sometime. The question that is decided by our behavior is when and, to a certain extent, how. This book, and especially this unit, is designed to assist students to develop the cognitive skills and knowledge that, when put to use, help make the moment of our death come as late as possible in our lives, and to maintain our health as long as possible. While we cannot control many of the things that happen to us, we must all strive to accept personal responsibility for, and make informed decisions about, things that we can control. This is no minor task, but it is one in which the potential reward is life itself. Perhaps the best way to start this process is by educating ourselves on the relative risks associated with the various behaviors and lifestyle choices we make. To minimize all the risks to life and health would be to significantly limit the quality of our lives, and while this might be a choice that some would make, it certainly is not the goal of health education. A more logical approach to risk reduction would be to educate the public on the relative risks associated with various behaviors and lifestyle choices so that they are capable of making informed decisions. While it may seem obvious that certain behaviors, such as smoking, entail a high level of risk, the significance of others such as toxic waste sites and food additives are frequently blown out of proportion to the actual risks involved. The net result of this type of distortion is that many Americans tend to minimize the dangers of known hazards such as tobacco and alcohol and focus attention instead on potentially minor health hazards over which they have little or no control.

Educating the public on the relative risk of various health behaviors is only part of the job that health educators must tackle in order to assist individuals in making informed choices regarding their health. They must also teach the skills that will enable people to evaluate the validity and significance of new information as it becomes available. Just how important informed decision making is in our daily lives is evidenced by the numerous health-related media announcements and articles that fill our newspapers, magazines, and television broadcasts. Rather than informing and enlightening the public on significant new medical discoveries, many of these announcements do little more than add to the level of confusion or exaggerate or sensationalize health issues.

Let's assume for a minute that the scientific community is in general agreement that certain behaviors clearly promote our health while others damage our health. Given this information, are you likely to make adjustments to your lifestyle to comply with the findings? Logic would suggest that of course you would, but experience has taught us that information alone isn't enough to bring about behavioral change in many people. Why is it that so many people continue to make bad choices regarding their health behaviors when they are fully aware of the risks involved? And why do women take better care of themselves than men?

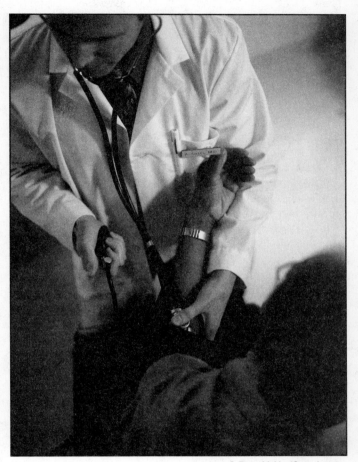

© Ryan McVay/Getty Images

In "Mars vs. Venus: The Gender Gap in Health," the authors discuss health behaviors such as alcohol, substance abuse, and lack of consistent health care among men, which contributes to men getting sick younger and dying faster than women. Another article addressing health behaviors explains why people tend to take better care of themselves during hard economic times. See "Are Bad Times Healthy?" by Tara Parker-Pope.

We can take vows to try and undo or minimize the negative health behaviors of our past. However, while strategies such as these may work for those who feel they are at risk, how do we help those who do not feel that they are at risk, or those who feel that it is too late in their lives for the changes to matter? In "The Perils of Higher Education," Steven Kotler maintains that while college is a place to learn and grow, for many students it becomes four years of bad diet, too little sleep, and too much alcohol. These negative health behaviors affect not only the students' health, but their grades too. "Carrots, Sticks, and Health Care Reform—Problems with Wellness Incentives" addresses the issue of using incentives to influence positive health behaviors.

Are Bad Times Healthy?

Tara Parker-Pope

M ost people are worried about the health of the economy. But does the economy also affect your health?

It does, but not always in ways you might expect. The data on how an economic downturn influences an individual's health are surprisingly mixed.

It's clear that long-term economic gains lead to improvements in a population's overall health, in developing and industrialized societies alike.

But whether the current economic slump will take a toll on your own health depends, in part, on your health habits when times are good. And economic studies suggest that people tend not to take care of themselves in boom times—drinking too much (especially before driving), dining on fat-laden restaurant meals and skipping exercise and doctors' appointments because of work-related time commitments.

"The value of time is higher during good economic times," said Grant Miller, an assistant professor of medicine at Stanford. "So people work more and do less of the things that are good for them, like cooking at home and exercising; and people experience more stress due to the rigors of hard work during booms."

1936 In hard times, as in the Great Depression, laborers have more time to care for their children.

Similar patterns have been seen in some developing nations. Dr. Miller, who is studying the effects of fluctuating coffee prices on health in Colombia, says that even though falling prices are bad for the economy, they appear to improve health and mortality rates. When prices are low, laborers have more time to care for their children.

"When coffee prices suddenly rise, people work harder on their coffee plots and spend less time doing things around the home, including things that are good for their children," he said. "Because the things that matter most for infant and child health in rural Colombia aren't expensive, but require a substantial amount of time—such as breast-feeding, bringing clean water from far away, taking your child to a distant health clinic for free vaccinations—infant and child mortality rates rise."

In this country, a similar effect appeared in the Dust Bowl during the Great Depression, according to a 2007 paper by Dr. Miller

and colleagues in The Proceedings of the National Academy of Sciences.

The data seem to contradict research in the 1970s suggesting that in hard times there are more deaths from heart disease, cirrhosis, suicide and homicide, as well as more admissions to mental hospitals. But those findings have not been replicated, and several economists have pointed out flaws in the research.

In May 2000, the *Quarterly Journal of Economics* published a surprising paper called "Are Recessions Good for Your Health?" by Christopher J. Ruhm, professor of economics at the University of North Carolina, Greensboro, based on an analysis measuring death rates and health behavior against economic shifts and jobless rates from 1972 to 1991.

Dr. Ruhm found that death rates declined sharply in the 1974 and 1982 recessions, and increased in the economic recovery of the 1980s. An increase of one percentage point in state unemployment rates correlated with a 0.5 percentage point decline in the death rate—or about 5 fewer deaths per 100,000 people. Over all, the death rate fell by more than 8 percent in the 20-year period of mostly economic decline, led by drops in heart disease and car crashes.

The economic downturn did appear to take a toll on factors having less to do with prevention and more to do with mental well-being and access to health care. For instance, cancer deaths rose 23 percent, and deaths from flu and pneumonia increased slightly. Suicides rose 2 percent, homicides 12 percent.

The issue that may matter most in an economic crisis is not related to jobs or income, but whether the slump widens the gap between rich and poor, and whether there is an adequate health safety net available to those who have lost their jobs and insurance.

1999 In Japan, people who lost jobs and insurance were likely to be in poorer health than those who didn't.

During a decade of economic recession in Japan that began in the 1990s, people who were unemployed were twice as likely to be in poor health than those with secure jobs. During Peru's severe economic crisis in the 1980s, infant mortality jumped 2.5 percentage points—about 17,000 more children died as public health spending and social programs collapsed.

In August, researchers from the Free University of Amsterdam looked at health studies of twins in Denmark. They found that individuals born in a recession were at higher risk for heart problems later in life and lived, on average, 15 months less than those born under better conditions.

Gerard J. van den Berg, an economics professor who was a co-author of the study, said babies in poor households suffered the most in a recession, because their families lacked access to good health care. Poor economic conditions can also cause stress that may interfere with parent bonding and childhood development, he said.

He noted that other studies had found that recessions can benefit babies by giving their parents more time at home.

"This scenario may be relevant for well-to-do families where one of the parents loses a job and the other still brings in enough money," he said. "But in a crisis where the family may have to incur huge housing-cost losses and the household income is insufficient for adequate nutrition and health care, the adverse effects of being born in a recession seem much more relevant."

2008 The rising cost of prepared foods in the United States is forcing people to cook from scratch.

In this country, there are already signs of the economy's effect on health. In May, the market research firm Information Resources reported that 53 percent of consumers said they were cooking from scratch more than they did just six months before—in part, no doubt, because of the rising cost of prepared foods. At the same time, health insurance costs are rising. With premiums and co-payments, the average employee with insurance pays nearly one-third of medical costs—about twice as much as four years ago, according to Paul H. Keckley, executive director of the Deloitte Center for Health Solutions.

In the United States, which unlike other industrialized nations lacks a national health plan, the looming recession may take a greater toll. About 46 million Americans lack health insurance, Dr. Keckley says, and even among the 179 million who have it, an estimated 1 in 7 would be bankrupted by a single health crisis.

The economic downturn "is not good news for the health care industry," he said. "There may be slivers of positive, but I view this as sobering."

Assess Your Progress

1. What motivates people to engage in healthy behaviors?
2. Why does a poor economy contribute to better health practices?

The Perils of Higher Education

Can't remember the difference between declensions and derivatives? Blame college. The undergrad life is a blast, but it may lead you to forget everything you learn.

Steven Kotler

We go to college to learn, to soak up a dazzling array of information intended to prepare us for adult life. But college is not simply a data dump; it is also the end of parental supervision. For many students, that translates into four years of late nights, pizza banquets and boozy week ends that start on Wednesday. And while we know that bad habits are detrimental to cognition in general—think drunk driving—new studies show that the undergrad urges to eat, drink and be merry have devastating effects on learning and memory. It turns out that the exact place we go to get an education may in fact be one of the worst possible environments in which to retain anything we've learned.

Dude, I Haven't Slept in Three Days!

Normal human beings spend one-third of their lives asleep, but today's college students aren't normal. A recent survey of undergraduates and medical students at Stanford University found 80 percent of them qualified as sleep-deprived, and a poll taken by the National Sleep Foundation found that most young adults get only 6.8 hours a night.

All-night cramfests may seem to be the only option when the end of the semester looms, but in fact getting sleep—and a full dose of it—might be a better way to ace exams. Sleep is crucial to declarative memory, the hard, factual kind that helps us remember which year World War I began, or what room the French Lit class is in. It's also essential for procedural memory, the "know-how" memory we use when learning to drive a car or write a five-paragraph essay. "Practice makes perfect," says Harvard Medical School psychologist Matt Walker, "but having a night's rest after practicing might make you even better."

Walker taught 100 people to bang out a series of nonsense sequences on a keyboard—a standard procedural memory task. When asked to replay the sequence 12 hours later, they hadn't improved. But when one group of subjects was allowed to sleep overnight before being retested, their speed and accuracy improved by 20 to 30 percent. "It was bizarre," says Walker. "We were seeing people's skills improve just by sleeping."

For procedural memory, the deep slow-wave stages of sleep were the most important for improvement—particularly during the last two hours of the night. Declarative memory, by contrast, gets processed during the slow-wave stages that come in the first two hours of sleep. "This means that memory requires a full eight hours of sleep," says Walker. He also found that if someone goes without sleep for 24 hours after acquiring a new skill, a week later they will have lost it completely. So college students who pull all-nighters during exam week might do fine on their tests but may not remember any of the material by next semester.

Walker believes that the common practice of back-loading semesters with a blizzard of papers and exams needs a rethink. "Educators are just encouraging sleeplessness," says Walker. "This is just not an effective way to force information into the brain."

Who's up for Pizza?

Walk into any college cafeteria and you'll find a smorgasbord of French fries, greasy pizza, burgers, potato chips and the like. On top of that, McDonald's, Burger King, Wendy's and other fast-food chains have been gobbling up campus real estate in recent years. With hectic schedules and skinny budgets, students find fast food an easy alternative. A recent Tufts University survey found that 50 percent of students eat too much fat, and 70 to 80 percent eat too much saturated fat.

But students who fuel their studies with fast food have something more serious than the "freshman 15" to worry about: They may literally be eating themselves stupid. Researchers have known since the late 1980s that bad eating habits contribute to the kind of cognitive decline found in diseases like Alzheimer's. Since then, they've been trying to find out exactly how a bad diet might be hard on the brain. Ann-Charlotte Granholm, director of the Center for Aging at the Medical University of South Carolina, has recently focused on trans fat, widely used in fast-food cooking because it extends the shelf life of foods. Trans fat is made by bubbling hydrogen through unsaturated fat, with copper or zinc added to speed the chemical reaction along. These metals are frequently found in the brains of people with Alzheimer's, which sparked Granholm's concern.

To investigate, she fed one group of rats a diet high in trans fat and compared them with another group fed a diet that was just as greasy but low in trans fat. Six weeks later, she tested the animals in a water maze, the rodent equivalent of a final exam in organic chemistry. "The trans-fat group made many more errors," says Granholm, especially when she used more difficult mazes.

When she examined the rats' brains, she found that trans-fat eaters had fewer proteins critical to healthy neurological function. She also saw inflammation in and around the hippocampus, the part of the brain responsible for learning and memory. "It was alarming," says Granholm. "These are the exact types of changes we normally see at the onset of Alzheimer's, but we saw them after six weeks," even though the rats were still young.

Students who fuel their studies with fast food have something serious to worry about: They may literally be eating themselves stupid.

Her work corresponds to a broader inquiry conducted by Veerendra Kumar Madala Halagaapa and Mark Mattson of the National Institute on Aging. The researchers fed four groups of mice different diets—normal, high-fat, high-sugar and high-fat/high-sugar. Each diet had the same caloric value, so that one group of mice wouldn't end up heavier. Four months later, the mice on the high-fat diets performed significantly worse than the other groups on a water maze test.

The researchers then exposed the animals to a neurotoxin that targets the hippocampus, to assess whether a high-fat diet made the mice less able to cope with brain damage. Back in the maze, all the animals performed worse than before, but the mice who had eaten the high-fat diets were most seriously compromised. "Based on our work," says Mattson, "we'd predict that people who eat high-fat diets and high-fat/high-sugar diets are not only damaging their ability to learn and remember new information, but also putting themselves at much greater risk for all sorts of neurodegenerative disorders like Alzheimer's."

Welcome to Margaritaville State University

It's widely recognized that heavy drinking doesn't exactly boost your intellect. But most people figure that their booze-induced foolishness wears off once the hangover is gone. Instead, it turns out that even limited stints of overindulgence may have long-term effects.

Less than 20 years ago, researchers began to realize that the adult brain wasn't just a static lump of cells. They found that stem cells in the brain are constantly churning out new neurons, particularly in the hippocampus. Alcoholism researchers, in turn, began to wonder if chronic alcoholics' memory problems had something to do with nerve cell birth and growth.

In 2000, Kimberly Nixon and Fulton Crews at the University of North Carolina's Bowles Center for Alcohol Studies subjected lab rats to four days of heavy alcohol intoxication. They gave the rats a week to shake off their hangovers, then tested them on and off during the next month in a water maze. "We didn't find anything at first," says Nixon. But on the 19th day, the rats who had been on the binge performed much worse. In 19 days, the cells born during the binge had grown to maturity—and clearly, the neurons born during the boozy period didn't work properly once they reached maturity. "[The timing] was almost too perfect," says Nixon.

While normal rats generated about 2,500 new brain cells in three weeks, the drinking rats produced only 1,400. A month later, the sober rats had lost about half of those new cells through normal die-off. But all of the new cells died in the brains of the binge drinkers. "This was startling," says Nixon. "It was the first time anyone had found that alcohol not only inhibits the birth of new cells but also inhibits the ones that survive." In further study, they found that a week's abstinence produced a twofold burst of neurogenesis, and a month off the sauce brought cognitive function back to normal.

What does this have to do with a weekend keg party? A number of recent studies show that college students consume far more alcohol than anyone previously suspected. Forty-four percent of today's collegiates drink enough to be classified as binge drinkers, according to a nationwide survey of 10,000 students done at Harvard University. The amount of alcohol consumed by Nixon's binging rats far exceeded intake at a typical keg party—but other research shows that the effects of alcohol work on a sliding scale. Students who follow a weekend of heavy drinking with a week of heavy studying might not forget everything they learn. They just may struggle come test time.

Can I Bum a Smoke?

If this ledger of campus menaces worries you, here's something you really won't like: Smoking cigarettes may actually have some cognitive benefits, thanks to the power of nicotine. The chemical improves mental focus, as scientists have known since the 1950s. Nicotine also aids concentration in people who have ADHD and may protect against Alzheimer's disease. Back in 2000, a nicotine-like drug under development by the pharmaceutical company Astra Arcus USA was shown to restore the ability to learn and remember in rats with brain lesions similar to those found in Alzheimer's patients. More recently Granholm, the scientist investigating trans fats and memory, found that nicotine enhances spatial memory in healthy rats. Other researchers have found that nicotine also boosts both emotional memory (the kind that helps us *not* put our hands back in the fire after we've been burned) and auditory memory.

There's a catch: Other studies show that nicotine encourages state-dependent learning. The idea is that if, for example, you study in blue sweats, it helps to take the exam in blue sweats. In other words, what you learn while smoking is best recalled while smoking. Since lighting up in an exam room might cause problems, cigarettes probably aren't the key to getting on the dean's list.

Nonetheless, while the number of cigarette smokers continues to drop nationwide, college students are still lighting up: As many as 30 percent smoke during their years of higher education. The smoking rate for young adults between the ages of 18 and 24 has actually risen in the past decade.

All this news makes you wonder how anyone's ever managed to get an education. Or what would happen to GPAs at a vegetarian university with a 10 P.M. curfew. But you might not need to go to such extremes. While Granholm agrees that the excesses of college can be "a perfect example of what you shouldn't do to yourself if you are trying to learn," she doesn't recommend abstinence. "Moderation," she counsels, "just like in everything else. Moderation is the key to collegiate success."

Assess Your Progress

1. Why do so many college students engage in negative health behaviors?
2. Discuss the relationship between fast food and the brain.

STEVEN KOTLER, based in Los Angeles, has written for *The New York Times Magazine*, *National Geographic*, *Details*, *Wired* and *Outside*.

Mars vs. Venus: The Gender Gap in Health

Ask any guy, and he'll tell you that men are the stronger sex. His reasoning is obvious: in general, men are bigger and more muscular than women. They can run faster, lift more, and throw things farther. Men rule on the playing field, but in medical terms, it's a very different story. When it comes to health, men are the weaker sex.

The Longevity Gap

Much has changed in the United States over the past 100 years. Medicine has evolved as much as any field, with dramatic advances in diagnosis and treatment. Changing, too, is the American lifestyle, with its new emphasis on healthier diets and regular exercise and its declining dependence on tobacco. As a result of these developments, life expectancy is also changing, rising slowly but steadily year after year (see Table 1). One thing, though, has not changed—the gender gap. People of both sexes are living longer, but decade after decade, women continue to outpace men. In fact, the gap is wider now than it was a century ago.

When all Americans are taken together, the longevity gap is 5.1 years, but there is a racial gap as well. In 2007, the life expectancy for African American women was 77 but only 70.2 for men, a gap of 6.8 years.

The longevity gap is responsible for the striking demographic characteristics of older Americans. More than half of all women older than 65 are widows, and widows outnumber widowers by at least three to one. At age 65, for every 100 American women, there are only 77 men. At age 85, the disparity is even greater, with women outnumbering men by 2.6 to 1. And the longevity gap persists even into very old age, long after hormones have passed their peak; among centenarians, there are four females for every male.

The gender gap is not unique to America. In fact, every country with reliable health statistics reports that women live longer than men. The longevity gap is present both in industrialized societies and in developing countries (see Table 2). It's a universal observation that suggests a basic difference between the health of men and women.

The Health Gap

Men die at a faster rate than women; the overall mortality rate is 41% higher for men than for women, and it's also higher for men for eight of the 10 leading causes of death (see Table 3). In addition, American men are 2.1 times more likely to die from liver disease, 2.7 times more likely to die from HIV/AIDS, 4.1 times more likely to commit suicide, and 3.8 times more likely to be murder victims than women.

Men die younger than women, and they are more burdened by illness during life. They fall ill at a younger age and have more chronic illnesses than women. For example, men are nearly 10 times more

Table 1 Life Expectancy in America

Year	Females	Males	Gender Gap
1900	48.3	46.3	2 years
1950	71.1	65.6	5.5 years
2000	79.7	74.3	5.4 years
2007	80.4	75.3	5.1 years

Source: National Center for Health Statistics

Table 2 The International Longevity Gap

Country	Overall Life Expectancy	Females	Males	Gap (in years)
Japan	82.1	85.6	78.8	6.8
Canada	81.2	83.9	78.7	5.2
Italy	80.2	83.3	77.3	6.0
U.K.	79.0	81.6	76.5	5.1
Jordan	78.9	81.6	76.3	5.3
Bosnia	78.5	82.3	74.9	7.4

Source: *CIA World Factbook* (2009 estimates)

likely to get inguinal hernias than women, and five times more likely to have aortic aneurysms. American men are about four times more likely to contract AIDS or be hit by gout; they are more than three times more likely than women to develop kidney stones, to become alcoholics, or to have bladder cancer. And they are about twice as likely to suffer from emphysema or a duodenal ulcer. Although women see doctors more often than men, men cost our society much more for medical care beyond age 65.

A Lifelong Gap

The health disparity between males and females begins during fetal life and continues from cradle to grave. About 115 males are conceived for every 100 females, but males are much more likely to die before birth, so there are only 104 newborn boys for every 100 girls. Boys are about 60% more likely to be born prematurely, to have conditions related to prematurity such as neonatal respiratory distress syndrome, and to suffer birth injuries. Boys are about 18% more likely to die before their first birthday than girls.

Table 3 America's 10 Leading Killers

Disease	Male: Female Death Rate Ratio
1. Heart disease	1.5
2. Cancer	1.4
3. Stroke	1.0
4. Chronic obstructive lung disease	1.3
5. Accidents	2.2
6. Diabetes	1.4
7. Alzheimer's disease	0.7
8. Influenza and pneumonia	1.4
9. Kidney disease	1.4
10. Septicemia (blood infection)	1.2
All causes	1.4

Source: National Center for Health Statistics

Table 4 Why Do Men Lag?

Biological factors
- Sex chromosomes
- Hormones
- Reproductive anatomy (?)
- Metabolism

Social factors
- Work stress
- Lack of social networks and supports

Behavioral factors
- Risky behavior
- Aggression and violence
- Smoking
- Alcohol and substance abuse
- Diet
- Lack of exercise
- Lack of routine medical care

When it comes to health, males are the weaker sex throughout life. But why? It's the $64,000 question, but there is no single answer. Instead, the gap depends on a complex mix of biological, social, and behavioral factors (see Table 4).

Biological Factors
Genes and Chromosomes

Males and females are different from the very moment of conception. Each has 23 pairs of chromosomes, which carry the body's 20,000 to 25,000 genes. Twenty-two of these pairs are present in both males and females, but the 23rd separates the sexes. This final pair contains the sex chromosomes. In women, both members of the pair are X chromosomes, but in men one is an X and the other a Y.

The Y chromosome is only about a third as large as the X and contains far fewer genes than the female sex chromosome. Some of these genes may be linked to diseases that contribute to the excess male mortality throughout life. In addition, if a woman has a disease-producing gene on one of her X chromosomes, it may be counterbalanced by a normal gene on the other X, but if a man has the same bad gene on his X chromosome, he lacks the potential protection of a matching gene.

Hormones

It used to be so simple: testosterone got the blame for premature heart disease in men, while estrogen got the credit for protecting women. The theory was based on the observation that athletes who abuse androgens—male hormones—develop unfavorable cholesterol profiles and suffer an increased risk of cardiovascular disease. But new research shows that in physiologic doses, testosterone neither impairs cholesterol levels nor damages the heart. In fact, small studies suggest that testosterone treatment may even help some men with heart disease. Moreover, women who take estrogen well beyond menopause, when their natural levels plummet, experience an increased risk of heart attacks, strokes, and blood clots.

Even if hormones don't account for the lion's share of the gender gap, they do play a role. Estrogen raises HDL ("good") cholesterol levels, perhaps explaining why heart disease typically begins about 10 years later in women than men. On the other hand, testosterone may contribute to the risk-taking and aggressive behavior that causes problems for many young men. And testosterone also fuels diseases of the prostate, both benign and malignant. Even so, the testosterone-prostate connection can't account for the longevity gap, since there are more deaths from breast cancer (about 40,000 a year in the U.S.) than prostate cancer (about 27,000).

Both sex hormones keep bones strong, but here, men actually have the edge. As men age, testosterone levels decline slowly, about 1% a year, but estrogen levels drop abruptly at menopause, boosting the risk of osteoporosis. (see *Harvard Men's Health Watch,* December 2008).

Reproductive Anatomy

Many men view the prostate gland as a vulnerability. That may be, but reproductive factors actually hold down the health gap between men and women. The number of new prostate and breast cancers are closely matched, but women are about 45% more likely to die from their disease. Add malignant and benign diseases of the uterus and the perils of pregnancy and childbirth, and you'd suppose that women are the more fragile sex. Since they're not, males must have important problems in other areas.

Metabolism

Cholesterol may account for some of the health gap. Males and females have similar LDL ("bad") cholesterol levels, but women have substantially higher levels of HDL ("good") cholesterol (60.3 milligrams per deciliter, or mg/dL, versus 48.5 mg/dL on average). HDL cholesterol protects against heart disease (see *HMHW,* August and September 2007), but triglycerides may increase risk—and American men average 158 mg/dL, while women come in at only 135 mg/dL.

Diabetes is a major problem for both sexes, and its prevalence is increasing in both. But this metabolic risk factor affects a somewhat higher percentage of men (11%) than women (10%).

Like diabetes, obesity is rapidly increasing in the United States. More than two-thirds of American adults are overweight or obese. As compared to men with a healthy weight, an average 40-year-old nonsmoker will lose three years of life to overweight and almost six years to obesity. The prevalence of obesity is slightly higher in American women than men; still, excess weight is more of a problem for males. That's because women tend to carry excess weight on their hips and thighs (the "pear shape"), while men add it to their waistlines (the "apple shape," or "beer belly"). Excess body fat is never a good thing, but abdominal obesity is much riskier than lower body obesity, sharply increasing the risk of heart attack and stroke (see *HMHW,* January 2009). Aesthetics aside, women are shaped better.

Although obesity is often classified as a metabolic problem, it usually results from unwise health behaviors, another major misfortune for males. In fact, although metabolic, genetic, and hormonal factors may explain part of the health gap, particularly very early in life, social and behavioral factors play a larger role in adults.

Social Factors
Work Stress and Hostility

It's a common explanation for excess male mortality, and there may be something to it. Indeed, the stereotype of the harried, hard-driving, overworked male executive has a basis in fact, and work stress can increase the risk of hypertension, heart attack, and stroke. In fact, *karoshi,* "death from overwork," is a recognized diagnosis in Japan, and it triggers compensatory payments to survivors. Type A behavior, stress, hostility, and anger have all been implicated as heart disease risk factors, and these traits tend to have a higher prevalence in men than women.

Work-related stress and heart-breaking personality factors may contribute to male vulnerability. But as more women enter the workplace and add financial obligations to their traditional roles at home, they may have the dubious honor of closing the gender gap by moving in the wrong direction.

Social Networks and Supports

It's true: people are good medicine. Strong interpersonal relationships and support networks reduce the risk of many problems, ranging from the common cold and depression to heart attacks and strokes. In contrast, social isolation has been identified as a heart disease risk factor.

Women have much larger and more reliable social networks than men. A study by the New England Research Institute found that 28% of women but only 9% of men report they can rely on friends for support, and men were 2.5 times more likely than women to lack social supports.

Some 400 years ago, poet and pastor John Donne proclaimed, "No man is an island." In 21st century America, though, many men seem very insular indeed. There is more than a germ of truth in the quip that two men can't take a walk together unless one is carrying a ball. In general, women are in touch with their feelings and with other women, and they have a remarkable ability to express their thoughts and emotions. Women may not really be from Venus any more than men are from Mars, but strong relationships and good communication seem to help explain why women live longer on Earth.

Behavioral Factors

Biological factors account for part of the gender gap, social factors for another portion. But from adolescence onward, male behavior is the main reason that men fall ill sooner and die off faster than women.

Risky Behavior

Is it nature or nurture, the Y chromosome and testosterone, or daredevil role models and cultural norms? Nobody knows, but the answer is not likely to be either/or but all of the above. Whatever the cause, from boyhood on, males take more risks than females, and they often pay the price in terms of trauma, injury, and death. Simple precautions like seat belts and bike helmets can help, but more complex measures involving education about alcohol, drugs, firearms, and safe sex are also essential. More than ever before, young males need role models who demonstrate that common sense and prudence are manly traits.

Aggression and Violence

These are extreme forms of risky behavior, and they all have many of the same root causes. But there is a difference between risk taking and aggressive or violent behavior. A man who takes risks places himself in harm's way, but his unwise choices may not endanger others. Violent behavior, though, directly threatens the health and well-being of others, both male and female. A man is nearly four times more likely to die from homicide or suicide than a woman, but women are much more likely to be victims of domestic violence. Men need to learn self-control and anger management if they are to close this portion of the gender gap. Understanding that real men have feelings and that strong emotions are best expressed with words, not acts, is also important.

Smoking

It's the riskiest of all health habits, and since secondhand smoke is dangerous to others, it's also a form of undercover hostility.

In the old days, men smoked but women didn't. Those were good old days for women, but not for men. Times are changing; when women began to smoke in large numbers, they started to catch up to men in heart disease, lung cancer, and emphysema. Now, at last, both sexes are trying to break the habit, but more men (24%) than women (18%) are hooked on cigarettes. And since 30% of male and 21% of female high school students use tobacco, smoking is likely to continue fueling the gender gap for years to come.

Smoking is a terrible hazard for men and women, young and old.

Alcohol and Substance Abuse

Like smoking, drinking and drug abuse are traditionally male problems that are increasingly threatening to women as well. Still, males dominate in these self-destructive habits.

Small to modest amounts of alcohol (one to two drinks a day) appear to protect a man's health, reducing his risk of heart attack and the most common type of stroke. But larger amounts shorten life by increasing the likelihood of hypertension, heart failure, liver disease, various cancers, accidents, and traumatic death. Alcoholism also takes a terrible toll on employment, personal happiness, and family life. Men are twice as likely as women to be binge drinkers and to become dependent on alcohol. Alcohol is responsible for about 85,000 American deaths annually; that's 85,000 too many.

Illicit drugs claim about 17,000 lives a year. It's a tragedy for both sexes, but males are 80% more likely to abuse drugs than females.

Diet

Meat is bad, veggies are good. It's an oversimplification, but it may help explain why women are generally healthier than men: in most cases, they eat better. In a Massachusetts survey, for example, women were about 50% more likely than men to meet the goal of eating at least five servings of fruits and vegetables a day. The masculine ideal of meat and potatoes should give way to vegetables, fruits, grains, and fish.

Exercise

When human survival depended on physical work, both men and women got plenty of exercise. As men moved behind desks, women who continued to haul groceries, climb stairs, scrub, and wash continued to get the many health benefits of physical activity. But as modern appliances replace muscles at home and women join men in sedentary jobs, American women have fallen slightly behind in exercise. It's small comfort to men, though, since most men don't come close to getting the exercise they need for health.

Medical Care

Women think about health, and they do more about it. Women are more likely than men to have health insurance and a regular source of health care. According to a major survey conducted by the Commonwealth Fund, three times as many men as women had not seen a doctor in the previous year; more than half of all men had not had a physical exam or cholesterol test in the previous year; among men over 50 years of age, 41% had not been screened for prostate cancer, and 60% had not been screened for colon cancer in the previous year; and 25% of men said they would handle worries about health by waiting as long as possible before seeking help. In general, men who have the most traditional, macho views about masculinity are the least likely to get routine check-ups and necessary medical care.

Call it the ostrich mentality or the John Wayne Syndrome; by any name, men who skip tests and treatments, minimize symptoms, and disregard medical advice are asking for trouble. Men who look under the hood every time the engine coughs should be as quick to get help when they cough.

It is hard to know why men make such poor patients; busy work schedules and competing responsibilities and interests may play a role, but the macho mentality appears to be the chief culprit. Who can blame men for wanting to be John Wayne? But by following the example of that quintessential American he-man, men fail to take the simple steps that can protect them from heart disease and lung cancer—the very same illnesses that plagued John Wayne before his death at age 72.

Closing the Gap

Men can't change their chromosomes and genes, and very few would change their hormones. Still, men can catch up to women in some other areas. That doesn't mean "going girly," though it does mean following some simple rules. But will men change their behavior?

An incident reported in *The Wall Street Journal* may help you decide about making changes. In the 1960s, when Muhammad Ali was a brash and fearless boxing sensation still known as Cassius Clay, he boarded a plane to fly to a big fight. While preparing for takeoff, a flight attendant noticed that the boxer had not fastened his seat belt. She asked him to buckle up, but he ignored her. When she asked again, he replied, "Superman don't need no seat belt." Her retort: "Superman don't need no airplane. Buckle up." And he did.

Men who think they are too tough to get sick are risking a medical crash-landing. To stay healthy, we all need to follow the rules (including the one about seat belts). Here are 10 tips to help you wing your way to a long and healthy life.

1. **Avoid tobacco** in all its forms.
2. **Eat well.** That means eating more healthful foods and fewer harmful foods.
   - Eat more: whole grains, fruits, vegetables and legumes, fish, low- or non-fat dairy products, and nuts and seeds.
   - Eat less: red meat, whole-milk dairy products, poultry skin, high-sodium (salty) processed foods, sweets, sugary drinks and refined carbohydrates, trans fats, and, if you need to lose weight, calories.
3. **Exercise regularly,** including:
   - 30 minutes of moderate exercise nearly every day.
   - Exercises for strength two to three times a week.
   - Exercises for flexibility and balance according to need.
4. **Stay lean.** It's equally hard for men and women, but even partial success will help.
5. **If you choose to drink, limit yourself to one to two drinks a day,** counting 5 ounces of wine, 12 ounces of beer, and 1.5 ounces of liquor as one drink.
6. **Reduce stress.** Get enough sleep. Build social ties and community support.
7. **Avoid risky behavior,** including drug abuse, unsafe sex, dangerous driving, unsafe firearm use, and living in hazardous household conditions.
8. **Reduce exposure to toxins and radiation,** including sunlight and medical x-rays.
9. **Get regular medical check-ups,** screening tests, and immunizations. Listen to your body and report sounds of discord to your doctor.
10. **Seek joy and share it with others.** Laughter is good medicine. Fun and optimism improve health as well as happiness. And if you make changes 1 to 9 slowly, steadily, and reasonably, you will actually come to enjoy your healthful lifestyle.

As things now stand, men are from Mars, women from Venus. But gents who get their planets aligned correctly can enjoy the best of both worlds—and good health right here on Earth.

Assess Your Progress

1. Why are women more likely to see physicians on a regular basis?
2. Why do many men neglect their health?
3. Give three examples of positive health behaviors.
4. Distinguish the differences in access to health care by gender.

From *Harvard Men's Health Watch,* January 2010, pp. 1–6. Copyright © 2010 by Harvard Health Publications Group. Reprinted by permission.

Carrots, Sticks, and Health Care Reform—Problems with Wellness Incentives

HARALD SCHMIDT, MA, KRISTIN VOIGT, DPHIL, AND DANIEL WIKLER, PHD

C hronic conditions, especially those associated with overweight, are on the rise in the United States (as elsewhere). Employers have used both carrots and sticks to encourage healthier behavior.

The current health care reform bills seek to expand the role of incentives, which promise a win–win bargain: employees enjoy better health, while employers reduce health care costs and profit from a healthier workforce.

However, these provisions cannot be given an ethical free pass. In some cases, the incentives are really sticks dressed up as carrots. There is a risk of inequity that would further disadvantage the people most in need of health improvements, and doctors might be assigned watchdog roles that might harm the therapeutic relationship. We believe that some changes must be made to reconcile incentive use with ethical norms.

Under the 1996 Health Insurance Portability and Accountability Act (HIPAA), a group health plan may not discriminate among individuals on the basis of health factors by varying their premiums. But HIPAA does not prevent insurers from offering reimbursements through "wellness programs." These include what could be called participation incentives, which offer a premium discount or other reimbursement simply for participating in a health-promotion program, and attainment incentives, which provide reimbursements only for meeting targets—for example, a particular body-mass index or cholesterol level. Subsequent regulations specified that attainment incentives must not exceed 20% of the total cost of an employee's coverage (i.e., the combination of the employer's and employee's contributions).[1]

The health care reform measures currently before Congress would substantially expand these provisions (see box). However, ethical analysis and empirical research suggest that the current protections are inadequate to ensure fairness.

Attainment incentives provide welcome rewards for employees who manage to comply but may be unfair for those who struggle, particularly if they fail. The law demands the provision of alternative standards for those who cannot or should not participate because of medical conditions, but those categories are narrowly defined. For all others, the implicit assumption is that they can achieve targets if they try. This assumption is hard to reconcile with what we know about lifestyle change. Most diets, for example, do not result in long-lasting weight reduction, even though participants want and try to lose weight. Attainment-incentive programs make no distinction between those who try but fail and those who do not try.

Proponents of attainment incentives typically do not view this situation as inequitable. Steven Burd, the chief executive officer of Safeway, whose "Healthy Measures" program offers reimbursements for meeting weight, blood-pressure, cholesterol, and tobacco-use targets, compared his company's program to automobile insurance, in which for decades "driving behavior has been correlated with accident risk and has therefore translated into premium differences among drivers." In other words, says Burd, "the auto-insurance industry has long recognized the role of personal responsibility. As a result, bad behaviors (like speeding, tickets for failure to follow the rules of the road, and frequency of accidents) are considered when establishing insurance premiums. Bad driver premiums are not subsidized by the good driver premiums."[2]

If people could lose weight, stop smoking, or reduce cholesterol simply by deciding to do so, the analogy might be appropriate. But in that case, few would have had weight, smoking, or cholesterol problems in the first place. Moreover, there is a social gradient. A law school graduate from a wealthy family who has a gym on the top floor of his condominium block is more likely to succeed in losing weight if he

Summary of Wellness Incentives in the Current Legislation

The "Affordable Health Care for America Act" (House of Representatives), section 112, requires that qualifying programs:

- Be evidence-based and certified by the Department of Health and Human Services.
- Provide support for populations at risk for poor health outcomes.
- Include designs that are "culturally competent [and] physically and programmatically accessible (including for individuals with disabilities)."
- Be available to all employees without charge.
- Not link financial incentives to premiums.
- Entail no cost shifting.

The "Patient Protection and Affordable Care Act" (Senate), section 2705, proposes to increase reimbursement levels to 30% of the cost of employee-only coverage, or up to 50% with government approval. In part restating provisions for current wellness programs, it also requires that qualifying programs:

- Be "available to all similarly situated individuals."
- Have "a reasonable chance of improving the health of, or preventing disease in, participating individuals."
- Not be "overly burdensome, [be] a subterfuge for discriminating based on a health status factor, [or be] highly suspect in the method chosen to promote health or prevent disease."
- Provide an alternative standard for employees whose medical condition—as certified by a physician—precludes participation in attainment-incentive programs.
- Not pose an "undue burden for individuals insured in the individual insurance market."
- Entail no cost shifting.
- Be evaluated in pilot studies and a 10-state demonstration project.

The reform proposals prohibit cost shifting, but provisions in the Senate bill could result in a substantial increase in financial burden on employees who do not meet targets (or alternative standards). On the basis of the average cost of $4700 for employee-only coverage, a 20% incentive amounts to $940; 30% would equal $1410 and 50%, $2350. In practice, insurers may stay below the maximum levels. Some may elect to absorb the full cost of reimbursements, in part because some or all of these costs may be offset by future savings from a healthier workforce. Alternatively, however, insurers might recoup some or all of the costs by increasing insurance contributions from insurance holders. In the extreme case, the incentive might then simply consist of being able to return to the previous level of contributions. Similar effects can be achieved by varying applicable copayments or deductibles.[4] Direct and indirect increases would disproportionately hurt lower-paid workers, who are generally less healthy than their higher-paid counterparts and thus in greater need of health care, less likely to meet the targets, and least likely to be able to afford higher costs. Some employees might decide to opt out of employer-based health insurance—and indeed, one wellness consulting firm, Benicomp, implies in its prospectus that such a result might be desirable, pointing out that employees who do not comply might be "motivated to consider other coverage options" and highlighting the savings that would result for employers.[4]

Proponents emphasize that wellness incentives are voluntary. But the scenarios above show that voluntariness can become dubious for lower-income employees, if the only way to obtain affordable insurance is to meet the targets. To them, programs that are offered as carrots may feel more like sticks. It is worth noting that countries such as Germany generally use far lower reimbursements ($45 to $130 per year, or a maximum of 6% of an employee's contribution) and often use in-kind incentives (such as exercise equipment, heart-rate monitors, or vouchers contributing to the cost of a "wellness holiday") rather than cash.[3]

There are also questions about the effect on the therapeutic relationship. When the German Parliament passed a law making lower copayments conditional on patients' undergoing certain cancer screenings and complying with therapy, medical professionals rejected it, partly out of concern about being put in a policing position.[3] American physicians expressed concern when West Virginia's Medicaid program charged participating doctors with monitoring patients' adherence to the requirements set out in the member agreement.[5] Requiring physicians to certify an employee's medical unsuitability for an incentive scheme or to attest to their achievement of a target might similarly introduce an adversarial element into the doctor–patient relationship.

Incentives for healthy behavior may be part of an effective national response to risk factors for chronic disease. Wrongly implemented, however, they can introduce substantial inequity into the health insurance system. It is a problem if the people who are less likely to benefit from the

tries than is a teenage mother who grew up and continues to live and work odd jobs in a poor neighborhood with limited access to healthy food and exercise opportunities. And he is more likely to try. In Germany, where both participation and attainment incentives have been offered since 2004, participation rates among people in the top socioeconomic quintile are nearly double the rates among those in the poorest quintile.[3]

Incentive schemes are defended on the grounds of personal responsibility, but as Kant observed, "ought" implies "can." Although alternative standards must be offered to employees for whom specific targets are medically inappropriate, disadvantaged people with multiple coexisting conditions may refrain from making such petitions, seeing them as degrading or humiliating. These potential problems are important in view of the proposed increases in reimbursement levels.

programs are those who may need them more. The proposed increases in reimbursement levels threaten to further exacerbate inequities. Reform legislation should therefore not raise the incentive cap. Attainment incentives that primarily benefit the well-off and healthy should be phased out, and the focus should shift to participation-incentive schemes tailored to the abilities and needs of lower-paid employees. Moreover, it is crucial that the evaluation of pilots include an assessment of the socioeconomic and ethnic backgrounds of both users and nonusers to ascertain the equitability of programs.

Notes

1. Mello MM, Rosenthal MB. Wellness programs and lifestyle discrimination—the legal limits. *N Engl J Med* 2008;359:192–9.

2. Burd SA. How Safeway is cutting health-care costs. *Wall Street Journal.* June 12, 2009.

3. Schmidt H, Stock S, Gerber A. What can we learn from German health incentive schemes? *BMJ* 2009;339:b3504.

4. Detailed overview, 2009. Ft. Wayne, IN: BeniComp Advantage. (Accessed December 22, 2009, at www.benicompadvantage.com/products/overview.htm.)

5. Bishop G, Brodkey A. Personal responsibility and physician responsibility—West Virginia's Medicaid plan. *N Engl J Med* 2006;355:756–8.

Assess Your Progress

1. Distinguish between the carrot and stick approach to health practices.
2. Discuss the advantages and disadvantages of wellness incentives.

Financial and other disclosures provided by the authors are available with the full text of this article at NEJM.org.

From the Harvard School of Public Health and the Harvard University Program in Ethics and Health, Boston.

UNIT 2
Stress and Mental Health

Unit Selections

Learning Outcomes

After reading this unit, you should be able to:

- Explain why it is difficult to diagnose depression.
- Describe the behaviors of pathologic hoarders.
- Explain the causes of obsessive compulsive disorder.
- Discuss how the presence or absence of sunlight affects mental health in people with Seasonal Affective Disorder.
- Describe the major stressors in life.
- Explain how stressors have changed over the last 5,000 years.
- Contrast positive and negative stressors in shaping one's life.
- Explain how one can cope with harmful stress.

Student Website
www.mhhe.com/cls

Internet References

The American Institute of Stress
    www.stress.org
National Mental Health Association (NMHA)
    www.nmha.org/index.html
Self-Help Magazine
    www.selfhelpmagazine.com/index.html

The brain is one organ that still mystifies and baffles the scientific community. While more has been learned about this organ in the last decade than in all the rest of recorded history, our understanding of the brain is still in its infancy. What has been learned, however, has spawned exciting new research, and has contributed to the establishment of new disciplines, such as psychophysiology and psychoneuroimmunology (PNI).

Traditionally, the medical community has viewed health problems as either physical or mental, and has treated each type separately. This dichotomy between the psyche (mind) and soma (body) is fading in the light of scientific data that reveal profound physiological changes associated with mood shifts. What are the physiological changes associated with stress? Hans Selye, the father of stress research, described stress as a nonspecific physiological response to anything that challenges the body. He demonstrated that this response could be elicited by both mental and physical stimuli. Stress researchers have come to regard this response pattern as the "flight or fight" response, perhaps an adaptive throwback to our primitive ancestors. Researchers now believe that repeated and prolonged activation of this response can trigger destructive changes in our bodies and contribute to the development of several chronic diseases. So profound is the impact of emotional stress on the body, that current estimates suggest that approximately 90 percent of all doctor visits are for stress-related disorders. If emotional stress elicits a generalized physiological response, why are there so many different diseases associated with it? Many experts believe that the answer may best be explained by what has been termed "the weak-organ theory." According to this theory, every individual has one organ system that is most susceptible to the damaging effects of prolonged stress.

Mental illness, which is generally regarded as a dysfunction of normal thought processes, has no single identifiable etiology. One may speculate that this is due to the complex nature of the organ system involved. There is also mounting evidence to suggest that there is an organic component to the traditional forms of mental illness such as schizophrenia, chronic depression, and manic depression. The fact that certain mental illnesses tend to occur within families has divided the mental health community into two camps: those who believe that there is a genetic factor operating and those who see the family tendency as more of a learned behavior. In either case, the evidence supports mental illness as another example of the weak-organ theory. The reason one person is more susceptible to the damaging effects of stress than another may not be altogether clear, but evidence is mounting that one's perception or attitude plays a key role in the stress equation. A prime example demonstrating this relationship comes from the research that relates cardiovascular disease to stress. The realization that our attitude has such a significant impact on our health has led to a burgeoning new movement in psychology termed "positive psychology." Dr. Martin Segilman, professor of psychology at the University of Pennsylvania and father of the positive psychology movement, believes that optimism is a key factor in maintaining not only our mental health, but our physical health as well. Dr. Segilman notes that while some people are naturally more optimistic than others, optimism can be learned.

© Jules Frazier

One area in particular that appears to be influenced by the "positive psychology movement" is the area of stress management. Traditionally, stress management programs have focused on the elimination of stress, but that is starting to change as new strategies approach stress as an essential component of life and a potential source of health. It is worth noting that this concept, of stress serving as a positive force in a person's life, was presented by Dr. Hans Selye in 1974 in his book *Stress Without Distress.* Dr. Selye felt that there were three types of stress: negative stress (distress), normal stress, and positive stress (eustress). He maintained that positive stress not only increases a person's self-esteem but also serves to inoculate the person against the damaging effects of distress. Only time will tell if this change of focus, in the area of stress management, makes any real difference in patient outcome.

The causes of stress are many, but for some individuals, the coming of winter is a very difficult time. Many of these folks experience periods of depression during the shorter days of winter, as described in "Seasonal Affective Disorder," by Stephen J. Lurie et al. Workplace stress is another form of distress. In "Dealing with the Stressed," Ken MacQueen notes that stress in the workplace costs the economy billions of dollars per year due to sick leave and loss of productivity. Researchers have made significant strides in their understanding of the mechanisms that link emotional stress to physical ailments, but they are less clear on the mechanisms by which positive emotions bolster one's health. Although significant gains have been made in our understanding of the relationship between body and mind, much remains to be learned. What is known indicates that perception and one's attitude are the key elements in shaping our responses to stressors.

Two articles in this section address mental health issues including depression and obsessive compulsive disorders. In "Redefining Depression as Mere Sadness," Ronald Pies believes it's valuable to treat individuals with profound sadness as depressed and to provide whatever therapeutic approaches that make the patient feel better. "I Can't Let Anything Go:" A Case Study with Psychological Testing of a Patient with Pathologic Hoarding, discusses pathologic hoarding and obsessive compulsive disorder.

Redefining Depression as Mere Sadness

RONALD PIES, MD

Let's say a patient walks into my office and says he's been feeling down for the past three weeks. A month ago, his fiancée left him for another man, and he feels there's no point in going on. He has not been sleeping well, his appetite is poor and he has lost interest in nearly all of his usual activities.

Should I give him a diagnosis of clinical depression? Or is my patient merely experiencing what the 14th-century monk Thomas à Kempis called "the proper sorrows of the soul"? The answer is more complicated than some critics of psychiatric diagnosis think.

To these critics, psychiatry has medicalized normal sadness by failing to consider the social and emotional context in which people develop low mood—for example, after losing a job or experiencing the breakup of an important relationship. This diagnostic failure, the argument goes, has created a bogus epidemic of increasing depression.

A debate over when and how to treat a patient reeling from a loss.

In their recent book "The Loss of Sadness" (Oxford, 2007), Allan V. Horwitz and Jerome C. Wakefield assert that for thousands of years, symptoms of sadness that were "with cause" were separated from those that were "without cause." Only the latter were viewed as mental disorders.

With the advent of modern diagnostic criteria, these authors argue, doctors were directed to ignore the context of the patient's complaints and focus only on symptoms—poor appetite, insomnia, low energy, hopelessness and so on. The current criteria for major depression, they say, largely fail to distinguish between "abnormal" reactions caused by "internal dysfunction" and "normal sadness" brought on by external circumstances. And they blame vested interests—doctors, researchers, pharmaceutical companies—for fostering this bloated concept of depression.

But while this increasingly popular thesis contains a kernel of truth, it conceals a bushel basket of conceptual and scientific problems.

For one thing, if modern diagnostic criteria were converting mere sadness into clinical depression, we would expect the number of new cases of depression to be skyrocketing compared with rates in a period like the 1950s to the 1970s. But several new studies in the United States and Canada find that the incidence of serious depression has held relatively steady in recent decades.

Second, it may seem easy to determine that someone with depressive complaints is reacting to a loss that touched off the depression. Experienced clinicians know this is rarely the case.

Most of us can point to recent losses and disappointments in our lives, but it is not always clear that they are causally related to our becoming depressed. For example, a patient who had a stroke a month ago may appear tearful, lethargic and depressed. To critics, the so-called depression is just "normal sadness" in reaction to a terrible psychological blow. But strokes are also known to disrupt chemical pathways in the brain that directly affect mood.

What is the "real" trigger for this patient's depression? Perhaps it is a combination of psychological and neurological factors. In short, the notion of "reacting" to adverse life events is complex and problematic.

Third, and perhaps most troubling, is the implication that a recent major loss makes it more likely that the person's depressive symptoms will follow a benign and limited course, and therefore do not need medical treatment. This has never been demonstrated, to my knowledge, in any well-designed studies. And what *has* been demonstrated, in a study by Dr. Sidney Zisook, is that antidepressants may help patients with major depressive symptoms occurring just after the death of a loved one.

Yes, most psychiatrists would concede that in the space of a brief "managed care" appointment, it's very hard to understand much about the context of the patient's depressive complaints. And yes, under such conditions, some doctors are tempted to write that prescription for Prozac or Zoloft and move on to the next patient.

But the vexing issue of when bereavement or sadness becomes a disorder, and how it should be treated, requires much more study. Most psychiatrists believe that undertreatment of severe depression is a more pressing problem than overtreatment of "normal sadness." Until solid research persuades me otherwise, I will most likely see people like my jilted patient as clinically depressed, not just "normally sad"—and I will provide him with whatever psychiatric treatment he needs to feel better.

Assess Your Progress

1. Distinguish between depression and sadness.
2. Discuss the relationship between adverse life events and depression.

RONALD PIES is a professor of psychiatry at Tufts and SUNY Upstate Medical Center in Syracuse.

"I Can't Let Anything Go:" A Case Study with Psychological Testing of a Patient with Pathologic Hoarding

Pathologic hoarding is a symptom generally recognized as related to obsessional dynamics (Gutheil, 1959). The hoarder cannot, without great anxiety, tolerate separation from or dispose of his possessions. Thus the hoarder accumulates vast amount of possessions, often in such amounts as to compromise freedom of movement in the residence. Popular in tabloid reportage, such news items portray persons found dead among floor-to-ceiling piles of old newspapers and similar detritus, while in actual clinical practice such dramatic cases are not common (Bryk, 2005; Duenwald, 2004). More importantly, such individuals are rarely available for psychological intervention or testing both because of social isolation and injury or death caused by the hoarded materials. Additionally, a majority of the current literature regarding hoarding is linked with Obsessive Compulsive Disorder (OCD), though other major disorders have been noted.

This report describes a particular individual with characteristic features of hoarding which is explored through formal psychological testing.

JANNA KORETZ AND THOMAS G. GUTHEIL

Hoarding—Definition

Frost and Hard (1996) define hoarding as follows:

a. The acquisition of, and failure to, discard a large number of possessions that appear to be useless or of limited value.

b. Living spaces sufficiently cluttered so as to preclude activities for which these spaces were designed.

c. Significant distress or impairment in functioning caused by the hoarding.

d. Reluctance or inability to return borrowed items. As boundaries blur, impulsive acquisitiveness could lead to kleptomania or stealing (p. 341).

Case Examples in Literature

The small but striking literature on hoarding contains a number of dramatic case examples, such as that of a 32-year-old singer, which captures some of the classic features of hoarding dynamics (Gutheil, 1959).

> The patient's separation anxiety included . . . separation from objects. The patient was unable to throw away or discard anything. The result was that her apartment, in the course of time, resembled a huge garbage bin.

The patient considered all objects in her possession, even the most insignificant ones, such as burnt out matchsticks, cigarette butts, or candy wrappers, as parts of her ego, and discarding them as tantamount to weakening of her ego integration. Giving them away was like giving away parts of herself (p. 799).

Perhaps the most famous example of hoarding was that of the Collyer brothers (Lidz, 2003). Set in the later 1940s, two brothers Homer and Langley lived a highly reclusive hermit-like existence in a Harlem brownstone, which at the time of their death contained over 100 tons of trash that they had collected over a lifetime. The material in the house included:

> baby carriages, rusted bicycles, old food, potato peelers, guns, glass chandeliers, bowling balls, camera equipment, the folding top of a horsedrawn carriage, a saw horse, three dressmaking dummies, painted portraits, pinup girl photos, plaster busts, Mrs. Collyer's hope chests, rusty bedsprings, a kerosene stove, a child's chair . . . , more than 25,000 books, human organs pickled in jars, eight live cats, the chassis of [a model T Ford], tapestries, hundreds of yards of unused silks and fabric, clocks, fourteen pianos . . . , a clavichord, two organs, banjos, violins, bugles, accordions, a gramophone and records and countless bundles of newspapers and magazines, some of them decades old (p. 5).

Based on their expressed fears of intruders, both realistic and paranoid, the brothers had rigged a number of booby traps within their residence. Langley, who had been crawling through tunnels in the debris to bring food to his blind and paralyzed brother, was caught in one of his own traps and killed. Then Homer starved to death. The stench of Langleys' decaying corpses led the police to attempt to break into their house, only to find infinite piles of objects blocking their way. Police confronted rat-infested piles of detritus stacked to the ceilings in rooms and stairwells. While Homer was found dead in his chair shortly after the police entered, Langley was not found until nearly a month later, a short distance away from his brother, but concealed under debris from the trap (Lidz, 2003).

Discover Magazine Online (Duenwald, 2004) provides another succinct case of hoarding:

> [For years] . . . Patrice Moore received . . . load[s] of mail—newspapers, magazines, book, catalogs and random solicitations. Each day the 43-year-old recluse piled the new with the old, until floor-to-ceiling stacks of disorganized paper nearly filled his windowless 10-by-10-foot apartment in New York City. In late December, the avalanche came, and Moore was buried standing up. He stood alone for two days, until neighbors heard his muffled moaning. The landlord broke in with a crowbar; it took another hour for neighbors and firefighters to dig Moore out and get him medical help (p. 1).

New avenues of understanding about hoarding have opened through brain imaging and cortical function studies (Saxena et al., 2008; Anonymous, 2008; Steller, 1943). However, our focus here is on the psychological aspects of hoarding.

Report of the Case
Prelude to Admission

Michael (identifying data in this case report have been altered to preclude recognition) is a middle-aged, white, unmarried male who attended two years of community college and briefly worked as a box cutter until 1992, after which he subsisted solely on Social Security income. He is a tall, balding man with hair grown out on the sides of his head to his shoulders; he refuses to cut his hair and nails. He wears thick glasses, which magnify his eyes, and tends to stare intensely at others, sometimes without speaking.

Michael was brought to the hospital after being evicted from his apartment for causing disturbances, playing music very loudly, calling the police with allegations of the neighbors' making noise, and knocking on neighbors' doors late at night. His landlord had offered to let him stay if he engaged in treatment, but Michael was very erratic about attending therapy: During conversation he was agreeable to the plan but then did not appear. Eventually, when his landlord took him to court, he was ordered to attend a treatment program if he wanted to leave his possessions in his apartment. As treatment, Michael entered a daytime partial hospital program and resided in the evenings in the adjacent shelter.

At the point of his planned eviction, the landlord, without informing Michael, entered his apartment in order to clean it. There he encountered piles of magazines, trash, sheet music, and many other items stacked all over the apartment's floor space up to the ceiling. Ultimately, a cleaning team required two weeks to clear out the apartment contents sufficiently to open fully the front door.

On an unauthorized visit home, Michael arrived at the apartment while the landlord and his team were cleaning it. Upon seeing his things being thrown away, he became acutely anxious and defecated on himself. He returned, in great distress, to the partial hospital program shelter.

Family and Social History

Michael has no known living relatives or friends and had interpersonal difficulties throughout his life. His mother died of cancer when he was in early grade school, and his father died when Michael was in his mid-thirties, and his stepmother died roughly around the same time. During this time, Michael's stepfamily pushed him from his father's house so that they could sell it, and Michael moved to the above-mentioned apartment mentioned. Some of the items from his stepfamily's house were of high emotional significance to Michael and were part of the hoarded materials.

The diagnoses for the current hospitalization included Major Depressive Disorder (MDD) with psychotic features and paranoid personality disorder with a history of treatment noncompliance. Michael had a significant depressive history. He had been hospitalized five times for suicidal ideation and attempts, the most recent of which was 12 years before this admission, though he experienced a waxing and waning depressive mood throughout that time.

Mental Status

At the time of the interview, Michael was oriented to person, place, and time. He had an unusual cadence of speech, but did maintain a regular rate. His thought form was goal oriented, and he was preoccupied with relational difficulties with others, primarily women. Michael denied any current or past auditory and visual hallucinations.

Psychological Testing
Instruments Used

Interview, Wechsler Adult Intelligence Scale (WAIS-III), Rorschach, Thematic Apperception Test (TAT), Minnesota Multiphasic Personality Inventory (MMPI-2)

Behavioral Observations

Michael appeared on time for each of the four sessions of the evaluation, and was cooperative and pleasant throughout. He stated repeatedly that he enjoyed the testing process very much. Michael, who had previously displayed only a flat affect with the examiner, smiled and laughed a few times during the testing sessions. Michael did not appear to be anxious, except during the inquiry section of the Rorschach when the question, "What made it look like that?" was repeated. He became visibly

Table 1   Full Scale IQ

76/5th Percentile			
Verbal IQ (Left Brain) 79/8th Percentile		**Performance IQ (Right Brain) 77/6th Percentile**	
Verbal Comprehension (CVI) 93/32nd percentile	Working Memory Index (WMI) 61/. 5th percentile	Perceptual Organization Index (POI) 82/12th percentile	Processing Speed Index (PSI) 66/1st percentile
Digit Span-5	Information-12	Picture Completion-6	Symbol Search-l
Lemer Number Sequencing-2	Comprehension-4	Block Design-7	Coding-5
Arithmetic-4	Similarities-7	Matrix Reasoning-8	
	Vocabulary-7	Object Assembly-5	
		Picture Arrangement-6	

agitated. These observations were confirmed by Michael's verbal acknowledgment of his anxiety during that particular time as well as his denial of anxiety during any other tests. His speech was perfunctory but appropriate, and his affect was usually flat with intermittent episodes of more appropriate affect.

Michael's thinking appeared confused, as many of his answers were not appropriate to the questions asked. For example, on the vocabulary section of the WAIS-III, when asked the definition of breakfast, Michael gave elements of what could be considered breakfast, such as "eggs, food," but also included "energy and vitamins," material not entirely appropriate to the definition. Although Michael's stated his mood was "good," he appeared to be somewhat morose.

Generally, Michael was very aware of his personal struggles and his differences compared to others. Cognitively, his dysregulation created an inability to change his behavior or cognitive sets. Because of this Michael appears to be somewhat lost in his world, which has increased his desire for self-harm, social isolation, and paranoid thought.

The following table describes the breakdown of Michael's full-scale IQ. In testing terms, "index scores" break down the categories of Verbal and Performance into slightly smaller subcategories that narrow the focus of the tasks tested. It is important to note that Michael's total Performance and Verbal IQ scores do not adequately describe the significant discrepancies *within* each of these categories. These discrepancies, seen through Michael's index scores in the VCI, WMI, POI and PSI cells shown above, much more accurately elucidate Michael's cognitive fingerprint.

Michael's profile reveals relative strengths and weaknesses in both his right and left hemispheres. Michael scored high on the Verbal Comprehension index in comparison to his other scores, showing that he retained a good base of knowledge from his formal education, which stayed with him throughout the years. In comparison to his other scores, Michael also scored high on the Perceptual Organization index, demonstrating that he was able to organize and work with data fairly well. Interestingly, Michael's answers to many items on the Information, Comprehension, and Vocabulary sections were not as integrated, as his scores indicate; though he received credit for many of his answers, they tended to be superficial and tangential.

Michael also showed weaknesses in his profile. He scored lowest on the Working Memory index, which primarily tests auditory memory. Michael's lowest subtest score within this index was on Letter-Number Sequencing, a task that requires the individual to remember numbers and letters while rearranging their order. Letter-Number Sequencing requires a high level of planning as well as flexibility. Michael is a concrete thinker, so that the complexity of this task may have been too difficult for him. Additionally, because of the concreteness of his thinking, Michael might not have had the ability to think flexibly enough to engage well in this task. Furthermore, this task can be highly influenced by anxiety; if the individual is experiencing anxiety, then the ability to remember numbers and letters while reorganizing their sequence is highly compromised.

Michael also had relative difficulty in the Processing Speed index, which falls under the Performance IQ composite score. Michael received a scaled score of 1, a very low score, on the Symbol Search subtest, a test that requires an individual to determine whether a series of symbols contains any symbols presented in another group. This task also requires quick visual-motor speed, efficiency, and graphomotor output. Michael might not have these skills, partially due to his poor working memory; thus it would be nearly impossible for Michael to hold the figure designs in his mind while searching for them in a new location. An alternative explanation would be that Michael might have had an obsessive concern with detail, which would prevent him from moving quickly through the task. This reason is plausible given Michael's history with hoarding and its obsessional roots.

In the emotional realm, the results from the Rorschach, MMPI-2, and TAT are convergent in many regards. Michael's awareness of his own differences can be seen through his high level of dependency and narcissistic defenses as shown by his responses on the Rorschach, which indicate that he may rely on others for direction and support and may believe that people will be more tolerant of his demands than they may actually be. Michael appears to be experiencing more needs for closeness than are being met; he is, therefore, likely to feel lonely, emotionally deprived, and interpersonally needy. This also is observed in Michael's responses on the TAT, which were primarily about family and loss. One of the cards indicated that, when fear is evoked in Michael, he becomes extremely disorganized and confused.

This disorganization leads Michael to become cognitively rigid. Michael's Rorschach responses show an avoidant style in which he tends to view himself in an overly narrow focus of attention. This was seen in the multitude of solely form-determinant responses on the Rorschach and his refusal to use the whole card in many of his responses. This rigidity and confusion about events in his daily life would likely cause Michael to feel depressed and trigger him to isolate from others.

Michael's cognitive rigidity, in combination with his impairment in reality testing, leads him to have an unusual and incorrect perception of reality. Michael's adaptation is compromised by instances of arbitrary and circumstantial reasoning and moments in which loose and scattered ideation confuses him. Although his insight is limited, Michael is able to recognize that his confusion and perception do not fit into the world in which he lives. This awareness significantly contributes to his low self-esteem, desire for self-harm, social isolation, and paranoid thinking. This is confirmed on the MMPI-2, where Michael scores extremely high on the sections outlining paranoid thinking and schizophrenia characteristics, and he endorses such ideas as "It is safer to trust no one," and "If people had not had it in for me, I would have been much more successful."

Michael's feelings of social isolation can be surmised from his answers to Card 13 B on the TAT, in which it seems that Michael projects his feelings of being different. He states: "A boy is sitting outside his house . . . watching the world go by . . . he is wondering' Why can't I go to school? Why can't I do what they're doing?'" This response illustrates that Michael feels different from the world he lives in and that he knows he is not fully incorporated into the world around him.

Michael's responses on the Rorschach also show that he tends to overvalue his personal worth and to become preoccupied with his own needs as a defense against the continual rejection he feels in his world. Michael exhibits narcissistic tendencies such as entitlement and externalization of blame and responsibility as defenses against his substantial self-doubt and low self-esteem.

An example of Michael's low self-esteem and sadness can be seen in his response to Card 3 BM on the TAT where Michael says:

Woman that is crying. She is very sad and depressed . . . she just lost her house, case, and family . . . she is homeless and doesn't know what to do. Fragile. She has lost everything . . . lost her family too.

This response captures Michael's apparent feeling that he is upset about the substantial loss in his life.

Michael's hoarding behaviors can be connected to these neuropsychological findings. Although hoarding can be understood in terms of obsessive and compulsive symptoms, it can also be seen through the lens of loss. Michael's history shows that he has suffered many losses throughout his life, leading to anxiety around separation, which he viewed as equivalent to death. This explains why Michael refused to get rid of a multitude of items. As in the literature excerpts at the start of this article illustrate about those who hoard, Michael might have experienced objects as being a part of his ego and therefore, a loss of these items would feel to him like a loss of a part of himself. Similarly, if Michael suffered a loss through rejection, he might overcompensate his own feelings of rejection by refusing to reject anything.

Discussion

Michael is a 50-year-old man with a diagnosis of recurrent MDD, with psychotic features, ruling out anxiety disorder and paranoid personality disorder. Michael suffers from significant depression and suicidal ideation, anxiety, coping deficiencies, disordered thinking, social isolation, paranoia, hoarding behaviors, and a possible history of trauma. Michael is also painfully aware of his lack of connectedness and deficits in fitting in with his peers. Although Michael has a borderline IQ, he has some relative strength in both verbal competence as well as perceptual organization. Despite experiencing high anxiety, Michael is somewhat willing to engage in situations that increase his anxiety level. Michael would likely benefit from a psychopharmacological evaluation to clarify whether his medication suits his needs, continued individual therapy, and continued group therapy aimed at practicing social and therapeutic skills.

Hoarding behaviors, though usually connected with OCD dynamics, have been linked to major depression, information processing deficits, problems with emotional attachment, decision-making deficits, and behavioral avoidance (all of which Michael experiences), as well as schizophrenia and other disorders. As in the case of the Collyer brothers, death can result from physical dangers associated with hoarding; death may also occur following separation from the hoarded objects.

Hoarders tend to view their possessions as extensions of themselves, "with objects valued as safety signals because of the sense of security derived from them . . . hoarders often report that discarding possessions becomes akin to losing a loved one" (Kyrios et al., 2004, p. 244). This distorted view of their processions may bring a sense of safety to hoarders because they lack an appropriate alternative attachment (Kyrios et al., 2004). Previous studies have indicated the correlation between ambivalent attachments and low self-worth. A family environment characterized by overprotective, yet highly demanding parenting styles, not only leads an individual to seek security elsewhere, but also strengthens their alternative attachments to objects as a compensation for the high levels of perceived parental criticism that the individual received (Kyrios et al., 2004). Although not much is known about Michael's past, it is possible that he possessed this kind of attachment style and similar familial environment, possibly leading him to develop hoarding behaviors.

Michael was discharged from the partial hospital program to a day program in the area. Michael's attendance has been nearly nonexistent, and he declined group or congregate housing options. Michael has also been inconsistent in making his appointments with any of his outpatient treaters.

Conclusion

Our case report with psychological testing has illuminated some of the underlying dynamics of hoarding behavior. Although hoarding is a recognized aspect of mental illness, hoarding unrelated to OCD has been given very little attention. In cases such as Michael's, treatment plans would likely be more effective with a deeper understanding of the origin of his hoarding. Future research is needed to understand hoarding in a broader context and in relation to mental disorders beyond OCD.

References

Anonymous, Secret of compulsive hoarding revealed (New Scientist, 15 November, 2003, Magazine issue 2421 (www.newscientist.com/article/mg18024212.800.html) retrieved 8/1/09

Bryk, W. (2005, April 13). The Collyer Brothers. *The New York Sun.* Retrieved 3/12/09 from www.nysun.com/on-the-town/collyer-brothers/12165

Duenwald, M. (2004, October). The psychology of . . . hoarding. What lies beneath the pathological desire to hoard tons of stuff [Electronic version]. *Discover Magazine.* Retrieved 3/17/09 (http://discovermagazine.com/2004/oct/psychology-of-hoarding)

Frost, R.O. & Hard, T.L. (1996). A cognitive behavioral model of compulsive hoarding. *Behavior Research and Therapy,* 34:341–350.

Gutheil, E.A. (1959). Problems of therapy in obsessive-compulsive neurosis. *American Journal of Psychotherapy,* 13: 793–808.

Kyrios, M., Frost, R.O., & Steketee, G. (2004). Cognitions in compulsive buying and acquisition. *Cognitive Therapy and Research,* 28:241–258.

Lidz, F: The paper chase. New York Times: October 26, 2003. Retroeved 8/1/09 www.nytimes.com/2003/10/26/nyregion/26feat.html

Saxena, S., Brody, A.L., Maidment, K.M., Smith, E.C., Zohrabi, N., Katz, E., Baker, S.K., Baxter, Lewis R., Jr. (2004). Cerebral Glucose Metabolism in Obsessive-Compulsive Hoarding. *American Journal of Psychiatry,* 161: 1038–1048. Retrieved 8/1/09 from Psychiatry Online (http://ajp.psychiatryonline.org/cgi/content/full/161/6/1038)

Steller, E. The effect of epinephrine, insulin, and glucose upon hoarding in rats. Brown University: January 28, 1943.

Assess Your Progress

1. What are the signs and symptoms of pathological hoarding?
2. Distinguish between clutter and pathological hoarding.

Acknowledgments—The authors thank June Wolf, PhD for the review of the psychological testing.

From *American Journal of Psychotherapy,* November 3, 2009, pp. 257–266. Copyright © 2009 by Association for the Advancement of Psychotherapy. Reprinted by permission.

Seasonal Affective Disorder

Patients with seasonal affective disorder have episodes of major depression that tend to recur during specific times of the year, usually in winter. Like major depression, seasonal affective disorder probably is underdiagnosed in primary care settings. Although several screening instruments are available, such screening is unlikely to lead to improved outcomes without personalized and detailed attention to individual symptoms. Physicians should be aware of comorbid factors that could signal a need for further assessment. Specifically, some emerging evidence suggests that seasonal affective disorder may be associated with alcoholism and attention-deficit/hyperactivity disorder. Seasonal affective disorder often can be treated with light therapy, which appears to have a low risk of adverse effects. Light therapy is more effective if administered in the morning. It remains unclear whether light is equivalent to drug therapy, whether drug therapy can augment the effects of light therapy, or whether cognitive behavior therapy is a better treatment choice. (Am Fam Physician 2006;74:1521–24. Copyright © 2006 American Academy of Family Physicians.)

STEPHEN J. LURIE ET AL.

The *Diagnostic and Statistical Manual of Mental Disorders*, 4th ed., (DSM-IV) categorizes seasonal affective disorder (SAD) not as a unique mood disorder, but as a specifier of major depression.[1] Thus, patients with SAD experience episodes of major depression that tend to recur at specific times of the year. These seasonal episodes may take the form of major depressive or bipolar disorders.

Epidemiology

The overall lifetime prevalence of SAD ranges from 0 to 9.7 percent.[2] This estimate depends on the specific population studied, as well as whether SAD is diagnosed by a screening questionnaire or a more rigorous clinical interview. In one U.S. study that used DSM-IV-based criteria, the lifetime prevalence of major depression with a seasonal pattern was 0.4 percent.[3] Prevalence may be higher at northern latitudes, and it may vary within ethnic groups at the same latitude.[4]

Patients with SAD are more likely to have family members with SAD, although this may be subject to reporting bias.[5] Twin studies have found that there may be a genetic component to susceptibility. Several genes code for serotonin transport, but the overall pattern of heritability likely is complex and polygenomic.[6]

Patients with SAD have more outpatient visits, more diagnostic testing, more prescriptions, and more referrals throughout the year compared with age- and sex-matched controls.[7] Patients with SAD visit their primary care physician more often in the winter than other patients, but rates between the groups are similar the rest of the year.[8]

Screening for SAD

Primary care physicians routinely fail to diagnose nearly one half of all patients who present with depression and other mental health problems.[9] Because SAD is a subtype of major depression, screening for depression should theoretically help identify patients with this disorder. The U.S. Preventive Services Task Force (USPSTF) concluded that there is good evidence that screening improves the accurate identification of patients with depression in primary care settings, and that treatment decreases clinical morbidity. The USPSTF concluded that the benefits of screening likely outweigh any potential harms.[10]

There are several instruments for detecting depression in primary care, ranging in length from one to 30 items with an average administration time of two to six minutes. Typically, the reading level of these instruments is between the third- and fifth-grade levels.[11] Some standardized instruments focus more narrowly on SAD. Reports on the sensitivity and specificity of these instruments can be difficult to interpret because of the small sizes and heterogeneity of patient samples tested, the possibility of differential recall bias (depending on the time of year the test is administered), and ongoing controversy over the criteria standard for SAD.

The Seasonal Pattern Assessment Questionnaire (SPAQ) is perhaps the most widely studied tool. It has been reported to have a high specificity (94 percent) for SAD but a low sensitivity (41 percent).[12] Other authors, however, have reported a much lower specificity.[13] The Seasonal Health Questionnaire has been reported to have higher specificity and sensitivity than the SPAQ,[14] but these results must be confirmed in larger and more diverse patient groups.

Sort: Key Recommendations for Practice

Clinical Recommendation	Evidence Rating	References
Standardized screening instruments for SAD probably are not sensitive enough to be used for routine screening.	C	12
Light therapy may be used for treating SAD, with effect sizes similar to those for antidepressant medications in treating depression. The total daily dosage should be approximately 5,000 lux, administered in the morning over 30 to 120 minutes.	A	23
Cognitive behavior therapy may be considered as an alternative to light therapy in the treatment of SAD.	B	28

SAD = seasonal affective disorder.
A = consistent, good-quality patient-oriented evidence; B = inconsistent or limited-quality patient-oriented evidence; C = consensus, disease-oriented evidence, usual practice, expert opinion, or case series. For information about the SORT evidence rating system, see page 1463 or www.aafp.org/afpsort.xml.

Although benefits from screening are less likely to be achieved without an accurate diagnostic work-up, effective treatment interventions, and close follow-up, it is unclear whether screening ultimately improves the care and outcomes of patients with major depression. When deciding to implement a screening instrument in a practice, office personnel should consider the administration time, scoring ease, reading level, and usefulness in identifying major depression and assessing change in the depression scores over time.[15]

Once patients have been identified as having major depression, questions must be asked to determine if the depression is linked to SAD. These questions concern the relationship between depression and time of year (if remission occurs during certain times of the year) and whether the depression has occurred at the same time during the past two years.

Associated Diagnoses

Because SAD is associated with serotonergic dysregulation and possibly with noradrenergic mechanisms, it may overlap with other diagnoses that share similar mechanisms, including generalized anxiety disorder, panic disorder, bulimia nervosa, late luteal phase dysphoric disorder, and chronic fatigue syndrome.[16] SAD also may be associated with attention-deficit/hyperactivity disorder (ADHD). Both conditions have been described as "disorders of central underarousal coupled with a heightened sensitivity to stimuli from the physical environment," and both are more common in women with a particular genotype for *HTR2A*, a gene that codes for a serotonin receptor.[17,18]

A pattern of seasonal alcohol use also may be associated with SAD. A summary of current research findings concluded that some patients with alcoholism may be self-medicating an underlying depression with alcohol or manifesting a seasonal pattern to alcohol-induced depression.[19] Such patterns appear to have a familial component and, like the link between ADHD and SAD, may be related to serotonergic functioning.

Treatment

Treatment options for SAD include light therapy, cognitive behavior therapy, and pharmacotherapy. Each option has been proven beneficial in treating SAD, but no large studies have found any treatment to be superior.

Light Therapy

Among susceptible persons, decreased seasonal exposure to light may mediate SAD through phase shifts in circadian rhythms, with resulting alterations in several aspects of serotonin metabolism. Thus, light replacement has been the most widely studied treatment for SAD.[20] In a review of studies of light therapy, an average dosage of 2,500 lux daily for one week was superior to placebo, as indicated by improvements on a depression rating scale.[21] The dosage most often found to be effective is 5,000 lux per day, given as 2,500 lux for two hours or 10,000 lux for 30 minutes.[22] A recent meta-analysis of 23 studies of light therapy found that the odds ratio for remission was 2.9 (95% confidence interval, 1.6 to 5.4); this ratio is similar to those of many pharmaceutical treatments for depression.[23] Like drug therapy for depression, light therapy carries some risk of precipitating mania.[24]

Light therapy generally is most effective when administered earlier in the day.[21,25,26] Early morning light therapy regulates the circadian pattern of melatonin secretion, whereas the use of light in the evening delays the normal melatonin phase shift.[27]

To ensure adequate response, patients should be treated with light therapy units that are specifically designed to treat SAD. Units that are not specifically designed for SAD treatment may not provide adequate brightness and may not have appropriate ultraviolet light filtration.[22]

Cognitive Behavior Therapy

Although cognitive behavior therapy (CBT) has some effectiveness in improving dysfunctional automatic thoughts and attitudes, behavior withdrawal, low rates of positive reinforcement, and ruminations in patients with major depression, few studies have assessed its effectiveness in the treatment of SAD. In one small clinical trial, patients with SAD were randomized to six weeks of treatment with CBT or light therapy, or CBT plus light therapy.[28] At the end of treatment, all three groups had significantly decreased levels of depression, but there was no difference between groups. However, this study only enrolled 26 subjects. To date, there have been no studies large enough to establish the effectiveness of CBT in the treatment of SAD.

Pharmacotherapy

Because patients with SAD also must fulfill criteria for depression, several randomized trials have assessed the use of antidepressants for this condition.[29–33] Most of these studies have compared pharmacotherapy with placebo rather than light therapy, making it difficult to determine if one treatment is superior. In the largest of these trials, patients with SAD had significantly better response on several measures of depression after eight weeks of sertraline (Zoloft) therapy compared with control patients.[29] Patients were excluded if they were receiving light therapy or other psychoactive medications, or if they had a history of alcoholism, drug abuse, or "emotional or intellectual problems."

A smaller study found that, in some statistical analyses, fluoxetine (Prozac) was better than placebo in the treatment of SAD.[30] Another small study found that the monoamine oxidase inhibitor moclobemide (not available in the United States) was similar to placebo in terms of changes on several general depression scales.[31]

Small trials of other agents (i.e., carbidopa/levodopa [Sinemet] and vitamin B_{12}) found no benefit over placebo.[34,35] Although there may be some theoretical justification for these treatments, there have not been trials of sufficient size to assess their effects.

Few randomized trials have assessed the effect of light therapy compared with pharmacotherapy.[32,36] These trials failed to find a difference between the effect of 6,000 lux and that of 20 mg of fluoxetine daily,[32] or between 10,000 lux and 20 mg of fluoxetine daily.[36] Larger trials will be required to establish whether there is a difference in effect size between light therapy and pharmacotherapy.

It is also possible that pharmacotherapy may preserve an initial therapeutic response to light therapy. Among 168 patients who had a positive response to light therapy, citalopram (Celexa) was found to be no more effective than placebo at preventing relapse; however, it was superior in terms of some secondary measures of depression.[33] In general, current evidence does not provide clear guidance as to whether antidepressant treatment is superior to light therapy, or whether antidepressants are useful as an adjunct to light therapy.

References

1. American Psychiatric Association. Task Force on DSM-IV. Diagnostic and Statistical Manual of Mental Disorders. 4th ed. Washington, D.C.: American Psychiatric Association, 1994.
2. Magnusson A. An overview of epidemiological studies on seasonal affective disorder. Acta Psychiatr Scand 2000;101:176–84.
3. Blazer DG, Kessler RC, Swartz MS. Epidemiology of recurrent major and minor depression with a seasonal pattern. The National Comorbidity Survey. Br J Psychiatry 1998;172:164–7.
4. Mersch PP, Middendorp HM, Bouhuys AL, Beersma DG, van den Hoofdakker RH. Seasonal affective disorder and latitude: a review of the literature. J Affect Disord 1999;53:35–48.
5. Sher L, Goldman D, Ozaki N, Rosenthal NE. The role of genetic factors in the etiology of seasonal affective disorder and seasonality. J Affect Disord 1999;53:203–10.
6. Sher L. Genetic studies of seasonal affective disorder and seasonality. Compr Psychiatry 2001;42:105–10.
7. Eagles JM, Howie FL, Cameron IM, Wileman SM, Andrew JE, Robertson C, et al. Use of health care services in seasonal affective disorder. Br J Psychiatry 2002;180:449–54.
8. Andrew JE, Wileman SM, Howie FL, Cameron IM, Naji SA, Eagles JM. Comparison of consultation rates in primary care attenders with and without seasonal affective disorder. J Affect Disord 2001;62:199–205.
9. Higgins ES. A review of unrecognized mental illness in primary care. Prevalence, natural history, and efforts to change the course. Arch Fam Med 1994;3:908–17.
10. U.S. Preventive Services Task Force. Screening for depression: recommendations and rationale. Ann Intern Med 2002;136:760–4.
11. Williams JW Jr, Pignone M, Ramirez G, Perez Stellato C. Identifying depression in primary care: a literature synthesis of case-finding instruments. Gen Hosp Psychiatry 2002;24:225–37.
12. Mersch PP, Vastenburg NC, Meesters Y, Bouhuys AL, Beersma DG, van den Hoofdakker RH, et al. The reliability and validity of the Seasonal Pattern Assessment Questionnaire: a comparison between patient groups. J Affect Disorder 2004;80:209–19.
13. Raheja SK, King EA, Thompson C. The Seasonal Pattern Assessment Questionnaire for identifying seasonal affective disorders. J Affect Disord 1996;41:193–9.
14. Thompson C, Thompson S, Smith R. Prevalence of seasonal affective disorder in primary care; a comparison of the seasonal pattern assessment questionnaire. J Affect Disord 2004;78:219–26.
15. Nease DE Jr, Malouin JM. Depression screening: a practical strategy. J Fam Pract 2003;52:118–24.
16. Partonen T, Magnusson A. Seasonal Affective Disorder: Practice and Research. New York, N.Y.: Oxford University Press, 2001.
17. Levitan RD, Masellis M, Basile VS, Lam RW, Jain U, Kaplan AS, et al. Polymorphism of the serotonin-2A receptor gene (HTR2A) associated with childhood attention deficit hyperactivity disorder (ADHD) in adult women with seasonal affective disorder. J Affect Disord 2002;71:229–33.
18. Levitan RD, Jain UR, Katzman MA. Seasonal affective symptoms in adults with residual attention-deficit hyperactivity disorder. Compr Psychiatry 1999;40:261–7.
19. Sher L. Alcoholism and seasonal affective disorder. Compr Psychiatry 2004;45:51–6.
20. Partonen T, Lonnqvist J. Seasonal affective disorder. Lancet 1998;352:1369–74.
21. Terman M, Terman JS, Quitkin FM, McGrath PJ, Stewart JW, Rafferty B. Light therapy for seasonal affective disorder. A review of efficacy. Neuropsychopharmacology 1989;2:1–22.
22. Levitan RD. What is the optimal implementation of bright light therapy for seasonal affective disorder (SAD)? J Psychiatry Neurosci 2005;30:72.
23. Golden RN, Gaynes BN, Ekstrom RD, Hamer RM, Jacobsen FM, Suppes T, et al. The efficacy of light therapy in the treatment of mood disorders: a review and meta-analysis of the evidence. Am J Psychiatry 2005;162:656–62.
24. Sohn CH, Lam RW. Treatment of seasonal affective disorder: unipolar versus bipolar differences. Curr Psychiatry Rep 2004;6:478–85.
25. Eastman CI, Young MA, Fogg LF, Liu L, Meaden PM. Bright light treatment of winter depression: a placebo-controlled trial. Arch Gen Psychiatry 1998;55:883–9.
26. Terman M, Terman JS, Ross DC. A controlled trial of timed bright light and negative air ionization for treatment of winter depression. Arch Gen Psychiatry 1998;55:875–82.
27. Terman JS, Terman M, Lo ES, Cooper TB. Circadian time of morning light administration and therapeutic response in winter depression. Arch Gen Psychiatry 2001;58:69–75.
28. Rohan KJ, Lindsey KT, Roecklein KA, Lacy TJ. Cognitive-behavioral therapy, light therapy, and their combination in treating seasonal affective disorder. J Affect Disord 2004;80:273–83.

29. Moscovitch A, Blashko CA, Eagles JM, Darcourt G, Thompson C, Kasper S, et al., for the International Collaborative Group on Sertraline in the Treatment of Outpatients with Seasonal Affective Disorders. A placebo-controlled study of sertraline in the treatment of outpatients with seasonal affective disorder. Psychopharmacology (Berl) 2004;171:390–7.

30. Lam RW, Gorman CP, Michalon M, Steiner M, Levitt AJ, Corral MR, et al. Multicenter, placebo-controlled study of fluoxetine in seasonal affective disorder. Am J Psychiatry 1995;152:1765–70.

31. Lingjaerde O, Reichborn-Kjennerud T, Haggag A, Gartner I, Narud K, Berg EM. Treatment of winter depression in Norway. II. A comparison of the selective monoamine oxidase A inhibitor moclobemide and placebo. Acta Psychiatr Scand 1993;88:372–80.

32. Ruhrmann S, Kasper S, Hawellek B, Martinez B, Hoflich G, Nickelsen T, et al. Effects of fluoxetine versus bright light in the treatment of seasonal affective disorder. Psychol Med 1998;28:923–33.

33. Martiny K, Lunde M, Simonsen C, Clemmensen L, Poulsen DL, Solstad K, et al. Relapse prevention by citalopram in SAD patients responding to 1 week of light therapy. A placebo-controlled study. Acta Psychiatr Scand 2004;109:230–4.

34. Oren DA, Moul DE, Schwartz PJ, Wehr TA, Rosenthal NE. A controlled trial of levodopa plus carbidopa in the treatment of winter seasonal affective disorder: a test of the dopamine hypothesis. J Clin Psychopharmacol 1994;14:196–200.

35. Oren DA, Teicher MH, Schwartz PJ, Glod C, Turner EH, Ito YN, et al. A controlled trial of cyanocobalamin (vitamin B12) in the treatment of winter seasonal affective disorder. J Affect Disord 1994;32:197–200.

36. Lam RW, Levitt AJ, Levitan RD, Enns MW, Morehouse R, Michalek EE, et al. The Can-SAD study: a randomized controlled trial of the effectiveness of light therapy and fluoxetine in patients with winter seasonal affective disorder. Am J Psychiatry 2006;163:805–12.

Assess Your Progress

1. What are the reasons people with SAD become depressed in the winter?

2. What are the signs and symptoms of seasonal affective disorder?

STEPHEN J. LURIE, MD, PhD, is assistant professor of family medicine at the University of Rochester (N.Y.) School of Medicine and Dentistry. BARBARA GAWINSKI, PhD, is director of psychosocial curriculum in the Department of Family Medicine at the University of Rochester School of Medicine and Dentistry. DEBORAH PIERCE, MD, MPH, is clinical associate professor of family medicine at the University of Rochester School of Medicine and Dentistry. SALLY J. ROUSSEAU, MSW, is administrator of the Family Medicine Research Center at the University of Rochester School of Medicine and Dentistry.

Address correspondence to Stephen J. Lurie, MD, PhD, Dept. of Family Medicine, University of Rochester School of Medicine and Dentistry, 1381 South Ave., Rochester, NY 14620 (e-mail: Stephen_Lurie @urmcrochester.edu). Reprints are not available from the authors.

Dealing with the Stressed

Workplace stress costs the economy more than $30 billion a year, and yet nobody knows what it is or how to deal with it.

KEN MACQUEEN

Life is hard. You work in a "fabric-covered box," as Dilbert puts it. Some troll in the IT department monitors your every keystroke. Lunch is a greasy slab of *pizza al desko,* eaten under heavy email fire. Your eyesight is shot, you're going to flab, you've vowed to make this just a 50-hour week because your spouse—toiling in another cubicle across town—needs every night and the weekend to meet her ridiculous deadline. It's 4:59 P.M., and if you're late again the daycare's gonna dump the kid on the street and call Children's Aid. Grab the cell. Grab the BlackBerry. You just know the boss is going to tug your electronic leash if he sees you leaving this early. Yeah, yeah, life is hard.

It's, you know, stressful. Whatever that means.

Stress is part of an explosion in workplace mental health issues now costing the Canadian economy an estimated $33 billion a year in lost productivity, as well as billions more in medical costs. It's become a political priority for Prime Minister Stephen Harper, who recently announced a new Mental Health Commission of Canada. With almost one million Canadians suffering from a mental health disorder, "it's now the fastest-growing category of disability insurance claims in Canada," Harper said. The cause is unclear. "Some blame the hectic pace of modern life, the trend to smaller and fragmented families, often separated by great distances, or the mass migration from small stable communities to huge, impersonal cities," he said. If there was a false note in his speech, it was his optimistic view of society's comprehension of the issue. "We now understand," he said, "that mental illness is not a supernatural phenomenon, or a character flaw."

Well, maybe. Such understanding is hardly universal in the workplace, where, as Harper noted, "stress or worse" exacts a heavy toll. It's as likely that stress-related maladies will be viewed with a combination of cynicism, incomprehension, and a skepticism bordering on hostility. To critics—a field that includes many employers, some academics, and co-workers resentful at picking up the slack—stress is the new whiplash, except bigger, more expensive, harder to define, and even more difficult to prove. Or to disprove.

"Stress," says U.S. author and workplace counsellor Scott Sheperd, "is probably the most overused and misused word in the English language—with the possible exception of love." It means everything and nothing. It is, he argues in *Attacking the Stress Myth*, "The Great Excuse." Look at the numbers: stress leaves are off the charts and some of the zombies who do show up accomplish little more than draining the company coffee pot.

The cause of this growing hit on productivity is indeed a mystery. Did the world get harder, or did people get softer? Or are employers stuck with an addled labour force of their own creation? It's not as if today's children will be sent to work in the mines. Women aren't struggling to raise six kids, while mourning several more who died in infancy. Men aren't spending 12 hours a day plowing fields behind a mule, or sweating over some mechanical monster of the Industrial Revolution, waiting for an arm or a leg to be dragged into its innards. No, odds are you've got indoor work, no heavy lifting, a 40-hour week (in theory), holiday time, and a big-screen TV waiting at home. How hard can life be?

Well, one person's dream job can be another's nightmare.

Nights, weekends, Janie Toivanen, an employee on the Burnaby campus of video game giant Electronic Arts (Canada) Ltd., gave her all to her job. She was part of the team producing EA's wildly popular NHL game series. EA prides itself on being a work-hard/play-hard kind of place. The complex looks like a workers' paradise, complete with a sand-covered beach volleyball court, an artificial turf soccer pitch, a full-on fitness centre, massage, yoga classes and a steam room. There's a gourmet cafeteria, and an employee concierge service to look after such mundanities as dry cleaning and car washing. In exchange, EA expects a huge degree of worker commitment.

Toivanen, an employee since 1996, earned strong performance ratings in her early years, regular bonuses and stock options. She rose through the ranks, often using what downtime she had to catch up on her sleep. "Ms. Toivanen's career was her life," says a decision last year by the British Columbia Human Rights Tribunal. But life caught up with her. By 2002, at age 47, she was carrying a heavy load, and looming deadlines preyed on her mind and ruined her sleep. Dealings with co-workers were strained, questions from supervisors were met with tears or anger.

She resisted her doctor's urging to take stress leave, fearing it would hurt her career. Finally, on the edge of a breakdown in September 2002, she handed her doctor's note to a supervisor and requested leave, only to be told EA had already decided to fire her. Big mistake. The failure to investigate her deteriorating condition or to accommodate her medical condition violated the provincial human rights code, the tribunal concluded. "She thought that EA was a company that prided itself on looking after employees," it said. "Instead of investing any time and energy in bringing her back, healthy, to her workplace, it fired her." She spiralled into depression and was placed on long-term disability by her former employer's insurer. At the time of the ruling in 2006 she was still on paid disability. The tribunal ordered EA to pay almost $150,000 in costs, severance, stock option losses and damages, "for injury to her dignity, feelings and self-respect."

Chronic job stress has emerged in epidemic terms. Our job is to make a business case for mental health.

Employers neglect the work environment at their peril, warns Bill Wilkerson, a former insurance company president and now CEO of the Global Business and Economic Roundtable on Addiction and Mental Health. "Chronic job stress has emerged in what you might call epidemic terms," he says. He co-founded the group 10 years ago, as private insurers grew alarmed at the runaway impact of mental health issues.

The first indicator was the spiralling costs of prescription drugs for maladies that were "imprecise in their nature," says Wilkerson, who also now serves as chairman of the workplace advisory board of the Canadian Mental Health Commission. Depression, insomnia, hypertension were all part of the mix. "As a business guy I was focused on how we tackled these as costs," he says. After a decade immersed in the science, Wilkerson has no doubt stress is a trigger for mental health issues, and such physical ailments as hypertension and heart attack. But there remains, he concedes, skepticism in boardrooms and corner offices. "We have to talk tough love to business leaders all the time," he says. "Our job isn't to make a case for business, it's to make a business case for mental health."

Still, the skepticism remains. In the case of politicians, for example, some think stress leave is just an excuse to escape political problems. Consider some examples: veteran NDP MP Svend Robinson walked into a public auction in 2004 and stole an expensive ring. Days later, he turned himself in, held a tearful news conference and embarked on stress leave. He was subsequently diagnosed with a bipolar disorder. A year

later, Conservative Gurmant Grewal, then an MP from Surrey, B.C., took stress leave after being embroiled in a scandal over secretly recording conversations with senior Liberal officials, among other bizarre incidents. "One of the things that makes me pretty cynical is when I hear a politician or a CEO who's gotten into trouble leave to spend more time with his family, or to take stress leave," says stress researcher Donna Lero of the University of Guelph.

Even when companies think they have clear evidence of malingering, they may find the courts decide otherwise. James Symington, a Halifax police officer and aspiring actor, left work June 11, 2001, citing an elbow injury. He was found fit for duty; instead, he booked off on stress leave. Months later, still on leave, Symington took his service dog to New York to help search for bodies after the terror attacks of Sept. 11. He also worked acting gigs. Symington was fired in early 2005, while still on leave, after the force said he wouldn't co-operate with attempts to get him back to work. This August, the Nova Scotia Court of Appeal cleared the way for Symington to sue the police for malicious prosecution for conducting a fraud investigation into his alleged misuse of stress leave. He's also suing his union, claiming it failed to protect him from a hostile work environment.

Understandably, many employers have become highly skeptical of complaints about excessive stress, and they vent their frustration to people like employment law specialist Howard Levitt, a Toronto-based lawyer for Lang Michener. He says stress issues have mushroomed during his 28 years in the field. "It's become for most employers the single biggest bugaboo in terms of workplace law issues," he says. Companies are "infuriated" by doctors who recommend stress leaves "without any real substantiation." For one thing, the family doctor isn't diagnosing the problem behind the alleged stress. Nor does the doctor know if there are other jobs in the workplace the patient is still capable of doing. The end result, ironically, is a more stressful workplace. "It's a bad motivation for other employees who see these employees getting away with it, and then have to work harder to pick up the slack," says Levitt. "So, often they say, 'Why shouldn't I participate in this scam?' And everybody works a little less hard."

A vocal minority of academics and others share a view that stress is a bogus concept. British author and former Fulbright Scholar Angela Patmore took on the "stress industry" in her 2006 book, *The Truth About Stress*. She doesn't buy that life in Britain is more stressful than it was, for instance, during the war years or the disease-ridden Victorian era. "The concept of mitigating stress is bollocks," she told *Maclean's*. "Everywhere in the West we see this message, 'you will drop dead, you will go mad, avoid negative emotions, avoid emotional situations.' None of our ancestors would have understood a word of this." She has an ally in Bob Briner, an occupational psychologist teaching at London University's Birkbeck College. He considers stress a meaningless concept; one that is creating a generation of "emotional hypochondriacs." As he writes, "One of the main explanations for the popularity of stress is that people like simple catch-all ways of 'explaining' why bad things happen, particularly illness."

The concept of mitigating stress is bollocks. Our ancestors wouldn't have understood a word of this.

Whether you believe stress is a real condition with debilitating effects, or the product of a generation of weak-minded workers, this much is indisputable: the costs are real, and spectacular. "Today, our estimate is that mental health conditions—with stress a risk factor—clearly cost the economy $33 billion per annum in lost industrial output," says Wilkerson. Those losses, he adds, "are excessively higher than the cost of health care associated with treating these conditions."

But one of the central problems with treating the apparent stress epidemic is that it remains exceptionally difficult to cure a problem that can't be easily defined. If you ask experts for a definition of stress, you often get a pause and then something like this: it is a highly individualistic, multi-faceted response to a set of circumstances that place a demand on physical or mental energy. There is "distress," a negative response to disturbing circumstances. And there is "eustress," so-called good stress. Eustress might come on the day you marry the love of your life. Distress might come on the day the love of your life marries someone else. Stress is a kind of personal weather system, ever changing, its components unique to the individual. It may consist of overwork and job insecurity, combined with colicky children and a sickly mother. It may be an unrealistic deadline, vague expectations and hostile co-workers. It may be the thing that gets you up in the morning, the challenge that makes work bearable, the risk of failure that makes success sweeter. Stress is bad. Stress is good. Stress is a mess. It is also a constantly moving target.

"Is stress quantitatively growing, I don't know," says Shannon Wagner, a clinical psychologist and a specialist in workplace stress research at the University of Northern British Columbia. "What we do know is it is qualitatively changing." Jobs may not be as physically laborious as they were but they're more relentless, she says. "A lot of people now are identifying techno-stress and the 24/7 workday, which we didn't have even 10 or 15 years ago, this feeling of being constantly plugged in, of checking email 500 times a day."

There is ample evidence that people are working longer and harder, skimping on holidays, and paying a price. The work-life balance is out of whack, says Donna Lero, who holds the Jarislowsky Chair in Families and Work at the University of Guelph. She says the stresses today's families face are different, and come from all directions. Workdays are longer, and for most families, including three-quarters of those with children, both parents work. "What used to be three people's work is being done by two, with nobody home when the child is sick," she says. Families are smaller, but they're also scattered. The sandwich generation is often simultaneously handling both child and elder care. "At a time when employers and certainly individuals are voicing concerns about work-family conflict, we're seeing things go in the opposite direction we'd like them to."

Consider the impact on the federal public service. A newly released Treasury Board study of remuneration for some 351,000 public servants notes that disability claims for its two main insurance plans have more than doubled between 1990 and 2002. "Much of the increase," the report concludes, "resulted from growth in cases relating to depression and anxiety." In fact, more than 44 per cent of all new public service disability claims were for depression and anxiety—up from less than 24 per cent a decade earlier. Stress and mental health issues are now the leading reason for long-term disability claims, ahead of cancer. The problem seems to be especially acute in Quebec, where civil servants are off the job an average of 14 days a year, an increase of 33 per cent since 2001, according to a recent report.

Nationally, an estimated 35 million workdays are lost to mental conditions among our 10 million workers. A six-year-old Health Canada report estimates the annual cost of just depression and distress at $14.4 billion: $6.3 billion in treatment and $8.1 billion in lost productivity. And all that only measures the number of people who actually miss time at work. Just as serious may be "presenteeism"— the phenomenon of stressed-out workers who show up to work anyway and accomplish little. It's estimated to cost Canadian employers $22 billion a year. "It's the silent scourge of productivity," says Paul Hemp, who wrote a definitive article on the subject for *The Harvard Business Review* in 2004. A U.S. study of 29,000 adults calculated the total cost of presenteeism at more than US$150 billion.

So what is an enlightened, conscientious employer to do? That's a quandary: in some cases, a generous benefits plan actually *increases* the likelihood of workers booking off. A study on sick leave published last year by Statistics Canada found unionized workers with disability insurance are far more likely to take extended leaves. The recent federal public service pay study uncovered an interesting fact: prison guards, dockyard workers, heating plant operators and hospital service groups consistently used the most sick leave per capita during the 13-year period under examination. It's understandable that those in "difficult environments like penitentiaries or dockyards" would make more claims, the study notes. But their consistent use of leave over the years "suggests that cultural and management factors may also play a role in the level of demand for sick leave." Translation: some workers take stress leave simply because they can.

Nationally, an estimated 35 million workdays are lost each year due to mental and emotional distress.

It seems the key is to strike a difficult balance between compassion and coddling. It's not easy, but for those who get it right, the results are dramatic. For example, the Vancouver City Savings Credit Union—Vancity—has been repeatedly ranked among *Maclean's* Top 100 employers, in part because of an ingrained employee assistance program and management training in spotting employee problems before they reach a crisis.

Few jobs are as stressful as front-line tellers, especially in Vancouver, with an average 237 bank robberies a year, about the highest rate in Canada. Ann Leckie, Vancity's director of human resources, concedes "one of the greatest negative situations we can face is robbery." Vancity set out in the mid-1980s to limit the personal and financial fallout by contracting Daniel Stone & Associates Inc., its employee assistance provider, to design a robbery recovery program. Branch employees who wish to gather after a robbery can meet with Stone, a clinical counsellor, and others of his staff. Those who wish can have one-on-one sessions later. All have access to a 24-hour help line. Managers keep watch for delayed signs of stress: absenteeism, increased mistakes or mood swings. These workers are urged to seek help.

If it all seems too touchy-feely, consider the results. In B.C., the average post-robbery absence per branch—as paid out by the Workers Compensation Board—is 62 days. "In Vancity [in 2005] 17 of our 19 robberies had no days absent," says Leckie. The other two robberies had an average absence of two days. Leckie does a quick calculation: "That's 1,054 days not lost," she says. "There's a big financial incentive to doing it right."

Doing it right means building mutual trust and respect between employer and employee. It means heading off problems in advance and believing in those employees who need help. "The sense that there are non-sick people obtaining benefits fraudulently is an urban myth," Leckie says. The Vancity program is much copied, but rarely duplicated. "I have seen the program fail," she says. "In a cynical organization you get comments like, 'Well, the only time I get to talk to anyone important is when I have a gun to my head.'"

Sometimes the gun is real, more often it's a metaphor. Maybe bad stress is exactly that: a robbery. It steals joy and purpose and health; and it takes from the bottom line. In that sense it is real, no matter how it is defined, or how cynically it is viewed.

Assess Your Progress

1. Give examples that demonstrate the interaction between mental and physical health.
2. Name three modern stressors that didn't exist 5,000 years ago.
3. How do positive and negative stressors impact health?

With Martin Patriquin and John Intini.

UNIT 3
Nutritional Health

Unit Selections

Learning Outcomes

After reading this unit, you should be able to:

- Distinguish between healthy and less healthy foods.

- Discuss how one can eat healthy on a limited budget.

- Discuss what dietary changes will improve health.

- Contrast the nutritional advantages of breastfeeding versus bottle feeding.

- Describe the functions of vitamin D and its effect on health.

- Explain why it is important to eat breakfast.

Student Website
www.mhhe.com/cls

Internet References

The American Dietetic Association
 www.eatright.org
Center for Science in the Public Interest (CSPI)
 www.cspinet.org
Food and Nutrition Information Center
 www.nalusda.gov/fnic/index.html

For years, the majority of Americans paid little attention to nutrition, other than to eat three meals a day and, perhaps, take a vitamin supplement. While this dietary style was generally adequate for the prevention of major nutritional deficiencies, medical evidence began to accumulate linking the American diet to a variety of chronic illnesses. In an effort to guide Americans in their dietary choices, the U.S. Dept. of Agriculture and the U.S. Public Health Service review and publish Dietary Guidelines every 5 years. The year 2000 Dietary Guidelines recommendations are no longer limited to food choices; they include advice on the importance of maintaining a healthy weight and engaging in daily exercise. In addition to the Dietary Guidelines, the Department of Agriculture developed the *Food Guide Pyramid* to show the relative importance of food groups.

Despite an apparent ever-changing array of dietary recommendations from the scientific community, five recommendations remain constant: (1) eat a diet low in saturated fat, (2) eat whole grain foods, (3) drink plenty of fresh water daily, (4) limit your daily intake of sugar and salt, and (5) eat a diet rich in fruits and vegetables. These recommendations, while general in nature, are seldom heeded and in fact many Americans don't eat enough fruits and vegetables and eat too much sugar and saturated fat.

Of all the nutritional findings, the link between dietary fat and coronary heart disease remains the most consistent throughout the literature. Current recommendations suggest that the types of fats consumed may play a much greater role in disease processes than the total amount of fat consumed. As it currently stands, most experts agree that it is prudent to limit our intake of trans fat that appears to raise LDLs (the bad cholesterol) and lower HDLs (the good cholesterol) and thus increases the risk of heart disease. There's also evidence that trans fats increase the risk of diabetes.

While the basic advice on eating healthy remains fairly constant, many Americans are still confused over exactly what to eat. Should their diet be low carbohydrate, high protein, or low fat? When people turn to standards such as the *Food Guide Pyramid,* even here there is some confusion. The *Pyramid,* designed by the Department of Agriculture over 20 years ago, recommends a diet based on grains, fruits, and vegetables with several servings of meats and dairy products. It also restricts the consumption of fats, oils, and sweets. While the *Pyramid* offers guidelines as to food groups, individual nutrients are not emphasized. One nutrient, vitamin D, has been in the news recently. New research on the "sunshine" vitamin suggests current recommendations may not be adequate, especially for senior citizens, as explained in "An Oldie Vies for Nutrient of the Decade" by Jane E. Brody. The data also indicate that vitamin D may help lower the incidence of cancers, type 1 diabetes, and multiple sclerosis.

While the public continues to be confused about which foods are healthy, the media continually bombards us with articles and

© PunchStock/Corbis

television segments on nutrition-related issues. In "Eating Well on a Downsized Food Budget," Jane E. Brody advises that with the recent downturn in the economy, it may be time to return to the basics: healthy and reasonably priced foods. Catherine Marshall addresses the benefits of breastfeeding in "Breastfeeding Is Not Obscene."

Of all the topic areas in health, food and nutrition is certainly one of the most interesting, if for no other reason than the rate at which dietary recommendations change. One recommendation that hasn't changed is the adage that a good breakfast is the best way to start the day. In "What Good Is Breakfast?" author Amanda Fortini addresses the relationship between breakfast and a reduced risk of obesity. She also discusses the link between better grades and breakfast among schoolchildren. Despite all the controversy and conflict, the one message that seems to remain constant is the importance of balance and moderation in everything we eat.

Eating Well on a Downsized Food Budget

Jane E. Brody

Now may be a good time to bring back the basics—the nutritious and affordable foods that have been all but forgotten by many affluent families since the Great Depression.

I'm not going to suggest a nightly diet of stone soup or the cheap fat- and sugar-rich menus of the urban poor. But many people who once gave little thought to dining on steak, lobster, asparagus, baby spinach or crème brûlée are now having to spend less on just about everything, including food.

Those who have lost jobs may be able to turn some of their unwanted spare time toward the grocery and kitchen. Others, like families with two working parents or working single parents, have to carve out time to provide economical, nourishing meals.

Not only is it possible, but it can improve the health and reduce the girth of Americans, regardless of socioeconomic status.

A Little Effort Goes a Long Way

"We need to look at real foods for real people, the foods that got us through the last depression," said Adam Drewnowski, an epidemiologist at the University of Washington's Center for Public Health Nutrition. "We must avoid the temptation to turn to cheap, empty calories—the refined grains, added sugars and added fats that give you the most calories you can get for your food dollar."

Instead, Dr. Drewnowski said, "there are many foods that are affordable and nutrient-rich and not loaded with empty calories."

And eating for good health does not have to mean eating less. "If you have equal portions of foods that are nutrient-dense, you will end up eating fewer calories," he said.

For families accustomed to eating out and ordering in, shopping for and preparing meals can take more time. According to the Economic Research Service of the United States Department of Agriculture, low-income women who work full time spend just over 40 minutes a day on meal preparation. With a little planning, another 20 or 30 minutes can provide healthy, economical fare.

Households not accustomed to home cooking may have to make small investments in kitchen equipment and ingredients that can speed food preparation and will remain useful long after the economy improves. Even families using food stamps can afford the foods discussed below to make recipes like those posted with this column at nytimes.com/health. And no one need go hungry.

Value-Added Foods

To assess which foods provide the best value of balanced nutrients for less money, Dr. Drewnowski said, "we need to calculate nutrients per calorie and nutrients per dollar and make those foods part of the mainstream diet."

Researchers at the State University of New York at Buffalo who studied families in a program for overweight children found that basing the family diet on low-calorie, high-nutrient foods not only improved the health of the entire family but also reduced the amount spent on food.

One myth to dispel is that fruits and vegetables must be fresh to be nutritious. Not only do canned and frozen versions usually cost less and require less preparation, but nutrient value is as good or better and less food is wasted. Fresh produce is often harvested before it is fully ripe and so comes to the consumer with fewer than optimal nutrients. But fruits and vegetables that are canned or frozen are picked at the peak of ripeness. There is more vitamin C in a glass of orange juice made from frozen concentrate than in freshly squeezed juice.

So let's welcome back to the American table meals made from potatoes, eggs, beans, low-fat or nonfat yogurt and milk (including reconstituted powdered milk), carrots, kale or collards, onions, bananas, apples, peanut butter, almonds, lean ground beef, chicken and turkey, along with canned or frozen corn, peas, tomatoes, broccoli and fish. For nutrient-dense beverages, Dr. Drewnowski suggests 100 percent fruit juice blends and fruit-and-vegetable juice blends.

To his suggestions I would add pasta and rice (the whole-wheat kinds cost just pennies more), which can be a base for many quick, nutritious meals. Combining leftover vegetables and meat or poultry with a pot of pasta or rice takes just minutes, and has the added benefit of reducing potential waste.

For dessert, try frozen yogurt or low-fat ice cream topped with seasonal fruit for the best nutrient-to-calorie ratio and value.

Potatoes: One of the Good Guys

Some perfectly good foods have been unfairly smeared by a broad brush. Potatoes are an example, deplored by nutrition advocates for how they are most often consumed—fried and heavily salted—and by the low-carb set for their high glycemic index.

In fact, potatoes are highly versatile, they are easily prepared in many delicious ways with little or no added fat, and they are nearly always consumed with other foods, which greatly reduces their effect on blood sugar. And they are nutritious. A five-ounce potato provides just 100 calories, for which you get 35 percent of a day's recommended vitamin C, 20 percent of the vitamin B6, 15 percent of the iodine, 10 percent each of niacin, iron and copper, and 6 percent of the protein.

Try potatoes baked, boiled or steamed and topped with low-fat yogurt or sour cream seasoned with your favorite herbs or spices.

Beans, whether prepared from scratch (soaked overnight and then cooked) or taken from a can, are a low-cost nutritional powerhouse. They are low in fat, rich sources of B vitamins and iron, and richer in protein than any other plant food. When combined in a meal with a grain like rice (preferably brown), bulgur or whole-wheat bread, the protein quality is as good as that of meat.

Cabbage, too, gives you more than your money's worth of nutrients, including vitamin C and potassium, at only 17 calories a cup eaten shredded and raw, 29 calories a cup when cooked. Collards are high in vitamins A and C, potassium, calcium (cup for cup, on a par with milk), iron, niacin and protein, and yet low in sodium and calories. Kale has only 43 calories a cup when cooked.

In the fruit category, it's hard to beat apples for year-round, economical, nutritious and versatile fare that can be a part of any meal or served as a snack or dessert (as in baked apples). Bananas are also handy; even when overripe, they can be mashed and used to make banana bread or a smoothie.

Here are some other tips for busy cooks concerned about nutrition and cost:

- Buy family-size packages of meat or poultry; divide them up and freeze meal-size portions, labeled and dated.
- Choose the less expensive store brands of canned and frozen produce.
- Use powdered reconstituted milk for cooking.
- Cook in batches, enough for two or more meals, and freeze single portions for lunch.
- Use meat, poultry and fish as a condiment, in small amounts added to main-dish salads, soups and sauces.
- Try main-dish soups and salad for filling yet low-calorie meals. Soups can also be made in large amounts and frozen.
- Consider buying a slow cooker for efficient, one-dish meals.

Assess Your Progress

1. How can people eat a healthy diet when the economy is weak?
2. What are the benefits of canned and frozen fruits and vegetables against fresh produce?

Breastfeeding Is Not Obscene

CATHERINE MARSHALL

Breasts are everywhere these days. They saturate our media in guises both trivial and sombre. Whether grotesquely augmented, stricken with cancer or tumbling unbidden from the frocks of soccer wives, breasts guarantee rapt attention and ongoing debate.

But never are these appendages more hotly debated than when they are being used according to their very purpose and design—that is, for the nourishment of babies.

Although the west's growing technological sophistication is inversely proportionate to its tolerance for organic activities such as breastfeeding, the negative attitudes are hardly new. History is littered with wet nurses to whom this distasteful activity was outsourced and modern mothers who dispensed with the biological process altogether in favour of Nestle's magical infant formula.

Buoyed by groups like the World Health Organisation, breastfeeding is creeping back into the public square, but western newborns still enter a world riven with dissent over their right to a ready meal.

It was refreshing to see the lactating Mexican actress and UNICEF ambassador Salma Hayek instinctively suckle a malnourished Sierra Leonean baby while visiting that country earlier this year. Hayek told reporters it was a compassionate act for a dying child, and that it came naturally to her to reach out to this baby when her own milk supply was plentiful. It was also an attempt to diminish the stigma of breastfeeding.

Not since Rose of Sharon breastfed a dying man in John Steinbeck's *The Grapes of Wrath* had breasts been used to commit such a revolutionary act. This Hollywood sex symbol wasn't just sharing her milk with a stranger's baby; she was doing so under the full public gaze.

How could it possibly be, then, that just last month in culturally diverse and thoroughly modern Australia a mother was asked by a flight attendant to conceal her breastfeeding activity from the puritanical eyes of fellow travellers? And that as recently as 2007 the NSW state government was forced to pass legislation making it illegal to discriminate against women breastfeeding in public?

Opinions around this issue are violently split between the supporters who believe babies should be allowed to feed wherever they please and the detractors who accuse nursing mothers of indecent exposure.

Could this really be happening in the same laissez-faire society where, not long before Kevin Rudd became Prime Minister, he was praised as being 'red-blooded' for visiting a New York strip club? Where young women flaunt their cleavages on city streets and semi-naked models stare out from the covers of men's magazines in service stations and news agencies across the country? Where prostitutes advertise their ware on the classified pages of suburban family newspapers?

Or, to put it more bluntly: is female nakedness culturally acceptable only when it is aimed exclusively at the arousal and satisfaction of men?

The reaction from some quarters to the Salma Hayek story seems to reinforce this hypothesis. As a presenter on the American talk show *The Young Turks* remarked, 'I wanted to be turned on by her breasts, but in that context I just couldn't do it.'

Of course, the reverse is true in traditional societies, where women tend to dress conservatively and the natural function of breasts is well-respected. In the many years I breastfed my own children, it never occurred to me that I might offend anyone. The fact that I lived in Africa contributed, no doubt, to the ease with which I was able to conduct this ritual.

In Africa, breasts exist primarily as vessels of nourishment rather than as sexual objects. Women breastfeed their children on trains, buses and taxis, in restaurants and on park benches, in church and at work. Mostly they do so discreetly, but it's hardly newsworthy when they don't.

Using these African mamas as role models, I fed my babies on demand, regardless of where we happened to be at the time. The only person to object was a friend's mother, who believed vehemently that breasts were for sex, not babies. As if the two were somehow mutually exclusive.

And herein, perhaps, lies the absurd conundrum facing Australian women, who live in a strangely dichotomous society which tolerates them lying topless on the beach but chokes on its collective latte when they expose their nursing bras. In its typically prurient way, Western culture has co-opted breasts and sexualised them so thoroughly that their basic function is no longer accommodated.

This primordial act, upon which every other mammal relies for survival, has been twisted from its nurturing premise into an act of awful obscenity.

Sadly, society's fixation on the 'perversion' of public breastfeeding obscures the inordinate benefits that flow from it: breast milk improves infants' health and intellectual outcomes and decreases their carbon footprints; its production results in elevated levels of oxytocin within the nursing mother's brain, contributing to her emotional equilibrium, and decreases her risk of developing ovarian and breast cancer.

Almost a decade into the new century, it's a disgrace that women are still made to feel uncomfortable while using their breasts to nourish their babies. Breastfeeding is neither primitive nor obscene; it is an act of love and generosity, a forward-thinking deposit into society's depleted bank account.

Asssess Your Progress

1. What are the health benefits of breastfeeding?
2. Describe why public breastfeeding is considered obscene by some people.

An Oldie Vies for Nutrient of the Decade

JANE E. BRODY

The so-called sunshine vitamin is poised to become the nutrient of the decade, if a host of recent findings are to be believed. Vitamin D, an essential nutrient found in a limited number of foods, has long been renowned for its role in creating strong bones, which is why it is added to milk.

Now a growing legion of medical researchers have raised strong doubts about the adequacy of currently recommended levels of intake, from birth through the sunset years. The researchers maintain, based on a plethora of studies, that vitamin D levels considered adequate to prevent bone malformations like rickets in children are not optimal to counter a host of serious ailments that are now linked to low vitamin D levels.

To be sure, not all medical experts are convinced of the need for or the desirability of raising the amount of vitamin D people should receive, either through sunlight, foods, supplements or all three. The federal committee that establishes daily recommended levels of nutrients has resisted all efforts to increase vitamin D intake significantly, partly because the members are not convinced of assertions for its health-promoting potential and partly because of time-worn fears of toxicity.

This column will present the facts as currently known, but be forewarned. In the end, you will have to decide for yourself how much of this vital nutrient to consume each and every day and how to obtain it.

Where to Obtain It

Through most of human history, sunlight was the primary source of vitamin D, which is formed in skin exposed to ultraviolet B radiation (the UV light that causes sunburns). Thus, to determine how much vitamin D is needed from food and supplements, take into account factors like skin color, where you live, time of year, time spent out of doors, use of sunscreens and coverups and age.

Sun avoiders and dark-skinned people absorb less UV radiation. People in the northern two-thirds of the country make little or no vitamin D in winter, and older people make less vitamin D in their skin and are less able to convert it into the hormone that the body uses. In addition, babies fed just breast milk consume little vitamin D unless given a supplement.

In addition to fortified drinks like milk, soy milk and some juices, the limited number of vitamin D food sources include oily fish like salmon, mackerel, bluefish, catfish, sardines and tuna, as well as cod liver oil and fish oils. The amount of vitamin D in breakfast cereals is minimal at best. As for supplements, vitamin D is found in prenatal vitamins, multivitamins, calcium-vitamin D combinations and plain vitamin D. Check the label, and select brands that contain vitamin D3, or cholecalciferol. D2, or ergocalciferol, is 25 percent less effective.

Vitamin D content is listed on labels in international units (I.U.). An eight-ounce glass of milk or fortified orange juice is supposed to contain 100 I.U. Most brands of multivitamins provide 400 a day. Half a cup of canned red salmon has about 940, and three ounces of cooked catfish about 570.

Myriad Links to Health

Let's start with the least controversial role of vitamin D—strong bones. Last year, a 15-member team of nutrition experts noted in The American Journal of Clinical Nutrition that "randomized trials using the currently recommended intakes of 400 I.U. vitamin D a day have shown no appreciable reduction in fracture risk."

"In contrast," the experts continued, "trials using 700 to 800 I.U. found less fracture incidence, with and without supplemental calcium. This change may result from both improved bone health and reduction in falls due to greater muscle strength."

A Swiss study of women in their 80s found greater leg strength and half as many falls among those who took 800 I.U. of vitamin D a day for three months along with 1,200 milligrams of calcium, compared with women who took just calcium. Greater strength and better balance have been found in older people with high blood levels of vitamin D.

In animal studies, vitamin D has strikingly reduced tumor growth, and a large number of observational studies in people have linked low vitamin D levels to an increased risk of cancer, including cancers of the breast, rectum, ovary, prostate, stomach, bladder, esophagus, kidney, lung, pancreas and uterus, as well as Hodgkin's lymphoma and multiple myeloma.

Researchers at Creighton University in Omaha conducted a double-blind, randomized, placebo-controlled trial (the most reliable form of clinical research) among 1,179 community-living, healthy postmenopausal women. They reported last year in The American Journal of Clinical Nutrition that over the course of four years, those taking calcium and 1,100 I.U. of vitamin D3 each day developed about 80 percent fewer cancers than those who took just calcium or a placebo.

Vitamin D seems to dampen an overactive immune system. The incidence of autoimmune diseases like Type 1 diabetes and multiple sclerosis has been linked to low levels of vitamin D. A study published on Dec. 20, 2006, in The Journal of the American Medical Association examined the risk of developing multiple sclerosis among more than seven million military recruits followed for up to 12 years. Among whites, but not blacks or Hispanics, the risk of developing M.S. increased with ever lower levels of vitamin D in their blood serum before age 20.

A study published in Neurology in 2004 found a 40 percent lower risk of M.S. in women who took at least 400 I.U. of vitamin D a day.

Likewise, a study of a national sample of non-Hispanic whites found a 75 percent lower risk of diabetes among those with the highest blood levels of vitamin D.

Vitamin D is a fat-soluble vitamin that when consumed or made in the skin can be stored in body fat. In summer, as little as five minutes of sun a day on unprotected hands and face can replete the body's supply. Any excess can be stored for later use. But for most people during the rest of the year, the body needs dietary help.

Furthermore, the general increase in obesity has introduced a worrisome factor, the tendency for body fat to hold on to vitamin D, thus reducing its overall availability.

As for a maximum safe dose, researchers like Bruce W. Hollis, a pediatric nutritionist at the Medical University of South Carolina in Charleston, maintain that the current top level of 2,000 I.U. is based on shaky evidence indeed—a study of six patients in India. Dr. Hollis has been giving pregnant women 4,000 I.U. a day, and nursing women 6,000, with no adverse effects. Other experts, however, are concerned that high vitamin D levels (above 800 I.U.) with calcium can raise the risk of kidney stones in susceptible people.

Assess Your Progress

1. Name three functions of vitamin D.
2. What health benefits have been linked to vitamin D?
3. Why has vitamin D been called the "nutrient of the decade"?

What Good Is Breakfast?

The New Science of the Loneliest Meal

How I learned to love breakfast (or at least what to eat for it).

AMANDA FORTINI

As meals go, breakfast is something of a celebrity. It is one of the most studied, analyzed, parsed, discussed, and advised-about subjects of nutritional science. Never more so than today, as doctors, and nutritionists, and countless articles and academic papers prescribe breakfast as both prophylactic and cure-all: The morning meal is said to stoke metabolism, stop late-night grazing, thwart obesity, reduce diabetes risk, improve nutritional intake, sharpen concentration—even increase longevity. In March, a new study more conclusively linked breakfast with body-mass index, with weight increasing as the frequency of breakfast consumption decreased. Breakfast, it seems, is highly influential: the power broker of repasts.

Are we making ourselves hungrier, dumber, shorter-lived, slow metabolizers by not eating a proper breakfast?

Yet despite all the fussing over and fetishizing of breakfast, most of us have only the vaguest notion of what we should be ingesting. Each new study of breakfast seems to contradict the last. Are eggs advisable, or will they raise one's cholesterol? Is a meal of toast anemic or adequate? What is a whole grain, anyway? And most important, are we really making ourselves fatter, hungrier, dumber, shorter-lived, slow metabolizers by not eating a so-called proper breakfast? As the experts continue to debate, most of us shrug and make choices not out of any real knowledge but for lack of time. If we don't slurp down a bowl of cereal at home, or succumb to the buxom muffin beckoning from the glass case at the deli, then an enormous caffeinated drink with a hyphenated name becomes our de facto morning meal.

Or we have nothing at all. National survey data cited by the Breakfast Research Institute indicates that between 1965 and 1991, the number of adults who regularly skip breakfast increased from 14 to 25 percent. The attrition of breakfast-eaters is understandable. After all, what's to love about breakfast? The first meal of the day tends not to be celebratory or communal; unless we're talking about brunch, breakfast's fashionably late cousin, the morning meal is usually a solitary, functional affair. "Breakfast is the proper meal, the one that's usually prepared by oneself and eaten alone," David Heber, director of the UCLA Center for Human Nutrition, told me. "It's not as much fun as going out with friends for lunch or dinner. It's a chore. Breakfast is a meal people are ready to dump."

The multifarious reasons people cite for dumping breakfast shed some light on the psychology of the meal. Some simply don't like to eat in the morning; a handful of friends, none of them pregnant, tell me that even the smell of food before eleven makes them nauseated. Chronic dieters pass on breakfast with an eye toward shaving a few hundred calories off their day. Others can't seem to squeeze in a meal amid the chaos of their morning: the dog to walk, the children to dress, the in-box fires to extinguish, the enervating commute. Still others, and I count myself among this crowd, sometimes abstain because the received wisdom about breakfast seems possibly spurious— one of those persistent nutrition myths, like the notion that you need eight to ten glasses of water per day or that celery has negative calories: If breakfast is supposed to curb your appetite, then why, shortly after partaking, am I ravenous, unable to focus on anything but foraging for more food, hungrier than when I don't eat anything?

I am not the only breakfast skeptic out there (though this is, to be sure, a decidedly less populous camp). "I think it's a nonissue for adults," said Marion Nestle, professor of nutrition and food studies at New York University and a breakfast skipper herself. "I think people should eat when they're hungry. Some people are really hungry in the morning and some are not." In her book *What to Eat,* she writes, "I am well aware that everyone says breakfast is the most important meal of the day, but I am not convinced. What you eat—and how much—matters more to your health than when you eat."

But since so many researchers argue that breakfast does matter, I began to investigate. How, exactly, are we harming ourselves by failing to eat breakfast? The simplified answer is that it depends on how young you are. Even Nestle concedes that there is strong evidence that children who skip breakfast do not fare as well academically or physically as those who eat it. A study conducted by researchers at Tufts University found that children who consumed a breakfast of Quaker instant oatmeal displayed better spatial memory and an increased ability to stay on task (what the study called "vigilance attention") when performing a battery of cognitive tests than children who ate Cap'n Crunch, and, perhaps surprisingly, those who ate the sweetened cereal performed better than those who ate nothing. Another study, this one by researchers at the University of Reading, found that adolescents fed a sugary drink in the morning will subsequently display all the mental agility of a 70-year-old. It's not much of a leap to assume that an adult who skips breakfast will have the same difficulty concentrating at work as a kid sitting in a classroom—hunger is distracting whatever your age—but distracted office workers have not been a major concern for breakfast researchers.

Researchers are interested in breakfast because they are interested in obesity, and they suspect that skipping the former plays a role in fostering the latter. "The frequency of eating breakfast has declined over the past several decades, during which time the obesity epidemic has also unfolded," write researchers Maureen T. Timlin and Mark A. Pereira in an excellent meta-analysis of all the scientific literature on breakfast to date, published in the June 2007 issue of *Nutrition Reviews*. Timlin and Pereira—the pair appear to be the Boswells of breakfast—also conducted the study about breakfast and body-mass index (BMI) published in *Pediatrics* in March. They tracked 2,216 Minnesota adolescents for five years, and found that subjects who skipped breakfast were consistently heavier than those who did not.

The relationship appears to hold for adults as well. A 2003 study published in the *American Journal of Epidemiology* concluded that subjects who habitually skipped breakfast (at least 75 percent of the time) had a four and a half times higher risk of obesity than those who habitually consumed it. (Those who missed breakfast even once during the study had an increased risk of obesity.) And of the 5,000-plus members of the National Weight Control Registry—registrants have lost an average of 66 pounds and have kept it off for more than five years—78 percent claim to be regular breakfast eaters.

But breakfast-eating and weight management may not be connected in the way that we think: Despite what women's magazines, and pop health magazines, and legions of mothers say, the mere act of consuming breakfast does not miraculously speed up one's metabolism. In fact, it's hard to pinpoint exactly why eating breakfast tends to coincide with healthier weight. It may be that eating breakfast simply creates a feeling of satiety, which prevents trips to the vending machine or the drive-through in the afternoon or evening. (Eating at regular intervals maintains insulin and blood-sugar levels, preventing the peaks and valleys that cause voracity.) The *American Journal of Epidemiology* study found that adults consumed more calories on the days they eschewed a morning meal.

The real problem, from a researcher's point of view, is that breakfast consumption is a habit that tends to occur along with a constellation of other healthy behaviors—like exercising, not smoking, and maintaining a healthy diet—that may confound or influence the effect of breakfast on obesity. (Unhealthy behaviors, too, tend to stick together: Fewer than 5 percent of smokers eat breakfast daily.) In at least one study, when confounding variables were accounted for, the relationship between breakfast and body-mass index was not significant. The eating of breakfast was only an ancillary factor, one salubrious practice among several that contributed to slimness. Breakfasting and forgoing the gym will probably do little to reduce or control one's weight. In the *Pediatrics* study, for example, it seemed surprising the breakfast eaters often had a higher daily caloric intake and yet also a lower BMI than their breakfast-skipping peers, but when I asked Pereira what explained this finding—had eating a morning meal somehow increased the subjects' metabolism?—he emphasized that the eaters were exercisers as well.

This is all to say that it is not yet clear to researchers whether the relationship between breakfast and obesity is causal (i.e., breakfast consumption directly influences weight) or merely associational. Breakfast may play a supporting role in weight management, rather than a starring one. Few prospective studies (in which breakfast-eating subjects are followed over a period of time) or clinical trials (in which breakfast eating is tested as an interventional therapy, as a drug might be) have been done. This is why the *Pediatrics* study, conducted prospectively over the course of five years, was a significant contribution to the field of breakfast studies: We can observe the correlation between breakfast consumption and BMI over time, which approximates cause and effect.

If mere consumption is not itself transformative, the question remains: What are we to eat? People have been fretting about what constitutes an ideal breakfast since at least the 1800s. Sylvester Graham, of cracker fame, promoted his high-fiber, additive-free wheat flour as a remedy for the dyspepsia epidemic of the time, which he felt was caused by the meatcentric, multicourse American breakfast: an extravaganza of pancakes, biscuits, eggs, bacon, fried ham, salt pork, and potatoes. (Such hearty fare had been fuel for the farmer but was fattening to the more sedentary industrialist.) As Scott Bruce and Bill Crawford write in *Cerealizing America,* the ascetic Graham believed that "meat eating inflamed the 'baser properties,'" leading to masturbation—what he called "the vice"—and that "tea drinking led to delirium tremens." Sixty years later, John Harvey Kellogg, who breakfasted on graham crackers and apples himself, also peddled grains, in the form of the first flake cereal, as a vegetarian cure for digestive trouble. You might say that breakfast has a long history of having the fun drained out of it.

The warring of the diet factions continues today in a slightly more scientific fashion. A 2003 paper published in the *Journal of the American College of Nutrition* claimed that individuals who consumed ready-to-eat cereal, cooked cereal, or, oddly, "quick breads"—waffles, pancakes, pastries, and the like—had lower BMIs than those who ate meat and eggs or abstained from breakfast entirely. But a 2007 study found the opposite: Obese women who ate two eggs for breakfast daily for eight weeks lost 65 percent more weight than their bagel-fed counterparts. Like most prescriptive studies, however, these two must be taken with a grain of salt (or, in the case of the cereal study, a few granules of sugar): Kellogg funded the former; the American Egg Board funded the latter. Among those in the field of nutrition research, it is widely acknowledged that, for a variety of reasons ranging from flawed study design to buried negative results, industry-funded studies tend to find industry-favorable results. For instance: The Tufts study that found that Quaker instant oatmeal (and, to a lesser degree, Cap'n Crunch) improved cognitive performance was funded by Quaker, the maker of both products.

The studies and advice grow ever more specific and contradictory: If your aim is to optimize attention span and memory—especially in children—then, according to one study, the best breakfast is ham and hard cheese on whole-grain bread. If you want to prevent heart disease (and who doesn't?), try whole-grain cereal; one bowl per day is associated with a 28 percent lower risk of heart failure. If you're a woman hoping to conceive a boy, then, according to a recent study from the University of Exeter, you should increase your breakfast consumption by approximately 400 calories daily. (Women with the highest caloric intake had boys 56 percent of the time, compared with 45 percent with the lowest caloric intake.) It's enough to make one feel inclined to take refuge in Vonnegut's breakfast of champions: a morning martini.

And yet, even as they disagree on the specifics, the majority of researchers seem to agree that what we put into our bodies in the morning is a critical decision. Because it occurs after eight, ten, or even twelve hours of sleep, the breakfasting moment is physiologically unique. "The nature of the food we eat affects hormones in profound ways for many hours after a meal, and that's more important after breakfast," said Dr. David Ludwig, associate professor of pediatrics at Harvard Medical School and author of *Ending the Food Fight*. "We've been fasting and stress hormones are elevated and we're insulin-resistant, so we can use the properties of food at this time to our benefit or our detriment." A fasting body is particularly sensitive to, say, a sugary, refined-starch, low-fiber muffin; blood sugar will soar and then plummet, leaving you famished once again.

What's preferable, according to Ludwig, is to choose breakfast foods with a low glycemic index (GI). The term refers to the rate at which glucose is absorbed from carbohydrates—or, put another way, how rapidly carbohydrates affect blood sugar. This is important because controlling insulin and blood-glucose levels in turn controls appetite and, ultimately, weight. In a 1999 study led by Ludwig, twelve obese teenage boys were fed

at various occasions high-GI ("instant oatmeal"), medium-GI ("steel-cut oats"), and low-GI ("a vegetable omelette and fruit") breakfasts and lunches, and then were allowed to consume all the food they wanted for the rest of the day. The high-GI cohort, in a state of crashing blood sugar and surging adrenaline induced by the instant oatmeal, devoured 500 to 600 extra calories. (This phenomenon likely explains that postprandial ravenousness I often experience—my morning mainstays, toaster waffles and quick-cooking oats, rank fairly high on the GI list.) Low-glycemic foods may even help breakfasters achieve that dietary holy grail: speeding up metabolism. In another study, subjects kept on such a diet saw their metabolic rate shift slightly to burn approximately 80 more calories per day—not a lot, but every little bit helps.

How to tell if a food has a low glycemic index? A quick rule of thumb: The more processed the food, the higher its GI; the higher a food's fiber content, the lower its GI. Breakfast, in other words, should be a high-fiber affair. This means vegetables and fruits (but not juices—the fiber is in the pulp and skin) and whole grains. For the record, a whole grain is an intact, unrefined grain that retains the bran and germ, its nutrient- and fiber-rich components.

Eggs too may help to control blood sugar (protein stimulates the release of glucagon, a hormone that counterbalances insulin), but don't defect to the Atkins camp just yet. Eggs are also high in cholesterol. Many doctors, noting that sensitivity to dietary cholesterol varies, advise limiting eggs to several per week.

So what, then, to eat? The path of bread crumbs—or cereal flakes—through the thicket of breakfast suggestions is this: Breakfast is not dessert. Most muffins and bagels are out, as are those breakfast bars with the creepy strip of ersatz milk, and the many cereals that claim to be "whole grain" but are in fact sugary and fiberless. Out too are my beloved toaster waffles, unless I find a version containing the recommended five grams of fiber per serving. What remains are the foods that we probably should have been eating all along: unprocessed, low-GI, fiber-rich foods like fruits, vegetables (in omelettes if nowhere else), oatmeal (slow-cooking or steel-cut rather than instant), whole-grain breads and cereals (that are also high in fiber and low in sugar), protein in the form of low-fat dairy, and eggs in moderation. Nothing too exciting, but then, breakfast is all business. It you're looking for thrills, try dinner.

Assess Your Progress

1. Name three benefits of eating a healthy breakfast. Give an example of a healthy breakfast.

2. Why it is important to choose breakfast foods with a low glycemic index?

UNIT 4

Exercise and Weight Management

Unit Selections

Learning Outcomes

After reading this unit, you should be able to:

- Discuss why the number of athletic injuries is rising among young children.

- Discuss why there is a need for balanced exercise among young athletes.

- Explain why the rate of eating disorders among college women is so high.

- Distinguish between healthy and disordered eating.

- Explain how one can lose weight on a limited budget.

- Explain why it is important to exercise to achieve optimal health.

- Discuss why eliminating one particular food item a day will not likely lead to permanent weight loss.

Student Website
www.mhhe.com/cls

Internet References

American Society of Exercise Physiologists (ASEP)
    www.asep.org
Cyberdiet
    www.cyberdiet.com/reg/index.html
Shape Up America!
    www.shapeup.org

Recently, a new set of guidelines, dubbed "Exercise Lite," has been issued by the U.S. Centers for Disease Control and Prevention in conjunction with the American College of Sports Medicine. These guidelines call for 30 minutes of exercise, 5 days a week, which can be spread over the course of a day. The primary focus of this approach to exercise is improving health, not athletic performance. Examples of activities that qualify under the new guidelines are walking your dog, playing tag with your kids, scrubbing floors, washing your car, mowing the lawn, weeding your garden, and having sex. From a practical standpoint, this approach to fitness will likely motivate many more people to become active and stay active. Remember, since the benefits of exercise can take weeks or even months before they become apparent, it is very important to choose an exercise program that you enjoy so that you will stick with it.

While a good diet cannot compensate for the lack of exercise, exercise can compensate for a less than optimal diet. Exercise not only makes people physically healthier, it also keeps their brains healthy. While the connection hasn't been proven, there is evidence that regular workouts may cause the brain to better process and store information which results in a smarter brain.

Too much exercise, however, can have negative effects, as addressed by Gina Kolata in "A Big-Time Injury Striking Little Players' Knees." Because more and more children are playing sports competitively, there has been a rise in the diagnoses of torn ligaments, which can pose a serious risk for growing bones.

Although exercise and a nutritious diet can keep people fit and healthy, many Americans are not heeding this advice. For the first time in our history, the average American is now overweight when judged according to the standard height/weight tables. In addition, more than 25 percent of Americans are clinically obese, and the number appears to be growing. Why is this happening, given the prevailing attitude that Americans have toward fat? One theory that is currently gaining support suggests that while Americans have cut back on their consumption of fatty snacks and desserts, they have actually increased their total caloric intake by failing to limit their consumption of carbohydrates. The underlying philosophy goes something like this: fat calories make you fat, but you can eat as many carbohydrates as you want and not gain weight. The truth is that all calories count when it comes to weight gain, and if cutting back on fat calories prevents you from feeling satiated, you will naturally eat more to achieve that feeling. While this position seems reasonable enough, some groups, most notably supporters of the Atkins diet, have suggested that eating a high-fat diet will actually help people lose weight because of fat's high satiety value in conjunction with the formation of ketones (which suppress appetite). Whether people limit fat or carbohydrates, they will not lose weight unless their total caloric intake is less than their energy expenditure.

America's preoccupation with body weight has given rise to a billion-dollar industry. When asked why people go on diets, the predominant answer is for social reasons such as appearance and group acceptance, rather than concerns regarding health. Why do diets and diet aids fail? One of the major reasons lies in the mind-set of the dieter. Many dieters do not fully

understand the biological and behavioral aspects of weight loss, and consequently they have unrealistic expectations regarding the process. While many people reasonably need to lose weight, many college women strive and compete with each other for the thinnest and most perfect body. This practice has led to an increase in the number of young women suffering from eating disorders. Hara Estroff Marano discusses this issue in "The Skinny Sweepstakes."

Being overweight not only causes health problems; it also carries with it a social stigma. Overweight people are often thought of as weak-willed individuals with little or no self-respect. The notion that weight control problems are the result of personality defects is being challenged by new research findings. Evidence is mounting that suggests that physiological and hereditary factors may play as great a role in obesity as do behavioral and environmental factors. Researchers now believe that genetics dictate the base number of fat cells an individual will have, as well as the location and distribution of these cells within the body.

The study of fat metabolism has provided additional clues as to why weight control is so difficult. These metabolic studies have found that the body seems to have a "setpoint," or desired weight, and it will defend this weight through alterations in basal metabolic rate and fat-cell activities. While this process is thought to be an adaptive throwback to primitive times when food supplies were uncertain, today, with our abundant food supply, this mechanism only contributes to the problem of weight control.

It should be apparent by now that weight control is both an attitudinal and a lifestyle issue. Fortunately, a new, more rational approach to the problem of weight control is emerging. This approach is based on the premise that you can be perfectly healthy and good looking without being pencil-thin. The primary focus of this approach to weight management is the attainment of your body's "natural ideal weight" and not some idealized, fanciful notion of what you would like to weigh. The concept of achieving your natural ideal body weight suggests that we need to take a more realistic approach to both fitness and weight control, and also serves to remind us that a healthy lifestyle is based on the concepts of balance and moderation. Tara Parker-Pope discusses reducing extra calories through small changes as a means of weight control in "In Obesity Epidemic, What's One Cookie?" while "Dieting on a Budget?" explains how to lose weight without spending a fortune.

A Big-Time Injury Striking Little Players' Knees

Gina Kolata

Last year, when Collin Link was 11 years old, he was tackled as he went in for a touchdown in pee-wee football. "He didn't get up," his mother, Crystal Link, said. "He kept saying his knee hurt real bad." But Mrs. Link was not overly concerned, thinking it was just a sprain.

But the next morning when the family was getting ready to go to church near their home in The Woodlands, Tex., Collin said he could not walk. That Monday, a doctor told the Links what was wrong.

Torn ligament poses a greater risk for growing bones.

Collin had an injury that doctors used to think almost never occurred in children. He had torn the anterior cruciate ligament, or A.C.L., in his left knee, the main ligament that stabilizes the joint.

The standard and effective treatment for such an injury in adults is surgery. But the operation poses a greater risk for children and adolescents who have not finished growing because it involves drilling into a growth plate, an area of still-developing tissue at the end of the leg bone.

Although there are no complete or official numbers, orthopedists at leading medical centers estimate that several thousand children and young adolescents are getting A.C.L. tears each year, with the number being diagnosed soaring recently. Some centers that used to see only a few such cases a year are now seeing several each week.

And contrary to the old belief that boys are more prone to the injury than girls, as many as eight times more girls than boys are suffering the tears, doctors report.

It is not an overuse injury from playing one sport too intensively, like shoulder injuries in young pitchers. Instead, doctors say, the injury occurs simply from twisting the knee, and diagnoses are on the rise partly because it can now be easily detected and partly because the very nature of youth sports has changed.

In the old days, said Dr. Theodore J. Ganley, director of sports medicine at the Children's Hospital of Philadelphia and a spokesman for the American Academy of Orthopedic Surgeons, a child would develop a "trick knee" that made sports difficult, but the real reason was not understood. And most doctors, thinking children did not get A.C.L. tears, did not suspect the real reason.

Now that almost every child with a hurt knee gets a magnetic resonance imaging, doctors are finding the ligament tears on a regular basis.

The other reason for the reported surge in A.C.L. tears, doctors speculate, is that the best athletes are more or less constantly at risk. They play year-round and on multiple teams with frequent games, in which the risk of injury is higher than in practice because of the intensity of play.

"The kids are playing at really highly competitive levels at earlier and earlier ages," said Dr. Mininder S. Kocher, the associate director of the division of sports medicine at Children's Hospital in Boston.

Whatever the reason, the increase in diagnoses has created a new problem: what to do about the injury.

Every orthopedist is familiar with A.C.L. tears, but in adults. It is "the most common and most dreaded injury in professional sports," Dr. Kocher said. The well-established operation to repair it often results in a full return to function. And doctors often recommend that adults have the operation because without the ligament the knee is not stable.

After a tear, any sport, like soccer or basketball, that can twist the knee is dangerous. Without an anterior cruciate ligament, even everyday activities can injure the smooth, shock-absorbing cartilage that caps the knee joint. "Then you are on your way to arthritis," Dr. Kocher said.

But the standard A.C.L. repair operation, with its drilling into the growth plate, may cause permanent damage to the still-growing bones of young children. After drilling, surgeons replace the torn ligament with a tendon taken from elsewhere in the body, like the hamstring, or from a cadaver. But if the drilling damages a child's growth plate, the leg bone will not develop normally.

An injury once thought adults-only is a special problem for the young.

That happened recently to a 14-year-old boy who was referred to Dr. Freddie H. Fu, an orthopedic surgeon at the University of Pittsburgh. A year after the operation, Dr. Fu said, the leg with the repair was bowed 20 degrees on one side and was shorter than the other leg.

"I had to go in on the other side and stop the growth," Dr. Fu said. "Now, about six months later, the leg is still crooked. There still is a two-inch difference in length which I have to fix." The boy, he said, "will be a little bit shorter" as a result, although both legs will be the same length.

Doctors often suggest putting a brace on the injured knee and limiting a child's activities, delaying surgery until the child finishes growing. But the children who tear A.C.L.'s tend to be highly competitive athletes who chafe under the restrictions.

Ashley Hammond, owner of Soccer Domain, a domed facility in Montclair, N.J., said that parents of young soccer stars often wanted them to keep playing and that children were the type who would forget or resist instructions to wear a brace, putting their knees at risk.

"All kids feel they are indestructible," Mr. Hammond said. "The kids want to play no matter what we say." A result can be injuries to their knee cartilage and its attendant risk of arthritis in young adulthood.

Some surgeons are developing new and technically demanding methods to repair A.C.L. tears in children, drilling holes to create little tunnels in bone that is already finished growing and threading tendons around the growth plate. Different surgeons have different versions of the technique, Dr. Ganley said.

But the tendons are not anchored where they would normally be and the long-term effects of the operation are not known.

Dr. Kocher has perhaps the most extensive data, on 59 young patients. His results are encouraging; the implanted ligaments failed in only two patients and no patients had severe growth abnormalities. But the patients have been followed less than four years.

"We don't know the long-term results, 20, 30 years out," Dr. Willis said. "Are these people going to end up with arthritis? Some feel there's a chance of that, but we feel that surgery lessens the chance that will happen."

It is only with the new increase in diagnosed A.C.L. tears in children, orthopedists say, that they discovered how mistaken they once were about this injury.

Doctors used to think the tears did not occur or were extremely rare in children because children's ligaments were stronger than their bones. They thought an injury that would rip an adult's A.C.L. would, in children, result in a broken bone.

Another myth, Dr. Ganley said, is that A.C.L. tears arise mostly in contact injuries, like a tackle in football, and almost exclusively affect boys. Now, though, it appears that girls are more susceptible, although no one really knows why, said Dr. Baxter Willis, an orthopedist at Children's Hospital in Ottawa.

Doctors have also learned that contact injuries are not the most common cause of A.C.L. injuries. It turns out, Dr. Ganley said, that tears occur more often from twisting and jumping. A child can be running and step in a hole, twisting a leg. Or they can fall off a bike, like Malinda McCartney of Pembroke, Mass., who tore her ligament last year when she was 9.

Other times, a young athlete can tear an A.C.L. by coming down from a rebound in basketball or by accelerating and decelerating. Now, though, with doctors looking for the injury and surgeons finding new ways to repair it without touching the growth plate, parents often face difficult decisions, as Mrs. Link discovered. The first orthopedist told her that Collin should wear a knee brace and wait to have the operation until he stopped growing, which could take five years or more.

"He told Collin he was completely out of sports—soccer, basketball, baseball and football," Mrs. Link said. "They were his whole life. That was devastating to him."

So the Links took Collin to Children's Hospital in Dallas, where they saw another orthopedist. He said he could operate on Collin and that he had operated on a few children with A.C.L. tears, using one of the new methods that could avoid the growth plate. But first, he said, he wanted to put a brace on Collin's leg and see how he did before trying the surgery. The Links ended up traveling to Boston where Dr. Kocher operated on Collin. For the Links, it was the best of a bad set of choices. And the surgery and its aftermath were more difficult than they anticipated.

Collin was in intense pain and on a morphine drip after the operation and then spent much of the next six weeks lying down with his leg in a machine that moved his knee slowly through a range of motions. That was followed by six months of physical therapy, which was often painful and always difficult, physically and emotionally, Mrs. Link said.

Now, a year after the operation, Collin is starting to play a nontackle form of football, worried about injury if he played regular football and got tackled again. And he is running track.

Having the operation "was a difficult decision to make," Mrs. Link said. "But if they can play sports, it's the only option."

Assess Your Progress

1. For young athletes, is there a need for balanced exercising? When should one begin to regard something as too much exercise?

2. Describe some of the problems associated with the standard A.C.L. repair operation.

The Skinny Sweepstakes

In the push for achievement, the perfect body is now part of the perfect résumé. Deprived of an internal compass, girls compete to be "hottest," turning colleges into incubators of eating disorders.

HARA ESTROFF MARANO

"I started starving myself when I was 12 or 13," Chloe, an absolute beauty, recalls. "I wasn't overweight, but I wasn't as thin as a lot of my friends. It was just something I noticed."

Around that time, "a lot of problems" erupted in her family. "Dieting made me feel like I was in control of something. It was the one thing I knew I could change on my own. I would diet and get positive feedback and feel really good. So I wouldn't eat for a few days at a time."

Dieting also bound her to her peers. "A lot of girls at school would skip meals. We'd do it together. We went on fad diets together, too." Her family never noticed her food fetishes. "I had trouble impressing my mother. I could never achieve enough for her. But she definitely noticed when I lost weight."

From the beginning, starving consumed her life. "You think about it everywhere you go. And you compare yourself to other people. Each of my friends was vying to be better than the others. I was in a restaurant with my boyfriend and a girl walked in who was really pretty and much thinner than me. I saw him glance at her. I went into the bathroom and cried."

She couldn't look at a picture of a celebrity without feeling bad, either. The boys at her public school didn't help. "They're constantly comparing women to each other: 'That girl is really hot; she's so much hotter than her friends.' So we compete to be the hotter friend. Some days it makes you feel fat. On particularly bad days, I can look at children and think that when I'm older, that little 3-year-old girl is going to steal my husband."

In a culture of plenty where the young are pressured to succeed even before birth, the achievement package has come to include, especially for girls, a "perfect" body. Starting at puberty, sometimes before, the mounting pressure launches girls into the stratosphere of fat fear, in part fueled by the ubiquity of food, in part by new sensitivities adolescence brings to the judgments of others.

But perhaps the greatest accelerant of fat fear and distorted eating is the peer culture to which adolescents have been consigned for the past few decades. Age segregation isn't new to America's schools. But since the middle of the 20th century, it has gathered critical mass until it has also come to dominate the extracurricular life of the young in their insular march through middle school, high school, and beyond.

Between 1960 and 2000, the percentages of 20-, 25-, and 30-year-olds enrolled in school more than doubled, with females becoming an increasingly larger part of the total.

The extension of schooling for more young people, especially girls—now the majority of college attendees—requires them to be warehoused together for years with those deliberately selected to share many of the same attributes, constraining exposure to the broader range of humanity. Ongoing shifts in communication technology (think: MySpace, YouTube, and mp3 files) may employ up-to-the-nanosecond science, but they turn out to be extraordinarily conservative social and developmental forces, keeping the young tightly tethered to each other, cloistered among those like themselves, and sharing sights, sounds, and other cultural effusions targeted exclusively at them, further age-stratifying their souls.

Superimpose on that nature's compulsory contribution, the mating sweepstakes, and each cohort of girls seems forced to make ever more minute distinctions between themselves—just as they compete to distinguish themselves on their college application essays. Thus does dieting become a competitive sport with the gold medal going to the thinnest, a triumph of the cultural ideal for appearance that almost every American girl will unwittingly internalize by middle school.

The strongest predictor of eating disorders among middle-school girls today is the importance that peers place on weight and eating, researchers report in the *International Journal of Eating Disorders*. The perceptions of peers outweighs, as it were, such traditional factors as confidence level, actual body mass, trying to look like the girls and women appearing on television and in magazines, even being teased by family and others about weight.

In highly age-stratified education, particularly for females, whose attractiveness depends so heavily on youth, "all the most attractive females of a cohort are competing with each other" for the attention of males, explains Geoffrey Miller. "They are seeing only rivals who are quite similar to themselves," says the University of New Mexico psychologist. "They're not seeing the mating market as a whole. Their frame of reference is artificially constricted."

The result is "extreme intensification of sexual competition." And with increasing numbers of young women not merely going to college but getting advanced degrees, age segregation and stratification continue much later in life than they did even a few decades ago.

On bad days, I can look at children and think that when I'm older, that little 3-year-old girl is going to steal my husband.

Modern schools, Miller points out, are often so homogenous in terms of class and race as well as age that "kids have to invent ways to be different from each other that they never would have had to invent a hundred years ago." As they jockey intensely for skinny status, their very limited involvement with the outside world helps keep them highly focused on themselves.

Adrift Amid Peer Pressure

Richard Hersh calls it the culture of neglect: kids grow up overly dependent on their peers—"in essence, kids raising kids"—without developing a strong sense of self. A RAND scholar, former director of Harvard's Center for Moral Education, as well as former president of Trinity College and William Smith and Hobart Colleges, Hersh contends that adults—parents, neighbors, teachers, professors—have inadvertently done children and adolescents an injustice. They allow them to be socialized by television, the Internet, and by their peers rather than by caring, demanding, and mentoring adults. At the same time, the adults view kids as helpless, sheltering them from a wide range of experiences, "the risk of failure and being hurt being so great."

Both forms of deprivation weaken the young from within, so that kids go off to college socially and emotionally fragile, manifest in a rising tide of distress: anorexia and bulimia, along with depression, physical violence, alcohol and other drug abuse, and suicide attempts. Approximately 40 percent of females now experience an eating disorder at some point during their years of college, data show.

Missing in action is a rich internal life independent of peers. Hersh sees residential college life perpetuating and intensifying an adolescent pattern of overreliance on peer approval. It also, he says, elevates the body over the mind. And that combination subverts the developmental challenge of finding something far more durable: a stable identity.

The way New York psychotherapist Steven Levenkron sees it, the adults essentially outsource parenting. Levenkron has been treating young women with eating disorders for more than 30 years. He wrote one of the first books about anorexia, *The Best Little Girl in the World,* in 1978, and he has written textbooks on treatment of the disorder. Why is it, he asks, that some

girls succumb to the peer pressure and some don't? "Those who aren't mentored by parents are not inoculated against peer pressure. They wind up turning to their peers and to the media, to the outside society, for guidance on how to appeal to men." Without a strong, healthy attachment to parents, kids become fair game for what he sees as destructive messages about femininity from Hollywood.

But the damage goes especially deep because contemporary adolescents "have no language for reflection," he says. "They don't know how to think about hurts. That makes them feel alone in the world." Anorexics, he contends, have only a very primitive language. "They can talk your head off about body measurements and fats. It's all transacted with about 12 words."

From Comparison to Cutthroat Competition

It's bad enough that teens are swaddled in software and bound by a branch of consumer culture crafted exclusively for them. But there is something about herding them together 24/7 that actively distorts their thinking, specifically about bodies. As a result, America's universities have become incubators of eating disorders. Attending a residential college actually warps perception of self in relation to others, finds psychologist Catherine Sanderson. At a time and place where people should be getting smarter about everything, they are getting a lot less smart about themselves.

A professor of psychology at Amherst College, Sanderson looked at perceptions of the norms of thinness among women at Amherst, Princeton, and Smith colleges. When women arrive at college as freshmen, they believe that all the other women at their school are highly motivated to be thin—much thinner than they themselves want to be.

Mistakenly, they assume that other people's statements accurately reflect their behavior. They know that they themselves talk the talk in the dining hall and other public places—but privately slip out later for a bag of Doritos. They feel ashamed and isolated, without realizing that almost everyone else is wolfing down chips in private, too. Students develop a false impression of the norm.

But the damage is done. The feelings of shame and isolation lead almost directly to bingeing and purging and other forms of disordered eating. "The more women perceive themselves as different, the more symptoms they show of anorexia or bulimia," Sanderson finds.

"The problem with college is that the norms are in your face," she notes. You eat in a common dining hall, exercise in a common fitness center, shower together, and get dressed together. "The togetherness surrounds people at the key life period in which this stuff matters."

Norms matter especially at times of transition, such as going off to boarding school or starting college. In order to make it in their new environment, students look to others there to figure out what's normal. We all navigate the social universe by making comparisons to others, but researchers have long known that widespread insecurity (Will I get into Harvard? Is my family coming apart at the seams? Do I even have an identity of my own? Why do I feel so different from everyone?) exacerbates the process, turning comparison—with peers, with media figures—into cutthroat competition.

In such environments, misperception accelerates over time. Asked what they weigh, freshmen say "around 130," exactly what they believe other women weigh. But surveyed again the next year, after gaining about five pounds, the same women say—accurately—that they weigh 135. However, they think others weigh "around 125." "You're gaining weight and you know it, yet you believe that other women are losing weight," explains Sanderson. It's ironic, she notes, that this is a topic about which college actually makes people stupid: The more time they spend in school, the less accurate they become in their perceptions.

Puppets of Fear . . .

Columbia University psychologist Barbara Von Bulow co-runs a day-treatment program in Manhattan for eating disordered students who have been sent home on leave, asked by their out-of-town colleges to take time off for treatment. So competitive are the women about their weight-control strategies that the program has had to separate the bulimics from the anorexics.

"It's difficult to treat anorexics if they don't see themselves as unhealthy," Von Bulow observes. "Yet the bulimics look at the anorexics as successes because they are so thin." On the other hand, the anorexics "are terrified when they look at the bulimics, most of whom are normal weight. They see them as failed anorexics."

In reality, as in the dictionary, anorexia comes before bulimia; about 50 percent of the time, restrictive eating begets binge eating. Candice Sombrero, 19, a sophomore at Babson College outside Boston, endured six months of anorexia while a student at the prestigious Iolani School in Honolulu, where she grew up. "I'd grab coffee at home and tell my parents I'd get breakfast at school, which I never did. For lunch I prided myself on sipping an extra-large Diet Coke." The endless hunger made her preoccupied with food. "Once you get your hands on food, you stuff yourself. Then you feel physically uncomfortable and guilty for eating, so you start to purge." For the next year and a half, she was "stuck in the bulimic cycle, throwing up eight to 10 times a day."

Bulimia testifies to the difficulty of the restrictive eating that defines anorexia. On the other hand, not every girl can make herself throw up. Katy Palmer is one of the latter.

At 17, she was at the top of her high school class in Atlanta, looking at colleges and locked into competition with another girl for class valedictorian. "We knew each other's GPA down to the hundredth of a point," she recalls. The academic pressure was intense. That year her grandfather died, and suddenly family life was dominated by grieving. "I didn't have control over the college application process and I couldn't make any school accept me; I knew it was an arbitrary process. I didn't have control over what was happening in my family. Eating became the least complicated thing I could do that was under my control. I read an article in *Self* magazine all about calories. Cause and effect were clear: Fewer calories equal less weight."

Pressure Control

Just as there is no single cause of eating disorders among the young—they are rooted in conditions set long before college—there is no one solution. But many contributing elements can be addressed by schools, parents, and the culture at large.

- Attenuate the competitive pressure on kids; dispute the idea that the only path to success runs through Harvard Yard.
- Combat the pursuit of perfection: Discuss the impossibility of being perfect, the self-preoccupation that dogs perfectionists, and perfectionism's ultimately self-defeating nature.
- Allow the young meaningful engagement in a broad range of experiences beyond their usual routines.
- Encourage kids to experiment by giving them permission to fail, so they can claim their own experience and construct a strong sense of self.
- Discard helicopter parenting for real parenting, because authentic connection inoculates kids against the excesses of peer culture.
- Expose kids to alternatives to the pseudo culture mass manufactured for their consumption.
- Lobby upper schools to dampen the college-entrance sweepstakes. This in turn could force colleges to revamp admissions policies predicated on excess selectivity favoring ultracompetitive overachievers.

Today, kids have to invent ways to be different from each other that they never would have had to invent years ago.

Gradually, she shriveled into her five-foot-10-inch frame, until she weighed 115 pounds. "I was always in a bad mood. I stopped having a personality. I stopped thinking about boys. All I thought about was food. Everything had to be carefully portioned. Any spread of food, any open box, was dangerous waters. I was always hungry. My dreams were nightmares about eating too much."

But people told her she looked great. And her parents never picked up on her calorie restriction. In fact, she became locked into competition with her mother, a true peer in weight obsession. "She'd say, 'Your thighs are skinnier than mine; let's get out the tape measure.' We never actually did, but we did feed off each other. We talked about how good it feels to be hungry. She told me she wouldn't be attracted to my father if he were overweight.

"Initially it's a choice," she says now. "You start dieting to be in control. But then it veers out of control. Anorexia is so dictated by fear. You're just a puppet of fear." That sleight of slight is likely accomplished through an array of cognitive changes, purely the effects of starvation on the brain.

. . . But Perfect on Paper

Fear is the dark heart of contemporary girl culture. Courtney Martin, an instructor at Barnard College and author of *Perfect Girls, Starving Daughters: The Frightening New Normalcy of Hating Your Body,* contends that a whole generation of young women was told that they could be anything. What they heard was slightly different: "We have to be everything." And that's terrifying. The pre-college emphasis on achievement leads them "to compose the self as perfect, with a perfect résumé and a perfect body," since they were socialized to believe they can look any way they want if they just try hard enough. Unfortunately, it's hard to create a sustainable self-image without a sense of self.

The pursuit of perfection is always self-consuming, and it locks young women into a vicious cycle. The struggle to achieve so much in so many different areas overwhelms them with anxiety, and anxiety generates constant comparison, which only makes them see themselves more negatively, which pressures them to try harder.

Martin regards the rising rate of suicide among girls 10 to 14 as alarming proof that girls today increasingly lack the inner resources to disarm the anxiety of achievement pressure and fat fear. "Neither parents nor schools are nurturing kids' well-being," she says, "because they themselves are caught up in the anxiety dance."

Psychologist Janell Mensinger views it as fallout of the Superwoman Syndrome. Head of health research at Reading Hospital in Pennsylvania, Mensinger has been looking at eating disorders among girls for over a decade. In a recent study reported in the journal *Sex Roles,* she and her colleagues found that the more adolescent girls perceived behavioral commands for excellence in academics, appearance, and dating, the more they subscribed to the superwoman ideal and the more disordered their eating became.

What's more, in surveying 1,200 students in 11 schools in New York City and Philadelphia, she found that the all-girls schools fostered greater competitiveness on appearance-related issues than did the coed schools. "Girls at single-sex schools appear to be at a disadvantage in that they are more dissatisfied with their bodies," she reports.

That body competition is worse among students at all-girls schools makes perfect sense to Geoffrey Miller. The psyche reads the environment as a scarcity of males. And that only ups the mate competition among females. "It's a supply-and-demand effect," he suggests. Candice Sombrero would agree. A transfer student, she finds that eating disorders are much less prevalent at Babson than at most other schools. "This is a business college, and the ratio of males to females is 60:40 or 70:30."

If it is indeed a supply-and-demand effect, then America's campuses ought to be bracing for a near epidemic of eating disorders. The ratio of males to females is shrinking dramatically at most colleges; even Babson, able to draw from a larger pool of women, aims to add more female students.

It is a particularly cruel irony that, through unforeseen shifts in gender balance, higher education as it's now constituted winds up lowering the threshold for one of the most mentally and physically disabling disorders of our time.

Assess Your Progress

1. Why do girls experience "fat fear?"
2. What are the physical risks associated with eating disorders?

From *Psychology Today,* January/February 2008. Copyright © 2008 by Sussex Publishers, LLC. Reprinted by permission.

Dieting on a Budget

Plus the secrets of thin people, based on our survey of 21,000 readers.

With jobs being cut and retirement accounts seemingly shrinking by the day, it's too bad our waistlines aren't dwindling, too. We can't rectify that cosmic injustice, but in this issue we aim to help you figure out the most effective, least expensive ways to stay trim and fit.

Though most Americans find themselves overweight by middle age, an enviable minority stay slim throughout their lives. Are those people just genetically gifted? Or do they, too, have to work at keeping down their weight?

To find out, the Consumer Reports National Research Center asked subscribers to *Consumer Reports* about their lifetime weight history and their eating, dieting, and exercising habits. And now we have our answer:

People who have never become overweight aren't sitting in recliners with a bowl of corn chips in their laps. In our group of always-slim respondents, a mere 3 percent reported that they never exercised and that they ate whatever they pleased. The eating and exercise habits of the vast majority of the always-slim group look surprisingly like those of people who have successfully lost weight and kept it off.

Both groups eat healthful foods such as fruits, vegetables, and whole grains and eschew excessive dietary fat; practice portion control; and exercise vigorously and regularly. The only advantage the always-slim have over the successful dieters is that those habits seem to come a bit more naturally to them.

"When we've compared people maintaining a weight loss with controls who've always had a normal weight, we've found that both groups are working hard at it; the maintainers are just working a little harder," says Suzanne Phelan, Ph.D., an assistant professor of kinesiology at California Polytechnic State University and co-investigator of the National Weight Control Registry, which tracks people who have successfully maintained a weight loss over time. For our respondents, that meant exercising a little more and eating with a bit more restraint than an always-thin person—plus using more monitoring strategies such as weighing themselves or keeping a food diary.

A total of 21,632 readers completed the 2007 survey. The always thin, who had never been overweight, comprised 16 percent of our sample. Successful losers made up an additional 15 percent. We defined that group as people who, at the time of the survey, weighed at least 10 percent less than they did at their heaviest, and had been at that lower weight for at least three years. Failed dieters, who said they would like to slim down yet still weighed at or near their lifetime high, were, sad to say, the largest group: 42 percent. (The remaining 27 percent of respondents, such as people who had lost weight more recently, didn't fit into any of the categories.)

An encouraging note: More than half of our successful losers reported shedding the weight themselves, without aid of a commercial diet program, a medical treatment, a book, or diet pills. That confirms

Price vs. Nutrition: Making Smart Choices

Although healthful foods often cost more than high-calorie junk such as cookies and soda, we unearthed some encouraging exceptions. As illustrated below, two rich sources of nutrients, black beans and eggs, cost mere pennies per serving—and less than plain noodles, which supply fewer nutrients. And for the same price as a doughnut, packed with empty calories, you can buy a serving of broccoli.

- **Cooked black beans**
  - Serving size 1/2 cup
  - Calories per serving 114
  - Cost per serving 74¢
- **Hard-boiled egg**
  - Serving size one medium
  - Calories per serving 78
  - Cost per serving 94¢
- **Cooked noodles**
  - Serving size 3/4 cup
  - Calories per serving 166
  - Cost per serving 134¢
- **Glazed doughnut**
  - Serving size 1 medium
  - Calories per serving 239
  - Cost per serving 324¢
- **Cooked broccoli**
  - Serving size 1/2 cup chopped
  - Calories per serving 27
  - Cost per serving 334¢
- **Chicken breast**
  - Serving size 4 oz.
  - Calories per serving 142
  - Cost per serving 364¢

Sources: Adam Drewnowski, Ph.D., director of the Center for Public Health Nutrition, University of Washington: USDA Nutrient Database for Standard Reference.

what we found in our last large diet survey, in 2002, in which 83 percent of "superlosers"—people who'd lost at least 10 percent of their starting weight and kept it off for five years or more—had done it entirely on their own.

Stay-Thin Strategies

Successful losers and the always thin do a lot of the same things—and they do them more frequently than failed dieters do. For the dietary strategies below, numbers reflect those who said they are that way at least five days a week, a key tipping point, our analysis found. (Differences of less than 4 percentage points are not statistically meaningful.)

Lifetime Weight History

Failed dieters: overweight and have tried to lose, but still close to highest weight. **Always thin:** never overweight. **Successful losers:** once overweight but now at least 10 percent lighter and have kept pounds off for at least three years.

Strength Train at Least Once a Week

Always thin	31%
Successful loser	32%
Failed dieter	23%

Do Vigorous Exercise at Least Four Days a Week

Always thin	35%
Successful loser	41%
Failed dieter	27%

Eat Fruit and Vegetables at Least Five Times a Day

Always thin	49%
Successful loser	49%
Failed dieter	38%

Eat Whole Grains, Not Refined

Always thin	56%
Successful loser	61%
Failed dieter	49%

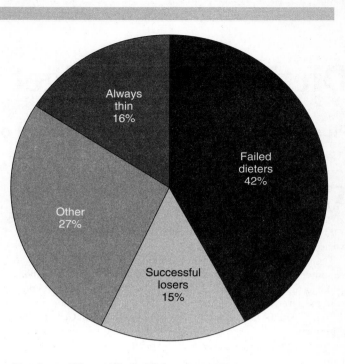

Failed dieters 42%

Always thin 16%

Other 27%

Successful losers 15%

Eat Less Than 1/3 Calories from Fat

Always thin	47%
Successful loser	53%
Failed dieter	35%

Observe Portion Control at Every Meal

Always thin	57%
Successful loser	62%
Failed dieter	42%

Count Calories

Always thin	9%
Successful loser	47%
Failed dieter	9%

6 Secrets of the Slim

Through statistical analyses, we were able to identify six key behaviors that correlated the most strongly with having a healthy body mass index (BMI), a measure of weight that takes height into account. Always thin people were only slightly less likely than successful losers to embrace each of the behaviors—and significantly more likely to do so than failed dieters. By following the behaviors, you can, quite literally, live like a thin person.

Watch portions. Of all the eating behaviors we asked about, carefully controlling portion size at each meal correlated most strongly with having a lower BMI. Successful losers—even those who were still overweight—were especially likely **(62 percent) to report practicing portion control at least five days per week. So did** 57 percent of the always thin, but only 42 percent of failed dieters.

Portion control is strongly linked to a lower BMI.

Limit fat. Specifically, that means restricting fat to less than one-third of daily calorie intake. Fifty-three percent of successful losers and 47 percent of the always thin said they did that five or more days a week, compared with just 35 percent of failed dieters.

Eat fruits and vegetables. The more days that respondents are five or more servings of fruits or vegetables, the lower their average BMI score. Forty-nine percent of successful losers and the always thin said they ate that way at least five days a week, while 38 percent of failed dieters did so.

Choose whole grains over refined. People with lower body weights consistently opted for whole-wheat breads, cereals, and other grains over refined (white) grains.

Eat at home. As the number of days per week respondents are restaurant or takeout meals for dinner increased, so did their weight. Eating at home can save a lot of money, too.

Exercise, exercise, exercise. Regular **vigorous exercise— the type that increases breathing and heart rate for 30 minutes** or longer—was strongly linked to a lower BMI. Although only about one quarter of **respondents said they did strength training at least once a week, that practice was significantly more prevalent among successful losers (32 percent) and always thin** respondents (31 percent) than it was among failed dieters (23 percent).

What Didn't Matter

One weight-loss strategy is conspicuously absent from the list: going low-carb. Of course we asked about it, and it turned out that limiting carbohydrates was linked to higher BMIs in our survey. That doesn't necessarily mean low-carb plans such as the Atkins or South Beach diets don't work. "If you go to the hospital and everyone there is sick, that doesn't mean the hospital made them sick," says Eric C. Westman, M.D., associate professor of medicine and director of the Lifestyle Medicine Clinic at Duke University Medical School. "just as people go to hospitals because they're ill, people may go to carb restriction because they have a higher BMI, not the other way around." At the same time, the findings do suggest that cutting carbs alone, without other healthful behaviors such as exercise and portion control, might not lead to great results.

Eating many small meals, or never eating between meals, didn't seem to make much difference one way or another. Including lean protein with most meals also didn't by itself predict a healthier weight.

Realistic Expectations

Sixty-six percent of our respondents, all subscribers to *Consumer Reports,* were overweight as assessed by their body mass index; that's the same percentage as the population as a whole. One third of the overweight group, or 22 percent of the overall sample, qualified as obese.

Although that might seem discouraging, the survey actually contains good news for would-be dieters. Our respondents did much better at losing weight than published clinical studies would predict. Though such studies are deemed successful if participants are 5 percent lighter after a year, our successful losers had managed to shed an average of 16 percent of their peak weight, an average of almost 34 pounds. They had an impressive average BMI of 25.7, meaning they were just barely overweight.

One key to weight loss success is having realistic goals and our subscribers responses proved encouraging. A staggering 70 percent of them said they currently wanted to lose weight. But when we asked how many pounds they hoped to take off, we found that their goals were modest: The vast majority reported wanting to lose 15 percent or less of their overall body weight; 65 percent sought to lose between 1 and 10 percent. Keeping expectations in check might help dieters from becoming discouraged when they don't achieve, say, a 70-pound

---

Are You Overweight?

A body mass index under 25 is considered normal weight: from 25 to 29, overweight; and 30 or above, obese. To calculate your BMI, multiply your weight in pounds by 703, then divide by your height squared in inches.

---

weight loss or drop from a size 20 to a size 6—a common problem in behavioral weight loss studies.

Realistic goals are one key to weight loss.

What You Can Do

Weight loss is a highly individual process, and what matters most is finding the combination of habits that work for you. But our findings suggest that there are key behaviors common to people who have successfully lost weight and to those who have never gained it in the first place. By embracing some or all of those behaviors, you can probably increase your chances of weight-loss success, and live a healthier life in the process. In addition to following the steps above, consider these tips:

Don't get discouraged. Studies show that prospective dieters often have unrealistic ideas about how much weight they can lose. A 10 percent loss might not sound like much, but it significantly improves overall health and reduces risk of disease.

Ask for support. Though only a small minority of respondents overall reported that a spouse or family member interfered with their healthful eating efforts, that problem was much more likely among failed dieters, 31 percent of whom reported some form of spousal sabotage in the month prior to the survey. Ask housemates to help you stay on track by, for example, not pestering you to eat foods you're trying to avoid, or not eating those foods in front of you.

Get up and move. While regular vigorous exercise correlated most strongly with healthy body weight, our findings suggest that any physical activity is helpful, including activities you might not even consider exercise. Everyday activities such as housework, yard work, and playing with kids were modestly tied to lower weight. By contrast, hours spent sitting each day, whether at an office desk or at home watching television, correlated with higher weight.

Assess Your Progress

1. Is it possible to diet on a limited food budget? Explain.
2. Why should exercise be included in any weight control program?

In Obesity Epidemic, What's One Cookie?

Tara Parker-Pope

The basic formula for gaining and losing weight is well known: a pound of fat equals 3,500 calories.

That simple equation has fueled the widely accepted notion that weight loss does not require daunting lifestyle changes but "small changes that add up," as the first lady, Michelle Obama, put it last month in announcing a national plan to counter childhood obesity.

In this view, cutting out or burning just 100 extra calories a day—by replacing soda with water, say, or walking to school—can lead to significant weight loss over time: a pound every 35 days, or more than 10 pounds a year.

While it's certainly a hopeful message, it's also misleading. Numerous scientific studies show that small caloric changes have almost no long-term effect on weight. When we skip a cookie or exercise a little more, the body's biological and behavioral adaptations kick in, significantly reducing the caloric benefits of our effort.

Small caloric changes have almost no long-term effect on weight, studies show.

But can small changes in diet and exercise at least keep children from gaining weight? While some obesity experts think so, mathematical models suggest otherwise.

As a recent commentary in *The Journal of the American Medical Association* noted, the "small changes" theory fails to take the body's adaptive mechanisms into account. The rise in children's obesity over the past few decades can't be explained by an extra 100-calorie soda each day, or fewer physical education classes. Skipping a cookie or walking to school would barely make a dent in a calorie imbalance that goes "far beyond the ability of most individuals to address on a personal level," the authors wrote—on the order of walking 5 to 10 miles a day for 10 years.

This doesn't mean small improvements are futile—far from it. But people need to take a realistic view of what they can accomplish.

"As clinicians, we celebrate small changes because they often lead to big changes," said Dr. David Ludwig, director of the Optimal Weight for Life program at Children's Hospital Boston and a co-author of the JAMA commentary. "An obese adolescent who cuts back TV viewing from six to five hours each day may then go on to decrease viewing much more. However, it would be entirely unrealistic to think that these changes alone would produce substantial weight loss."

Why wouldn't they? The answer lies in biology. A person's weight remains stable as long as the number of calories consumed doesn't exceed the amount of calories the body spends, both on exercise and to maintain basic body functions. As the balance between calories going in and calories going out changes, we gain or lose weight.

But bodies don't gain or lose weight indefinitely. Eventually, a cascade of biological changes kicks in to help the body maintain a new weight. As the JAMA article explains, a person who eats an extra cookie a day will gain some weight, but over time, an increasing proportion of the cookie's calories also goes to taking care of the extra body weight. Eventually, the body adjusts and stops gaining weight, even if the person continues to eat the cookie.

Similar factors come into play when we skip the extra cookie. We may lose a little weight at first, but soon the body adjusts to the new weight and requires fewer calories.

Regrettably, however, the body is more resistant to weight loss than weight gain. Hormones and brain chemicals that regulate your unconscious drive to eat and how your body responds to exercise can make it even more difficult to lose the weight. You may skip the cookie but unknowingly compensate by eating a bagel later on or an extra serving of pasta at dinner.

"There is a much bigger picture than parsing out the cookie a day or the Coke a day," said Dr. Jeffrey M. Friedman, head of Rockefeller University's molecular genetics lab, which first identified leptin, a hormonal signal made by the body's fat cells that regulates food intake and energy expenditure. "If you ask anyone on the street, 'Why is someone obese?,' they'll say, 'They eat too much.'"

"That is undoubtedly true," he continued, "but the deeper question is why do they eat too much? It's clear now that there are many important drivers to eat and that it is not purely a conscious or higher cognitive decision."

This is not to say that the push for small daily changes in eating and exercise is misguided. James O. Hill, director of the Center for Human Nutrition at the University of Colorado Denver, says that while weight loss requires significant lifestyle changes, taking away extra calories through small steps can help slow and prevent weight gain.

In a study of 200 families, half were asked to replace 100 calories of sugar with a noncaloric sweetener and walk an extra 2,000 steps a day. The other families were asked to use pedometers to record their exercise but were not asked to make diet changes.

During the six-month study, both groups of children showed small but statistically significant drops in body mass index; the group that also cut 100 calories had more children who maintained or reduced body mass and fewer children who gained excess weight.

The study, published in 2007 in Pediatrics, didn't look at long-term benefits. But Dr. Hill says it suggests that small changes can keep overweight kids from gaining even more excess weight.

"Once you're trying for weight loss, you're out of the small-change realm," he said. "But the small-steps approach can stop weight gain."

While small steps are unlikely to solve the nation's obesity crisis, doctors say losing a little weight, eating more heart-healthy foods and increasing exercise can make a meaningful difference in overall health and risks for heart disease and diabetes.

"I'm not saying throw up your hands and forget about it," Dr. Friedman said. "Instead of focusing on weight or appearance, focus on people's health. There are things people can do to improve their health significantly that don't require normalizing your weight."

Dr. Ludwig still encourages individuals to make small changes, like watching less television or eating a few extra vegetables, because those shifts can be a prelude to even bigger lifestyle changes that may ultimately lead to weight loss. But he and others say that reversing obesity will require larger shifts—like regulating food advertising to children and eliminating government subsidies that make junk food cheap and profitable.

"We need to know what we're up against in terms of the basic biological challenges, and then design a campaign that will truly address the problem in its full magnitude," Dr. Ludwig said. "If we just expect that inner-city child to exercise self-control and walk a little bit more, then I think we're in for a big disappointment."

Assess Your Progress

1. Can eliminating one food serving a day contribute to a lasting weight loss? Explain.

2. How important is exercise to achieving optimal health? Explain.

UNIT 5

Drugs and Health

Unit Selections

Learning Outcomes

After reading this unit, you should be able to:

- Describe how statin drugs work.

- Distinguish between the risks versus benefits of statin drugs.

- Describe the potential harmful effects of drinking alcohol during pregnancy.

- Describe the physical and behavioral characteristics of fetal alcohol syndrome.

- Discuss the risks associated with alcohol use among the young.

- Explain the increased use of prescription drugs to get high.

- Describe the risks of taking over-the-counter pain medications.

- Explain the health risks associated with smoking.

- Explain what companies can do to help their employees quit smoking.

Student Website

www.mhhe.com/cls

Internet References

Food and Drug Administration (FDA)
www.fda.gov
National Institute on Drug Abuse (NIDA)
www.nida.nih.gov

As a culture, Americans have come to rely on drugs not only as a treatment for disease but also as an aid for living normal, productive lives. This view of drugs has fostered a casual attitude regarding their use and resulted in a tremendous drug abuse problem. Drug use and abuse has become so widespread that there is no way to describe the typical drug abuser. There is no simple explanation for why America has become a drug-taking culture, but there certainly is evidence to suggest some of the factors that have contributed to this development.

From the time that we are children, we are constantly bombarded by advertisements about how certain drugs can make us feel and look better. While most of these ads deal with proprietary drugs, the belief created is that drugs are a legitimate and effective way to help us cope with everyday problems. Certainly drugs can have a profound effect on how we feel and act, but research has also demonstrated that our mind plays a major role in the healing process. For many people, it's easier to take a drug than to adopt a healthier lifestyle. Tara Parker-Pope addresses the usage of statin drugs, one of the most commonly prescribed medicines in the United States, in "Great Drug, but Does It Prolong Life?"

Growing up, most of us probably had a medicine cabinet full of prescription and over-the-counter (OTC) drugs, freely dispensed to family members to treat a variety of ailments. This familiarity with drugs, coupled with rising health care costs, has prompted many people to diagnose and medicate themselves with OTC medications without sufficient knowledge of the possible side effects. Though most of these preparations have little potential for abuse, it does not mean that they are innocuous. Generally speaking, OTC drugs are relatively safe if taken at the recommended dosage by healthy people, but the risk of dangerous side effects rises sharply when people exceed the recommended dosage. Another potential danger associated with the use of OTC drugs is the drug interactions that can occur when they are taken in conjunction with prescription medications. The gravest danger associated with the use of OTC drugs is that an individual may use them to control symptoms of an underlying disease and thus prevent its early diagnosis and treatment.

While OTC drugs can be abused, an increasing number of drug-related deaths over the past five years have been linked to prescription drugs. These drugs, opiate-based painkillers such as OxyContin, Darvon, and Vicodin, are often used as an alternative to an illicit high. Karmen Hanson handles this issue in "A Pill Problem."

As a culture, we have grown up believing that there is, or should be, a drug to treat any malady or discomfort that befalls us. Would we have a drug problem if there was no demand for drugs? One drug which is used widely in the United States is alcohol, especially on college campuses. Every year over 1,000

© PunchStock/Image Source

students die from alcohol-related causes, mostly drinking and driving. In "Drinking Too Much, Too Young," author Garry Boulard discusses other risks associated with students drinking, including missed classes, falling behind in school work, damage to property, and injuries which occur while under the influence of alcohol.

While alcohol abuse among college students is a serious issue, drinking among pregnant women is also a concern. Women who drink during their pregnancies risk delivering a baby which could suffer from a range of effects including physical, emotional, mental, behavioral, and cognitive abnormalities. In "Vital Signs," Mark Cohen describes a child he treated for attention deficit disorder. The child was adopted at birth and there was an indication that the birth mother drank heavily during her pregnancy which contributed to the child's condition.

In addition to alcohol, another widely used legal drug is tobacco. Millions still smoke despite all the well-publicized health effects linked to smoking. Many Americans have quit and many others would like to quit. To facilitate this process, some companies have developed programs to help employees stop smoking. Since smoking and its related diseases cost approximately $150 billion each year, the stakes are enormous. Pamela Babcock addresses this issue in "Helping Workers Kick the Habit."

Great Drug, but Does It Prolong Life?

Tara Parker-Pope

Statins are among the most prescribed drugs in the world, and there is no doubt that they work as advertised—that they lower not only cholesterol but also the risk for heart attack.

But in the fallout from the headline-making trial of Vytorin, a combination drug that was found to be no more effective than a simple statin in reducing arterial plaque, many people are asking a more fundamental question about statins in general: Do they prolong your life?

And for many users, the surprising answer appears to be no.

Some patients do receive significant benefits from statins, like Lipitor (from Pfizer), Crestor (AstraZeneca) and Pravachol (Bristol-Myers Squibb). In studies of middle-aged men with cardiovascular disease, statin users were less likely to die than those who were given a placebo.

But many statin users don't have established heart disease; they simply have high cholesterol. For healthy men, for women with or without heart disease and for people over 70, there is little evidence, if any, that taking a statin will make a meaningful difference in how long they live.

"High-risk groups have a lot to gain," said Dr. Mark H. Ebell, a professor at the University of Georgia who is deputy editor of the journal American Family Physician. "But patients at low risk benefit very little if at all. We end up overtreating a lot of patients." (Like the other doctors quoted in this column, Dr. Ebell has no ties to drug makers.)

How is this possible, if statins lower the risk of heart attack? Because preventing a heart attack is not the same thing as saving a life. In many statin studies that show lower heart attack risk, the same number of patients end up dying, whether they are taking statins or not.

"You may have helped the heart, but you haven't helped the patient," said Dr. Beatrice Golomb, an associate professor of medicine at the University of California, San Diego, and a co-author of a 2004 editorial in *The Journal of the American College of Cardiology* questioning the data on statins. "You still have to look at the impact on the patient over all."

A 2006 study in The Archives of Internal Medicine looked at seven trials of statin use in nearly 43,000 patients, mostly middle-aged men without heart disease. In that review, statins didn't lower mortality.

Nor did they in a study called Prosper, published in The Lancet in 2002, which studied statin use in people 70 and older. Nor did they in a 2004 review in The Journal of the American Medical Association, which looked at 13 studies of nearly 20,000 women, both healthy and with established heart disease.

Indications are that statins aren't all they're cracked up to be.

A Pfizer spokeswoman notes that a decline in heart disease death rates reported recently by the American Heart Association suggests that medications like statins are having an impact. But to consistently show a mortality benefit from statins in a research setting would take years of study. "We've concentrated on whether Lipitor reduces risk of heart attacks and strokes," says Halit Bander, medical team leader for Lipitor. "We've proven that again and again."

This month, *The Journal of the American College of Cardiology* published a report combining data from several studies of people 65 and older who had a prior heart attack or established heart disease. This "meta-analysis" showed that 18.7 percent of the placebo users died during the studies, compared with 15.6 percent of the statin users.

This translates into a 22 percent lower mortality risk for high-risk patients over 65. A co-author of the study, Dr. Jonathan Afilalo, a cardiology fellow at McGill University in Montreal, says that for every 28 patients over 65 with heart disease who take statins, one life will be saved.

"If a patient has had a heart attack," Dr. Afilalo said, "they generally should be on a statin."

Of course, prolonging life is not the only measure that matters. If preventing a heart attack improved the quality of life, that would be an argument for taking statins even if it didn't reduce mortality. But critics say there's no evidence that statin users have a better quality of life than other people.

"If you can show me one study that people who have a disability from their heart are worse off than people who have a disability from other causes, I would find that a compelling argument," Dr. Golomb said. "There's not a shred of evidence that you've mitigated suffering in the groups where there is not a mortality benefit."

One big concern is that the side effects of statins haven't been well studied. Reported side effects include muscle pain, cognitive problems and impotence.

"Statins have side effects that are underrated," said Dr. Uffe Ravnskov, a retired Swedish physician and a vocal critic of statins. "It's much more frequent and serious than has been reported."

Dr. Ebell acknowledges that there are probably patients with heart disease who could benefit from a statin but who aren't taking it.

But he added, "There are probably more of the opposite—patients who are taking a statin when they probably don't need one."

Assess Your Progress

1. What are the risks versus benefits of using statin drugs?
2. How do statin drugs reduce the risk of heart disease?

Vital Signs

MARK COHEN

A 3-year-old boy shows signs of hyperactivity. Is it ADHD, or is it something else that happened to him before he was born?

Hey, Mom! Mom! Watch me! Look, Mom!" I could hear the excited cries through the closed door of the examining room, even though I was still 20 feet down the hall. The happy shouts were followed by a loud thump and then a cascade of muted crashes. As I headed toward the commotion, my medical assistant smiled and handed me the chart for this patient.

"You'd better get in to see this little guy quickly, Dr. Cohen, before he totally wrecks your room!"

The brief information on the consultation request said, "Tyler Winters, 3-year-old boy, hyperactive." As I often tell medical students, nearly all 3-year-olds are hyperactive at least some of the time. Often the parents of a child whose development and behavior are perfectly normal insist on a referral to a developmental pediatrician like myself because they are sure there is something wrong—or someone has told them as much. I generally look forward to those consultations; it's enjoyable to reassure an anxious parent that her child is developing normally.

Before leaving my office I had briefly looked through Tyler's medical record on the computer. Other than his having been adopted at birth, there was nothing that stood out as unusual.

When I knocked and opened the door, Tyler was clambering onto the exam table while his mother, Sandi, was attempting to move a pile of books from the floor back onto the book rack. They had apparently been knocked off (the crashes) when he jumped from the table to the floor (the loud thump). Sandi glanced at me with a nervous smile, then quickly turned to scoop her child off the table.

"Hi, I'm Dr. Cohen," I said. "Why don't we go across the hall to the testing room, where all the toys are?"

Tyler immediately shouted, "Toys! Yeah! Toys!" and squirmed to get out of his mother's grasp. She managed to hold onto him long enough for us to move across the hall into the other room, where he broke free and ran to the toy shelf with glee.

"I'm sorry, doctor. He's like this all the time," she said.

"Oh, that's OK; I'm used to it," I answered. I was about to reassure her by telling her that I'd seen some children who were so active that they took all the toys off the shelves and threw them on the floor, when I noticed that Tyler was starting to do just that.

"People tell me he has ADHD and that I should get him on medication."

I was beginning to think the same thing, although it isn't common for me to diagnose attention deficit/hyperactivity disorder in a 3-year-old. For that diagnosis, a child's behavior must be significantly different from that of other children his age. But because most 3-year-olds are hyperactive, one with ADHD may not look very different from his friends. Then again, sometimes the ADHD symptoms are so severe that the child clearly stands out as having excessive impulsivity and hyperactivity. This might be one of those cases, I realized.

"Hey, look, Thomas train!" Tyler held the toy high above his head, then slammed it into the table. "Crash! Thomas crash!" he cried, laughing furiously.

This looked like a pretty clear case of ADHD. But then he stopped moving long enough for me to get a good look at his face, and his features told a different story. This wasn't going to be so simple. It was time for me to get back to the basics of medicine history and physical exam.

"What do you know about his birth mother?" I asked Sandi.

"Not much. We know that she was in her late teens and didn't have much prenatal care."

"Did she use any drugs or alcohol?"

"People said she did both drugs and alcohol, but the drug tests were negative on both her and the baby," Sandi replied. "The doctors told us that he was born full term, but he weighed only about four pounds at birth. He went right from the hospital to foster care with us, and then we adopted him about a year later. He was always incredibly active. We kept hoping he'd grow out of it, but it hasn't happened yet."

What I had observed when I looked at Tyler's face was that his eyes appeared small and his upper lip was quite thin. The distance from his nose to his upper lip was longer than average, and the philtrum (the vertical groove below the nose) was flattened, with a near-absence of the ridges that result from the fusion of embryonic elements of the face in this area. In addition, Tyler was quite short for his age, and his head seemed small relative to the rest of his body. His appearance triggered a tentative visual diagnosis. I had seen faces like this before, and the rest of the picture—hyperactivity, shortness, small head circumference, and a mother who may have abused alcohol—was consistent with my clinical impression. This boy might have fetal alcohol syndrome (FAS).

Some people trace the recognition of FAS all the way back to the Bible, when an angel tells Samson's future mother, "Behold . . . thou shalt conceive, and bear a son" and instructs her to "drink no wine nor strong drink." Other cultures have had similar proscriptions. But it wasn't until 1973 that a professor of pediatrics named David Smith and a student of his, Kenneth Jones, at the University of Washington Medical School (UWMS) described a cluster of physical and cognitive problems in children whose mothers had abused alcohol during their pregnancy. Studies by another UWMS pediatrician, Sterling Clarren, more directly established that alcohol can cause damage to the developing brain.

Physicians and researchers now recognize a whole range of conditions, known as fetal alcohol spectrum disorders, that can occur in children who are exposed to alcohol in utero. The effects may include physical, mental, behavioral, and learning disabilities with possible lifelong implications. The most severe condition on this spectrum is FAS. Three criteria are necessary for the diagnosis of FAS: characteristic facial features, poor growth, and abnormalities of the central nervous system.

The brain problems associated with FAS are manifold. Like Tyler, a child with FAS may be hyperactive and impulsive and so would meet the diagnostic criteria for ADHD. But the damage that alcohol causes to the developing brain results in a constellation of mental and behavioral characteristics that go well beyond what is seen in ADHD. Some children have a generalized cognitive impairment, or mental retardation. Others are not mentally retarded but still have significant learning disorders and other developmental issues, including motor delays, problems with social skills, memory deficits, language problems, and difficulties with the complex set of mental skills—including planning, flexibility, and decision making—that are known as "executive functioning."

If my diagnosis was found to be correct, it was likely that Tyler would require a comprehensive intervention program, including medications to help decrease his impulsivity, anxiety, and disruptive behavior. In addition, he would need special educational services, beginning in preschool and continuing through his school years, and an intensive behavioral intervention program both in school and at home. Tyler's concrete thinking, poor short-term memory, and limited tolerance for overstimulation would require plenty of patience from his teachers. Repetition, structure, and simplification are essential in teaching children with FAS.

When I told Sandi that I thought Tyler had fetal alcohol syndrome, she didn't seem surprised. "We had heard about FAS and wondered if Tyler could have it," she said. "But he didn't seem that bad, and we kept hoping he would get better as he matured. "So," she continued, "what do we do now?" I told her how to contact the school district and ask for an evaluation so her son could start receiving special education services. I also told her about several parent support groups in the area.

Most important, I told Sandi, Tyler would need firm support, guidance, encouragement, and love from his parents. Although children with FAS can be very challenging to raise and to teach, they can be immensely rewarding as well. Each successful step, each time the child smiles and shouts, "Mom, I did it!" can be a moment to enjoy.

I referred Tyler to our genetics clinic, where a complete evaluation confirmed the diagnosis of FAS. Six months later I saw him and his mother again when they came back for a follow-up visit.

"He's doing well," Sandi told me. "He's in a developmental preschool program with a one-on-one aide and a behavioral specialist, and he likes it a lot. He even has a friend now. I know it's not going to be easy, but I think we're on the right track."

Tyler looked at the toy shelf and then at me. "Can I play with Thomas, please?" he said.

I smiled at him and at his mother. "You sure can," I told him. "Thanks for asking!"

"Hey, look, Thomas train!" Tyler held the toy high above his head, then slammed it into the table. "Crash! Thomas crash!" he cried, laughing furiously.

Assess Your Progress

1. What are the behavioral and physical effects of fetal alcohol syndrome?
2. What are the potential harmful effects of maternal drinking?

MARK COHEN is a developmental pediatrician with Kaiser Permanente in Santa Clara, California. The cases described in Vital Signs are real, but names and certain details have been changed.

Drinking Too Much, Too Young

Trying to find an answer to the persistent habit of binge drinking among young people vexes the nation's policymakers.

GARRY BOULARD

The stories have been shocking, abruptly reminding a nation of a problem that remains unsolved: in the last half of 2004, six college-age students in Colorado died as a result of binge drinking.

Although each fatality was different in its circumstance—Samantha Spady, 19, a sophomore at Colorado State University, died after drinking vanilla vodka and more than two dozen beers, while Benett Bertoli, 20, also a CSU student, was found dead on a couch at an off-campus party from a combination of alcohol, methadone and benzodiazepene—the events leading up to the deaths were maddeningly familiar.

In almost every case, the fatalities were the unexpected ending to a boisterous party almost always involving large gatherings of young people on weekend nights consuming prodigious amounts of alcohol, sometimes for two days straight.

The number of Colorado deaths from binge drinking in late 2004 was exceptionally large, but the state is not alone. It killed Thomas Ryan Hauser, 23, a student at Virginia Tech in September. Blake Hammontree, 19, died at his fraternity house at the University of Oklahoma, also in September. Bradley Kemp, 20, died in October at his home near the University of Arkansas, where he was a student. Steven Judd died celebrating his 21st birthday with fraternity friends at New Mexico State University in November.

Those deaths did not occur in a vacuum. According to statistics from the National Institute for Alcohol Abuse and Alcoholism, more than 1,400 college students die from alcohol-related deaths each year including motor vehicle crashes. Unfortunately, that number has remained constant even though both high school and college-age drinking has decreased.

"The numbers have been going in the right direction," says Peter Cressy, the president of the Distilled Spirits Council of the United States. "There is today less regular use of alcohol on college campuses than there was 20 years ago. There has been a drop in the number of college students both of age and not of age who drink at all during any given month. And the data for eighth, 10th, and 12th graders who consume alcohol has also shown a downward trend."

Bucking the Trend

But what hasn't changed, industry, health and alcohol experts all agree, is the stubborn number of young people who continue to engage in destructive behavior.

"The issue is not the 30,000 kids on the campus of the University of Colorado, or any other school, who drink legally or illegally, but somehow manage to do it without any great peril," says Ralph Blackman, the president of the Century Council, a not-for-profit organization dedicated to fighting drunk driving and underage drinking.

"The issue is binge drinking and the continuing large numbers of kids who insist on over consumption to a level that has a very decided risk for a dangerous result," continues Blackman. "That is a phenomenon that very much remains with us."

Trying to find a specific reason for the persistence of binge drinking among the young is a subject that both vexes and causes great debate among the nation's policymakers. Do younger people just naturally like to get drunk, or in some cases, very drunk? Is it a matter of upbringing or income? Is it a reflection of a troubled and anxious society?

"You could ask questions like that all day, and not really get any solid answers," says Paul Hanson, a professor emeritus of sociology at the State University of New York, Potsdam.

"The only thing you could be sure of is that no matter how many different ways we approach it with different solutions, binge drinking continues among the very young, generation after generation."

But some experts believe one thing that is different with those who are a part of what demographers call the Millennials—those born in 1980 or after—and their predecessors, is that binge drinking today is out of the closet and celebrated on almost a worldwide basis due to the Internet.

"There is a huge difference from when many of us went to school in the 1960s and '70s and today," says Stephen Bentley, a coordinator of substance abuse services at the Wardenberg Health Center at the University of Colorado.

"Back in our day we really did not want any attention of any kind, we did not want adults or the world to know that we were drinking and partying excessively," continues Bentley.

"But today young people who engage in this kind of behavior are actually very proud of what they are doing, they post their own websites about their parties so that everyone else can see what they did."

One of the websites, called shamings.com, features pictures of drunken young men, updated on a regular basis, sometimes sleeping in their own vomit, often half naked, and many times covered with magic marker salutations alluding to their drinking prowess or lack thereof.

One of the website creators, Ricky Van Veen, explained to the Washington Post the guidelines used by the website in determining whether or not to post a binge drinker's picture: "The standard rule is, if you fall asleep with your shoes on, you're fair game," he said.

Youth Targets

For Julia Sherman, field director with the Center on Alcohol Marketing and Youth, binge drinking self-promotion is almost a natural outgrowth of what she says is the alcohol industry's "preoccupation with the young."

"The ads that are being put out there today are not your Mom and Pop, 'Mabel, Black Label,' ads of another era, but ads that are very much geared toward an exceedingly young demographic," she says.

"The whole ad focus of the alcohol industry has changed both in tenor and in numbers," says Sherman. "Their Web site ads now feature computer games and premiums for downloading music. They run ads in what are called the 'laddie magazines,' that are edgier than anything adults are seeing in their magazines. It is all part of a non-stop, never-ending pitch for the youth market."

According to a study released by the Center on Alcohol Marketing and Youth last October, the number of alcohol ads on TV jumped by nearly 90,000 between 2001 and 2003, with some 23 percent of the ads "more likely to be seen by the average underage person for every four seen by the average adult."

Cressey of the Distilled Spirits Council, among other industry leaders, disputes that there has been any concerted targeting of young people, and notes that his group will not permit any member to advertise where the media is not at least a 70/30, adult to minor, demographic.

"We also require through our code that all models in our ads be at least 25 years old," adds Cressey, a requirement that is also generally followed by members of the Beer Institute.

But even working within those parameters, the impact of drinking ads, usually showing young people at a beach party, rap concert, or skate boarding, remains a matter of contention.

"The problem is that how we view television has changed greatly in the last generation," says Sherman. "It used to be that there was one TV and the entire family was watching it, which meant that there would probably be some sort of adult filtering or response to whatever the ad message was. But that is much harder today when over 30 percent of kids aged two to eight, and two-thirds over the age of eight, have their own TVs in their own rooms."

The end result may not only be a message received early on that drinking alcohol is attractive, but an actual inability at

---

Binge Drinking—The Facts

- In 2001, 44% of U.S. college students engaged in binge drinking; this rate has not changed since 1993.
- 51% of the men drank five or more drinks in a row.
- 40% of the women drank four or more drinks in a row.
- Students more likely to binge drink are white, age 23 or younger, and are residents of a fraternity or sorority.
- 75.1% of fraternity residents and 62.4% of sorority residents report binge drinking.
- Binge drinkers in high school are three times more likely to binge in college.
- From 1993 to 2001, more students abstained from alcohol (16% to 19%), but more also frequently drank heavily (19.7% to 22.8%).
- Just as many freshman (those under 21) as seniors binge drink.
- Frequent binge drinkers are eight times more likely than others to miss a class, fall behind in schoolwork, get hurt or injured, and damage property.
- 91% of women and 78% of the men who are frequent binge drinkers consider themselves to be moderate or light drinkers.
- 1,400 college students every year die from alcohol-related causes; 1,100 of these deaths involve drinking and driving.

Sources: Harvard University's School of Public Health; Robert Wood Johnson Foundation.

---

an age leading all the way up to college to discern alcohol's potential danger. "There is a lot of research out there showing that even up to the age of 21 and beyond a young body is not fully developed and it does not absorb alcohol as well as it might in an older person," says Blackman of the Century Council. "Just as important is the evidence that your brain is not fully developed at that point either, so that issues of risk-taking and behavior are assessed in a different way."

To make matters worse, State University of New York's Hanson says, zero tolerance alcohol programs or efforts to make campuses virtually alcohol-free have a funny way of backfiring. "Prohibition is a classic example of how the laws in these matters can end up being counterproductive by actually making the thing that is being prohibited more attractive. That remains especially true for young people who don't like to be told what not to do."

"And when that happens," says Hanson, "young people very often find themselves involved in these dangerous events centered around heavy episodic drinking, which is the very last thing we want to see happen."

Teaching Moderation

Hanson has also noticed in his own research that the percentage of students who drink tends to decrease as they go from being freshmen to seniors. He says policymakers would be wiser to focus on what he calls "harm reduction policies" that acknowledge young people are going to drink no matter what, but emphasize responsible drinking through education—even to minors.

Similarly Colorado University's Bentley has noticed the effectiveness of the restorative justice approach on many college campuses that require students who have engaged in binge drinking to face the people who suffered the consequences of their behavior when they were drunk.

"That means the neighbors who were trying to study when the party was blaring," says Bentley, "or friends who had to take care of them when they were throwing up all over themselves or were otherwise dead drunk."

Legislatively, some lawmakers are looking at keg-registration laws in order to keep better track of who buys what for whom, particularly when such kegs end up at parties heavily populated with minors. So far, 24 states and the District of Columbia have adopted keg registration laws of varying severity.

"It is only a tool that might possibly reduce binge drinking and underage drinking," says Arizona Representative Ted Downing, who has introduced legislation requiring the state to put tracking numbers on every keg of beer sold.

"The way my legislation reads is that if you want to buy a keg, you have to show identification, fill out a form, leave a deposit, and detail where the keg is going to go and for what purpose" says Downing.

Other lawmakers believe that by making underage consumption and distribution more legally challenging, they can, at the very least, chip away at the roughly 33 percent of the nation's college students who are below the age of 21.

"It's worth a try," says Colorado Representative Angie Paccione, who has introduced legislation making it a class one misdemeanor to distribute alcohol to someone under the age of 21, with jail time of up to 18 months and fines topping out at $5,000.

"We want to give the DAs a tool that they can use for prosecuting and that the police can use in order to effect behavior changes," Paccione says, adding that problem college drinking is very often preceded by problem high school drinking.

"I was a dean in a high school and have seen more than my share of kids who have had liquid lunches," she says. "So I know that this is a problem that begins very early."

Education Works

And although a new look at both underage and binge drinking from the legislative perspective may be in order, Jeff Becker, president of the Beer Institute, says lawmakers should not lose sight of the progress that has already been made in reducing both high school and college drinking.

"The education and awareness programs have really worked, whether it is at the college or high school level; and I think lawmakers should take credit for any support they have given to those efforts and continue those programs," says Becker.

"Maybe these most recent deaths will serve as a wake-up call and get all of us to look once more at what works and what doesn't work," he adds. "But from the community, family and school level it is very clear that making kids aware of the dangers has also made them smarter. And I don't think we should stop doing that."

In Connecticut, Senator Biagio "Billy" Ciotto, a long-time advocate of programs that educate high school students on the harmful effects of both drinking and driving and binge drinking, says he remains convinced that lawmakers should concentrate on what he calls the "realistic goal of reduction" vs. the "impossible ideal," of elimination.

"You are never going to get rid of this kind of drinking completely," Ciotto says. "But I have no doubt in my mind that you can reduce the abuse simply by staying with it, never giving up, always trying to let kids know, without lecturing them, about the harmful effects of alcohol abuse."

Ciotto's efforts have even won the support of the Connecticut Coalition to Stop Underage Drinking, which named him "Outstanding Legislator in Reducing Underage Drinking" in 2004.

"I think they and just about everyone else recognize that we have to work on the big majority of kids who will not abuse alcohol if they know the dangers, and just figure that there is always going to be a minority that will do what they want to do no matter what," he says.

Arizona's Downing agrees: "It would be very foolish for any state representative or senator to feel that you can propose a bill that will somehow magically get rid of the problems of binge drinking or underage drinking."

"You can't," says Downing. "And we have to admit that. All you can really do is nudge things in a certain direction, which is what so many of our laws do anyway. If people are going to behave in the wrong way no matter what, there is only so much we can do. But we can help those who want to do the right thing, or don't want to break any laws just to have a little fun. That is the group we need to appeal to."

Assess Your Progress

1. Describe the health risks associated with teenage drinking.
2. What can be done to prevent binge drinking and underage drinking?

Freelancer **Garry Boulard** is a frequent contributor to *State Legislatures*.

From *State Legislatures*, April 2005, pp. 12–15. Copyright © 2005 by National Conference of State Legislatures. Reprinted by permission.

A Pill Problem

Prescription drug abuse is the fastest growing form of substance abuse.

KARMEN HANSON

The figure is startling: A 96.6 percent increase in drug-related deaths in a five-year period.

What's most shocking is that the drugs involved are not cocaine or heroin or even methamphetamine. They are prescription drugs—medication prescribed every day by doctors, mostly for pain.

"The prescription drug problem is a crisis that is steadily worsening," says Dr. Len Paulozzi, a medical epidemiologist with the Centers for Disease Control and Prevention. "The vast majority of unintentional drug overdose deaths are not the result of toddlers getting into medicines or the elderly mixing up their pills. Our scientific evidence suggests that these deaths are related to the increasing use of prescription drugs, especially opioid painkillers, among people during the working years of life."

> **"The prescription drug problem is a crisis that is steadily worsening."**
>
> —Dr. Len Paulozzi, Centers for Disease Control and Prevention

Opioid analgesic painkillers, one of the largest growing segments of prescription drugs, are medications such as Oxy-Contin, Darvon and Vicodin. They include ingredients such as oxycodone, hydrocodone, fentanyl and propoxyphene. More than 201 million prescriptions were written in 2007 for products that have a potential for abuse—opioid analgesics, methylphenidates and amphetamines—according to Verispan, a prescription information database.

It was a CDC study that found the 96.6 percent increase in prescription opioid analgesic-related deaths in 28 metropolitan areas from 1997 to 2002. During the same period, deaths from cocaine overdoses increased 12.9 percent, and deaths from heroin or morphine decreased 2.7 percent.

The problem is growing faster than previously estimated. Some 4.7 million people used various prescription drugs—pain relievers, sedatives and stimulants—nonmedically for the first time in 2008, according to the National Survey on Drug Use and Health.

As Paulozzi points out, "drug overdoses are now the second leading cause of unintentional injury death in the United States, exceeded only by motor vehicle fatalities."

People who initially take prescriptions for legitimate pain relief may go on to abuse these drugs for a recreational high. Others are abusing prescription drugs from the beginning as an alternative to illegal drugs.

State legislators are hoping to reverse this growing trend. In 2009, at least 11 state legislatures enacted Drug Abuse Awareness months, regulated pain clinics, and created prescription drug monitoring programs and unused prescription drug disposal programs to help prevent fraud and abuse and to rehabilitate current abusers.

Going after the Supply

The problem is widespread across the country, hitting every type of community. It began to increase after doctors started treating chronic pain with new, stronger medications in the 1990s. While thousands of people use these products legitimately every day, they may become addicted if the drugs are not used as prescribed.

More than half the nonmedical users of prescription pain relievers get them from a friend or relative for free, according to the national drug survey. The majority of those people had obtained the drugs from one doctor. Fewer than 10 percent bought the pain relievers from a friend or relative.

In Iowa, the Division of Narcotics Enforcement opened 243 percent more pharmaceutical abuse cases and seized 412 percent more prescription drugs in 2009 than in 2008. And the Statewide Poison Control Center reported a 1,225 percent increase since 2002 in calls about suspected hydrocodone and oxycodone overdoses.

To combat such increases, Iowa launched the first statewide prescription and over-the-counter drug abuse awareness campaign, called Take a Dose of Truth. A website features information for teens, parents, older adults and professionals on recognizing, educating and treating prescription drug abuse.

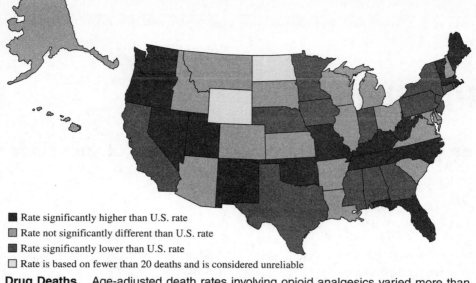

Rate significantly higher than U.S. rate
Rate not significantly different than U.S. rate
Rate significantly lower than U.S. rate
Rate is based on fewer than 20 deaths and is considered unreliable

Drug Deaths. Age-adjusted death rates involving opioid analgesics varied more than eightfold among states in 2006.

Florida's "Pill Mills"

In some states, such as Florida, pain clinics are popping up everywhere, including in shopping centers. In fact, Florida has one of the highest concentrations of pain clinics in the country. Doctors in Broward County, for example, handed out more than 6.5 million oxycodone pills, and 45 south Florida doctors gave out nearly 9 million oxycodone pills in the second half of 2008, according to an interim report of the Broward County Grand Jury.

Florida's numbers are potentially larger than nearby states because it does not have a prescription drug monitoring program. Pill seekers from across state lines may prey on neighboring states that do not track who is filling prescriptions for products prone to abuse and recreational use.

John Burke, president of the National Association of Drug Diversion Investigators, says he saw the problem play out before when Kentucky had a prescription drug monitoring program, and Ohio did not.

"Scores of folks from the Bluegrass State came into Ohio to obtain their medication at our pharmacies. Only after Ohio put their [program] in place did the influx of Kentucky illegal drug-seekers subside."

"Unfortunately this same situation exists today in Florida," he says. "The migration of Ohio drug diverters to Florida to obtain prescriptions for oxycodone is partly fueled by the fact that no [monitoring program] exists yet in Florida."

Florida legislators are considering bills to better regulate pain clinics and ensure legitimate medical need. For example, Senator Dan Gelber is sponsoring legislation that would require private pain management clinics to be registered with the department of health.

"Last year's effort to stem the tide of 'pill mills' didn't preclude felons from owning and operating pain-management clinics. This industry has attracted far too many bad apples, and this loophole needs to be closed," says Gelber. "This new provision is just common sense. The public expects, and the state should guarantee, that we do not allow convicted felons to be in the business of providing powerful narcotics to people who need legitimate pain management."

A House bill proposed by Representative Joseph Abruzzo would allow only licensed physicians to own and operate the pain clinics. "This is a national issue, as law enforcement agencies across the country are finding pill bottles with Broward or Palm Beach county addresses on them," Abruzzo says. "We need to make sure that the people who own and operate these clinics are licensed medical professionals."

> **"This is a national issue. We need to make sure that the people who own and operate these clinics are licensed medical professionals."**
>
> Joseph Abruzzo, Florida Representative

Another House bill from Representative John Legg would limit pain prescriptions to a 72-hour supply. This effectively would eliminate abusive pain clinics, Legg says, that we make money from volume dispensing, not physician visits or prescribing. Patients requiring more than a 72-hour dose would have to go to a licensed pharmacy to fill their prescriptions, instead of getting the drugs directly from their doctor's office or a questionable pill mill.

Texas lawmakers recently passed legislation to regulate pill mills because of concerns similar to those in Florida.

"The legitimate practice of pain management clinics has a valuable role in the state," says Representative Mike Hamilton, one supporter of the new law. "However, some pain management clinics work as an illegal drug diversion, causing great harm to many families and communities. We have seen an increase in the demand of controlled substances throughout the state, and part of the problem is the proliferation of these pill mills."

Role for Doctors and Pharmacists

Physicians and pharmacists play pivotal roles in curbing abuse. They are expected to identify and care for patients who are dependent on or addicted to prescription medicines and to help prevent prescription drug abuse. It is often difficult, however, to determine if a patient is one of the 70 million Americans who experience pain every day or among the 10 percent who struggle with addiction.

Physicians, including most in primary care and emergency medicine, are often trained to recognize drug-seeking behavior and how to thwart drug abuse. They may also rely on validated questionnaires or interview instruments to recognize uncontrolled pain, and have recently begun using clinician-patient agreements defining the expectations and responsibilities of patients receiving addictive substances. Doctors also can refer to prescription drug monitoring programs for more information about a patient's history with controlled substances.

These approaches, however, can increase time-consuming paperwork. And even the well-trained and methodical physician can fall victim to dishonest patients.

Pharmacists are responsible for ensuring that patients get the most benefit from their medications. They can also be part of the first line of defense in recognizing prescription drug abuse. By monitoring prescriptions for falsification or alterations and being aware of potential "doctor shopping"—patients who obtain multiple prescriptions from different doctors—pharmacists play a valuable role in prevention. They are trained to detect suspicious behaviors, including fraudulent prescriptions.

About half the states require security features such as watermarks on prescription pads to help prevent fraud. Pharmacy and insurance company computer systems may also issue a warning if patients are taking too many controlled substances or refilling their prescriptions too quickly.

State and local pharmacy associations have historically relied on "phone trees" to contact each other when a physician reports a stolen prescription pad or a customer attempts to pass a fraudulent prescription. Greater use of electronic health records, electronic prescribing and the exchange of information may help prevent drug abuse and diversion.

"The best way for a pharmacist to balance the risks of drug abuse and undertreatment is to have a relationship with the patient and the physician," says Dr. John O'Brien of the College of Notre Dame of Maryland School of Pharmacy. "A pharmacist-physician conversation can identify more information helpful in preventing a chronic pain sufferer from being branded an addict, and also identify a patient in need of assistance with addiction or dependency."

Assess Your Progress

1. Do you think America has a drug problem? Defend your answer.

2. What are the risks of taking over-the-counter pain medications?

KARMEN HANSON covers prescription drug issues for NCSL.

Helping Workers Kick the Habit

**Programs aimed at helping employees give up tobacco
can pay off in lower health care costs.**

PAMELA BABCOCK

Smoking is more than a health threat for the 45 million Americans who use tobacco. It's also an employers' problem because it raises health cost issues and productivity concerns.

Smoking and the illnesses that link to it, such as cancer and heart disease, account for annual medical costs of $150 billion or more, by some estimates. In turn, those costs affect the premiums for employer-sponsored health care. As employers try to exert control over their fast-rising health costs through wellness programs and other efforts to improve employees' health, some are adopting smoking-cessation programs as one of their tools.

Smoking-cessation approaches range from reminding employees of the health effects of smoking, to offering them multifaceted assistance programs, to requiring them to quit smoking if they want to keep their jobs.

In that middle ground between encouragement and ultimatum reside a number of generally affordable programs that typically offer counseling—sometimes one-on-one—and various types of drugs formulated to help smokers quit. Health coverage companies, behavioral health organizations, stand-alone wellness companies, hospitals and others number among the providers.

As the availability of smoking-cessation programs increases and as new drugs arrive in the market, it's important for benefits specialists to know how to choose a cessation approach that will work best for their employees, and where to turn when looking for a program.

The Will to Quit

Although about 47 million Americans say they have quit smoking, almost as many still smoke. About 70 percent of those who smoke say they want to quit, but only 5 percent succeed long term, the U.S. Centers for Disease Control and Prevention reports.

Indeed, quitting is difficult. Less than 7 percent of smokers who try to quit on their own abstain for longer than a year; most light up within a few days of attempting to quit, according to pharmaceutical manufacturer Pfizer Inc. It takes about 10 attempts, with or without treatment, before the average smoker kicks the habit for good, says Pfizer. The company recently introduced a smoking-cessation drug.

"Although we have made significant progress, tobacco use is still the leading cause of preventable illness and death," says Susan Butterworth, director of Health Management Services within the School of Nursing at Oregon Health & Science University (OHSU), based in Portland. "Nicotine dependency is more than a lifestyle choice. It's an addiction, and employees need assistance in addressing it," she says.

How Programs Work

Butterworth and many other smoking-cessation experts recommend a strategic approach that includes "quit medications" and health counseling.

Medications available over the counter include nicotine patches and nicotine gum; prescription drugs include nasal sprays, inhalers and pills. An article on the U.S. Food and Drug Administration's website describes how these medications work: "Most medical aids to smoking cessation are nicotine replacement products. They deliver small, steady doses of nicotine into the body to relieve some of the withdrawal symptoms, without the 'buzz' that keeps smokers hooked. . . . Like cigarettes, the products deliver nicotine into the blood, but they don't contain the tar and carbon monoxide that are largely responsible for cigarettes' dangerous health consequences."

Nicotine dependency is . . . an addiction, and employees need assistance in addressing it.

Many programs that operate under an employer-sponsored wellness initiative include a personal health assessment that identifies smoking as a health risk. Follow-up efforts often involve counseling—increasingly delivered by the Internet with threaded discussion, chat or e-mail. The vast majority, Butterworth says, deliver counseling by phone, while others deliver it in person.

One of the largest cessation companies, Free & Clear Inc., a coaching-based provider in Seattle, has been named the official quit-smoking program for 16 states and more than 100 large employers and health plans. Last year, the company registered more than 115,000 people into tobacco-cessation programs and completed nearly 700,000 intervention calls, says Dr. Tim McAfee, senior vice president for clinical and behavioral sciences at Free & Clear.

The company offers a personal Internet application, called Web Coach, in its Quit For Life Program. It also offers Vital Signs, a real-time, online reporting tool for clients. OHSU's Health Management Services competes in the field, offering smoking cessation as one of its health-coaching services for outside clients.

Other major providers of smoking-cessation programs include QuitNet, WebMD and the Mayo Clinic. For more

Online Resources

For additional information about helping employees to quit smoking, see the online version of this article at www.shrm.org/hrmagazine/07September for links to:

- A SHRM article on employers who want to help employees quit smoking.
- An *HR Magazine* article on the legal issues in providing smoking-cessation programs.
- An *HR News* article on tobacco's drain on employee productivity.
- A SHRM article about a Rhode Island law mandating employer health plan coverage of smoking-cessation treatment programs.
- Information from the Centers for Disease Control and Prevention on helping employees who smoke to quit.
- The American Legacy Foundation's survey on smoking cessation as an employer-sponsored health benefit.

on those organizations, including their smoking-cessation approaches, see the online version of this article at www.shrm.org/hrmagazine/07September.

Employers should avoid "going with a canned or low-cost program that doesn't embrace best practice in nicotine dependence treatment," says Butterworth, also an associate professor in OHSU's School of Nursing. Look for programs that use best practices—a combination of quit medications and coaching—and that demonstrate measurable outcomes, she says.

Measurable outcomes are determined by quit rates at one year compared with the rates in a control group in a random controlled study, Butterworth says. When the quit rate significantly exceeds the rate in the control group, the treatment is considered effective.

The combined use of coaching and quit medications—she calls it "the gold standard"— seems to work equally well across demographic and cultural differences within workplaces, but she adds that it's important for health coaches "to understand the culture, to be sensitive to employee norms, and to be acquainted with their benefits and other resources."

Employees may prefer accessing information in different ways, for example. Office workers who have desktops may prefer Internet products, while those on a manufacturing line may do better with telephone coaching or printed handouts.

Costs and Savings

Employers can provide programs such as a telephone "quit line"—generally the lowest-price approach—for under 5 cents per employee per month, a figure based on the total population of employees and their covered dependents, not on the number of employees using the service. The figure is in the results of research commissioned by the American Legacy Foundation, a Washington, D.C., organization that focuses on smoking prevention and cessation, and carried out by Milliman, a global consulting organization based in Seattle.

The research report, *Covering Smoking Cessation as a Health Benefit: A Case for Employers*, released last December, found that more-comprehensive coverage that includes therapy and selected pharmaceuticals costs 28 cents to 45 cents per health plan member per month.

The annual savings for each smoker who quits, according to the report, is about $210 through reductions in costs for smoking-related conditions such as stroke, coronary heart disease, pneumonia, childhood respiratory disease and low birth weight. The dollar savings alone may not fully offset an employer's annual cost for a cessation program, but they can make a difference over time, since they accrue each year the employee remains a nonsmoker.

In addition, smoking cessation reduces annual medical and life insurance costs almost immediately, says the study's author, Bruce Pyenson, a principal and consulting actuary with Milliman in New York.

Among the approaches compared in the study, telephonic quit lines, with no face-to-face contact with employees, had quit rates of 4.5 percent, Pyenson says. Programs with more features, such as counseling and a range of medications, cost more but had higher quit rates, up to about 30 percent.

Noting that the costs of cessation programs vary according to the type of service provided and the vendor providing it, Butterworth says one-time fees for each health-coaching participant range from $100 to $250.

Building the Base

Before settling on a particular program, benefits specialists should determine the incidence of smoking among the company's employees, experts suggest, and start their searches by tapping their trusted sources of information, such as brokers and health plan providers.

Christopher J. Mathews, a Washington, D.C.-based senior health consultant and vice president of the Segal Co., a benefits consulting organization headquartered in New York, recommends working with your health plan or advisor to find out whether smoking is a real problem in your employee population. Employee surveys can be used to determine how many smokers you have and whether any are really interested in quitting.

If your CEO is a cigar smoker and there's no way he's going to quit, there's a problem.

If your organization's smoker population is made up of those who have been smoking for 30 years, you might not get a lot of traction. "But if the smoker population is comprised of those who sincerely wish to quit, then the prospects for success are greatly improved," Mathews explains.

Karen Roberts, a senior vice president in Aon Consulting's Health and Benefits Practice in Las Vegas, recommends making sure that the program has support from the top. "If your CEO is a cigar smoker and there's no way he's going to quit, there's a problem," she says. "You really have to walk the talk with these programs."

Take inventory of your physical premises to determine how committed you are to the cessation program. Are you going to push cessation but still have designated smoking areas on your property or allow smoking in company cars?

Also, take inventory of provisions in your health benefits plan to determine if there are barriers to a program's success, such as lack of coverage for smoking-cessation drugs or for coaching or counseling, Mathews says. If such coverage isn't provided, he says, and your plan, in effect, becomes "a barrier to providing the necessary support needed for smokers to quit, it will need to be modified."

As sponsor of your health plan, you should decide how many attempts to quit smoking by an individual will be covered by your plan and whether there would be a maximum on the benefit per employee, Mathews says.

For OHSU's own tobacco-cessation program, provided by Health Management Services, the university has structured its employee health plan so that over-the-counter quit medications such as patches and gum are free, and there are no co-payments for prescription-only quit medicines approved by the U.S. Food and Drug Administration. Employees who sign up also receive an individual quit plan.

Butterworth and her staff acknowledge that some smokers may want to try alternative cessation approaches such as acupuncture and hypnosis; they are not included in any OHSU plan, however.

Butterworth recommends motivational interviewing, an approach "used by many reputable vendors" to help tobacco users develop the self-confidence necessary to quit. It's important, she says, to "engage smokers who aren't ready to quit" to "help them consider their options, draw out their ambivalence and help them weigh the pros and cons of quitting."

OHSU's smoking-cessation campaign expands this month to its entire Portland campus—12,000 employees, thousands of patients and students. All smoking will be banned, even on streets and sidewalks.

Try a Little Tenderness

Roger Reed, a nurse practitioner and executive vice president of Gordian Health Solutions, a health management provider based in Franklin, Tenn., says a positive and benevolent approach can go a long way in a smoking-cessation initiative. "The biggest mistake," he says, "is to start taking a list of smokers and singling them out with some kind of punitive action, such as saying you have 12 months to quit or you won't work here anymore."

Gordian provides one-on-one coaching, online information and health materials via mail to large employers, health plans and government entities. Last year, the company had 6,755 people enrolled in tobacco-cessation programs.

"Most people try to stop smoking multiple times, and it's just that one time when they make that one more attempt that it actually works," Reed says, adding, "You never know." It could be that when their employer provides that extra opportunity, it just might be the employee's time to quit for good.

Assess Your Progress

1. What can companies do to help workers quit smoking?
2. Why should companies support smoking cessation programs?

PAMELA BABCOCK is a freelance writer based in the New York City area.

UNIT 6

Sexuality and Relationships

Unit Selections

Learning Outcomes

After reading this unit, you should be able to:

- Describe the relationship between scent and sexual attraction.
- Describe the biological basis for using scent to attract a mate.
- Explain what is meant by the "expectations trap."
- Explain what is meant by the following sentence: Searching for perfection is common because people believe that they are entitled to the best option there is.
- Describe how gender is identified before birth.
- Explain why or why not parents should be permitted to choose the sex of their baby.
- Explain what role pornography may play in relationships.
- Describe why pornography may be considered adultery.

Student Website
www.mhhe.com/cls

Internet References

Planned Parenthood
www.plannedparenthood.org
Sexuality Information and Education Council of the United States (SIECUS)
www.siecus.org

Sexuality is an important part of both self-awareness and intimate relationships. But how important is physical attraction in establishing and maintaining intimate relationships? Researchers in the area of evolutionary psychology have proposed numerous theories that attempt to explain the mutual attraction that occurs between the sexes. The most controversial of these theories postulates that our perception of beauty or physical attractiveness is not subjective, but rather a biological component hard-wired into our brains. It is generally assumed that perceptions of beauty vary from era to era and culture to culture, but evidence is mounting that suggests that people all over share a common sense of beauty that is based on physical symmetry. In addition to a sense of physical beauty, researchers believe that scent plays an important role in who we end up with. In "Scents and Sensibility," Elizabeth Svoboda explains that physical attraction based on smell may be a significant component of what we think of as "chemistry" between partners.

While physical attraction is clearly an important issue when it comes to dating, how important is it in long-term loving relationships? For many Americans the answer may be very important because we tend to be a "Love Culture" that places a premium on passion in the selection of our mates. Is passion an essential ingredient in love, and can passion serve to sustain a long-term meaningful relationship? Since most people can't imagine marrying someone that they don't love, we must assume that most marriages are based on this feeling we call love. That being the case, why is it that so few marriages survive the rigors of day-to-day living? Perhaps the answer has more to do with our limited definition of love rather than love itself. An interesting look at relationships can be found in "The Expectations Trap," which addresses improving happiness and satisfaction in marriage. According to author Hara Estroff Marano, it appears that married individuals tend to see any unhappiness they experience as a failure of their partner to satisfy their needs. It's common for couples to search for perfection because people believe that they are entitled to the best option there is. Spending time together in challenging activities is suggested to couples to enhance the feelings of closeness and satisfaction with the relationship.

Pornography can be another reason for dissatisfaction in a relationship. The idea that pornography is related to marital infidelity has been a topic of discussion in recent years. With the increase in online options to view pornography, there appears to be a connection to divorce as well. Ross Douthat addresses this problem in "Is Pornography Adultery?"

Two additional topics of interest and controversy in the area of human sexuality are sex education and sex selection. First, although most states mandate some type of school-based sex education, many parents believe that they should be the only source for their children's sex education. Next, should couples have the option of choosing the sex of their baby? Some doctors are willing to accommodate parents choices, while others question the ethics of choosing gender. Denise Grady addresses this issue in "Girl or Boy?"

Perhaps no topic in the area of human sexuality has garnered more publicity and public concern than the dangers associated with unprotected sex. Although the concept of "safe sex" is nothing new, the degree of open and public discussion regarding sexual behaviors is. With the emergence of AIDS as a disease of epidemic proportions and the rapid spreading of other sexually transmitted

© Royalty-Free/Corbis

diseases (STDs), the surgeon general of the United States initiated an aggressive educational campaign, based on the assumption that knowledge would change behavior. If STD rates among teens are any indication of the effectiveness of this approach, then we must conclude that our educational efforts are failing. Conservatives believe that while education may play a role in curbing the spread of STDs, the root of the problem is promiscuity, and that promiscuity rises when a society is undergoing a moral decline. The solution, according to conservatives, is a joint effort between parents and educators to teach students the importance of values such as respect, responsibility, and integrity. Liberals, on the other hand, think that preventing promiscuity is unrealistic, and instead the focus should be on establishing open and frank discussions between the sexes. Their premise is that we are all sexual beings, and the best way to combat STDs is to establish open discussions between sexual partners, so that condoms will be used correctly when couples engage in intercourse.

While education undoubtedly has had a positive impact on slowing the spread of STDs, perhaps it is unrealistic to think that education alone is the solution, given the magnitude and the nature of the problem. Most experts agree that for education to succeed in changing personal behaviors, the following conditions must be met: (1) The recipients of the information must first perceive themselves as vulnerable and, thus, be motivated to explore replacement behaviors, and (2) the replacement behaviors must satisfy the needs that were the basis of the problem behaviors. To date, most education programs have failed to meet these criteria. Given all the information that we now have on the dangers associated with AIDS and STDs, why is it that people do not perceive themselves at risk? It is not so much the denial of risks as it is the notion of most people that they use good judgment when it comes to choosing sex partners. Unfortunately, most decisions regarding sexual behavior are based on subjective criteria that bear little or no relationship to one's actual risk. Even when individuals do view themselves as vulnerable to AIDS and STDs, there are currently only two viable options for reducing the risk of contracting these diseases. The first is the use of a condom and the second is sexual abstinence, neither of which is an ideal solution to the problem.

Scents and Sensibility

"Sexual chemistry" is more than just a way of talking about heated attraction. Subtle chemical keys actually help determine who we fall for. But here comes news that our lifestyles may unwittingly undermine our natural sex appeal.

ELIZABETH SVOBODA

Psychologists Rachel Herz and Estelle Campenni were just getting to know each other, swapping stories about their lives over coffee, when Campenni confided something unexpected: She was living proof, she said, of love at first smell. "I knew I would marry my husband the minute I smelled him," she told Herz. "I've always been into smell, but this was different; he really smelled good to me. His scent made me feel safe and at the same time turned on—and I'm talking about his real body smell, not cologne or soap. I'd never felt like that from a man's smell before. We've been married for eight years now and have three kids, and his smell is always very sexy to me."

Everyone knows what it's like to be powerfully affected by a partner's smell—witness men who bury their noses in their wives' hair and women who can't stop sniffing their boyfriends' T-shirts. And couples have long testified to the ways scent-based chemistry affects their relationships. "One of the most common things women tell marriage counselors is, 'I can't stand his smell,'" says Herz, the author of *The Scent of Desire*.

Sexual attraction remains one of life's biggest mysteries. We might say we go for partners who are tall and thin, love to cook, or have a mania for exercise, but when push comes to shove, studies show, the people we actually end up with possess few of the traits we claim to want. Some researchers think scent could be the hidden cosmological constant in the sexual universe, the missing factor that explains who we end up with. It may even explain why we feel "chemistry"—or "sparks" or "electricity"—with one person and not with another.

Physical attraction itself may literally be based on smell. We discount the importance of scent-centric communication only because it operates on such a subtle level. "This is not something that jumps out at you, like smelling a good steak cooking on the grill," says Randy Thornhill, an evolutionary psychologist at the University of New Mexico. "But the scent capability is there, and it's not surprising to find smell capacity in the context of sexual behavior." As a result, we may find ourselves drawn to the counter attendant at the local drugstore, but have no idea why—or, conversely, find ourselves put off by potential dating partners even though they seem perfect on paper.

Though we may remain partially oblivious to scent signals we're sending and receiving, new research suggests that we not only come equipped to choose a romantic partner who smells good to us, but that this choice has profound biological implications. As we act out the complex rituals of courtship, many of them inscribed deep in our brain, scent-based cues help us zero in on optimal partners—the ones most likely to stay faithful to us and to create healthy children with us.

At first blush, the idea of scent-based attraction might seem hypothetical and ephemeral, but when we unknowingly interfere with the transmission of subtle olfactory messages operating below the level of conscious awareness, the results can be both concrete and devastating. When we disregard what our noses tell us, we can find ourselves mired in partnerships that breed sexual discontent, infertility, and even—in extreme cases—unhealthy offspring.

The Scent of Desire

When you're turned on by your partner's scent, taking a deep whiff of his chest or the back of her neck feels like taking a powerful drug—it's an instant flume ride to bliss, however momentary. Research has shown that we use scent-based signaling mechanisms to suss out compatibility. Claus Wedekind, a biologist at the University of Lausanne in Switzerland, created Exhibit A of this evidence by giving 44 men new T-shirts and instructing them to wear the shirts for two straight nights. To ensure that the sweat collecting on the shirts would remain "odor-neutral," he supplied the men with scent-free soap and aftershave.

After the men were allowed to change, 49 women sniffed the shirts and specified which odors they found most attractive. Far more often than chance would predict, the women preferred the smell of T-shirts worn by men who were immunologically dissimilar to them. The difference lay in the sequence of more than 100 immune system genes known as the MHC, or major histocompatibility complex. These genes code for proteins that help the immune system recognize pathogens. The smell of their favorite shirts also reminded the women of their past and current boyfriends, suggesting that MHC does indeed influence women's dating decisions in real life.

I knew I would marry my husband the minute I first smelled him. His body scent made me feel safe and turned on.

Women's preference for MHC-distinct mates makes perfect sense from a biological point of view. Ever since ancestral times, partners whose immune systems are different have produced offspring who are more disease-resistant. With more immune genes expressed, kids are buffered against a wider variety of pathogens and toxins.

But that doesn't mean women prefer men whose MHC genes are most different from theirs, as University of Chicago evolutionary biologist Martha McClintock found when she performed a T-shirt study similar to Wedekind's. Women are not attracted to the smell of men with whom they had no MHC genes in common. "This might be a case where you're protecting yourself against a mate who's too similar or too dissimilar, but there's a middle range where you're OK," McClintock says.

Women consistently outperform men in smell sensitivity tests, and they also make greater time and energy sacrifices on their children's behalf than men do—in addition to bearing off-spring, they look after them most of the time. These factors may explain why women are more discriminating in sniffing out MHC compatibility.

Men are sensitive to smell as well, but because women shoulder a greater reproductive burden, and are therefore choosier about potential mates, researchers are not surprised to find that women are also more discriminating in sniffing out MHC compatibility.

Unlike, say, blood types, MHC gene complements differ so much from one person to the next that there's no obvious way to reliably predict who's MHC-compatible with whom. Skin color, for instance, isn't much help,

Follow Your Nose

How to Put Your Nose to Work in Choosing a Partner—or Evaluating an Existing One

Think twice about opting for the pill if you're seeking a long-term partner. The first few weeks of a relationship are critical to assessing compatibility, so make sure your nose is up to the task.

Try a fragrance-free week. Eliminate factors that could throw your nostrils off. Have your partner set aside scented shower gels in favor of fragrance-free soap, nix the cologne, and use only unscented deodorant.

Keep smell's importance in context. If you sometimes find your partner's scent off-putting, don't panic; it doesn't necessarily mean fertility issues are in your future. Connections between MHC compatibility and conception problems have yet to be confirmed in large-scale population studies, so don't plunk down big bucks for MHC testing at this point.

since groups of people living in different areas of the world might happen to evolve genetic resistance to some of the same germs. "People of different ethnicities can have similar profiles, so race is not a good predictor of MHC dissimilarity," Thornhill says.

And because people's MHC profiles are as distinct as fingerprints—there are thousands of possible gene combinations—a potential sex partner who smells good to one woman may completely repel another. "There's no Brad Pitt of smell," Herz says. "Body odor is an external manifestation of the immune system, and the smells we think are attractive come from the people who are most genetically compatible with us." Much of what we vaguely call "sexual chemistry," she adds, is likely a direct result of this scent-based compatibility.

Typically, our noses steer us in the right direction when it comes to picking a reproductively compatible partner. But what if they fail us and we wind up with a mate whose MHC profile is too similar to our own? Carol Ober, a geneticist at the University of Chicago, explored this question in her studies of members of the Hutterite religious clan, an Amish-like closed society that consists of some 40,000 members and extends through the rural Midwest. Hutterites marry only other members of their clan, so the variety in their gene pool is relatively low. Within these imposed limits, Hutterite women nevertheless manage to find partners who are MHC-distinct from them most of the time.

The few couples with a high degree of MHC similarity, however, suffered higher rates of miscarriage and experienced longer intervals between pregnancies, indicating more difficulty conceiving. Some scientists speculate that miscarriages may be the body's way of curtailing investment in a child who isn't likely to have a strong immune system anyway.

What's more, among heterosexual couples, similar MHC profiles spell relational difficulty, Christine Garver-Apgar, a psychologist at the University of New Mexico, has found. "As the proportion of MHC alleles increased, women's sexual responsiveness to their partners decreased, and their number of sex partners outside the relationship increased," Garver-Apgar reports. The number of MHC genes couples shared corresponded directly with the likelihood that they would cheat on one another; if a man and woman had 50 percent of their MHC alleles in common, the woman had a 50 percent chance of sleeping with another man behind her partner's back.

The Divorce Pill?

Women generally prefer the smell of men whose MHC gene complements are different from theirs, setting the stage for the best biological match. But Wedekind's T-shirt study revealed one notable exception to this rule: women on the birth-control pill. When the pill users among his subjects sniffed the array of pre-worn T-shirts, they preferred the scent of men whose MHC profiles were similar to theirs—the opposite of their pill-free counterparts.

This dramatic reversal of smell preferences may reflect the pill's mechanism of action: It prevents the ovaries from releasing an egg, fooling the body into thinking it's pregnant. And since pregnancy is such a vulnerable state, it seems to activate a preference for kin, who are genetically similar to us and likely to serve as protectors. "When pregnant rodent females are exposed to strange males, they can spontaneously abort," Herz says. "The same may be true for human females." What's more, some women report a deficit in sex drive when they take the pill, a possible consequence of its pregnancy-mimicking function.

The tendency to favor mates with similar MHC genes could potentially hamper the durability of pill users' relationships in the long term. While Herz shies away from dubbing hormonal birth control "the divorce pill," as a few media outlets have done in response to her theories, she does think the pill jumbles women's smell preferences. "It's like picking your cousins as marriage partners," Herz says. "It constitutes a biological error." As a result, explains Charles Wysocki, a psychobiologist at Florida State University, when such a couple decides to have children and the woman stops taking birth control, she may find herself less attracted to her mate for reasons she doesn't quite understand. "On a subconscious level, her brain is realizing a mistake was made—she married the wrong guy," he says.

"Some couples' fertility problems may be related to the pill-induced flip-flop in MHC preferences," Garver-Apgar adds. No one has yet collected data to indicate whether the pill has created a large-scale problem in compatibility. Still, Herz recommends that women seeking a long-term partner consider alternative birth control methods, at least until they get to know their potential significant other well and are sure they like the way he smells. "If you're looking for a man to be the father of your child," she says, "go off the pill before you start your search."

If you were on the pill when you met your current partner, the situation is more complicated. Once a relationship has progressed to long-term commitment, says Herz, a woman's perception of her partner's smell is so intertwined with her emotional reaction to him that it could be difficult for her to assess his scent as if he were a stranger. "If she's in love, he could smell like a garbage can and she'd still be attracted to him."

Crossed Signals

The pill subverts a woman's ability to sniff out a compatible mate by causing her to misinterpret the scent messages she receives. But it may warp olfactory communication channels in the other direction as well, distorting the signals she sends—and making her seem less appealing to men, an irony given that women typically take the pill to boost their appeal in a partner's eyes.

Geoffrey Miller, an evolutionary psychologist at University of New Mexico and author of *The Mating Mind*, noticed the pill's connection to waning male desire while studying a group of exotic dancers—women whose livelihoods depend on how sexually appealing they are to male customers. Non-pill-using dancers made about 50 percent more in tips than dancers on oral contraceptives. In other words, women who were on the pill were only about two-thirds as sexy as women who weren't.

Why were the pill-takers in the study so much less attractive to men? "Women are probably doing something unconsciously, and men are responding to it unconsciously," says Miller. "We just don't know whether it has to do with a shift in their psychology, their tone of voice, or if it's more physical, as in the kind of pheromones they're putting out."

The biggest earners in Miller's study were non-pill-using dancers at the time of ovulation. Other studies have shown that men rate women as smelling best when they are at the most fertile point of their menstrual cycles, suggesting that women give offscent-based signals that broadcast their level of fecundity. "The pill might be producing cues that a woman is in the early stage of pregnancy, which would not tend to elicit a lot of male sexual

Solving the Mystery of Gaydar

The Ability to Discern Sexual Orientation May Be Based on Scent

Everyone knows someone with impeccable "gaydar," the seemingly telepathic ability to tell whether someone is gay or straight. New research is robbing gaydar of its sixth-sense mystique, revealing that some people literally have the power to sniff out another person's sexual orientation—and that the ability is strongly rooted in biology.

When Charles Wysocki, a geneticist at the University of Pennsylvania's Monell Chemical Senses Center, asked volunteers to sniff underarm sweat from donors of a variety of genders and sexual orientations, some clear patterns began to emerge. Gay men strongly preferred the odor of other gay men, lesbians gravitated toward the smell of other lesbians, and straight women rated the odor of straight men higher than that of gay men. Each group, in short, preferred the smell of their first-choice mates, indicating a scent-based ability to assess sexual orientation. Another study confirmed that gay men and lesbians can recognize and identify the odor of others who share their sexual preference. This kind of scent-based gaydar enables gays to pinpoint potential partners instantly.

Researchers at Karolinska University in Sweden have added to Wysocki's findings, identifying a potential reason why gay men find the smell of other males so enticing. They found that androstenone, a steroid compound men secrete in their sweat, excited brain areas that control sexual behavior in gay men but left the brains of straight men unaffected. This suggests the chemical may be an integral part of the scent-driven signaling mechanism that attracts gay men to each other.

interest," Miller says. "It makes sense for men to be sensitive to that and for them not to feel the same chemistry with the woman."

Drowning in Fragrance

The pill isn't the only way we might confound sexual chemistry. Every day, far more people may be subverting their quest for love with soap and bottled fragrances. In ancestral times, smelling ripe was just a fact of life, absent hot showers and shampoo. This held true well into the 19th century, when the miasma of body odor in Parisian streets grew so thick that it was dubbed "The Great Stink of 1880." Back when a person's scent could waft across a room, a mere handshake could provide valuable information about attraction.

The need to smell our mates—and the difficulty in doing so over the sensory din of modern perfumes and colognes—may drive the sexual disinhibition of modern society.

Since the 20th-century hygiene revolution and the rise of the personal-care industry, however, companies have pitched deodorants, perfumes, and colognes to consumers as the epitome of sex appeal. But instead of furthering our quest to find the perfect mate, such products may actually derail it, say researchers, by masking our true scent and making it difficult for prospects to assess compatibility. "Humans abuse body smell signals by hiding them, masking them, putting on deodorant," says Devendra Singh, a psychologist at the University of Texas. "The noise-to-signal ratio was much better in primitive society."

Miller argues that modern hygiene may be such an impediment to sexual signaling that it could explain why so many people in our culture get so physical so fast. "Hunter-gatherers didn't have to do a lot of kissing, because they could smell each other pretty clearly from a few feet away," Miller says. "With all the showering, scents, and soap, we have to get our noses and mouths really up close to people to get a good idea of their biochemistry. People are more motivated to do a lot more kissing and petting, to do that assessment before they have sex." In other words, the need to smell our mates—and the comparative difficulty of doing so in today's environment of perfumes and colognes—may actually be driving the sexual disinhibition of modern society.

Other scientists counter that odor detection is a bit subtler. For one thing, it's possible we select store-bought scents to complement our natural odorprints, rather than mask them entirely: One study found that people with similar MHC profiles tend to go for the same colognes. And Garver-Apgar points out that in spending hours together each day, partners have ample opportunity to experience each other sans artificial scents. "Once you're in a close enough relationship," she says, "you're going to get a real whiff at some point."

Scents and Sensibility

There's no way to know whether couples who shell out thousands of dollars to fertility clinics—and those who struggle to make a relationship work because "the chemistry just isn't there"—suffer MHC incompatibility. We might never know, since a multitude of factors contributes to every reproductive and romantic outcome. But we can, at least, be cognizant of the importance of natural scent.

"Scent can be a deal breaker if it's not right, just like someone being too stupid or unkind or short," says Miller. Nevertheless, smell isn't the be-all and end-all of attraction, but one of a constellation of important factors. Armed with knowledge of how scent-based attraction operates, we have some power to decide how much priority we want to accord it. Is it more important to be with the partner who smells amazing and with whom you have great chemistry, or with the one who may not attract you quite as much on a physical level but is honest and reliable?

"People tend to treat this as an either-or situation: Either we're completely driven by pheromones, like moths, or we're completely in charge of our own destiny," University of Chicago psychologist McClintock says. "But it's not a wild idea that both factors are involved." While people like Estelle Campenni have reaped untold benefits by trusting their scent impressions, it's ultimately up to us how highly we value what our noses tell us.

Assess Your Progress

1. What role does scent play in sexual attraction?
2. What is the biological role scent plays in mate selection?

ELIZABETH SVOBODA contributes regularly to the *New York Times, Discover,* and *Popular Science.* She lives in San Jose, California.

The Expectations Trap

Much of the discontent couples encounter today is really culturally inflicted, although we're conditioned to blame our partners for our unhappiness. Yet research points to ways couples can immunize themselves against unseen pressures now pulling them apart.

HARA ESTROFF MARANO

Six years, ten months, and eight days into their marriage, Sam and Melissa blew apart. Everyone was stunned, most of all the couple themselves. One day she was your basic stressed-out professional woman (and mother of a 3-year-old) carrying the major financial burden of their household. The next day she was a betrayed wife. The affair Sam disclosed detonated a caterwaul of hurt heard by every couple in their circle and her large coterie of friends and family. With speed verging on inevitability, the public knowledge of their private life commandeered the driver's seat of their own destiny. A surge of support for Melissa as the wronged woman swiftly isolated Sam emotionally and precluded deep discussion of the conditions that had long alienated him. Out of respect for the pain that his mere presence now caused, Sam decamped within days. He never moved back in.

It's not clear that the couple could have salvaged the relationship if they had tried. It wasn't just the infidelity. "We had so many background and stylistic differences," says Sam. "It was like we came from two separate cultures. We couldn't take out the garbage without a Geneva Accord." Constant negotiation was necessary, but if there was time, there was also usually too much accumulated irritation for Melissa to tolerate. And then, opening a public window on the relationship seemed to close the door on the possibility of working through the disappointments, the frustrations, the betrayal.

Within weeks, the couple was indeed in discussions—for a divorce. At least they both insisted on mediation, not litigation, and their lawyers complied. A couple of months, and some time and determination later, they had a settlement. Only now that Sam and Melissa have settled into their mostly separate lives, and their daughter appears to be doing well with abundant care from both her parents, are they catching their respective breaths—two years later.

Americans value marriage more than people do in any other culture, and it holds a central place in our dreams. Over 90 percent of young adults aspire to marriage—although fewer are actually choosing it, many opting instead for cohabitation. But no matter how you count it, Americans have the highest rate of romantic breakup in the world, says Andrew J. Cherlin, professor of sociology and public policy at Johns Hopkins. As with Sam and Melissa, marriages are discarded often before the partners know what hit them.

"By age 35, 10 percent of American women have lived with three or more husbands or domestic partners," Cherlin reports in his recent hook. *The Marriage-Go-Round: The State of Marriage and the Family in America Today.* "Children of married parents in America face a higher risk of seeing them break up than children born of unmarried parents in Sweden."

With general affluence has come a plethora of choices, including constant choices about our personal and family life. Even marriage itself is now a choice. "The result is an ongoing self-appraisal of how your personal life is going, like having a continual readout of your emotional heart rate," says Cherlin. You get used to the idea of always making choices to improve your happiness.

The constant appraisal of personal life to improve happiness creates a heightened sensitivity to problems that arise in intimate relationships.

The heightened focus on options "creates a heightened sensitivity to problems that arise in intimate relationships." And negative emotions get priority processing in our brains. "There are so many opportunities to decide that it's unsatisfactory," says Cherlin.

It would be one thing if we were living more satisfied lives than ever. But just gauging by the number of relationships wrecked every year, we're less satisfied, says Cherlin. "We're carrying over into our personal lives the fast pace of decisions and actions we have everywhere else, and that may not be for the best." More than ever, we're paying attention to the most volatile parts of our emotional makeup—the parts that are too reactive to momentary events to give meaning to life.

More than ever, we're paying attention to the most volatile parts of our emotional makeup—parts that are too reactive to momentary events to give meaning to life.

Because our intimate relationships are now almost wholly vehicles for meeting our emotional needs, and with almost all our emotions invested in one relationship, we tend to look upon any unhappiness we experience—whatever the source—as a failure of a partner to satisfy our longings. Disappointment inevitably feels so *personal* we see no other possibility but to hunt for individual psychological reasons—that is, to blame our partners for our own unhappiness.

But much—perhaps most—of the discontent we now encounter in close relationships is culturally inflicted, although we rarely interpret our experience that way. Culture—the pressure to constantly monitor our happiness, the plethora of choices surreptitiously creating an expectation of perfection, the speed of everyday life—always climbs into bed with us. An accumulation of forces has made the cultural climate hostile to long-term relationships today.

Attuned to disappointment and confused about its source, we wind up discarding perfectly good relationships. People work themselves up over "the ordinary problems of marriage, for which, by the way, they usually fail to see their own contributions," says William Doherty, professor of family sciences at the University of Minnesota. "They badger their partners to change, convince themselves nothing will budge, and so work their way out of really good relationships." Doherty believes it's possible to stop the careering disappointment even when people believe a relationship is over.

It's not going to happen by putting the genie back in the bottle. It's not possible to curb the excess of options life now offers. And speed is a fixture of the ongoing technological revolution, no matter how much friction it creates in personal lives. Yet new research points to ways that actually render them irrelevant. We are, after all, the architects of our own passions.

The Purpose of Marriage

Marriage probably evolved as the best way to pool the labor of men and women to enable families to subsist and assure that children survive to independence—and data indicate it still is. But beyond the basics, the purpose of marriage has shifted constantly, says Stephanie Coontz, a historian at Washington's Evergreen State College. It helps to remember that marriage evolved in an atmosphere of scarcity, the conditions that prevailed for almost all of human history. "The earliest purpose of marriage was to make strategic alliances with

---

Case Study
Stephen and Christina

Five years into his marriage, not long after the birth of his first son, most of Stephen G.'s interactions with his wife were not pleasant. "I thought the difficulties would pass," he recalls. "My wife, Christina, got fed up faster and wanted me to leave." He was traveling frequently and finances were thin; she'd gone back to school full-time after having worked until the baby was born. "Very few needs were being met for either of us. We were either yelling or in a cold war."

They entered counseling to learn how to co-parent if they indeed separated. "It helped restore our friendship: At least we could talk civilly. That led to deeper communication—we could actually listen to each other without getting defensive. We heard that we were both hurting, both feeling the stress of new parenthood without a support system of either parents or friends. We could talk about the ways we weren't there for each other without feeling attacked. It took a lot longer for the romance to return."

Stephen, now 37, a sales representative for a pharmaceutical company in San Francisco, says it was a time of "growing up. I had to accept that I had new responsibilities. And I had to accept that my partner, now 38, is not ideal in every way although she is ideal in many ways. But her short temper is not enough of a reason to leave the relationship and our two kids. When I wish she'd be different, I have to remind myself of all the ways she is the person I want to be with. It's not something you 'get over.' You accept it."

---

other people, to turn strangers into relatives," says Coontz. "As society became more differentiated, marriage became a major mechanism for adjusting your position."

It wasn't until the 18th century that anyone thought that love might have anything to do with marriage, but love was held in check by a sense of duty. Even through the 19th century, the belief prevailed that females and males had different natures and couldn't he expected to understand each other well. Only in the 20th century did the idea take hold that men and women should be companions, that they should be passionate, and that both should get sexual and personal fulfillment from marriage.

We're still trying to figure out how to do that—and get the laundry done, too. The hassles of a negotiated and constantly renegotiated relationship—few wish a return to inequality—assure a ready source of stress or disappointment or both.

From We to Me

Our mind-set has further shifted over the past few decades, experts suggest. Today, the minute one partner is faced with dissatisfaction—feeling stressed-out or neglected, having

Case Study
Susan and Tim

Susan Pohlman, now 50, reluctantly accompanied her workaholic husband on a business trip to Italy believing it would be their last together. Back home in Los Angeles were their two teenagers, their luxurious home, their overfurnished lives—and the divorce lawyer she had contacted to end their 18-year marriage.

They were leading such parallel lives that collaboration had turned to competition, with fights over things like who spent more time with the kids and who spent more time working. But knocked off balance by the beauty of the coast near Genoa toward the end of the trip, Tim asked, out of the blue, "What if we lived here?" "The spirit of this odd day overtook me," recalls Susan. At 6 P.M. on the evening before departure, they were shown a beautiful apartment overlooking the water. Despite knowing no Italian, they signed a lease on the spot. Two months later, with their house sold, they moved with their kids to Italy for a year.

"In L.A. we were four people going in four directions. In Italy, we became completely dependent on each other. How to get a phone? How to shop for food? Also, we had no belongings. The simplicity forced us to notice the experiences of life. Often, we had no idea what we were doing. There was lots of laughing at and with each other." Susan says she "became aware of the power of adventure and of doing things together, and how they became a natural bridge to intimacy."

Both Pohlmans found Italy offered "a more appreciative lifestyle." Says Susan: "I realized the American Dream was pulling us apart. We followed the formula of owning, having, pushing each other. You have all this stuff but you're miserable because what you're really craving is interaction." Too, she says, American life is exhausting, and "exhaustion distorts your ability to judge problems."

Now back in the U.S. and living in Arizona, the Pohlmans believe they needed to remove themselves from the culture to see its distorting effects. "And we needed to participate in a paradigm shift: 'I'm not perfect, you're not perfect; let's not get hung up on our imperfections.'" But the most powerful element of their move could be reproduced anywhere, she says: "The simplicity was liberating."

consumer mind-set is a major portal through which destructive forces gain entry and undermine conjoint life.

"Marriage is for *me*" is the way Austin, Texas, family therapist Pat Love puts it. "It's for meeting *my* needs." It's not about what *I do*, but how it makes me *feel*.

Such beliefs lead to a sense of entitlement: "I deserve better than I'm getting." Doherty sees that as the basic message of almost every advertisement in the consumer culture. You deserve more and we can provide it. You begin to think: This isn't the deal I signed up for. Or you begin to feel that you're putting into this a lot more than you're getting out. "We believe in our inalienable right to the intimate relationships of our choice," says Doherty.

In allowing such free-market values to seep into our private lives, we come to believe that a partner's job is, above all, to provide pleasure. "People do not go into relationships because they want to learn how to negotiate and master difficulties," observes Brown University psychiatrist Scott Haltzman. "They want the other person to provide pleasure." It's partner as service provider. The pleasure bond, unfortunately, is as volatile as the emotions that underlie it and as hollow and fragile as the hedonic sense of happiness.

The Expectations Trap: Perfection, Please

If there's one thing that most explicitly detracts from the enjoyment of relationships today, it's an abundance of choice. Psychologist Barry Schwartz would call it an *excess* of choice—the tyranny of abundance. We see it as a measure of our autonomy and we firmly believe that freedom of choice will lead to fulfillment. Our antennae are always up for better opportunities, finds Schwartz, professor of psychology at Swarthmore College.

Just as only the best pair of jeans will do, so will only the best partner—whatever that is. "People walk starry-eyed looking not into the eyes of their romantic partner but over their romantic partner's shoulder, in case there might be somebody better walking by. This is not the road to successful long-term relationships." It does not stop with marriage. And it undermines commitment by encouraging people to keep their options open.

Like Doherty, Schwartz sees it as a consequence of a consumer society. He also sees it as a self-fulfilling phenomenon. "If you think there might be something better around the next corner, then there will be, because you're not fully committed to the relationship you've got."

It's naïve to expect relationships to feel good every minute. Every relationship has its bumps. How big a bump does it have to be before you do something about it? As Hopkins's Cherlin says, if you're constantly asking yourself whether you should leave, "there may be a day when the answer is yes. In any marriage there may be a day when the answer is yes."

One of the problems with unrestrained choice, explains Schwartz, is that it raises expectations to the breaking point.

a partner who isn't overly expressive or who works too hard or doesn't initiate sex very often—then the communal ideal we bring to relationships is jettisoned and an individualistic mentality asserts itself. We revert to a stingier self that has been programmed into us by the consumer culture, which has only become increasingly pervasive, the current recession notwithstanding.

Psychologically, the goal of life becomes *my* happiness. "The minute your needs are not being met then you appropriate the individualistic norm," says Doherty. This accelerating

A sense of multiple alternatives, of unlimited possibility, breeds in us the illusion that perfection exists out there, somewhere, if only we could find it. This one's sense of humor, that one's looks, another one's charisma—we come to imagine that there will be a package in which all these desirable features coexist. We search for perfection because we believe we are entitled to the best—even if perfection is an illusion foisted on us by an abundance of possibilities.

If perfection is what you expect, you will always be disappointed, says Schwartz. We become picky and unhappy. The cruel joke our psychology plays on us, of course, is that we are terrible at knowing what will satisfy us or at knowing how any experience will make us feel.

> **A sense of multiple alternatives, of unlimited possibility, breeds in us the illusion that the perfect person is out there waiting to be found.**

If the search through all possibilities weren't exhausting (and futile) enough, thinking about attractive features of the alternatives not chosen—what economists call opportunity costs—reduces the potential pleasure in whatever choice we finally do make. The more possibilities, the more opportunity costs—and the more we think about them, the more we come to regret any choice. "So, once again," says Schwartz, "a greater variety of choices actually makes us feel worse."

Ultimately, our excess of choice leads to lack of intimacy. "How is anyone going to stack up against this perfect person who's out there somewhere just waiting to be found?" asks Schwartz. "It creates doubt about this person, who seems like a good person, someone I might even be in love with—but who knows what's possible *out* there? Intimacy takes time to develop. You need to have some reason to put in the time. If you're full of doubt at the start, you're not going to put in the time."

Moreover, a focus on one's own preferences can come at the expense of those of others. As Schwartz said in his 2004 book, *The Paradox of Choice: Why More Is Less,* "most people find it extremely challenging to balance the conflicting impulses of freedom of choice on the one hand and loyalty and commitment on the other."

And yet, throughout, we are focused on the partner we want to have, not on the one we want—or need—to be. That may be the worst choice of all.

Disappointment—or Tragedy?

The heightened sensitivity to relationship problems that follows from constantly appraising our happiness encourages couples to turn disappointment into tragedy, Doherty contends.

Inevitably, images of the perfect relationship dancing in our heads collide with our sense of entitlement; "I'm entitled to the best possible marriage." The reality of disappointment becomes intolerable. "It's part of a cultural belief system that says we are entitled to everything we feel we need."

Through the alchemy of desire, wants become needs, and unfulfilled needs become personal tragedies. "A husband who isn't very expressive of his feelings can be a disappointment or a tragedy, depending on whether it's an entitlement," says Doherty. "And that's very much a cultural phenomenon." We take the everyday disappointments of relationships and treat them as intolerable, see them as demeaning—the equivalent of alcoholism, say, or abuse. "People work their way into 'I'm a tragic figure' around the ordinary problems of marriage." Such stories are so widespread, Doherty is no longer inclined to see them as reflecting an individual psychological problem, although that is how he was trained—and how he practiced for many years as an eminent family therapist. "I see it first now as a cultural phenomenon."

First Lady Michelle Obama is no stranger to the disappointment that pervades relationships today. In *Barack and Michelle: Portrait of an American Marriage,* by Christopher Anderson, she confides how she reached a "state of desperation" while working full-time, bringing in the majority of the family income, raising two daughters, and rarely seeing her husband, who was then spending most of his week away from their Chicago home as an Illinois state senator, a job she thought would lead nowhere while it paid little. "She's killing me with this constant criticism," Barack complained. "She just seems so bitter, so angry all the time." She was annoyed that he "seems to think he can just go out there and pursue his dream and leave all the heavy lifting to me."

But then she had an epiphany: She remembered the guy she fell in love with. "I figured out that I was pushing to make Barack be something I wanted him to be for me. I was depending on him to make me happy. Except it didn't have anything to do with him. I needed support. I didn't necessarily need it from Barack."

Certainly, commitment narrows choice. But it is the ability to remember you really do love someone—even though you may not be feeling it at the moment.

Commitment is the ability to sustain an investment, to honor values over momentary feelings. The irony, of course, is that while we want happiness, it isn't a moment-by-moment experience; the deepest, most enduring form of happiness is the result of sustained emotional investments in other people.

Architects of the Heart

One of the most noteworthy findings emerging from relationship research is that desire isn't just something we passively feel when everything's going right; it develops in direct response to what we do. Simply having fun together, for example, is crucial to keeping the sex drive alive.

But in the churn of daily life, we tend to give short shrift to creating positive experiences. Over time, we typically become more oriented to dampening threats and insecurities—to resolving conflict, to eliminating jealousy, to banishing problems. But the brain is wired with both a positive and negative motivational system, and satisfaction and desire demand keeping the brain's positive system well-stoked.

Even for long-term couples, spending time together in novel, interesting, or challenging activities—games, dancing, even conversation—enhances feelings of closeness, passionate love, and satisfaction with the relationship. Couples recapture the excitement of the early days of being in love. Such passion naturally feeds commitment.

From Michelle to Michelangelo

Important as it is to choose the right partner, it's probably more important to *be* the right partner. Most people are focused on changing the wrong person in the relationship; if anyone has to change in a relationship, it's you—although preferably with the help of your partner.

> **Important as it is to choose the right partner, it's probably more important to *be* the right partner. We focus on changing the wrong person.**

Ultimately, "Marriage is an inside job," Pat Love told the 2009 Smart marriages Conference. "It's internal to the person. You have to let it do its work." And its biggest job is helping individuals grow up. "Marriage is about getting over yourself. Happiness is not about focusing on yourself." Happiness is about holding onto your values, deciding who you are and being that person, using your particular talent, and investing in others.

Unfortunately, says Margin family therapist and *PT* blogger Susan Pease Gadoua, not enough people today are willing to do the hard work of becoming a more mature person. "They think they have a lot more choices. And they think life will be easier in another relationship. What they don't realize is that it will be the same relationship—just with a different name."

The question is not how you want your partner to change but what kind of partner and person you want to be. In the best relationships, not only are you thinking about who you want to be, but your partner is willing to help you get there. Psychologist Caryl E. Rusbult calls it the Michelangelo phenomenon. Just as Michelangelo felt the figures he created were already "in" the stones, "slumbering within the actual self is an ideal form," explains Eli Finkel, associate professor of psychology at Northwestern University and frequent Rusbult collaborator. Your partner becomes an ally in sculpting your ideal self, in bringing out the person you dream of becoming, leading you to a deep form of personal growth as well as long-term satisfaction with life and with the relationship.

It takes a partner who supports your dreams, the traits and qualities you want to develop—whether or not you've

Case Study
Patty and Rod

Patty NewBold had married "a really great guy," but by the time their 13th anniversary rolled around, she had a long list of things he needed to change to make the marriage work. At 34, she felt depressed, frantic—and guilty, as Rod was fighting a chronic disease. But she had reached a breaking point, "I read my husband my list of unmet needs and suggested a divorce," even though what she really wanted was her marriage back. "I wanted to feel loved again. But it didn't seem possible."

Newbold has had a long time to think about that list. Her husband died the next day, a freak side effect of his medications. "He was gone, but the list remained. Out of perhaps 30 needs, only one was eased by losing him. I was free now to move the drinking glasses next to the sink."

As she read through the list the morning after he died, she realized that "marriage isn't about my needs or his needs or about how well we communicate about our needs. It's about loving and being loved. *Life* is about meeting (or letting go of) my own *needs. Marriage* is about loving another person and receiving love in return. It suddenly became oh so clear that receiving love is something I make happen, not him." And then she was flooded with memories of all the times "I'd been offered love by this wonderful man and rejected it because I was too wrapped up in whatever need I was facing at the time."

Revitalized is "a funny word to describe a relationship in which one party is dead," she reports, "but ours was revitalized. I was completely changed, too," Everything she learned that awful day has gone into a second marriage, now well into its second decade.

articulated them clearly or simply expressed vague yearnings. "People come to reflect what their partners see in them and elicit from them," Finkel and Rusbult report in *Current Directions in Psychological Science.*

Such affirmation promotes trust in the partner and strengthens commitment. And commitment, Rusbult has found, is a key predictor of relationship durability. "It creates positive bias towards each other," says Finkel. "It feels good to achieve our goals. It's deeply satisfying and meaningful." In addition, it immunizes the relationship against potential distractions—all those "perfect" others. Finkel explains, "It motivates the derogation of alternative partners." It creates the perception—the illusion—that even the most attractive alternative partners are unappealing. Attention to them gets turned off—one of the many cognitive gymnastics we engage in to ward off doubts.

Like growth, commitment is an inside job. It's not a simple vow. Partners see each other in ways that enhance their connection and fend off threats. It fosters the perception that the relationship you're in is better than that of others. It breeds the inclination to react constructively—by accommodation—rather than destructively when a partner does something inconsiderate. It even motivates that most difficult of tasks, forgiveness for the ultimate harm of betrayal, Rusbult has shown.

It is a willingness—stemming in part from an understanding that your well-being and your partner's are linked over the long term—to depart from direct self-interest, such as erecting a grudge when you feel hurt.

The Michelangelo phenomenon gives the lie to the soulmate search. You can't find the perfect person; there is no such thing. And even if you think you could, the person he or she is today is, hopefully, not quite the person he or she wants to be 10 years down the road. You and your partner help each other become a more perfect person—perfect, that is, according to your own inner ideals. You are both, with mutual help, constantly evolving.

Assess Your Progress

1. Why do many modern couples believe their partner must satisfy all their needs?

2. Why do many people search for perfection when selecting a partner?

Girl or Boy?

As Fertility Technology Advances, So Does an Ethical Debate

Denise Grady

If people want to choose their baby's sex before pregnancy, should doctors help?

Some parents would love the chance to decide, while others wouldn't dream of meddling with nature. The medical world is also divided. Professional groups say sex selection is allowable in certain situations, but differ as to which ones. Meanwhile, it's not illegal, and some doctors are already cashing in on the demand.

There are several ways to pick a baby's sex before a woman becomes pregnant, or at least to shift the odds. Most of the procedures were originally developed to treat infertility or prevent genetic diseases.

The most reliable method is not easy or cheap. It requires in vitro fertilization, in which doctors prescribe drugs to stimulate the mother's ovaries, perform surgery to collect her eggs, fertilize them in the laboratory and then insert the embryos into her uterus.

Before the embryos are placed in the womb, some doctors will test for sex and, if there are enough embryos, let the parents decide whether to insert exclusively male or female ones. Pregnancy is not guaranteed, and the combined procedures can cost $20,000 or more, often not covered by insurance. Many doctors refuse to perform these invasive procedures just for sex selection, and some people are troubled by what eventually becomes of the embryos of the unwanted sex, which may be frozen or discarded.

Another method, used before the eggs are fertilized, involves sorting sperm, because it is the sperm and not the egg that determines a baby's sex. Semen normally has equal numbers of male- and female-producing sperm cells, but a technology called MicroSort can shift the ratio to either 88 percent female or 73 percent male. The "enriched" specimen can then be used for insemination or in vitro fertilization. It can cost $4,000 to $6,000, not including in vitro fertilization.

MicroSort is still experimental and available only as part of a study being done to apply for approval from the Food and Drug Administration. The technology was originally developed by the Agriculture Department for use in farm animals, and it was adapted for people by scientists at the Genetics and IVF Institute, a fertility clinic in Virginia. The technique has been used in more than 1,000 pregnancies, with more than 900 births

so far, a spokesman for the clinic said. As of January 2006 (the most recent figures released), the success rate among parents who wanted girls was 91 percent, and for those who wanted boys, it was 76 percent.

Regardless of the method, the American College of Obstetricians and Gynecologists opposes sex selection except in people who carry a genetic disease that primarily affects one sex. But allowing sex selection just because the parents want it, with no medical reason, may support "sexist practices," the college said in an opinion paper published this month in its journal, Obstetrics and Gynecology.

Some people say sex selection is ethical if parents already have one or more boys and now want a girl, or vice versa. In that case, it's "family balancing," not sex discrimination. The MicroSort study accepts only people who have genetic disorders or request family balancing (they are asked for birth records), and a company spokesman said that even if the technique was approved, it would not be used for first babies.

The obstetricians group doesn't buy the family-balance argument, noting that some parents will say whatever they think the doctor wants to hear. The group also says that even if people are sincere about family balance, the very act of choosing a baby's sex "may be interpreted as condoning sexist values."

Much of the worry about this issue derives from what has happened in China and India, where preferences for boys led to widespread aborting of female fetuses when ultrasound and other tests made it possible to identify them. China's one-child policy is thought to have made matters worse. Last month, Chinese officials said that 118 boys were born for every 100 girls in 2005, and some reports have projected an excess of 30 million males in less than 15 years. The United Nations opposes sex selection for nonmedical reasons, and a number of countries have outlawed it, including Australia, Canada and Britain, and other nations in Asia, South America and Europe. Left unanswered is the question of whether societies, and families, that favor boys should just be allowed to have them, since attitudes are hard to change, and girls born into such environments may be abused.

The American Society for Reproductive Medicine, a group for infertility doctors, takes a somewhat more relaxed view of sex selection than does the college of obstetricians. Instead of opposing sex selection outright, it says that in people who already need in vitro fertilization and want to test the embryos' sex without a medical reason, the testing should "not be encouraged." And those who don't need in vitro fertilization but want it just for sex selection "should be discouraged," the group says.

But sperm sorting is another matter, the society says. It is noninvasive and does not involve discarding embryos of the "wrong" sex. The society concludes that "sex selection aimed at increasing gender variety in families may not so greatly increase the risk of harm to children, women or society that its use should be prohibited or condemned as unethical in all cases." The group also says it may eventually be reasonable to use sperm sorting for a first or only child.

Dr. Jamie Grifo, the program director of New York University's Fertility Center, said that he opposed using embryo testing just for sex selection, but that it was reasonable to honor the request in patients who were already having embryos screened for medical reasons, had a child and wanted one of the opposite sex. In those cases, he said, the information is already available and doesn't require an extra procedure.

"It's the patient's information, their desire," he said. "Who are we to decide, to play God? I've got news for you, it's not going to change the gender balance in the world. We get a handful of requests per year, and we're doing it. It's always been a controversy, but I don't think it's a big problem. We should preserve the autonomy of patients to make these very personal decisions."

Dr. Jeffrey M. Steinberg, from Encino, Calif., who has three clinics that offer sex selection and plans to open a fourth, in Manhattan, said: "We prefer to do it for family balancing, but we've never turned away someone who came in and said, 'I want my first to be a boy or a girl.' If they all said a boy first, we'd probably shy away, but it's 50-50."

"Reproductive choice, as far as I'm concerned, is a very personal issue," Dr. Steinberg said. "If it's not going to hurt anyone, we go ahead and give them what they want."

Many patients come from other countries, he said. John A. Robertson, a professor of law and bioethics at the University of Texas, said: "The distinction between doing it for so-called family balancing or gender variety would be a useful line to draw at this stage of the debate, just as maybe a practice guideline, and let's just see how it works out."

In the long run, Mr. Robertson said, he doubted that enough Americans would use genetic tests to skew the sex balance in the population, and he pointed out that so far, sperm sorting was more successful at producing girls than boys.

He concluded, "I think this will slowly get clarified, and people will see it's not as big a deal as they think."

Assess Your Progress

1. Should parents be permitted to choose the sex of their baby?
2. How is gender identified before birth?

Is Pornography Adultery?

Ross Douthat

The marriage of Christie Brinkley and Peter Cook collapsed the old-fashioned way in 2006, when she discovered that he was sleeping with his 18-year-old assistant. But their divorce trial this summer was a distinctly Internet-age affair. Having insisted on keeping the proceedings open to the media, Brinkley and her lawyers served up a long list of juicy allegations about Cook's taste in online porn: the $3,000 a month he dropped on adult Web sites, the nude photos he posted online, the user names he favored ("happyladdie2002," for instance, and "wannasee-all") while surfing swinger sites, even the videos he supposedly made of himself masturbating.

Perhaps the most interesting thing about the porn-related revelations, though, was the ambiguity about what line, precisely, Cook was accused of having crossed. Was the porn habit a betrayal in and of itself? Was it the financial irresponsibility that mattered most, or the addictive behavior it suggested? Was it the way his habit had segued into other online activities? Or was it about Cook's fitness as a parent, and the possibility that their son had stumbled upon his porn cache? Clearly, the court and the public were supposed to think that Cook was an even lousier husband than his affair with a teenager might have indicated. But it was considerably less clear whether the porn habit itself was supposed to prove this, or whether it was the particulars—the monthly bill, the swinger sites, the webcam, the danger to the kids—that made the difference.

The notion that pornography, and especially hard-core pornography, has *something* to do with marital infidelity has been floating around the edges of the American conversation for a while now, even as the porn industry, by some estimates, has swollen to rival professional sports and the major broadcast networks as a revenue-generating source of entertainment. A 2002 survey of the American Academy of Matrimonial Lawyers suggests that Internet porn plays a part in an increasing number of divorce cases, and the Brinkley-Cook divorce wasn't the first celebrity split to feature porn-related revelations. In 2005, at the start of their messy divorce, Denise Richards accused Charlie Sheen of posting shots of his genitalia online and cultivating a taste for "barely legal" porn sites. Two years later, Anne Heche,

Ellen DeGeneres's ex, accused her non-celeb husband of surfing porn sites when he was supposed to be taking care of their 5-year-old son. The country singer Sara Evans's 2006 divorce involved similar allegations, including the claim that her husband had collected 100 nude photographs of himself and solicited sex online.

But the attention paid to the connection between porn and infidelity doesn't translate into anything like a consensus on what that connection is. Polls show that Americans are almost evenly divided on questions like whether porn is bad for relationships, whether it's an inevitable feature of male existence, and whether it's demeaning to women. This divide tends to cut along gender lines, inevitably: women are more likely to look at pornography than in the past, but they remain considerably more hostile to porn than men are, and considerably less likely to make use of it. (Even among the Internet generation, the split between the sexes remains stark. A survey of American college students last year found that 70 percent of the women in the sample never looked at pornography, compared with just 14 percent of their male peers; almost half of the men surveyed looked at porn at least once a week, versus just 3 percent of the women.)

One perspective, broadly construed, treats porn as a harmless habit, near-universal among men, and at worst a little silly. This is the viewpoint that's transformed adult-industry icons like Jenna Jameson and Ron Jeremy from targets of opprobrium into C-list celebrities. It's what inspires fledgling stars to gin up sex tapes in the hope of boosting their careers. And it's made smut a staple of gross-out comedy: rising star funnyman Seth Rogen has gone from headlining Judd Apatow's *Knocked Up*, in which his character's aspiration to run a pornographic website was somewhat incidental to the plot, to starring in Kevin Smith's forthcoming *Zack and Miri Make a Porno*, in which the porn business promises to be rather more central.

A second perspective treats porn as a kind of gateway drug—a vice that paves the way for more-serious betrayals. A 2004 study found that married individuals who cheated on their spouses were three times as likely to have used Internet pornography as married people who hadn't committed adultery. In Tom Perrotta's bestselling *Little Children*, the female protagonist's husband—who is himself being cuckolded—progresses from obsessing over an online porn star named "Slurry Kay" to sending away for her panties to joining a club of fans who pay to vacation with her in person. Brinkley's husband may have followed a similar trajectory, along with many of the other porn-happy celebrity spouses who've featured in the gossip pages and divorce courts lately.

Maybe it's worth sharpening the debate. Over the past three decades, the VCR, on-demand cable service, and the Internet have completely overhauled the ways in which people interact with porn. Innovation has piled on innovation, making modern pornography a more immediate, visceral, and personalized experience. Nothing in the long history of erotica compares with the way millions of Americans experience porn today, and our moral intuitions are struggling to catch up. As we try to make sense of the brave new world that VHS and streaming video have built, we might start by asking a radical question: Is pornography use a form of adultery?

Nothing in the history of erotica compares with the way Americans experience porn today, and our moral intuitions are struggling to catch up.

The most stringent take on this matter comes, of course, from Jesus of Nazareth: "I tell you that anyone who looks at a woman lustfully has already committed adultery with her in his heart." But even among Christians, this teaching tends to be grouped with the Gospel injunctions about turning the other cheek and giving would-be robbers your possessions—as a guideline for saintliness, useful to Francis of Assisi and the Desert Fathers but less helpful to ordinary sinners trying to figure out what counts as a breach of marital trust. Jimmy Carter's confession to *Playboy* that he had "lusted in [his] heart" still inspires giggles three decades later. Most Americans, devout or secular, are inclined to distinguish lustful thoughts from lustful actions, and hew to the *Merriam-Webster* definition of adultery as "voluntary sexual intercourse between a married man and someone other than his wife or between a married woman and someone other than her husband."

On the face of things, this definition would seem to let porn users off the hook. Intercourse, after all, involves physicality, a flesh-and-blood encounter that Internet Explorer and the DVD player can't provide, no matter what sort of adultery the user happens to be committing in his heart.

But there's another way to look at it. During the long, late winter week that transformed the governor of New York, Eliot Spitzer, into an alleged john, a late-night punch line, and finally an ex-governor, there was a lively debate on blogs and radio shows and op-ed pages about whether prostitution ought to be illegal at all. Yet amid all the chatter about whether the FBI should have cared about Spitzer's habit of paying for extramarital sex, next to nobody suggested, publicly at least, that *his wife* ought not to care—that Silda Spitzer ought to have been grateful he was seeking only sexual gratification elsewhere, and that so long as he was loyal to her in his mind and heart, it shouldn't matter what he did with his penis.

Start with the near-universal assumption that what Spitzer did in his hotel room constituted adultery, and then ponder whether Silda Spitzer would have had cause to feel betrayed if the FBI probe had revealed that her husband had paid merely to *watch* a prostitute perform sexual acts while he folded himself into a hotel armchair to masturbate. My suspicion is that an awful lot of people would say yes—not because there isn't some distinction between the two acts, but because the distinction isn't morally significant enough to prevent both from belonging to the zone, broadly defined, of cheating on your wife.

You can see where I'm going with this. If it's cheating on your wife to watch while another woman performs sexually in front of you, then why isn't it cheating to watch while the same sort of spectacle unfolds on your laptop or TV? Isn't the man who uses hard-core pornography already betraying his wife, whether or not the habit leads to anything worse? (The same goes, of course, for a wife betraying her husband—the arguments in this essay should be assumed to apply as well to the small minority of women who use porn.)

Fine, you might respond, but there are betrayals and then there are betrayals. The man who lets his eyes stray across the photo of Gisele Bündchen, bare-assed and beguiling on the cover of *GQ*, has betrayed his wife in some sense, but only a 21st-century Savonarola would describe that sort of thing as adultery. The line that matters is the one between fantasy and reality—between the call girl who's really there having sex with you, and the porn star who's selling the *image* of herself having sex to a host of men she'll never even meet. In this reading, porn is "a fictional, fantastical, even allegorical realm," as the cultural critic Laura Kipnis described it in the mid-1990s—"mythological and hyperbolic" rather than realistic, and experienced not as a form of intercourse but as a "popular-culture genre" like true crime or science fiction.

This seems like a potentially reasonable distinction to draw. But the fantasy-versus-reality, pixels-versus-flesh binary feels more appropriate to the pre-Internet landscape than to one where people spend hours every day in entirely virtual worlds, whether they're accumulating "friends" on Facebook, acting out Tolkienesque fantasies in World of Warcraft, or flirting with a sexy avatar in Second Life. And it feels much more appropriate to the tamer sorts of pornography, from the increasingly archaic (dirty playing cards and pinups, smutty books and the *Penthouse* letters section) to the of-the-moment (the topless photos and sex-scene stills in the more restrained precincts of the online pornosphere), than it does to the harder-core material at the heart of the porn economy. Masturbating to a *Sports Illustrated* swimsuit model (like Christie Brinkley, once upon a time) or a *Playboy* centerfold is a one-way street: the images are intended to provoke fantasies, not to embody reality, since the women pictured aren't having sex for the viewer's gratification. Even strippers, for all their flesh-and-blood appeal, are essentially fantasy objects—depending on how you respond to a lap dance, of course. But hard-core pornography is real sex by definition, and the two sexual acts involved—the on-camera copulation, and the masturbation it enables—are interdependent: neither would happen without the other. The whole point of a centerfold is her unattainability, but with hard-core porn, it's precisely the reverse: the star isn't just attainable, she's already being attained, and the user gets to be in on the action.

Moreover, the way the porn industry is evolving reflects the extent to which the Internet subverts the fantasy-reality dichotomy. After years of booming profits, the "mainstream" porn studios are increasingly losing ground to start-ups and freelancers—people making sex videos on their beds and sofas and shag carpeting and uploading them on the cheap. It turns out that, increasingly, Americans don't want porn as a "kind of science fiction," as Kipnis put it—they want realistic porn, porn that resembles the sex they might be having, and porn that at every moment holds out the promise that they can join in, like Peter Cook masturbating in front of his webcam.

So yes, there's an obvious line between leafing through a *Playboy* and pulling a Spitzer on your wife. But the line between Spitzer and the suburban husband who pays $29.95 a month to stream hard-core sex onto his laptop is considerably blurrier. The suburbanite with the hard-core porn hookup is masturbating to real sex, albeit at a DSL-enabled remove. He's experiencing it in an intimate setting, rather than in a grind house alongside other huddled masturbators in raincoats, and in a form that's customized to his tastes in a way that mass-market porn like *Deep Throat and Debbie Does Dallas* never was. There's no emotional connection, true—but there presumably wasn't one on Spitzer's part, either.

This isn't to say the distinction between hiring a prostitute and shelling out for online porn doesn't matter; in moral issues, every distinction matters. But if you approach infidelity as a continuum of betrayal rather than an either/or

proposition, then the Internet era has ratcheted the experience of pornography much closer to adultery than I suspect most porn users would like to admit.

It's possible, of course, to consider hard-core porn use a kind of infidelity and shrug it off even so. After all, human societies have frequently made sweeping accommodations for extramarital dalliances, usually on the assumption that the male libido simply can't be expected to submit to monogamy. When apologists for pornography aren't making Kipnis-style appeals to cultural transgression and sexual imagination, they tend to fall back on the defense that it's pointless to moralize about porn, because men are going to use it anyway.

Here's Dan Savage, the popular Seattle-based sex columnist, responding to a reader who fretted about her boyfriend's porn habit—"not because I'm jealous," she wrote, "but because I'm insecure. I'm sure many of those girls are more attractive than me":

> All men look at porn . . . The handful of men who claim they don't look at porn are liars or castrates. Tearful discussions about your insecurities or your feminist principles will not stop a man from looking at porn. That's why the best advice for straight women is this: GET OVER IT. If you don't want to be with someone who looks at porn . . . get a woman, get a dog, or get a blind guy . . . While men shouldn't rub their female partners' noses in the fact that they look at porn—that's just inconsiderate—telling women that the porn "problem" can be resolved through good communication, couples counseling, or a chat with your pastor is neither helpful nor realistic.

Savage's perspective is hardly unique, and is found among women as well as men. In 2003, three psychology professors at Illinois State University surveyed a broad population of women who were, or had been, in a relationship with a man who they knew used pornography. About a third of the women described the porn habit as a form of betrayal and infidelity. But the majority were neutral or even positively disposed to their lover's taste for smut, responding slightly more favorably than not to prompts like "I do not mind my partner's pornography use" or "My partner's pornography use is perfectly normal."

This point of view—that looking at pornography is a "perfectly normal" activity, one that the more-judgmental third of women need to just stop whining about—has been strengthened by the erosion of the second-order arguments against the use of porn, especially the argument that it feeds misogyny and encourages rape. In the great porn debates of the 1980s, arguments linking porn to violence against women were advanced across the ideological spectrum.

Feminist crusaders like Andrea Dworkin and Catharine MacKinnon denounced smut as a weapon of the patriarchy; the Christian radio psychologist (and future religious-right fixture) James Dobson induced the serial killer Ted Bundy to confess on death row to a pornography addiction; the Meese Commission on Pornography declared, "In both clinical and experimental settings, exposure to sexually violent materials has indicated an increase in the likelihood of aggression." It all sounded plausible—but between 1980 and 2004, an era in which porn became more available, and in more varieties, the rate of reported sexual violence *dropped,* and by 85 percent. Correlation isn't necessarily causation, but the sharpness of the decline at least suggests that porn may reduce sexual violence by providing an outlet for some potential sex offenders. (Indeed, the best way to deter a rapist might be to hook him up with a high-speed Internet connection: in a 2006 study, the Clemson economist Todd Kendall found that a 10 percent increase in Internet access is associated with a 7 percent decline in reported rapes.)

And what's true of rapists could be true of ordinary married men, a porn apologist might argue. For every Peter Cook, using porn *and* sleeping around, there might be countless men who use porn as a substitute for extramarital dalliances, satisfying their need for sexual variety without hiring a prostitute or kicking off a workplace romance.

Like Philip Weiss's friends, for instance. In the wake of the Spitzer affair, Weiss, a New York-based investigative journalist, came closer than any mainstream writer to endorsing not only the legalization of prostitution but the destigmatization of infidelity in a rambling essay for *New York* magazine on the agonies that monogamy imposes on his buddies. Amid nostalgia for the days of courtesans and concubines and the usual plaints about how much more sophisticated things are in Europe, Weiss depicted porn as the modern man's "common answer" to the marital-sex deficit. Here's one of his pals dilating on his online outlets:

> "Porn captures these women [its performers] before they get smart," he said in a hot whisper as we sat in Schiller's Liquor Bar on the Lower East Side. Porn exploited the sexual desires, and naiveté, of women in their early twenties, he went on . . . He spoke of acts he observed online that his wife wouldn't do. "It's painful to say, but that's your boys' night out, and it takes an enlightened woman to say that."

The use of the term *enlightened* is telling, since the strongest argument for the acceptance of pornography—and the hard-core variety in particular—is precisely that it represents a form of sexual progress, a more civilized approach to the problem of the male libido than either the toleration of mass prostitution or the attempt, from the Victorian era onward, to simultaneously legislate prostitution away and hold married couples to an unreasonably high standard of fidelity. Porn may be an evil, this argument goes, but it's the least of several evils. The man who uses porn is cheating sexually, but he isn't involving himself in an emotional relationship. He's cheating in a way that carries none of the risks of intercourse, from pregnancy to venereal disease. And he's cheating with women who may be trading sex for money, but are doing so in vastly safer situations than streetwalkers or even high-end escorts.

Indeed, in a significant sense, the porn industry looks like what advocates of legalized prostitution hope to achieve for "sex workers." There are no bullying pimps and no police officers demanding sex in return for not putting the prostitutes in jail. There are regular tests for STDs, at least in the higher-end sectors of the industry. The performers are safely separated from their johns. And freelancers aren't wandering downtown intersections on their own; they're filming from the friendly confines of their homes.

If we would just accept Dan Savage's advice, then, and *get over it,* everyone would gain something. Weiss and his pals could have their "boys' night out" online and enjoy sexual experiences that their marriages deny them. The majority of wives could rest secure in the knowledge that worse forms of infidelity are being averted; some women could get into the act themselves, either solo or with their spouse, experiencing the thrill of a threesome or a '70s key party with fewer of the consequences. The porn industry's sex workers could earn a steady paycheck without worrying about pimps, police, or HIV. Every society lives with infidelity in one form or another, whether openly or hypocritically. Why shouldn't we learn to live with porn?

Live with it we almost, certainly will. But it's worth being clear about what were accepting. Yes, adultery is inevitable, but it's never been universal in the way that pornography has the potential to become—at least if we approach the use of hard-core porn as a normal outlet from the rigors of monogamy, and invest ourselves in a cultural paradigm that understands this as something all men do and all women need to live with. In the name of providing a low-risk alternative for males who would otherwise be tempted by "real" prostitutes and "real" affairs, we're ultimately universalizing, in a milder but not all that much milder form, the sort of degradation and betrayal that only a minority of men have traditionally been involved in.

Go back to Philip Weiss's pal and listen to him talk: *Porn captures these women before they get smart . . . It's painful to say, but that's your boys' night out.* This is the language of a man who has accepted, not as a temporary lapse but as a permanent and necessary aspect of his married life, a paid sexual relationship with women other than his wife. And it's the language of a man who has internalized a view of marriage as a sexual prison, rendered bearable only by frequent online furloughs with women more easily exploited than his spouse.

Calling porn a form of adultery isn't about pretending that we can make it disappear. The temptation will always be there, and of course people will give in to it. I've looked at porn; if you're male and breathing, chances are so have you. Rather, it's about what sort of people we aspire to be: how we define our ideals, how we draw the lines in our relationships, and how we feel about ourselves if we cross them. And it's about providing a way for everyone involved, men and women alike—whether they're using porn or merely tolerating it—to think about what, precisely, they're involving themselves in, and whether they should reconsider.

The extremes of anti-porn hysteria are unhelpful in this debate. If the turn toward an "everybody does it" approach to pornography and marriage is wrong, it's because that approach is wrong in and of itself, not because porn is going to wreck society, destroy the institution of marriage, and turn thousands of rapists loose to prey on unsuspecting women. Smut isn't going to bring down Western Civilization any more than Nero's orgies actually led to the fall of Rome, and a society that expects near-universal online infidelity may run just as smoothly as a society that doesn't.

Which is precisely why it's so easy to say that the spread of pornography means that we're just taking a turn, where sex and fidelity are concerned, toward realism, toward adulthood, toward sophistication. All we have to give up to get there is our sense of decency.

Assess Your Progress

1. What role does pornography play in relationships?
2. Why is pornography considered adultery among some couples?

Ross Douthat, an *Atlantic* senior editor, blogs at rossdouthat .theatlantic.com.

UNIT 7

Preventing and Fighting Disease

Unit Selections

Learning Outcomes

After reading this unit, you should be able to:

- Describe the relationship between obesity and diabetes (Type 2)?

- Describe the reasons why diabetes is increasing.

- Describe how the prison environment fosters the spread of HIV.

- Explain how prison inmates are able to engage in drug use while incarcerated.

- Contrast the new versus the previous mammogram guidelines.

- Describe why mammogram guidelines were changed.

- Explain why are people still dying from AIDS despite the many anti-viral drugs.

- Identify the lifestyle changes that you can make to reduce your risk of developing cardiovascular disease, cancer, diabetes, and AIDS.

- Describe why or why not all young girls should be vaccinated against HPV.

- Distinguish the risks versus the benefits of the HPV vaccination.

Student Website

www.mhhe.com/cls

Internet References

American Cancer Society
   www.cancer.org
American Diabetes Association Home Page
   www.diabetes.org
American Heart Association
   www.amhrt.org
National Institute of Allergy and Infectious Diseases (NIAID)
   www.niaid.nih.gov

Cardiovascular disease and cancer are the leading killers in this country. This is not altogether surprising given that the American population is growing increasingly older, and one's risk of developing both of these diseases is directly proportional to one's age. Another major risk factor, which has received considerable attention over the past 30 years, is one's genetic predisposition or family history. Historically, the significance of this risk factor has been emphasized as a basis for encouraging at-risk individuals to make prudent lifestyle choices, but this may be about to change as recent advances in genetic research, including mapping the human genome, may significantly improve the efficacy of both diagnostic and therapeutic procedures.

Just as cutting-edge genetic research is transforming the practice of medicine, startling new research findings in the health profession are transforming our views concerning adult health. This new research suggests that the primary determinants of our health as adults are the environmental conditions we experienced during our life in the womb. According to Dr. Peter Nathanielsz of Cornell University, conditions during gestation, ranging from hormones that flow from the mother to how well the placenta delivers nutrients to the tiny limbs and organs, program how our liver, heart, kidneys, and especially our brains function as adults. While it is too early to draw any firm conclusions regarding the significance of the "life in the womb factor," it appears that this avenue of research may yield important clues as to how we may best prevent or forestall chronic illness.

Of all the diseases in America, coronary heart disease is this nation's number one killer. Frequently, the first and only symptom of this disease is a sudden heart attack. Epidemiological studies have revealed a number of risk factors that increase one's likelihood of developing this disease. These include hypertension, a high serum cholesterol level, diabetes, cigarette smoking, obesity, a sedentary lifestyle, a family history of heart disease, age, sex, race, and stress. In addition to these well-established risk factors, scientists think they may have discovered several additional risk factors. These include the following: low birth weight, cytomegalovirus, *Chlamydia pneumoniae,* porphyromonasgingivalis, and c-reactive protein (CRP). CRP is a measure of inflammation somewhere in the body. In theory, a high CRP reading may be a good indicator of an impending heart attack.

One of the most startling and ominous health stories was the recent announcement by the Centers for Disease Control and Prevention (CDC) that the incidence of Type 2 adult onset diabetes increased significantly over the past 15 years. This sudden rise appears to cross all races and age groups, with the sharpest increase occurring among people ages 30 to 39 (about 70 percent). Health experts at the CDC believe that this startling rise in diabetes among 30- to 39-year-olds is linked to the rise in obesity observed among young adults (obesity rates rose from 12 to 20 percent nationally during this same time period). Experts at the CDC believe that there is a time lag of about 10–15 years between the deposition of body fat and the manifestation of Type 2 diabetes. This time lag could explain why individuals in their 30s are experiencing the greatest increase in developing Type 2 diabetes today. Current estimates suggest that 16 million Americans have diabetes, and it kills approximately 180,000 Americans each year. Many experts now believe that our couch potato culture is fueling the rising rates of both obesity and diabetes. Given what we know about the relationship between obesity and Type 2 diabetes, the only practical solution is for Americans to watch their total calorie intake and exercise regularly. 'Diabesity,' a Crisis in an Expanding Country" examines the rapid rise in the incidence of Type 2 diabetes among our youth and young adults, and suggests that the term "adult onset diabetes" may be a misnomer, given the growing number of young adults and teens with this form of diabetes.

Cardiovascular disease is America's number one killer, but cancer takes top billing in terms of the "fear factor." This fear of cancer stems from an awareness of the degenerative and disfiguring nature of the disease. Today, cancer specialists are employing a variety of

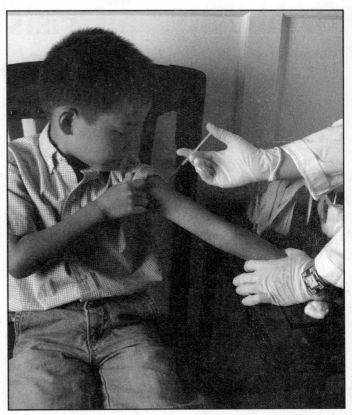

complex agents and technologies, such as monoclonal antibodies, interferon, and immunotherapy, in their attempt to fight the disease. Progress has been slow, however, and the results, while promising, suggest that a cure may be several years away. A very disturbing aspect of this country's battle against cancer is the fact that millions of dollars are spent each year trying to advance the treatment of cancer, while the funding for the technologies used to detect cancer in its early stages is quite limited. A reallocation of funds would seem appropriate, given the medical community posits that early detection and treatment are the key elements in the successful cure of cancer. An interesting issue related to early detection has arisen. A government task force recently announced that women in their 40s do not need annual mammograms, a long-held belief. This task force recommendation is addressed in "New Mammogram Guidelines Raise Questions." Until we have more effective methods for detecting cancer in the early stages our best hope for managing cancer is to prevent it through our lifestyle choices. The same lifestyle choices that may help prevent cancer can also help reduce the incidence of heart disease and diabetes.

The final three articles in this unit cover interesting topics such as fighting disease among prison inmates, the new cervical cancer vaccine, and the AIDS virus. In "Sex, Drugs, Prisons, and HIV," Susan Okie discusses the risky health behaviors that occur among inmates. These behaviors increase the risk of transmitting HIV. Kate O'Beirne focuses on the issue of the HPV vaccine and the questions that remain over who should be immunized in "A Mandate in Texas." And lastly, Gary Taubes explains why the AIDS virus can still trump modern medicine and kill its victims in "Who Still Dies of AIDS, and Why."

'Diabesity,' a Crisis in an Expanding Country

JANE E. BRODY

I can't understand why we still don't have a national initiative to control what is fast emerging as the most serious and costly health problem in America: excess weight. Are our schools, our parents, our national leaders blind to what is happening—a health crisis that looms even larger than our former and current smoking habits?

Just look at the numbers, so graphically described in an eye-opening new book, "Diabesity: The Obesity-Diabetes Epidemic That Threatens America—and What We Must Do to Stop It" (Bantam), by Dr. Francine R. Kaufman, a pediatric endocrinologist, the director of the diabetes clinic at Children's Hospital Los Angeles and a past president of the American Diabetes Association.

In just over a decade, she noted, the prevalence of diabetes nearly doubled in the American adult population: to 8.7 percent in 2002, from 4.9 percent in 1990. Furthermore, an estimated one-third of Americans with Type 2 diabetes don't even know they have it because the disease is hard to spot until it causes a medical crisis.

An estimated 18.2 million Americans now have diabetes, 90 percent of them the environmentally influenced type that used to be called adult-onset diabetes. But adults are no longer the only victims—a trend that prompted an official change in name in 1997 to Type 2 diabetes.

More and more children are developing this health-robbing disease or its precursor, prediabetes. Counting children and adults together, some 41 million Americans have a higher-than-normal blood sugar level that typically precedes the development of full-blown diabetes.

'Then Everything Changed'

And what is the reason for this runaway epidemic? Being overweight or obese, especially with the accumulation of large amounts of body fat around the abdomen. In Dr. Kaufman's first 15 years as a pediatric endocrinologist, 1978 to 1993, she wrote, "I never saw a young patient with Type 2 diabetes. But then everything changed."

Teenagers now come into her clinic weighing 200, 300, even nearly 400 pounds with blood sugar levels that are off the charts.

But, she adds, we cannot simply blame this problem on gluttony and laziness and "assume that the sole solution is individual change."

The major causes, Dr. Kaufman says, are "an economic structure that makes it cheaper to eat fries than fruit" and a food industry and mass media that lure children to eat the wrong foods and too much of them. "We have defined progress in terms of the quantity rather than the quality of our food," she wrote.

Her views are supported by a 15-year study published in January in The Lancet. A team headed by Dr. Mark A. Pereira of the University of Minnesota analyzed the eating habits of 3,031 young adults and found that weight gain and the development of prediabetes were directly related to unhealthful fast food.

Taking other factors into consideration, consuming fast food two or more times a week resulted, on average, in an extra weight gain of 10 pounds and doubled the risk of prediabetes over the 15-year period.

Other important factors in the diabesity epidemic, Dr. Kaufman explained, are the failure of schools to set good examples by providing only healthful fare, a loss of required physical activity in schools and the inability of many children these days to walk or bike safely to school or to play outside later.

Genes play a role as well. Some people are more prone to developing Type 2 diabetes than others. The risk is 1.6 times as great for blacks as for whites of similar age. It is 1.5 times as great for Hispanic-Americans, and 2 times as great for Mexican-Americans and Native Americans.

Unless we change our eating and exercise habits and pay greater attention to this disease, more than one-third of whites, two-fifths of blacks and half of Hispanic people in this country will develop diabetes.

It is also obvious from the disastrous patient histories recounted in Dr. Kaufman's book that the nation's medical structure is a factor as well. Many people do not have readily accessible medical care, and still many others have no coverage for preventive medicine. As a result, millions fall between the cracks until they are felled by heart attacks or strokes.

A Devastating Disease

There is a tendency in some older people to think of diabetes as "just a little sugar," a common family problem. They fail to take it seriously and make the connection between it and the costly, crippling and often fatal diseases that can ensue.

Diabetes, with its consequences of heart attack, stroke, kidney failure, amputations and blindness, among others, already ranks No. 1 in direct health care costs, consuming $1 of every $7 spent on health care.

Nor is this epidemic confined to American borders. Internationally, "we are witnessing an epidemic that is the scourge of the 21st century," Dr. Kaufman wrote.

Unlike some other killer diseases, Type 2 diabetes issues an easily detected wake-up call: the accumulation of excess weight, especially around the abdomen. When the average fasting level of blood sugar (glucose) rises above 100 milligrams per deciliter, diabetes is looming.

Abdominal fat is highly active. The chemical output of its cells increases blood levels of hormones like estrogen, providing the link between obesity and breast cancer, and decreases androgens, which can cause a decline in libido. As the cells in abdominal fat expand, they also release chemicals that increase fat accumulation, ensuring their own existence.

The result is an increasing cellular resistance to the effects of the hormone insulin, which enables cells to burn blood sugar for energy. As blood sugar rises with increasing insulin resistance, the pancreas puts out more and more insulin (promoting further fat storage) until this gland is exhausted. Then when your fasting blood sugar level reaches 126 milligrams, you have diabetes.

Two recent clinical trials showed that Type 2 diabetes could be prevented by changes in diet and exercise. The Diabetes Prevention Program Research Group involving 3,234 overweight adults showed that "intensive lifestyle intervention" was more effective than a drug that increases insulin sensitivity in preventing diabetes over three years.

The intervention, lasting 24 weeks, trains people to choose low-calorie, low-fat diets; increase activity; and change their habits. Likewise, the randomized, controlled Finnish Diabetes Prevention Study of 522 obese patients showed that introducing a moderate exercise program of at least 150 minutes a week and weight loss of at least 5 percent reduced the incidence of diabetes by 58 percent.

Many changes are needed to combat this epidemic, starting with schools and parents. Perhaps the quickest changes can be made in the workplace, where people can be encouraged to use stairs instead of elevators; vending machines can be removed or dispense only healthful snacks; and cafeterias can offer attractive healthful fare. Lunchrooms equipped with refrigerators and microwaves will allow workers to bring healthful meals to work.

Dr. Kaufman tells of a challenge to get fit and lose weight by Caesars Entertainment in which 4,600 workers who completed the program lost a total of 45,000 pounds in 90 days. Others could follow this example.

Assess Your Progress

1. What is the relationship between obesity and diabetes (Type 2)?
2. Name three reasons diabetes in increasing in the United States.

From *The New York Times*, March 29, 2005, p. 1. Copyright © 2005 by The New York Times Company. Reprinted by permission via PARS International.

Sex, Drugs, Prisons, and HIV

SUSAN OKIE, MD

One recent morning at a medium-security compound at Rhode Island's state prison, Mr. M, a middle-aged black inmate, described some of the high-risk behavior he has witnessed while serving time. "I've seen it all," he said, smiling and rolling his eyes. "We have a lot of risky sexual activities. . . . Almost every second or minute, somebody's sneaking and doing something." Some participants are homosexual, he added; others are "curious, bisexual, bored, lonely, and . . . experimenting." As in all U.S. prisons, sex is illegal at the facility; as in nearly all, condoms are prohibited. Some inmates try to take precautions, fashioning makeshift condoms from latex gloves or sandwich bags. Most, however, "are so frustrated that they are not thinking of the consequences except for later," said Mr. M.

Drugs, and sometimes needles and syringes, find their way inside the walls. "I've seen the lifers that just don't care," Mr. M said. "They share needles and don't take a minute to rinse them." In the 1990s, he said, "needles were coming in by the handful," but prison officials have since stopped that traffic, and inmates who take illicit drugs usually snort or swallow them. Tattooing, although also prohibited, has been popular at times. "A lot of people I've known caught hepatitis from tattooing," Mr. M said. "They use staples, a nail . . . anything with a point."

Mr. M had just undergone a checkup performed by Dr. Josiah D. Rich, a professor of medicine at Brown University Medical School, who provides him with medical care as part of a long-standing arrangement between Brown and the Adult Correctional Institute in Cranston. Two years ago, Mr. M was hospitalized with pneumonia and meningitis. "I was scared and in denial," he said. Now, thanks to treatment with antiretroviral drugs, "I'm doing great, and I feel good," he reported. "I am HIV-positive and still healthy and still look fabulous."

U.S. public health experts consider the Rhode Island prison's human immunodeficiency virus (HIV) counseling and testing practices, medical care, and prerelease services to be among the best in the country. Yet according to international guidelines for reducing the risk of HIV transmission inside prisons, all U.S. prison systems fall short. Recognizing that sex occurs in prison despite prohibitions, the World Health Organization (WHO) and the Joint United Nations Program on HIV/AIDS (UNAIDS) have recommended for more than a decade that condoms be made available to prisoners. They also recommend that prisoners have access to bleach for cleaning injecting equipment,

that drug-dependence treatment and methadone maintenance programs be offered in prisons if they are provided in the community, and that needle-exchange programs be considered.

Prisons in several Western European countries and in Australia, Canada, Kyrgyzstan, Belarus, Moldova, Indonesia, and Iran have adopted some or all of these approaches to "harm reduction," with largely favorable results. For example, programs providing sterile needles and syringes have been established in some 50 prisons in eight countries; evaluations of such programs in Switzerland, Spain, and Germany found no increase in drug use, a dramatic decrease in needle sharing, no new cases of infection with HIV or hepatitis B or C, and no reported instances of needles being used as weapons.[1] Nevertheless, in the United States, condoms are currently provided on a limited basis in only two state prison systems (Vermont and Mississippi) and five county jail systems (New York, Philadelphia, San Francisco, Los Angeles, and Washington, DC). Methadone maintenance programs are rarer still, and no U.S. prison has piloted a needle-exchange program.

The U.S. prison population has reached record numbers—at the end of 2005, more than 2.2 million American adults were incarcerated, according to the Justice Department. And drug-related offenses are a major reason for the population growth, accounting for 49% of the increase between 1995 and 2003. Moreover, in 2005, more than half of all inmates had a mental health problem, and doctors who treat prisoners say that many have used illicit drugs as self-medication for untreated mental disorders.

In the United States in 2004 (see table), 1.8% of prison inmates were HIV-positive, more than four times the estimated rate in the general population; the rate of confirmed AIDS cases is also substantially higher (see graph).[2] Some behaviors that increase the risk of contracting HIV and other bloodborne or sexually transmitted infections can also lead to incarceration, and the burden of infectious diseases in prisons is high. It has been estimated that each year, about 25% of all HIV-infected persons in the United States spend time in a correctional facility, as do 33% of persons with hepatitis C virus (HCV) infection and 40% of those with active tuberculosis.[3]

Critics in the public health community have been urging U.S. prison officials to do more to prevent HIV transmission, to improve diagnosis and treatment in prisons, and to expand programs for reducing high-risk behavior after release. The

HIV–AIDS among Prison Inmates at the End of 2004*

Jurisdictions with the Most Prisoners Living with HIV–AIDS	No. of Inmates Living with HIV–AIDS	Prevalence of HIV–AIDS %
New York	4500	7.0
Florida	3250	3.9
Texas	2405	1.7
Federal system	1680	1.1
California	1212	0.7
Georgia	1109	2.2

*Data are from Maruschak.[2]

debate over such preventive strategies as providing condoms and needles reflects philosophical differences, as well as uncertainty about the frequency of HIV transmission inside prisons. The UNAIDS and WHO recommendations assume that sexual activity and injection of drugs by inmates cannot be entirely eliminated and aim to protect both prisoners and the public from HIV, HCV, and other diseases.

But many U.S. prison officials contend that providing needles or condoms would send a mixed message. By distributing condoms, "you're saying sex, whether consensual or not, is OK," said Lieutenant Gerald Ducharme, a guard at the Rhode Island prison. "It's a detriment to what we're trying to enforce." U.S. prison populations have higher rates of mental illness and violence than their European counterparts, which, some researchers argue, might make providing needles more dangerous. And some believe that whereas European prison officials tend to be pragmatic, many U.S. officials adopt a "just deserts" philosophy, viewing infections as the consequences of breaking prison rules.

Studies involving state-prison inmates suggest that the frequency of HIV transmission is low but not negligible. For example, between 1988—when the Georgia Department of Corrections began mandatory HIV testing of all inmates on entry to prison and voluntary testing thereafter—and 2005, HIV seroconversion occurred in 88 male inmates in Georgia state prisons. HIV transmission in prison was associated with men having sex with other men or receiving a tattoo.[4] In another study in a southeastern state, Christopher Krebs of RTI International documented that 33 of 5265 male prison inmates (0.63%) contracted HIV while in prison.[5] But Krebs points out that "when you have a large prison population, as our country does . . . you do start thinking about large numbers of people contracting HIV."

Studies of high-risk behavior in prisons yield widely varying frequency estimates: for example, estimates of the proportion of male inmates who have sex with other men range from 2 to 65%, and estimates of the proportion who are sexually assaulted range from 0 to 40%.[5] Such variations may reflect differences in research methods, inmate populations, and prison conditions that affect privacy and opportunity. Researchers emphasize that classifying prison sex as either consensual or forced is often overly simplistic: an inmate may provide sexual favors to another in

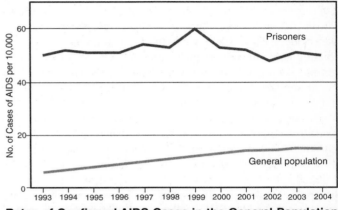

Rates of Confirmed AIDS Cases in the General Population and among State and Federal Prisoners, 1993–2004.

Data are from Maruschak.[2]

return for protection or for other reasons. Better information on sexual transmission of HIV in prisons may eventually become available as a result of the Prison Rape Elimination Act of 2003, which requires the Justice Department to collect statistics on prison rape and to provide funds for educating prison staff and inmates about the subject.

Theodore M. Hammett of the Domestic Health, Health Policy, and Clinical Research Division of Abt Associates, a Massachusetts-based policy research and consulting firm, acknowledged that for political reasons U.S. prisons are unlikely to accept needle-exchange programs, but he said adoption of other HIV-prevention measures is long overdue. "Condoms ought to be widely available in prisons," he said. "From a public health standpoint, I think there's little question that that should be done. Methadone, also—all kinds of drug [abuse] treatment should be much more widely available in correctional settings." Methadone maintenance programs for inmates have been established in a few jails and prisons, including those in New York City, Albuquerque, and San Juan, Puerto Rico. Brown University's Rich is currently conducting a randomized, controlled trial at the Rhode Island facility, sponsored by the National Institutes of Health, to determine whether starting methadone maintenance in heroin-addicted inmates a month before their release will lead to better health outcomes and reduced recidivism, as compared with providing either usual care or referral to community methadone programs at the time of release.

At the Rhode Island prison, the medical program focuses on identifying HIV-infected inmates, treating them, teaching them how to avoid transmitting the virus, addressing drug dependence, and when they're released, referring them to a program that arranges for HIV care and other assistance, including methadone maintenance treatment if needed. The prison offers routine HIV testing, and 90% of inmates accept it. One third of the state's HIV cases have been diagnosed at the prison. "These people are a target population and a captive one," noted Rich. "We should use this time" for health care and prevention. Nationally, 73% of state inmates and 77% of federal inmates surveyed in 2004 said they had been tested for HIV in prison. State policies vary, with 20 states reportedly testing all inmates and the rest offering tests for high-risk groups, at inmates' request, or in specific situations. Researchers said inmate acceptance rates also vary widely, depending on how the test is presented. Drugs for treating HIV-infected prisoners are not covered by federal programs, and prison budgets often contain inadequate funding for health services. "You can see how, in some cases, there could be a disincentive for really pushing testing," Hammett said.

Critics of U.S. penal policies contend that incarceration has exacerbated the HIV epidemic among blacks, who are disproportionately represented in the prison population, accounting for 40% of inmates. A new report by the National Minority AIDS Council calls for routine, voluntary HIV testing in prisons and on release, making condoms available, and expanding reentry programs that address HIV prevention, substance abuse, mental health, and housing needs as prisoners return to the community. "Any reservoir of infection that is as large as a prison would warrant, by simple public health logic, that we do our best . . . to reduce the risk of transmission" both inside and outside the walls, said Robert E. Fullilove of Columbia University's Mailman School of Public Health, who wrote the report. "The issue has never been, Do we understand what has to happen to reduce the risks? . . . It's always been, Do we have the political will necessary to put what we know is effective into operation?"

Notes

1. Dolan K, Rutter S, Wodak AD. Prison-based syringe exchange programmes: a review of international research and development. Addiction 2003;98:153–158.
2. Maruschak LM. HIV in prisons, 2004. Washington, DC: Bureau of Justice Statistics, November 2006.
3. Hammett TM, Harmon MP, Rhodes W. The burden of infectious disease among inmates of and releasees from US correctional facilities, 1997. Am J Public Health 2002;92:1789–1794.
4. HIV transmission among male inmates in a state prison system—Georgia, 1992–2005. MMWR Morb Mortal Wkly Rep 2006;55:421–6.
5. Krebs CP. Inmate factors associated with HIV transmission in prison. Criminology Public Policy 2006;5:113–36.

Assess Your Progress

1. Why are inmates able to abuse drugs while incarcerated?
2. How does the environment in prison foster the spread of HIV?

DR. OKIE is a contributing editor of the *Journal*.

New Mammogram Guidelines Raise Questions

Benefits of screening before age 50 don't outweigh risks, task force says.

For many women, getting a mammogram is already one of life's more stressful experiences.

Now, women in their 40s have the added anxiety of trying to figure out if they should even be getting one at all.

A government task force said Monday that most women don't need mammograms in their 40s and should get one every two years starting at 50—a stunning reversal and a break with the American Cancer Society's long-standing position. What's more, the panel said breast self-exams do no good, and women shouldn't be taught to do them.

The news seemed destined to leave many deeply confused about whose advice to follow.

"I've never had a scare, but isn't it better to be safe than sorry?" asked Beth Rosenthal, 41, sitting in a San Francisco cafe on Monday afternoon with her friend and their small children. "I've heard of a lot of women in their 40s, and even 30s, who've gotten breast cancer. It just doesn't seem right to wait until 50."

Her friend agreed. "I don't think I'll wait," said Leslie David-Jones, also 41, shaking her head.

For most of the past two decades, the American Cancer Society has been recommending annual mammograms beginning at 40, and it reiterated that position on Monday. "This is one screening test I recommend unequivocally, and would recommend to any woman 40 and over," the society's chief medical officer, Dr. Otis Brawley, said in a statement.

But the government panel of doctors and scientists concluded that getting screened for breast cancer so early and so often is harmful, causing too many false alarms and unneeded biopsies without substantially improving women's odds of surviving the disease.

"The benefits are less and the harms are greater when screening starts in the 40s," said Dr. Diana Petitti, vice chair of the panel.

The new guidelines were issued by the U.S. Preventive Services Task Force, whose stance influences coverage of screening tests by Medicare and many insurance companies. But Susan Pisano, a spokeswoman for America's Health Insurance Plans, an industry group, said insurance coverage isn't likely to change because of the new guidelines.

Experts expect the revisions to be hotly debated, and to cause confusion for women and their doctors.

"Our concern is that as a result of that confusion, women may elect not to get screened at all. And that, to me, would be a serious problem," said Dr. Len Lichtenfeld, the cancer society's deputy chief medical officer.

The guidelines are for the general population, not those at high risk of breast cancer because of family history or gene mutations that would justify having mammograms sooner or more often.

The new advice says:

Most women in their 40s should not routinely get mammograms.

Women 50 to 74 should get a mammogram every other year until they turn 75, after which the risks and benefits are unknown. (The task force's previous guidelines had no upper limit and called for exams every year or two.)

The value of breast exams by doctors is unknown. And breast self-exams are of no value.

Medical groups such as the cancer society have been backing off promoting breast self-exams in recent years because of scant evidence of their effectiveness. Decades ago, the practice was so heavily promoted that organizations distributed cards that could be hung in the shower demonstrating the circular motion women should use to feel for lumps in their breasts.

The guidelines and research supporting them were released Monday and are being published in Tuesday's issue of the Annals of Internal Medicine.

Sharp Criticism from Cancer Society

The new advice was sharply challenged by the cancer society.

"This is one screening test I recommend unequivocally, and would recommend to any woman 40 and over," the society's chief medical officer, Dr. Otis Brawley, said in a statement.

The task force advice is based on its conclusion that screening 1,300 women in their 50s to save one life is worth it, but that screening 1,900 women in their 40s to save a life is not, Brawley wrote.

That stance "is essentially telling women that mammography at age 40 to 49 saves lives, just not enough of them," he said. The cancer society feels the benefits outweigh the harms for women in both groups.

International guidelines also call for screening to start at age 50; the World Health Organization recommends the test every two years, Britain says every three years.

Breast cancer is the most common cancer and the second leading cause of cancer deaths in American women. More than 192,000 new cases and 40,000 deaths from the disease are expected in the U.S. this year.

Mammograms can find cancer early, and two-thirds of women over 40 report having had the test in the previous two years. But how much they cut the risk of dying of the disease, and at what cost in terms of unneeded biopsies, expense and worry, have been debated.

In most women, tumors are slow-growing, and that likelihood increases with age. So there is little risk by extending the time between mammograms, some researchers say. Even for the minority of women with aggressive, fast-growing tumors, annual screening will make little difference in survival odds.

The new guidelines balance these risks and benefits, scientists say.

The probability of dying of breast cancer after age 40 is 3 percent, they calculate. Getting a mammogram every other year from ages 50 to 69 lowers that risk by about 16 percent.

"It's an average of five lives saved per thousand women screened," said Georgetown University researcher Dr. Jeanne Mandelblatt.

False Alarms

Starting at age 40 would prevent one additional death but also lead to 470 false alarms for every 1,000 women screened. Continuing mammograms through age 79 prevents three additional deaths but raises the number of women treated for breast cancers that would not threaten their lives.

"You save more lives because breast cancer is more common, but you diagnose tumors in women who were destined to die of something else. The overdiagnosis increases in older women," Mandelblatt said.

She led six teams around the world who used federal data on cancer and mammography to develop mathematical models of what would happen if women were screened at different ages and time intervals. Their conclusions helped shape the new guidelines.

Several medical groups say they are sticking to their guidelines that call for routine screening starting at 40.

"Screening isn't perfect. But it's the best thing we have. And it works," said Dr. Carol Lee, a spokeswoman for the American College of Radiology. She suggested that cutting health care costs may have played a role in the decision, but Petitti said the task force does not consider cost or insurance in its review.

The American College of Obstetricians and Gynecologists also has qualms. The organization's Dr. Hal Lawrence said there is still significant benefit to women in their 40s, adding: "We think that women deserve that benefit."

But Dr. Amy Abernethy of the Duke Comprehensive Cancer Center agreed with the task force's changes.

"Overall, I think it really took courage for them to do this," she said. "It does ask us as doctors to change what we do and how we communicate with patients. That's no small undertaking."

Abernethy, who is 41, said she got her first mammogram the day after her 40th birthday, even though she wasn't convinced it was needed. Now she doesn't plan to have another mammogram until she is 50.

Barbara Brenner, executive director of the San Francisco-based Breast Cancer Action, said the group was "thrilled" with the revisions. The advocacy group doesn't support screening before menopause, and will be changing its suggested interval from yearly to every two years, she said.

Mammograms, like all medical interventions, have risks and benefits, she said.

"Women are entitled to know what they are and to make their best decisions," she said. "These guidelines will help that conversation."

Assess Your Progress

1. Why did the panel publish changes in mammogram requirements?
2. What are some of the benefits and risks associated with early screening?

Who Still Dies of AIDS, and Why

In the age of HAART, the virus can still outwit modern medicine.

GARY TAUBES

In the video, filmed last November, Mel Cheren appears understandably dismayed. He's being interviewed by a reporter for CBS News on *Logo,* a gay-themed news program; he's sitting in a wheelchair, and he's talking about the indignity and the irony of dying from AIDS at a time when AIDS should be a chronic disease, not a fatal one. Cheren, a music producer and founder of West End Records, had been an AIDS activist since the earliest days of the epidemic. It was Cheren, in 1982, who gave the Gay Men's Health Crisis its first home, providing a floor of his brownstone on West 22nd Street. In the interview, Cheren talks about what it's like to lose more than 300 friends to the AIDS epidemic, outlive them all, and then get diagnosed yourself at age 74.

Indeed, the fact that Cheren had plenty of sex through the height of the epidemic, had been tested regularly, and had apparently emerged uninfected had led him to believe that testing was no longer necessary, or at least so one doctor had told him half a dozen years earlier. He's only learned the truth after he began losing weight, had trouble walking, and was finally referred to a specialist who didn't consider AIDS an unreasonable diagnosis for a man of Cheren's experience and advanced years and so ordered up the requisite blood test. "There was one guy," Cheren says in the interview, explaining how he might have been infected. A male escort. "We really hit it off, sexually . . ."

By the time Cheren learned he had AIDS, he was already suffering from a rare, drug-resistant pneumonia, what infectious-disease specialists refer to as an opportunistic infection, and he had lymphoma, an AIDS-related cancer that had spread to his bones.

Within a month of his diagnosis, Cheren was dead. The official cause was pneumonia, although, as his cousin Mark Cheren points out, cause of death in these cases is a moot point. "Infection from pneumonia was probably the culprit," he says, "but only because that acts quickest when you don't stop it."

Dying from AIDS, or dying with an HIV infection, which may not be the same thing, is a significantly less common event than it was a decade ago, but it's not nearly as uncommon as anyone would like. Bob Hattoy, for instance, died last year as well. Hattoy, 56, was "the first gay man with AIDS many Americans had knowingly laid eyes on," as the *New York Times* described him after Hattoy announced his condition to the world in a speech at the 1992 Democratic National Convention. Hattoy went on the work in the Clinton White House as an advocate for gay and lesbian issues. In the summer of 1993, he told the *New York Times,* "I don't make real long-term plans." But the advent of an anti-retroviral drug known as a protease inhibitor, in 1995, and then, a year later multidrug cocktails called HAART—for highly active anti-retroviral therapy—gave Hattoy and a few hundred thousand HIV-infected Americans like him the opportunity to do just that.

If the pharmaceutical industry ever needed an icon for evidence of its good works, HAART would be it. Between 1995 and 1997, annual AIDS deaths in New York City dropped from 8,309 to 3,426, and that number has continued to decline ever since. The success of HAART has been so remarkable that it now tends to take us by surprise when anybody does succumb, although 2,076 New Yorkers died in 2006 (2007 figures are not yet available). Though many of the most prominent deaths, like Cheren's and Hattoy's, tend to be of gay men, the percentage of the dead who contracted the disease through gay sex is now reportedly as low as 15 percent (with a large proportion still reported as unknown). Intravenous-drug users make up the biggest group, 38.5 percent, and women account for almost one in three of total AIDS deaths.

One of the ironies of the success of HAART is that it has fostered the myth that the AIDS epidemic has come to an end, and that living with HIV is only marginally more problematic than living with herpes or genital warts. This is one obvious explanation for why HIV infection is once again on the rise among young men—specifically, MSMs, as they're now known in the public-health jargon, for men who have sex with men—increasing by a third between 2001 and 2006. Among those 30 and over, the infection rate is still decreasing, notes Thomas Frieden, commissioner of the city's Department of Health and Mental Hygiene, suggesting that the increased rate of infection among men under 30 is due in part to decreased awareness of the disease or the toll it can take.

"If you do the mathematics," Frieden says, "HAART became available in 1996. If you were of age before then, sexually active, and you saw a lot of people dying or sick or disfigured from AIDS, maybe you're more careful than if you came of age after 1996 and didn't see that. When we've done focus groups, what young men have told us is that the only thing they hear about HIV these days is that if you get it, you can climb mountains, like Magic Johnson. Certainly it's true that the treatment for HIV is very effective and it's possible to live a long and productive life with an HIV infection. It's also true that it remains an incurable infection. That the treatment is very arduous and sometimes unsuccessful. It remains a disease often fatal, and frequently disabling."

At the moment some 100,000 New Yorkers are infected with the HIV virus, and AIDS remains the third leading cause of death in men under 65, exceeded only by heart disease and cancer. The question of who will die from AIDS in the HAART era—or who dies with an HIV infection but not technically from AIDS—and what kills them is worth asking now that such deaths have become relatively infrequent.

Frieden's department of Health and Mental Hygiene tried to answer this question with a study it published in the summer of 2006. The newsworthy conclusions were that deaths among New Yorkers with AIDS were still dropping, thanks to HAART, and that one in four of these individuals was now living long enough to die of the same chronic diseases that are likely to kill the uninfected—particularly cancer or heart disease—although most of these non-HIV-related deaths were from the side effects of drug abuse. HIV-related illnesses were still responsible for the remaining three out of four deaths. Or at least "HIV disease," in these cases, was recorded as a cause of death on the death certificates.

What the Health Department study couldn't do is say precisely what these HIV-related deaths were. For the answer to this question, you have to go to physicians who specialize in treating HIV-infected patients. Michael Mullen, clinical director of infectious diseases at Mount Sinai School of Medicine, for instance, says the best way to think about AIDS deaths is to divide HIV-infected individuals into three groups.

The bulk of these deaths occur within the first group, those who either never started HAART to begin with or didn't stay on it once they did. For these patients, "it might as well still be the eighties," says Mullen, and they die from the same AIDS-defining illnesses that were the common causes of death twenty years ago—pneumocystis pneumonia, central-nervous system opportunistic infections (such as toxoplasmosis), lymphoma, Kaposi's sarcoma, etc.

A large proportion of these victims are indigent; many are intravenous-drug users—IVDUs, as they're known in the official jargon, accounted for 21 percent of HIV-positive New Yorkers in 2006, but, as noted above, 38.5 percent of the city's AIDS deaths. The virus is not more aggressive or virulent in these cases. Rather, these are the people who either don't or can't do what it takes to fight it. "These individuals are repeatedly admitted to the hospital," says Mullen, "sometimes for opportunistic infections, sometimes for drug-related issues, often for HIV-related lymphomas and malignancies. They will not take the medication, nine times out of ten, because of drug use." Often these individuals are co-infected with hepatitis, which increases the risk that the more toxic side effects of the anti-retroviral drugs will lead to permanent liver or kidney damage.

By far the highest death rates in this group are in what the authorities now refer to as concurrent HIV/AIDS diagnoses. These patients never get diagnosed with HIV infection until they already have active AIDS. (Cheren, because of his age and his AIDS awareness, is an extreme case.) These constituted more than a quarter of the 3,745 new cases of HIV infections diagnosed in New York in 2006. "Those people have never been tested before," says Mullen. "Believe it or not, people like this still exist." Typically, they've had the infection for ten years—the average time between HIV infection and the emergence of AIDS—but won't know it or acknowledge it until admitted to the emergency room with pneumonia or some other opportunistic infection. These individuals are twice as likely to die in the three to four years after their diagnosis as someone who was just diagnosed with HIV alone. Half of these deaths will occur in the first four months after diagnosis, often from whatever AIDS-related ailment led them to the emergency room in the first place.

It's because of these concurrent HIV/AIDS diagnoses that the Centers for Disease Control and Prevention and the city's Department of Health and Mental Hygiene have been lobbying for HIV tests to be given routinely to anyone who visits an emergency room for any reason. In one recent study from South Carolina, almost three out of four

of those people with concurrent HIV/AIDS diagnoses had visited a medical facility after their infection and prior to getting their blood tested for the virus—averaging six visits each before they were finally tested and diagnosed. "By remaining untested during their routine contacts with the health-care system," said Frieden, in testimony to the New York State Assembly Committee on Health, "they have missed the high-quality treatment that could improve their health and extend their lives. Many may have unknowingly infected their partners—and these partners may not learn that they are infected until they too are sick with AIDS. And so this cycle of death continues."

The second group of HIV-infected patients consists of those at the other extreme, the ones who are least likely to die from AIDS or its complications. These individuals were diagnosed with HIV after the advent of HAART and have taken their medications religiously ever since. In these cases, HAART is likely to suppress their virus for decades, and they're now significantly more likely to die of heart disease or cancer than of anything related to AIDS. To get an idea of the mortality rate among these patients, consider Alexander McMeeking's practice, on East 40th Street. McMeeking ran the HIV clinic at Bellevue from 1987 to 1989 and then left to start a private practice. To the best of his knowledge, only three of his 300-odd Bellevue patients survived long enough to get on HAART. They are still alive today. "Fortunately, thank God, all three are doing great," says McMeeking. "I tell them they will essentially die of old age."

McMeeking's practice now includes 600 HIV-infected patients, and last year he lost only two of those—one to lung cancer, another to liver cancer.

Now the question is whether these patients doing well with HAART are actually more susceptible to the kind of chronic diseases that kill the uninfected. Are they more likely to die from heart disease, cancers, liver and kidney failure, and other chronic diseases either because of the HIV itself or the anti-retroviral regimen keeping it under control? One observation made repeatedly in studies—including the 2006 report from the Department of Health and Mental Hygiene—is that these HIV-infected individuals appear to have higher rates of several different cancers, in particular lung cancer among smokers, non-Hodgkins lymphoma, and cancers of the rectal area. These cancers appear both more precocious and more aggressive in HIV-infected patients—they strike earlier and kill quicker. The reason is not yet clear, although a likely explanation is that the ability of the immune system to search out and destroy incipient malignancies is sufficiently compromised from either the anti-retroviral drugs, the virus, or the coexistence of several viruses—squamous-cell cancers of the rectal area are caused by the same human papilloma virus that causes cervical cancer in woman—that the cancers get a foothold they don't get in non-HIV-infected individuals.

One finding that's considered indisputable is that HAART, and particularly the protease inhibitors that are a critical part of the anti-retroviral cocktail, can play havoc with risk factors for heart disease. They raise cholesterol and triglyceride levels; they lower HDL, and they can cause increased resistance to the hormone insulin. These changes often accompany a condition known as HIV-related lipodystrophy, which afflicts maybe half of all individuals who go on HAART. Subcutaneous fat is lost on the face, arms, legs, and buttocks, while fat accumulates in the gut, upper back (a condition known as a buffalo hump), and breasts. The question is whether these metabolic disturbances actually increase the likelihood of having a heart attack. It's certainly reasonable to think they would, but it's remarkably difficult to demonstrate that the drugs or the virus itself is responsible: The fact that a relatively young man or woman with AIDS has a heart attack does not mean that the heart attack was caused by HIV or the disturbance in cholesterol and lipid levels induced by the therapy.

"If it's 1988, 1989," says one doctor, "and I have a patient with HIV disease and hypertension, he's not going to live long enough to die of hypertension. I want to treat the disease."

Any difference in disease incidence between HIV-infected and uninfected individuals, explains John Brooks, leader of the clinical-epidemiology team within the CDC's Division of HIV/AIDS Prevention, can be due to the infection itself, to the therapy—HAART—or to "the host, the person who has HIV infection, both physiologically and socioculturally." It's the last factor—the host—that complicates the science. Until recently, for instance, physicians saw little reason to worry about heart-disease risk factors in their HIV-infected patients and so didn't bother to aggressively treat risk factors in those patients, as they did the HIV-negative. "Think about it," says Brooks, "if it's 1988, 1989, and I have a patient with HIV disease and hypertension, he's not going to live long enough to die of hypertension. I want to treat the disease."

The rate of cigarette smoking among HIV-infected individuals is also twice as high as the national average. The rate of intravenous drug use is far higher, as is the rate of infection with hepatitis B or C, because intravenous drug use is a common route to getting both HIV and hepatitis. So the fact that an HIV-infected patient may seem to be suffering premature heart disease, diabetes, or liver or kidney disease earlier than seems normal for the population as a whole—or the fact that a study reports such a finding about a population of HIV-infected individuals—only raises the issue of whether the population as a whole is the relevant comparison group. "Since one of the major risk factors for HIV is intravenous drug use," says Brooks, "you have to ask, what's the contribution of heroin to somebody's kidney disease versus the HIV versus untreated high blood pressure versus smoking?"

I still expect most of my patients to live a normal life expectancy," says an AIDS doctor, "but they may do so with a bit more nips and scrapes.

From his own clinical experience, McMeeking agrees that heart disease, certain cancers, and liver and kidney disease do seem to pose a greater threat to his HIV-infected patients than might otherwise be expected in a comparable uninfected population. "I still expect most of my patients to live a normal life expectancy," he says, "but they may do so with a bit more nips and scrapes."

The third group of HIV-infected individuals consists of those in the middle of the two extremes. HAART, in these cases, has literally been a life saver, but has not guaranteed a normal life expectancy. These are the patients, like Bob Hattoy, who were diagnosed with AIDS in the late eighties or early nineties, before the advent of HAART. They began on one drug (AZT, for instance) and then stayed alive long enough to get on protease inhibitors and the HAART cocktails. These patients were on the cusp of the HIV transformation from a deadly to a chronic-disease epidemic; they were infected late enough to survive but too early to derive all the benefits from HAART.

The anti-retroviral drugs of HAART work by attacking the life cycle of the virus. The earliest generation of HAART drugs attacked the enzymes that the virus virus uses to reproduce in the cells. (Protease inhibitors, for instance, go after an enzyme called HIV-1 protease, which the virus uses to assemble itself during reproduction.) The latest drugs go after the methods that the virus uses to enter cells in which it will replicate. The key to the effectiveness of HAART, as researchers discovered in the mid-nineties, was to include at least three drugs in the cocktail to which the patient's specific virus had no resistance. This would suppress viral replication sufficiently so that the virus wouldn't be able to mutate fast enough to evolve resistance to any of the drugs. But patients who began on one or two anti-AIDS drugs and only then moved to HAART already had time to evolve resistance to a few of the drugs in the cocktail. This made the entire package less effective and increased the likelihood that they would evolve resistance to the other drugs as well.

"We call it 'sins of the past,'" says Mullen. "We gave these patients sequential monotherapy; it was state-of-the-art at the time, and a lot of those people are alive today because of that. It got them through until HAART came along, but their HAART is not highly active, only fairly active. Their virus has baseline mutations that interfere with the response." This group of patients also includes those who were infected initially with a strain of HIV already resistant to one or several of the components of HAART, or those patients who were less than 99 percent faithful in taking the regimen of pills that constitute HAART. Anything less than that and the virus has the opportunity to evolve resistance.

Perhaps a quarter of all new cases, says Mullen, are infected with a strain of the virus resistant to one or more drugs in the HAART cocktail. "You can't use the frontline regimen, because the virus has already seen those drugs," he says. "You have to go to more complicated regimens. This is why we do resistance testing before we start a person on medication. We see what drugs the virus has seen or is resistant to and can take that into account."

Sins-of-the-past patients have to have faith that the pharmaceutical industry can stay one step ahead of their disease. The prognosis, at the moment, is promising. There are several entirely new classes of AIDS drugs, including one by Merck, called an integrase inhibitor, that was just approved by the FDA last October. A recent report of the discovery of 270 new human proteins employed by the AIDS virus to hijack cells and start replicating—the definition of a successful infection—means the pharmaceutical industry will not run out of new targets to block the infection in the near future.

Still, some sins-of-the-past patients simply do worse than others, and the occasional patient will lose the battle before new drugs come along or simply give up. "I had a friend who died last week," one sins-of-the-past patient told me recently. "He just lost faith. He would get sick a lot, would get better, then sick again. Finally he decided to try Eastern medicine, and stopped taking his [HAART] medications entirely. It killed him. It's not a good example, other than to show that people can reach their breaking point."

Assess Your Progress

1. What are the lifestyle changes that you can make to reduce your risk of developing cardiovascular disease, cancer, diabetes, and AIDS?

2. Why are people still dying from AIDS?

3. What population groups are most likely to die from AIDS and why?

A Mandate in Texas
The Story of a Compulsory Vaccination and What It Means

KATE O'BEIRNE

On February 2, Texas became the first state to require that young girls be vaccinated against some sexually transmitted viruses. This happened when Gov. Rick Perry issued an executive order requiring that students receive a new vaccine before entering the sixth grade. Perry's order has met with criticism from state legislators who object to his unilateral action, medical groups that welcome the breakthrough vaccine but oppose a mandate, and parents who believe that such coercion usurps their authority. The vaccine's manufacturer is aggressively lobbying other state legislatures to back mandates, and legislation to require the new vaccine is pending in over a dozen states.

Last June, the Food and Drug Administration approved Merck & Co.'s Gardasil vaccine for females aged 9 to 26. When administered to girls before they become sexually active, the vaccine can protect against two of the strains of the human papillomavirus (HPV) that cause about 70 percent of cervical cancers. Within a few weeks of the approval, the vaccine was added to the federal list of recommended routine immunizations for eleven- and twelve-year-old girls. The duration of immunity for the three-dose vaccine series, at a cost of about $360, is not yet known. The federal, means-tested Vaccines for Children program will now include the HPV vaccine, and insurance companies are expected to begin covering its costs.

There is little controversy over the recommendation that the vaccine be broadly used. HPV is the most common sexually transmitted infection, with about half of those who are sexually active carrying it at some point in their lives and about 6.2 million infected annually. The number of sexual partners is the most important risk factor for genital HPV infection. There are no treatments to cure HPV infections, but most are cleared by the immune system, with 90 percent disappearing within two years. Some infections do persist, causing genital warts, cancers of the cervix, and other types of cancer. Each year, over 9,000 new cases of cervical cancer are diagnosed, and the disease kills 3,700 women. Routine Pap tests have dramatically reduced the incidence of cervical cancers over the past 50 years, and it is recommended that even those immunized with the new vaccine continue to be tested, as the vaccine doesn't guard against eleven other high-risk strains of HPV that cause cancer.

Governor Perry recognized that "the newly approved HPV vaccine is a great advance in the protection of women's health" in a "whereas" clause on the way to his "therefore" order that rules be adopted to "mandate the age appropriate vaccination of all female children for HPV prior to admission to the sixth grade." In turning a federal recommendation into a state mandate, Perry has thrilled the vaccine manufacturer, while acting against the balance of medical opinion. And critics object to an opt-out provision that puts the onus on parents to file an affidavit seeking approval of their objection.

The American College of Pediatricians opposes requiring the vaccination for school attendance, saying that such a mandate would represent a "serious, precedent-setting action that trespasses on the rights of parents to make medical decisions for their children as well as on the rights of the children to attend school." The chairman of the American Academy of Pediatrics Committee on Infectious Diseases, Dr. Joseph A. Bocchini, believes a vaccine mandate is premature. "I think it's too early," he said. "This is a new vaccine. It would be wise to wait until we have additional information about the safety of the vaccine." The Texas Medical Association also opposes the mandate, expressing concerns over liability and costs.

Mandatory-education laws create a responsibility to make sure that children are vaccinated against contagious diseases they might be exposed to at school. Now states are considering compelling vaccination in the name of a broad public good, even though the disease in question would not be spread at schools.

Dr. Jon Abramson, the chairman of the Advisory Committee on Immunization Practices of the Centers for Disease Control, explains that protecting children against a virus that is spread by sexual activity is different from preventing the spread of measles. Abramson believes that mandating the HPV vaccine "is a much harder case to make, because you're not going to spread it in a school unless you're doing something you're not supposed to be doing in school." Non-vaccinated students would pose no risk to others while at school.

Texas state senator Glenn Hegar has introduced legislation to reverse Governor Perry's order on the grounds that research trials are still underway and "such mandates take away parents' rights to make medical decisions for their children and usurp parental authority." Twenty-six of 31 state senators believe the governor has usurped legislative authority too, and are calling on him to rescind the executive order. Perry stands by the order, but the rising controversy has discouraged other supporters of mandates.

The *Washington Post* recently reported that Virginia and 17 other states are considering the vaccine requirement "at the urging of New Jersey–based pharmaceutical giant Merck & Co. . . . [which] stands to earn hundreds of millions of dollars annually on Gardasil, according to Wall Street estimates." Public-health organizations have joined Merck in urging that the vaccine be made available in public clinics and encouraging its coverage by private insurers, but they don't support Merck's push for a school requirement.

There were 210 cases of cervical cancer in Maryland last year. Democratic state senator Delores Kelley introduced a bill to require the HPV vaccine for sixth-grade girls. Following complaints from parents and recent non-compliance problems with current mandated vaccinations, Kelley has withdrawn her bill (though she has spoken openly of reintroducing it next session). She explains that she was unaware of Merck & Co.'s lobbying efforts, and that she learned about the new HPV vaccine through a nonpartisan group of female legislators called Women in Government. More than half of its listed supporters are pharmaceutical manufacturers or other health-related companies. Women in Government is spearheading the campaign to mandate the HPV vaccine through school requirements, and some watchdog groups question the support it receives from Merck & Co. "It's not the vaccine community pushing for this," explains the director of the National Network for Immunization Information. Governor Perry's critics point to his own connection with Gardasil's manufacturer: His former chief of staff is a lobbyist for Merck & Co. in Texas.

The profit motive of a company can coincide with public-health interests, but the case for an HPV-vaccine mandate has not been made. The new vaccine does not prevent cervical cancer, but is a welcome protection against some strains of HPV. It is already available to parents who can decide whether it is appropriate for their young daughters. In substituting his judgment for theirs, Governor Perry has attempted to intrude upon their prerogatives and responsibilities. He has also substituted his own judgment for expert medical opinion. State officials who follow his lead won't enjoy immunity from the firestorm of criticism they will rightly earn.

Assess Your Progress

1. Should all young girls be vaccinated against HPV?
2. What are the risks versus the benefits of the HPV vaccination?

UNIT 8

Health Care and the Health Care System

Unit Selections

Learning Outcomes

After reading this unit, you should be able to:

- Explain why or why not pharmacists should be permitted to refuse to fill certain prescriptions.
- Explain why some pharmacists refuse to dispense birth control pills.
- Discuss why women's health is threatened when pharmacists refuse to dispense certain medications.
- Describe what can be done to help reduce health care costs.
- Discuss whether individuals without health insurance die earlier than those who are insured.
- Distinguish whether quality health care is a right or a privilege.
- Explain why patients may be treated independent of their wishes.
- Discuss whether or not there should be limits on health care provided to the terminally ill.
- Explain whether or not health care is just another commodity.
- Explain who should be involved in making health care decisions for the terminally ill.
- Discuss why the use of lesser trained medical personnel can save health care dollars.
- Discuss why or why not health care should be treated differently from other consumer services.

Student Website

www.mhhe.com/cls

Internet References

American Medical Association (AMA)
www.ama-assn.org
MedScape: The Online Resource for Better Patient Care
www.medscape.com

Americans are healthier today than they have been at any time in this nation's history. Americans suffer more illness today than they have at any time in this nation's history. Which statement is true? They both are, depending on the statistics you quote. According to longevity statistics, Americans are living longer today and, therefore, must be healthier. Still, other statistics indicate that Americans today report twice as many acute illnesses as did our ancestors 60 years ago. They also report that their pain lasts longer. Unfortunately, this combination of living longer and feeling sicker places additional demands on a health care system that, according to experts, is already in a state of crisis.

Despite the clamor about the problems with our health care system, if you can afford it, then the American health care system is one of the best in the world. However, being the best does not mean that it is without problems. Each year, more than half a million Americans are injured or die due to preventable mistakes made by medical care professionals. In addition, countless unnecessary tests are preformed that not only add to the expense of health care, but may actually place the patient at risk. Reports such as these fuel the fire of public skepticism toward the quality of health care that Americans receive. While these aspects of our health care system indicate a need for repair, they represent just the tip of the iceberg. In "Curbing Medical Costs," Daniel Callahan discusses the number of Americans who are uninsured and the problems they face. As the number continues to rise, Callahan calls for the government to develop a universal system that covers all. He believes that universal coverage will not only insure all Americans, but it will also help to reduce the cost of health care. Callahan also believes that costs continue to rise due to the blockage of price controls by the pharmaceutical industry. A related article, "The Case for Killing Granny," addresses the cost of treating the elderly at the end of their lives. In "Docs and Doctorates," Shirley Svorny covers the issue of physician shortages and the high cost of medical care in the United States. Laws that affect the way health care is provided and less regulations that impact market forces might reduce the overall cost of medical care.

An issue related to access to health services is presented in "Pharmacist Refusals: A Threat to Women's Health." It relates to pharmacists who refuse to fill prescriptions for certain medications that violate their personal beliefs. These typically include oral contraceptives and morning after pills, which some pharmacists believe cause abortions.

While choices in health care providers are increasing, paying for services continues to be a challenge as medical costs continue to rise. In "Myth Diagnosis," author Megan McArdle discusses the myth that the uninsured are more likely to die than those with health insurance. She maintains that the uninsured have more health risks since they're more likely to be poor, smokers, less educated, obese, and unemployed.

Why have health care costs risen so much? The answer to this question is multifaceted, and includes such factors as physicians' fees, hospital costs, insurance costs, pharmaceutical costs, and health fraud. It could be argued that while these factors operate within any health care system, the lack of a meaningful form of outcomes assessment has permitted and encouraged waste and inefficiency within our system. Ironically, one of the major factors for the rise in the cost of health care is our rapidly expanding aging population—tangible evidence of an improving health care delivery system. This is obviously one factor that we hope will continue to rise. Another significant factor that is often overlooked is the constantly

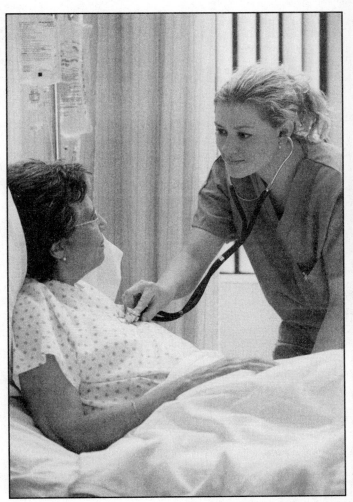

© Jose Luis Pelaez/Getty Images

expanding boundaries of health care. It is somewhat ironic that as our success in treating various disorders has expanded, so has the domain of health care, and often into areas where previously health care had little or no involvement. "Incapacitated, Alone and Treated to Death," offers an interesting perspective of how the care and treatment of patients is often made independent of their wishes.

Traditionally, Americans have felt that the state of their health was largely determined by the quality of the health care available to them. This attitude has fostered an unhealthy dependence upon the health care system and contributed to the skyrocketing costs. It should be obvious by now that while there is no simple solution to our health care problems, we would all be a lot better off if we accepted more personal responsibility for our health. While this shift would help ease the financial burden of health care, it might necessitate a more responsible coverage of medical news in order to educate and enlighten the public on personal health issues.

Pharmacist Refusals: A Threat to Women's Health

MARCIA D. GREENBERGER AND RACHEL VOGELSTEIN

Pharmacist refusals to fill prescriptions for birth control based on personal beliefs have been increasingly reported around the world. In the United States, reports of pharmacist refusals have surfaced in over a dozen states. These refusals have occurred at major drugstore chains like CVS and Walgreens and have affected everyone from rape survivors in search of emergency contraception to married mothers needing birth control pills. Pharmacists who refuse to dispense also often have refused to transfer a woman's prescription to another pharmacist or to refer her to another pharmacy. Other pharmacists have confiscated prescriptions, misled women about availability of drugs, lectured women about morality, or delayed access to drugs until they are no longer effective.

Pharmacist refusal incidents have also been reported in other countries. For example, a pharmacist at a popular London pharmacy chain recently refused to fill a woman's prescription for emergency contraception (EC), or the "morning-after pill," due to religious beliefs; two pharmacists refused to fill contraceptive prescriptions for women at a pharmacy in Salleboeuf, France; and in the small country town of Merriwa, Australia, the local pharmacist refuses to stock EC altogether.[1–3] Pharmacists for Life International, a group refusing to fill prescriptions for contraception, currently claims to have over 1600 members worldwide and represents members in 23 countries.[4]

Pharmacist refusals can have devastating consequences for women's health. Access to contraception is critical to preventing unwanted pregnancies and to enabling women to control the timing and spacing of their pregnancies. Without contraception, the average woman would bear between 12 and 15 children in her lifetime. For some women, pregnancy can entail great health risks and even life-endangerment. Also, women rely on prescription contraceptives for a range of medical reasons in addition to birth control, such as amenorrhea, dysmenorrhea, and endometriosis. Refusals to fill prescriptions for EC (a form of contraception approved by the U.S. Food and Drug Administration and relied on worldwide) are particularly burdensome, as EC is an extremely time-sensitive drug. EC is most effective if used within the first 12 to 24 hours after contraceptive failure, unprotected sex, or sexual assault. If not secured in a timely manner, this drug is useless. Rural and low-income women, as well as survivors of sexual assault, are at particular risk of harm.

In the United States, most states have an implied duty to dispense. Personal beliefs are omitted from the enumerated instances where pharmacists are authorized to refuse; such as where the pharmacist has concerns about therapeutic duplications, drug-disease contraindications, drug interactions, incorrect dosage, or drug abuse. In New Hampshire, the pharmacy regulations' Code of Ethics states that a pharmacist shall "[h]old the health and safety of patients to be of first consideration and render to each patient the full measure of his/her ability as an essential health practitioner."[5] Pharmacists who refuse to fill valid prescriptions based on personal beliefs do not hold patient health and safety as their first consideration.

Illinois explicitly charges pharmacies with a duty to ensure that women's prescriptions for birth control are filled without delay or interference.[6] Massachusetts and North Carolina have interpreted their laws to ensure that women's access to medication is not impeded by pharmacists' personal beliefs.[7,8] However, Arkansas, Georgia, Mississippi, and South Dakota explicitly grant pharmacists the right to refuse to dispense prescriptions for birth control based on personal beliefs.[9]

In addition, a small number of administrative and judicial bodies have considered challenges to pharmacist refusals. In the United States, the Wisconsin pharmacy board found that a pharmacist's failure to transfer a birth control prescription fell below the expected standard of care and constituted a danger to the health and welfare of the patient. The board formally reprimanded the pharmacist for his actions, charged him with the $20,000 cost of adjudication, and conditioned his license on provision of proper notification to his employer about anticipated refusals and his assurances about steps he will take to protect patient access to medication.[10]

Outside of the United States, the European Court of Human Rights rejected an appeal of a conviction of pharmacists under the French consumer code for a refusal to sell contraceptive pills. The Court held that the right to freedom of religion does not allow pharmacists to impose their beliefs on others, so long as the sale of contraceptives is legal.[2]

Some have questioned how such rules comport with the treatment of other medical professionals. In general, medical professionals have a duty to treat patients, with only limited exceptions. The majority of refusal laws apply to doctors and nurses and are limited to abortion services. Allowing pharmacists to refuse to dispense prescriptions for contraception would dramatically expand the universe of permissible refusals. Moreover, unlike doctors and nurses, pharmacists do not select or administer treatments or perform procedures. Therefore, pharmacists' involvement is not as direct, nor would patients' safety be potentially compromised in the same way as would be the case if a doctor or nurse were forced to perform a procedure that they personally oppose.

Since 1997, 28 states have introduced legislation that would permit pharmacists to refuse to dispense, and sometimes to refer or transfer, drugs on the basis of moral or religious grounds. Fifteen states have introduced such bills in the 2005 legislative session alone; while some are specific to contraception, others apply to all medication. These bills have implications for future refusals to fill prescriptions, such as in HIV regimens or treatments derived from embryonic stem cell research. On the other hand, bills have been introduced in four state legislatures and the U.S. Congress that would require pharmacists or pharmacies either to fill prescriptions for contraception or ensure that women have timely access to prescription medication in their pharmacies.

Some professional and medical associations have issued guidelines that protect women against pharmacist refusals. Value VIII of the *Code of Ethics* of the College of Pharmacists of British Columbia requires pharmacists to ensure "continuity of care in the event of . . . conflict with moral beliefs."[11] It permits pharmacists to refuse to dispense prescriptions based on moral beliefs, but only if there is another pharmacist "within a reasonable distance or available within a reasonable time willing to provide the service."

In the United States, several associations have issued similar, although not legally binding, policies. The American Public Health Association states that "[h]ealth systems are urged to establish protocols to ensure that a patient is not denied timely access to EC based on moral or religious objections of a health care provider."[12] The American Medical Women's Association has stated that "pharmacies should guarantee seamless delivery, without delay (within the standard practice for ordering), judgment, or other interference, of all contraceptive drugs and devices lawfully prescribed by a physician."[13]

The American Pharmacists Association (APhA) articulates a standard of professionalism in its *Code of Ethics* that is not legally binding. It mandates that pharmacists place "concern for the well-being of the patient at the center of professional practice."[14] The code also emphasizes that pharmacists are "dedicated to protecting the dignity of the patient" and must "respect personal and cultural differences . . ."[14] This language precludes refusals, lectures, and other barriers erected by pharmacists who disagree with a woman's decision, made in consultation with her health-care provider, to use birth control. Some state pharmacy associations have similar codes.

However, the APhA has another policy that conflicts with these principles. It allows for refusals based on personal beliefs, as long as pharmacists refer prescriptions to another pharmacist or pharmacy.[15] The APhA has not formally explained how to square this policy with its ethical principles of patient-protective care, let alone with state laws and regulations.

Recommendations

Women must be provided timely access to prescription medication. One solution is to require pharmacists to dispense all drugs despite their personal beliefs, in line with their professional duties and ethical obligations. Another solution is to shift the duty to fill from pharmacists onto pharmacies. Under this approach, pharmacies would be charged with ensuring that prescriptions for all drugs are filled without delay or other interference. Such a requirement would allow pharmacies to make arrangements to accommodate the personal beliefs of individual pharmacists. However, active obstruction by pharmacists of women's access to prescription medication—such as withholding or delaying prescriptions or providing misinformation—should be deemed unethical or unprofessional conduct subject to legal sanction.

References and Notes

1. "I Won't Sell Pill, It's Against My Religion," *Sunday Mirror* (27 February 2005).
2. Pichon and Sajous v. France, App. No. 49853/99, Eur. Court H.R. (2001).
3. "U.S. Firm Ships Free Contraceptives to Condom-Deprived Australian Town," *Financial Times,* 31 March 2005 [source: Agence France-Presse].
4. See www.pfli.org/main.php?pfli=locations
5. N.H. Code Admin. R. Ph. 501.01(b)(1) (2005).
6. Illinois Pharmacy Practice Act, § 1330.91 (j)(1) (2005).
7. Massachusetts Board of Pharmacy, letter on file with the National Women's Law Center, 6 May 2004.
8. Conscience concerns in pharmacist decisions, *North Carolina Board Pharm. Newsl.* **26** (3), 1 (2005), 1; available as item 2061 at www.ncbop.org/Newsletters/NC012005.pdf.
9. Ark. Code. Ann. § 20-16-304 (1973); Ga. Comp. R. & Regs. r. 480-5-.03(n) (2001); Miss. Code. Ann. § 41-107-1 (2004); S.D. Codified Laws § 36-11-70 (1998).
10. See www.naralwi.org/assets/files/noesendecision &finalorder.pdf
11. See www.bcpharmacists.org/standards/ethicslong/
12. American Public Health Association (APHA), Policy statement 2003-15 (APHA, Washington, DC, 2003).
13. American Medical Women's Association (AMWA), Statement of AMWA supporting pharmacies' obligation to dispense birth control (Alexandria, VA, 2005) (on file with the National Women's Law Center).
14. See www.aphanet.org/AM/Template.cfm ?Section=Pharmacy_ Practice&CONTENTID=2903&TEMPLATE=/CM/ HTMLDisplay.cfm
15. S. C. Winckler, American Pharmacists Association (1 July 2004) (letter to the editor, unpublished); available at www.aphanet.org/AM/Template.cfm? Section=Public_Relations&Template=/CM/HTML Display. cfm&ContentID=2689

Assess Your Progress

1. Should pharmacists be permitted to refuse to fill certain prescriptions?

2. Why do some pharmacists refuse to fill prescriptions for birth control pills?

3. Why is women's health compromised when pharmacists refuse to dispense certain medications?

The authors are with the National Women's Law Center, Washington, DC 20036, USA. For correspondence, e-mail: rlaser@nwlc.org.

Curbing Medical Costs

Daniel Callahan

It is no secret that the United States has a scandalously large number of uninsured people, now up to 47 million and growing. That number is vivid and evocative, but it has overshadowed a far more serious issue: the steady escalation of health care costs, currently increasing at an annual rate of 7 percent. As a consequence, it is projected that the Medicare program will be bankrupt in nine years and overall health care costs will rise from the present $2.1 trillion to $4 trillion in 10 years.

Those rising costs are an important reason why the number of uninsured people keeps going up. Businesses find it harder and harder to pay for employee health benefits, and only 61 percent of employers even provide them (from a high of close to 70 percent a decade ago). The employers who do provide benefits are cutting them and forcing employees to pay more in the form of co-payments and deductibles. The 15 percent of Americans who are uninsured are surely faced with both health and financial threats. The cost problem, however, now threatens everyone else as well, including those assisted by Medicare and Medicaid.

Universal care is the only tried and effective way to control costs. The European health care systems do so effectively by means of a strong government hand.

Yet even if most people are aware of the dangers of cost escalation—and many know it from personal experience—it has not gripped the public imagination, the presidential candidates or the media with the force of the problem of the uninsured (even though recent public opinion polls indicate it is catching up). Candidates and others have proposed a number of detailed plans for universal care, but nothing comparable for cost control. There is a reason for that.

The problem of the uninsured is the popular problem and the problem of cost control the unpopular one. The former is popular because it is easy to empathize with millions of people who cannot get decent care. Cost control, by contrast, is unpopular, or, perhaps more precisely put, it is dodged and evaded as if it were a nasty political virus to be avoided. Consider what serious cost control will require: moving from a 7 percent annual cost growth down to 3 percent—a rate of inflation for health

care costs that is no greater than the annual rise from general inflation. This amounts to a cost reduction of $1.5 trillion over the next 10 years, settling in at $2.5 trillion in a decade. That would represent an enormous and unprecedented drop in annual costs for a health care system that has never, since World War II, seen anything more than a short and temporary decline from time to time. But this will mean that just about everyone will be forced to give up something, obliged to accept a different, more austere kind of health care.

There are at bottom only three ways to deal with the high cost of health care. One of them is to increase revenues for the system. With government programs such as Medicare, this means raising taxes sharply; with private insurance it means raising premiums. Another approach is to cut benefits drastically, giving people less care. Still another way is to force individuals to pay more out of pocket for their care. Not one of these strategies, if openly embraced, could possibly become popular. They would just be different ways of inflicting pain.

Controlling Medical Technology

The feature of cost escalation that ought to catch our eye most is the role of medical technology. Health care economists estimate that 40 percent to 50 percent of annual cost increases can be traced to new technologies or the intensified use of old ones. That means that control of technology is the most important factor in bringing costs down. Technology also happens to be the most beloved feature of American medicine. Patients expect it; doctors are given extensive training to use it; the medical industries make billions of dollars selling it; and the media love to write about it. The economic and social incentives to develop and make it widely available are powerful, and the disincentives so far are weak and almost useless.

Even among economists and others who concede that technology plays a central role in the cost problem, there is considerable ambivalence about how to deal with it. Technological innovation is as fundamental a feature of American medicine as it is of our industrial sector. After all, innovation has given us vaccines, antibiotics, advanced heart disease care, splendid surgical advances and increasingly effective cancer treatments. And many diseases and crippling medical conditions call for still more innovation. No wonder a distinguished economist from the Brookings Institution, Henry Aaron, who has prominently called attention to all the problems of technology, has written nonetheless that any effort to curb the introduction of new technologies "beyond what is required for safety and efficacy would be sheer madness."

If there is ambivalence in many quarters about managing technology costs, there is outright resistance to such attempts among many American physicians and medical industry associations. Those groups were heavily responsible in the 1980s and 1990s for killing two federal agencies designed to assess medical technology from a scientific and economic perspective. Medical groups opposed them on the grounds that studies of that kind could interfere with the doctor-patient relationship (only they can decide about treatment evidence), and that since life is priceless, any economic assessment would be immoral. Congress, which has never shown much enthusiasm for the control of technology costs, did the actual killing. Ever since the advent of Medicare in 1965, Congress has not allowed it to take costs into account in determining which technologies and treatments it will cover. The medical device industry has been blamed for that resistance. Meanwhile, the pharmaceutical industry has blocked price controls on drugs for many decades.

While it will be hard enough to get universal health care in this country, it will be even harder to control costs. The opposition to such control is politically more intransigent; and in the case of technology, the opposition is deeply rooted in American culture, whose obsession with health is not matched in any other society. Comparative public opinion surveys in Europe and the United States indicate a much greater belief in technology in this country. An astonishing 40 percent of Americans believe that medical technology can always save their lives; not nearly as many Europeans share that fantasy. The old line that Americans believe death is just one more disease to be cured is no longer a joke.

Cost-Cutting Ideas

Can anything be done about costs? A number of ideas have been floated about how to meet the challenge, most of them not rooted in any experience or evidence. The longtime favorite has been to eliminate waste and inefficiency, which is like trying to keep dust out of a house located on the edge of a desert. Medical information technology is a more recent candidate, along with increased efforts to advance disease prevention efforts, consumer-directed health care and disease management programs.

Those are all attractive ideas, but they share a common and crippling handicap. In our messy and fragmented mixture of public and private health care, there is no effective leverage, government or otherwise, to put in place good but often painful ideas. Government might manage to act on some of them, but only after a long and difficult fight. The private sector has never shown much capacity to do so; and given its market philosophy, it would surely resist government efforts to impose cost control mechanisms upon it.

Universal care is the only tried and effective way to control costs. The European health care systems do so effectively by means of a strong government hand. They use, among other things, price controls, negotiated physician fees, hospital budgets with limits on expenditures and stringent policies on the adoption and diffusion of new technologies. The net result is that they keep annual cost increases within the range of 3 percent to 4 percent, have better health outcomes than we do and achieve both at significantly less cost. With the exception of the United Kingdom and Italy—despite what many American conservatives say—there is little rationing and there are no waiting lists for care.

But that is Europe, and this is America. The methods we are inclined to use here to control costs are generally mild and do not promise anything near the reduction in costs needed. The methods the Europeans use, dependent upon government, work well but are culturally and politically unacceptable here. That is the fundamental dilemma in trying to think through the problem.

Consequences of Cost Control

We need a change in culture, not just in the management of health care. Since many of the effective means of controlling costs will be painful for us because of our fascination with technology, the resistance to change will be formidable. Effective control will force patients to give up treatments they may need, doctors to sacrifice to a considerable extent their ancient tradition of treating patients the way they see fit and industry to reduce its drive for profit. Hardly anyone will want to do such things. Liberals will hate it, because though they favor universal health care, they are also children of the Enlightenment, champions of endless scientific progress and technological innovation. Economic conservatives will despise it as government interference with market freedom and consumer choice. Social conservatives will see the necessary rationing as a form of social euthanasia, killing off the burdensome in the name of cold-hearted economics.

The pharmaceutical industry has successfully blocked price controls for many decades.

Many commentators argue that if health care is not reformed, our system will collapse. I doubt that will happen. Instead, there is likely to be gradual deterioration, tolerable enough for the affluent but bringing to everyone else a gradual loss of quality, with more people uninsured, more expensive insurance, more bankruptcies and economic pain from medical debts and more economic anxiety about getting sick.

The frustrating part of all this is that in principle, cost control is a problem that can be solved. There is indeed waste and inefficiency, enormous and absurd variation in costs of care from one geographical region to the next, a great deal of useless or only marginally useful treatment, great possibilities in disease prevention programs, far too few primary care physicians and geriatricians and far too many specialists. The fact that the European countries can control costs and limit technologies without harming health is a patent rebuke to our way of doing things.

Looking for Solutions

Can we get there from here? To do so, both a huge economic gap and an equally huge cultural gap must be closed. We have become accustomed to living (and dying) with an expensive and disorganized system that serves many ends other than health. It is a system designed for reckless affluence. It builds upon a model of health and medical progress that is open-ended and infinite in its aspirations. Suffering, aging and death are enemies to be conquered, at whatever the cost to other social needs.

With the help of intensive marketing by industry and daily media hype, we have become fearful hypochondriacs, sensitive to every ache and pain and always anxious about that undiagnosed cancer or heart disease just waiting to get us. Our standard for good health constantly rises. Whatever the state of our health, it is never good enough. However high our life expectancy, we remain forever hopeful for medical miracles and endlessly dissatisfied with our health.

The nation needs a good dialogue on health care reform, but one that moves beyond organizational and management schemes. They are important but no more so than some deeper matters. Should death be seen as the greatest evil, which medicine should seek to combat, or would a good quality of life within a finite life span be a better goal?

Do the elderly need better access to intensive care units and more high-tech medicine to extend their lives, or better long-term and home care and improved economic and social support? Does it make any sense that the healthier we get in this country the more we spend on health care, not less? Should we be spending three times more of our gross domestic product on health care than on education (when 40 years ago it was about the same)?

Those are rhetorical questions. But they are the place to begin any serious discussion about the control of costs and technology. That discussion merits at least as much attention as does the plight of the uninsured; it will be harder to maintain and focus, but it is even more necessary.

Assess Your Progress

1. Describe the relationship between medical technology and health care costs.
2. What can you as an individual do to help reduce health care costs? Give specific actions that can be taken.

DANIEL CALLAHAN, director of the international program at the Hastings Center in Garrison, N.Y., is the author of *Setting Limits: Medical Goals in an Aging Society* (1987) and co-author of *Medicine and the Market: Equality vs. Choice* (2006).

Myth Diagnosis

Everyone knows that people without health insurance are more likely to die. But are they?

MEGAN MCARDLE

Outside of the few states where it is illegal to deny coverage based on medical history, I am probably uninsurable. Though I'm in pretty good health, I have several latent conditions, including an autoimmune disease. If I lost the generous insurance that I have through *The Atlantic,* even the most charitable insurer might hesitate to take me on.

So I took a keen interest when, at the fervid climax of the health-care debate in mid-December, a *Washington Post* blogger, Ezra Klein, declared that Senator Joseph Lieberman, by refusing to vote for a bill with a public option, was apparently "willing to cause the deaths of hundreds of thousands" of uninsured people in order to punish the progressives who had opposed his reelection in 2006. In the ensuing blogstorm, conservatives condemned Klein's "venomous smear," while liberals solemnly debated the circumstances under which one may properly accuse one's opponents of mass murder.

But aside from an exchange between Matthew Yglesias of the Center for American Progress and Michael Cannon of the Cato Institute, few people addressed the question that mattered most to those of us who cannot buy an individual insurance policy at any price—the question that was arguably the health-care debate's most important: Was Klein (not to mention other like-minded editorialists who cited similar numbers) *right?* If we lost our insurance, would this gargantuan new entitlement really be the only thing standing between us and an early grave?

Perhaps few people were asking, because the question sounds so stupid. Health insurance buys you health care. Health care is supposed to save your life. So if you don't have someone buying you health care . . . well, you can complete the syllogism.

Last year's national debate on health-care legislation tended to dwell on either heart-wrenching anecdotes about costly, unattainable medical treatments, or arcane battles over how many people in the United States lacked insurance.

Republicans rarely plumbed the connection between insurance and mortality, presumably because they would look foolish and heartless if they expressed any doubt about health insurance's benefits. It was politically safer to harp on the potential problems of government interventions—or, in extremis, to point out that more than half the uninsured were either affluent, lacking citizenship, or already eligible for government programs in which they hadn't bothered to enroll.

Even Democratic politicians made curiously little of the plight of the uninsured. Instead, they focused on cost control, so much so that you might have thought that covering the uninsured was a happy side effect of really throttling back the rate of growth in Medicare spending. When progressive politicians or journalists did address the disadvantages of being uninsured, they often fell back on the same data Klein had used: a 2008 report from the Urban Institute that estimated that about 20,000 people were dying every year for lack of health insurance.

But when you probe that claim, its accuracy is open to question. Even a rough approximation of how many people die because of lack of health insurance is hard to reach. Quite possibly, lack of health insurance has no more impact on your health than lack of flood insurance.

Part of the trouble with reports like the one from the Urban Institute is that they cannot do the kind of thing we do to test drugs or medical procedures: divide people randomly into groups that do and don't have health insurance, and see which group fares better. Experimental studies like this would be tremendously expensive, and it's hard to imagine that they'd attract sufficient volunteers. Moreover, they might well violate the ethical standards of doctors who believed they were condemning the uninsured patients to a life nasty, brutish, and short.

So instead, researchers usually do what are called "observational studies": they take data sets that include both insured and uninsured people, and compare their health outcomes—usually mortality rates, because these are unequivocal and easy to measure. For a long time, two of the best studies were Sorlie et al. (1994), which used a large sample of census data from 1982 to 1985; and Franks, Clancy, and Gold (1993), which examined a smaller but richer data set from the National Health and Nutrition Examination Survey, and its follow-up studies, between 1971 and 1987. The Institute of Medicine used the math behind these two studies to produce a 2002 report on an increase in illness and death from lack of insurance; the Urban Institute, in turn, updated those numbers to produce the figure that became the gold standard during the debate over healthcare reform.

The first thing one notices is that the original studies are a trifle elderly. Medicine has changed since 1987; presumably, so has the riskiness of going without health insurance. Moreover, the question of who had insurance is particularly dodgy: the studies counted as "uninsured" anyone who lacked insurance in the initial interview. But of course, not all of those people would have stayed uninsured—a separate study suggests that only about a third of those who reported being uninsured over a two-year time frame lacked coverage for the entire period. Most of the "uninsured" people probably got insurance relatively quickly, while some of the "insured" probably lost theirs. The effect of this churn could bias your results either way; the inability to control for it makes the statistics less accurate.

The bigger problem is that the uninsured generally have more health risks than the rest of the population. They are poorer, more likely to smoke, less educated, more likely to be unemployed, more likely to be obese, and so forth. All these things are known to increase your risk of dying, independent of your insurance status.

There are also factors we can't analyze. It's widely believed that health improves with social status, a quality that's hard to measure. Risk-seekers are probably more likely to end up uninsured, and also to end up dying in a car crash—but their predilection for thrills will not end up in our statistics. People who are suspicious of doctors probably don't pursue either generous health insurance or early treatment. Those who score low on measures of conscientiousness often have trouble keeping jobs with good health insurance—or following complicated treatment protocols. And so on.

The studies relied upon by the Institute of Medicine and the Urban Institute tried to control for some of these factors. But Sorlie et al.—the larger study—lacked data on things like smoking habits and could control for only a few factors, while Franks, Clancy, and Gold, which had better controls but a smaller sample, could not, as an observational study, categorically exclude the possibility that lack of insurance has no effect on mortality at all.

The possibility that no one risks death by going without health insurance may be startling, but some research supports it. Richard Kronick of the University of California at San Diego's Department of Family and Preventive Medicine,

an adviser to the Clinton administration, recently published the results of what may be the largest and most comprehensive analysis yet done of the effect of insurance on mortality. He used a sample of more than 600,000, and controlled not only for the standard factors, but for how long the subjects went without insurance, whether their disease was particularly amenable to early intervention, and even whether they lived in a mobile home. In test after test, he found no significantly elevated risk of death among the uninsured.

This result is not, perhaps, as shocking as it seems. Health care heals, but it also kills. Someone who lacked insurance over the past few decades might have missed taking their Lipitor, but also their Vioxx or Fen-Phen. According to one estimate, 80,000 people a year are killed just by "nosocomial infections"—infections that arise as a result of medical treatment. The only truly experimental study on health insurance, a randomized study of almost 4,000 subjects done by Rand and concluded in 1982, found that increasing the generosity of people's health insurance caused them to use more health care, but made almost no difference in their health status.

Health care heals, but it also kills. Someone who lacked insurance over the past decade might have missed taking Lipitor, but also Vioxx or Fen-Phen.

If gaining insurance has a large effect on people's health, we should see outcomes improve dramatically between one's early and late 60s. Yet like the Kronick and Rand studies, analyses of the effect of Medicare, which becomes available to virtually everyone in America at the age of 65, show little benefit. In a recent review of the literature, Helen Levy of the University of Michigan and David Meltzer of the University of Chicago noted that the latest studies of this question "paint a surprisingly consistent picture: Medicare increases consumption of medical care and may modestly improve self-reported health but has no effect on mortality, at least in the short run."

Of course, that might be an indictment of programs like Medicare and Medicaid. Indeed, given the uncertainties about their impact on mortality rates—uncertainties that the results from Sorlie et al. don't resolve—it's possible that, by blocking the proposed expansion of health care through Medicare, Senator Lieberman, rather than committing the industrial-scale slaughter Klein fears, might not have harmed anyone at all. We cannot use one study to "prove" that having government insurance is riskier than having none. But we also cannot use a flawed and conflicting literature to "prove" that Lieberman was willing to risk the deaths of hundreds of thousands. Government insurance should have some effect, but if that effect is not large enough to be unequivocally evident in the data we have, it must be small.

Even if we did agree that insurance rarely confers significant health benefits, that would not necessarily undermine the case for a national health-care program. The academics who question the mass benefits of expanding coverage still think that doing so improves outcomes among certain vulnerable subgroups, like infants and patients with HIV. Besides, a national health program has nonmedical benefits. Leaving tens of millions of Americans without health insurance violates our sense of equity—and leaves those millions exposed to the risk of mind-boggling medical bills.

But we should have had a better handle on the case for expanded coverage—and, more important, the evidence behind it—before we embarked on a year-long debate that divided our house against itself. Certainly, we should have had it before Congress voted on the largest entitlement expansion in 40 years. Unfortunately, most of us forgot to ask a fundamental question, because we were certain we already knew the answer. By the time we got around to challenging our assumptions, it was too late to do anything except scream at each other from the sidelines.

Assess Your Progress

1. Do individuals without health insurance die earlier than those who are insured? Why or why not?

2. Is quality health care a right or a privilege? Defend your answer.

MEGAN MCARDLE is *The Atlantic*'s business and economics editor, and the editor of the business channel at theatlantic.com.

The *Case for* Killing Granny

Evan Thomas et al.

Rethinking End-of-Life Care

My mother wanted to die, but the doctors wouldn't let her. At least that's the way it seemed to me as I stood by her bed in an intensive-care unit at a hospital in Hilton Head, S.C., five years ago. My mother was 79, a longtime smoker who was dying of emphysema. She knew that her quality of life was increasingly tethered to an oxygen tank, that she was losing her ability to get about, and that she was slowly drowning. The doctors at her bedside were recommending various tests and procedures to keep her alive, but my mother, with a certain firmness I recognized, said no. She seemed puzzled and a bit frustrated that she had to be so insistent on her own demise.

The hospital at my mother's assisted-living facility was sustained by Medicare, which pays by the procedure. I don't think the doctors were trying to be greedy by pushing more treatments on my mother. That's just the way the system works. The doctors were responding to the expectations of almost all patients. As a doctor friend of mine puts it, "Americans want the best, they want the latest, and they want it now." We expect doctors to make heroic efforts—especially to save our lives and the lives of our loved ones.

The idea that we might ration health care to seniors (or anyone else) is political anathema. Politicians do not dare breathe the R word, lest they be accused—however wrongly—of trying to pull the plug on Grandma. But the need to spend less money on the elderly at the end of life is the elephant in the room in the health-reform debate. Everyone sees it but no one wants to talk about it. At a more basic level, Americans are afraid not just of dying, but of talking and thinking about death. Until Americans learn to contemplate death as more than a scientific challenge to be overcome, our health-care system will remain unfixable.

Compared with other Western countries, the United States has more health care—but, generally speaking, not better health care. There is no way we can get control of costs, which have grown by nearly 50 percent in the past decade, without finding a way to stop overtreating patients. In his address to Congress, President Obama spoke airily about reducing inefficiency, but he slid past the hard choices that will have to be made to stop health care from devouring ever-larger slices of the economy and tax dollar. A significant portion of the savings will have to come from the money we spend on seniors at the end of life because, as Willie Sutton explained about why he robbed banks, that's where the money is.

As President Obama said, most of the uncontrolled growth in federal spending and the deficit comes from Medicare; nothing else comes close. Almost a third of the money spent by Medicare—about $66.8 billion a year—goes to chronically ill patients in the last two years of life. This might seem obvious—of course the costs come at the end, when patients are the sickest. But that can't explain what researchers at Dartmouth have discovered: Medicare spends twice as much on similar patients in some parts of the country as in others. The average cost of a Medicare patient in Miami is $16,351; the average in Honolulu is $5,311. In the Bronx, N.Y., it's $12,543. In Fargo, N.D., $5,738. The average Medicare patient undergoing end-of-life treatment spends 21.9 days in a Manhattan hospital. In Mason City, Iowa, he or she spends only 6.1 days.

Maybe it's unsurprising that treatment in rural towns costs less than in big cities, with all their high prices, varied populations, and urban woes. But there are also significant disparities in towns that are otherwise very similar. How do you explain the fact, for instance, that in Boulder, Colo., the average cost of Medicare treatment is $9,103, whereas an hour away in Fort Collins, Colo., the cost is $6,448?

The answer, the Dartmouth researchers found, is that in some places doctors are just more likely to order more tests and procedures. More specialists are involved. There is very little reason for them not to order more tests and treatments. By training and inclination, doctors want to do all they can to cure ailments. And since Medicare pays by procedure, test, and hospital stay—though less and less each year as the cost squeeze tightens—there is an incentive to do more and more. To make a good living, doctors must see more patients, and order more tests.

All this treatment does not necessarily buy better care. In fact, the Dartmouth studies have found worse outcomes in many states and cities where there is more health care. Why? Because just going into the hospital has risks—of infection, or error, or other unforeseen complications. Some studies estimate that Americans are overtreated by roughly 30 percent. "It's not about rationing care—that's always the bogeyman people use to block reform," says Dr. Elliott Fisher, a professor at Dartmouth Medical School. "The real problem is unnecessary and unwanted care."

But how do you decide which treatments to cut out? How do you choose between the necessary and the unnecessary? There has been talk among experts and lawmakers of giving more power to a panel of government experts to decide—Britain has one, called the National Institute for Health and Clinical Excellence (known by the somewhat ironic acronym NICE). But no one wants the horror stories of denied care and long waits that are said to plague state-run national health-care systems. (The criticism is unfair: patients wait longer to see primary-care physicians in the United States than in Britain.) After the summer of angry town halls, no politician is going to get anywhere near something that could be called a "death panel."

There's no question that reining in the lawyers would help cut costs. Fearing medical-malpractice suits, doctors engage in defensive medicine, ordering procedures that may not be strictly necessary—but why take the risk? According to various studies, defensive medicine adds perhaps 2 percent to the overall bill—a not-insignificant number when more than $2 trillion is at stake. A number of states have managed to institute some kind of so-called tort reform, limiting the size of damage awards by juries in medical-malpractice cases. But the trial lawyers—big donors to the Democratic Party—have stopped Congress from even considering reforms. That's why it was significant that President Obama even raised the subject in his speech last week, even if he was vague about just what he'd do. (Best idea: create medical courts run by experts to rule on malpractice claims, with no punitive damages.)

But the biggest cost booster is the way doctors are paid under most insurance systems, including Medicare. It's called fee-for-service, and it means just that. So why not just put doctors on salary? Some medical groups that do, like the Mayo Clinic, have reduced costs while producing better results. Unfortunately, putting doctors on salary requires that they work for someone, and most American physicians are self-employed or work in small group practices. The alternative—paying them a flat rate for each patient they care for—turned out to be at least a partial bust. HMOs that paid doctors a flat fee in the 1990s faced a backlash as patients bridled at long waits and denied service.

Ever-rising health-care spending now consumes about 17 percent of the economy (versus about 10 percent in Europe). At the current rate of increase, it will devour a fifth of GDP by 2018. We cannot afford to sustain a productive economy with so much money going to health care. Over time, economic reality may force us to adopt a national health-care system like Britain's or Canada's. But before that day arrives, there are steps we can take to reduce costs without totally turning the system inside out.

One place to start is to consider the psychological aspect of health care. Most people are at least minor hypochondriacs (I know I am). They use doctors to make themselves feel better, even if the doctor is not doing much to physically heal what ails them. (In ancient times, doctors often made people sicker with quack cures like bleeding.) The desire to see a physician is often pronounced in assisted-living facilities. Old people, far from their families in our mobile, atomized society, depend on their doctors for care and reassurance. I noticed that in my mother's retirement home, the talk in the dining room was often about illness; people built their day around doctor's visits, partly, it seemed to me, to combat loneliness.

Physicians at Massachusetts General Hospital are experimenting with innovative approaches to care for their most ill patients without necessarily sending them to the doctor. Three years ago, Massachusetts enacted universal care—just as Congress and the Obama administration are attempting to do now. The state quickly found it could not afford to meet everyone's health-care demands, so it's scrambling for solutions. The Mass General program assigned nurses to the hospital's 2,600 sickest—and costliest—Medicare patients. These nurses provide basic care, making sure the patients take their medications and so forth, and act as gatekeepers—they decide if a visit to the doctor is really necessary. It's not a perfect system—people will still demand to see their doctors when it's unnecessary—but the Mass General program cut costs by 5 percent while providing the elderly what they want and need most: caring human contact.

Other initiatives ensure that the elderly get counseling about end-of-life issues. Although demagogued as a "death panel," a program in Wisconsin to get patients to talk to their doctors about how they want to deal with death was actually a resounding success. A study by the Archives of Internal Medicine shows that such conversations between doctors and patients can decrease costs by about 35 percent—while improving the quality of life at the end. Patients should be encouraged to draft living wills to make their end-of-life desires known. Unfortunately, such paper can be useless if there is a family member at the bedside demanding heroic measures. "A lot of the time guilt is playing a role," says Dr. David Torchiana, a surgeon and CEO of the Massachusetts General Physicians Organization. Doctors can feel guilty, too—about overtreating patients. Torchiana recalls his unease over operating to treat a severe heart infection in a woman with two forms of metastatic cancer who was already comatose. The family insisted.

Studies show that about 70 percent of people want to die at home—but that about half die in hospitals. There has been an important increase in hospice or palliative care—keeping patients with incurable diseases as comfortable as possible while they live out the remainder of their lives. Hospice services are generally intended for the terminally ill in the last six months of life, but as a practical matter, many people receive hospice care for only a few weeks.

Our medical system does everything it can to encourage hope. And American health care has been near miraculous—the envy of the world—in its capacity to develop new lifesaving and life-enhancing treatments. But death can be delayed only so long, and sometimes the wait is grim and degrading. The hospice ideal recognized that for many people, quiet and dignity—and loving care and good painkillers—are really what's called for.

That's what my mother wanted. After convincing the doctors that she meant it—that she really was ready to die—she was transferred from the ICU to a hospice, where, five days later, she passed away. In the ICU, as they removed all the monitors and pulled out all the tubes and wires, she made a fluttery motion with her hands. She seemed to be signaling goodbye to all that—I'm free to go in peace.

Assess Your Progress

1. Why are terminally ill patients treated independent of their wishes?
2. Describe some of the initiatives that are being developed for terminally ill and elderly patients. What do you think of these programs?

EVAN THOMAS with Pat Wingert, Suzanne Smalley, and Claudia Kalb.

Incapacitated, Alone and Treated to Death

JOSEPH SACCO, MD

M r. Green lay in the bed next to the window, 15 floors above the Cross-Bronx Expressway. Fifty-nine years old and suffering from AIDS-related dementia, he was bedbound, permanently tethered to a ventilator and, though conscious, unaware of his medical condition. In medico-legal parlance, he was incapacitated: unable to understand the consequences of his decisions and unable to direct the doctors caring for him.

The view from his bedside was impressive—a thousand acres of worn, low-slung apartment buildings set off by the massed arc of Manhattan, rising from the distance like the Emerald City.

That no friend or family member would ever share this view was another of his mounting misfortunes. Referred to the hospital from a nursing home for fever and weight loss—he was so thin that the skin of his chest would not even hold EKG leads—he had no identified relatives or friends. His personal history had vanished into the maze of health care facilities that had been his home for more than a year. Other than name, Social Security number and date of birth, his life story had disappeared.

Mr. Green was one of thousands of New Yorkers—physically devastated, mentally depleted, without hope of recovery and without surrogates—for whom the prolongation of life at all costs was the only legally sanctioned course of treatment. Even if friends or relatives were found, New York prohibits the withholding or withdrawing of life-sustaining treatment without a signed health care proxy or "clear and convincing" evidence of a patient's wishes. A "do not resuscitate" order can be put in place by doctors, but only in the absence of identified surrogates and only if resuscitation is considered futile.

Other states, to varying extents, allow family members, friends or guardians to make the decision about life support, even without knowledge of a patient's prior wishes. A few states grant it to the doctor in the absence of such surrogates. A treatment that preserves a heartbeat but offers no hope of recovery—long-term ventilator support in a vegetative state, say—may be withdrawn. New York permits no such possibility. Physicians not wanting to find themselves at the center of precedent-setting

test cases on patients' rights will treat, treat and treat, no matter the cost to the patient or their own souls.

Mention the idea of withholding or withdrawing medical care from patients who cannot express their wishes, and people get uncomfortable. Advocacy groups use the term "medical killing," and despite the hyperbole, their concerns are merited. Doctors have no right to judge the value of a life. Many patients want their lives prolonged, regardless of prognosis, quality or need for invasive treatment.

Yet a 2007 study found that doctors in intensive-care units across the country commonly withheld or withdrew life support in critically or terminally ill patients who lacked surrogates, without knowledge of their wishes. Most such decisions were made by a single physician, without regard to hospital policy, professional society recommendations or state law. In other words, doctors are withholding treatment from this vulnerable population, a practice that is neither regulated nor publicly recognized.

Many things influenced the patient's care. Just not his own wishes.

Mr. Green's monetary value cannot be underestimated as an influence on his care. He was a valuable commodity. A ventilator-dependent patient, especially one undergoing the surgical incision necessary for long-term vent support, is among the highest-paying under Medicare's prospective hospital reimbursement system; his need for skilled care outside the hospital made him a lucrative nursing home patient.

Prognosis is not a factor in this equation. Forever on life support without hope of recovery, Mr. Green would develop pneumonias, urinary infections and other complications, each requiring transfer from the nursing home to the hospital, stabilization and transfer back again. The providers would be reimbursed for each of these procedures.

Extraordinary advances have been made in the treatment of H.I.V. Still, Mr. Green's dementia worsened, as did his terrible wasting and bedsores. In July, despite a full volley of high-tech interventions, he died, without ever having done anything volitional, never mind eating, talking or making eye contact. His well-intentioned hospital and doctors, fully aware of his dismal prognosis, continued the excruciating process of inserting pencil-thick IV catheters and cleaning fist-size bed sores.

No one asked if Mr. Green wanted these interventions, assuming instead that to do otherwise was both unethical and illegal, and he was treated to death. Modern American medicine owed him a better way.

Assess Your Progress

1. Should there be limits on health care provided to the terminally ill?

2. Who should be involved in making health care decisions for the mentally incapacitated, terminally ill patient?

JOSEPH SACCO is director of the palliative medicine consultation service at Bronx Lebanon Hospital Center.

Docs and Doctorates

Health care would be more accessible if you didn't need an MD to perform a colonoscopy.

SHIRLEY SVORNY

A report from the Association of American Medical Colleges (AAMC) lists 29 state studies that warn of looming physician shortages. Twenty-one specialty-specific studies and at least six national reports characterize the situation as critical.

The most recent comparable physician shortage occurred more than 40 years ago, when Medicare and Medicaid were introduced. At that time, the increased demand for physicians' services was met in part by changes in immigration law: In the 1970s, more than 40 percent of newly licensed physicians in the U.S. were trained overseas. At the same time, the output of domestic medical schools grew substantially, and together those changes helped alleviate the shortage. The concern now is that the large cohort of physicians who entered practice in the late 1960s and 1970s—one in three U.S. doctors is 55 or older—is nearing retirement.

The AAMC, which is involved in the accreditation of medical schools and other health-care education programs, has called for an increase in the number of medical-school graduates and corresponding increases in the number of residency positions. The enrollment increase is well under way. But even with new medical schools in several states and across-the-board increases in enrollment in existing schools, AAMC statistics suggest that a shortfall will be unavoidable as the population ages.

And we should be wary of the idea that training more doctors is a panacea for the supply shortage. Most physicians choose to settle in urban areas, and training additional physicians does not ensure that they will locate in underserved communities. In fact, it is mostly doctors' lack of interest in working in poor or remote communities that has prompted some states to overcome their opposition to the independent work of nurse practitioners.

The solution is rather to change the way medical care is provided in this country. Eliminating regulations and reforming reimbursement methods would free providers to innovate, reduce costs, and improve access to care. Directing public policy toward these ends is a tall order, but would certainly be no more disruptive of the status quo than the regulations proposed in the health-care bills before Congress. Deep, innovation-enabling reform would, however, lead to an outcome that the proposed health-care legislation wouldn't: more care at lower cost.

A 2008 report from the Association of Academic Health Centers (AAHC), "Out of Order, Out of Time," blames the shortage of medical professionals on piecemeal regulation and market forces. As a solution, the authors advocate the establishment of a national planning authority to develop a "coherent, overarching health work force policy," as well as a "harmonization in public and private standards, requirements and prevailing practices across jurisdictions." This, however, would make the health-care system even more rigid. It would also subject regulators to intense pressure from various stakeholders, the most prominent being organized groups of medical professionals and hospital associations seeking to promote their own interests. For example, the AAHC's plan—which calls for guessing where shortages may occur and then subsidizing education in those areas—would increase federal funding for its members. And while both the American Medical Association and the American College of Physicians recognize the role advanced-practice nurses and other non-physician clinicians can play, they are fearful of the competition and demand that non-physicians be allowed to practice only with physician supervision. They persist in this demand even though there is no evidence that direct physician oversight of nurse practitioners is necessary.

The reality is that federal and state regulations play a far larger role than market forces in the shortage of doctors and other medical practitioners we face today. Federal Medicare and state Medicaid reimbursement rates are set below market prices, predictably causing shortages. States insist on regulating exactly what health professionals are allowed to do and require excessive levels of education and training that limit providers' entry into the marketplace, thereby restricting patients' access to care. Some states micromanage health care with laws that mandate nurse-to-patient ratios and restrict the independent activities of non-physician caregivers such as advanced-practice nurses and dental hygienists.

Federal and state regulations play a far larger role than market forces in the shortage of doctors and other medical practitioners we face today.

These regulations stifle innovation in the provision of health care. In other markets, consumer demand for efficiency and convenience has motivated changes in the way goods and services are provided. But except for the growing use of advanced-practice nurses and physicians' assistants, medical care remains much as it was 40 years ago: One doctor sees one patient, face to face, even as we rely increasingly on the telephone and e-mail for a broad range of other exchanges. The high cost of these static practices is thrown into relief by the rare innovations that do occur. In 2004, Kaiser Permanente Hawaii put in place a system that allows patients to contact physicians via e-mail. By 2007, in-person office visits had fallen more than 25 percent. Tele-medicine also offers promise in meeting the health-care needs of underserved communities. It would benefit from the elimination of regulations that prohibit practicing across state lines.

Medical education in the United States is shaped by the Liaison Committee on Medical Education, a joint project of the AAMC and the American Medical Association; its accreditation of medical schools forms the basis for professional licensing by the states. It currently requires adherence to inflexible rules and fixed teaching methods, making innovation difficult.

Robert H. Brook of the RAND Corporation suggests an innovation in medical education that would expand access to care without increasing the number of physicians. He argues that a fully trained gastroenterologist or surgeon is not needed to perform a colonoscopy (a common screening for cancer), nor a fully credentialed ophthalmologist to perform routine cataract surgery. Instead, he suggests, two years of focused education and training would yield professionals qualified to perform these procedures, vastly expanding patients' access to these services.

And given the concern over provider shortages, it is troubling that certifying organizations continue to raise the education requirements for non-physicians. Following a decision by the Council on Academic Accreditation in Audiology and Speech-Language Pathology to accredit only doctoral programs, 18 states now require a doctorate of audiologists. The new requirement adds two years to the time it takes to train an audiologist, significantly raising the cost of entry into the profession. Until the 1990s, physical therapists needed only a bachelor's degree. Then a master's degree was required. Now the Commission on Accreditation in Physical Therapy Education has announced it will require doctorates by 2017. This adds three years of training beyond a bachelor's degree. Soon a doctorate will also be required for advanced-practice nurses and others. These decisions proceed from a self-interested desire to restrict the number of actors in the marketplace, and that is one reason no single organization should have the authority, under the law, to accredit medical schools or health-related educational programs.

State rules dictating how medical professionals must be trained and employed are ostensibly designed to protect consumers. It is, however, patently mistaken to defend these regulations on the basis that they offer protection beyond what private credentialing can provide. That is because the vetting process is already outsourced to private organizations, including specialty boards and malpractice-insurance underwriters. Taking into account its real costs—a false sense of security and the suppression of innovation—the existing regulatory structure cannot be justified. Economists agree that medical licensing is a constraint on the efficient use of resources and a drag on innovation.

Eliminating these burdensome rules would reduce supply constraints, but that alone will not be sufficient to generate more and better options for care. The prevalence of third-party reimbursement removes an incentive for consumers and medical professionals alike to use resources efficiently. For example, few consumers know what a physical exam actually costs or what it should include. Consequently, prices are rarely considered when patients and their physicians make decisions. The solution, as John C. Goodman of the National Center for Policy Analysis and others have pointed out, is to put health-care dollars directly into the hands of consumers. If health-savings accounts and similar measures were used to empower consumers while state regulations were simultaneously lifted, competition among suppliers would generate the type of innovation we enjoy in other service industries.

The elimination of regulatory constraints and third-party payment could also improve providers' earnings by expanding the scope of their practices and allowing market-rate fees, thereby drawing new practitioners into the marketplace. We won't really know how many physicians we need until we discover how the health-care industry can take advantage of technology and specialization. At that point, if we allow the markets to work, wages will adjust to reflect the real value of services instead of being arbitrarily set by a government agency.

Health-care providers would like us to believe that there is something unique about their business that requires heavy government regulation. They favor the low-competition status quo that has been secured through legislative and administrative mandates for education and practice, and their solution is more of the same. But it is government regulation that has brought us to this pass. Reducing regulation on the supply side while increasing consumers' power on the demand side is the combination most likely to produce better care at better prices.

Assess Your Progress

1. How can the use of lesser trained medical providers reduce health care costs?

2. Should health care be treated differently from other consumer services?

SHIRLEY SVORNY is a professor of economics at California State University, Northridge.

From *The National Review*, February 22, 2010, pp. 24–25, 26. Copyright © 2010 by National Review, Inc, 215 Lexington Avenue, New York, NY 10016. Reprinted by permission.

UNIT 9

Consumer Health

Unit Selections

Learning Outcomes

After reading this unit, you should be able to:

- Distinguish whether vaccination is more dangerous than getting the disease prevented by the vaccine.
- Explain why some parents opt out of vaccinating their children.
- Describe medical tourism.
- Discuss the risks versus benefits of medical tourism.
- Discuss why it is risky to try and kill all germs.
- Explain why sanitizers are not a good substitute for washing.
- Explain the risk associated with getting a tattoo.
- Explain the difficulties in having a tattoo removed.
- Discuss what consumers should look for when choosing health insurance.
- Distinguish between adequate and inadequate health care coverage.
- Describe why humans are getting less sleep these days.
- Explain the health implications of sleep deprivation.
- Explain why health care is compromised when you are overweight.

Student Website

www.mhhe.com/cls

Internet References

FDA Consumer Magazine
www.fda.gov/fdac
Global Vaccine Awareness League
www.gval.com
National Sleep Foundation
www.sleepfoundation.org

For many people the term "consumer health" conjures up images of selecting health care services and paying medical bills. While these two aspects of health care are indeed consumer health issues, the term consumer health encompasses all consumer products and services that influence the health and welfare of people. A definition this broad suggests that almost everything we see or do may be construed to be a consumer health issue, whether it is related to products or discussions such as the concept of getting enough sleep. In many ways consumer health is an outward expression of our health-related behaviors and decision-making processes, and as such, is based on our desire to make healthy choices, be assertive, and be in possession of accurate information on which to base our decisions.

Consumer health issues covered in this unit include the increasing number of Americans who travel overseas to combine surgery or medical treatments along with sightseeing. These travelers find that the costs of many treatments are much lower than in the United States. And, they can also seek those treatments that are not yet available back home. During the past few years, nearly half a million Americans went overseas for medical and dental treatment—a number that's expected to rise. Authors Lorene Burkhart and Lorna Gentry discuss this trend in "Medical Tourism: What You Should Know."

In "The Rough Road to *Dreamland*," Michael J. Breus provides an overview on the need for adequate sleep. Since the invention of electric lights, Americans have increasingly gotten by with less sleep. Unfortunately, sleep deprivation is linked to mortality and overall health status.

Another topic of concern is the use of antimicrobial soaps and gels to kill germs. Jerry Adler and Jeneen Interlandi discuss the latest research into the relationship between humans and the microbes that cover their bodies in "Caution: Killing Germs May Be Hazardous to Your Health." Many of these germs are not harmful and some are actually beneficial. Unfortunately, harmful germs are being strengthened by exposure to sanitizers and antibiotics used by a society obsessed with health and hygiene.

While being overweight may increase the risk for certain health problems, how much a person weighs may also affect the quality of health care that they receive. Ginny Graves addresses this issue in "The *Surprising Reason* Why Heavy Isn't Healthy."

Finally, this unit addresses the safety of getting tattooed in "Tattoos: Leaving Their Mark," the risk versus benefit of vaccination in "Vaccine Refusal, Mandatory Immunization, and the Risks of Vaccine-Preventable Diseases," and the adequacy of many health insurance plans in "Hazardous Health Plans."

© Goodshoot/PictureQuest

The health-conscious consumer seeks to be as informed as possible when making dietary and medical decisions—but the best intentions come to no avail when consumers base their decisions on inaccurate information, old beliefs, or media hype that lack a scientific base. Knowledge (based on accurate information) and critical thinking are the key elements required to become proactive in managing our daily health concerns.

Vaccine Refusal, Mandatory Immunization, and the Risks of Vaccine-Preventable Diseases

SAAD B. OMER ET AL.

Vaccines are among the most effective tools available for preventing infectious diseases and their complications and sequelae. High immunization coverage has resulted in drastic declines in vaccine-preventable diseases, particularly in many high- and middle-income countries. A reduction in the incidence of a vaccine-preventable disease often leads to the public perception that the severity of the disease and susceptibility to it have decreased.[1] At the same time, public concern about real or perceived adverse events associated with vaccines has increased. This heightened level of concern often results in an increase in the number of people refusing vaccines.[1,2]

In the United States, policy interventions, such as immunization requirements for school entry, have contributed to high vaccine coverage and record or near-record lows in the levels of vaccine-preventable diseases. Herd immunity, induced by high vaccination rates, has played an important role in greatly reducing or eliminating continual endemic transmission of a number of diseases, thereby benefiting the community overall in addition to the individual vaccinated person.

Recent parental concerns about perceived vaccine safety issues, such as a purported association between vaccines and autism, though not supported by a credible body of scientific evidence,[3-8] have led increasing numbers of parents to refuse or delay vaccination for their children.[9,10] The primary measure of vaccine refusal in the United States is the proportion of children who are exempted from school immunization requirements for nonmedical reasons. There has been an increase in state-level rates of nonmedical exemptions from immunization requirements.[11] In this article, we review the evidentiary basis for school immunization requirements, explore the determinants of vaccine refusal, and discuss the individual and community risks of vaccine-preventable diseases associated with vaccine refusal.

Evolution of U.S. Immunization Requirements

Vaccination was introduced in the United States at the turn of the 19th century. The first U.S. law to require smallpox vaccination was passed soon afterward, in 1809 in Massachusetts, to prevent and control frequent smallpox outbreaks that had substantial health and economic consequences.[12-14] Subsequently, other states enacted similar legislation.[13] Despite the challenges inherent in establishing a reliable and safe vaccine delivery system, vaccination became widely accepted as an effective tool for preventing smallpox through the middle of the 19th century, and the incidence of smallpox declined between 1802 and 1840.[15] In the 1850s, "irregular physicians, the advocates of unorthodox medical theories,"[16] led challenges to vaccination. Vaccine use decreased, and smallpox made a major reappearance in the 1870s.[15] Many states passed new vaccination laws, whereas other states started enforcing existing laws. Increased enforcement of the laws often resulted in increased opposition to vaccination. Several states, including California, Illinois, Indiana, Minnesota, Utah, West Virginia, and Wisconsin, repealed compulsory vaccination laws.[15] Many other states retained them.

In a 1905 landmark case, *Jacobson v. Massachusetts,* which has since served as the foundation for public health laws, the U.S. Supreme Court endorsed the rights of states to pass and enforce compulsory vaccination laws.[17] In 1922, deciding a case filed by a girl excluded from a public school (and later a private school) in San Antonio, Texas, the Supreme Court found school immunization requirements to be constitutional.[18] Since then, courts have been generally supportive of the states' power to enact and implement immunization requirements.

Difficulties with efforts to control measles in the 1960s and 1970s ushered in the modern era of immunization laws in the United States.[12] In 1969, a total of 17 states had laws that required children to be vaccinated against measles before entering school, and 12 states had legally mandated requirements for vaccination against all six diseases for which routine immunization was carried out at the time.[13] During the 1970s, efforts were made to strengthen and strictly enforce immunization laws.[12,13] During measles outbreaks, some state and local health officials excluded from school those students who did not comply with immunization requirements, resulting in minimal backlash, quick improvement in local coverage, and control of outbreaks.[19–22] Efforts by the public health community and other immunization advocates to increase measles vaccine coverage among school-age children resulted in enforcement of immunization requirements for all vaccines and the introduction of such requirements in states that did not already have them. By the beginning of the 1980s, all 50 states had school immunization requirements.

Recent School Immunization Requirements

Because laws concerning immunization are state-based, there are substantial differences in requirements across the country. The requirements from state to state differ in terms of the school grades covered, the vaccines included, the processes and authority used to introduce new vaccines, reasons for exemptions (medical reasons, religious reasons, philosophical or personal beliefs), and the procedures for granting exemptions.[23]

State immunization laws contain provisions for certain exemptions. As of March 2008, all states permitted medical exemptions from school immunization requirements, 48 states allowed religious exemptions, and 21 states allowed exemptions based on philosophical or personal beliefs.[23] Several states (New York, Arkansas, and Texas) have recently expanded eligibility for exemptions.

Secular and Geographic Trends in Immunization Refusal

Between 1991 and 2004, the mean state-level rate of nonmedical exemptions increased from 0.98 to 1.48%. The increase in exemption rates was not uniform.[11] Exemption rates for states that allowed only religious exemptions remained at approximately 1% between 1991 and 2004; however, in states that allowed exemptions for philosophical or personal beliefs, the mean exemption rate increased from 0.99 to 2.54%.[11]

Like any average, the mean exemption rate presents only part of the picture, since geographic clustering of nonmedical exemptions can result in local accumulation of a critical mass of susceptible children that increases the risk of outbreaks. There is evidence of substantial geographic heterogeneity in nonmedical-exemption rates between and within states.[24] For example, in the period from 2006 through 2007, the state-level nonmedical-exemption rate in Washington was 6%; however, the county-level rate ranged from 1.2 to 26.9%.[25] In a spatial analysis of Michigan's exemption data according to census tracts, 23 statistically significant clusters of increased exemptions were identified.[26] Similar heterogeneity in exemption rates has been identified in Oregon[27] and California (unpublished data).

The reasons for the geographic clustering of exemptions from school vaccination requirements are not fully understood, but they may include characteristics of the local population (e.g., cultural issues, socioeconomic status, or educational level), the beliefs of local health care providers and opinion leaders (e.g., clergy and politicians), and local media coverage. The factors known to be associated with exemption rates are heterogeneity in school policies[28] and the beliefs of school personnel who are responsible for compliance with the immunization requirements.[29]

Instead of refusing vaccines, some parents delay vaccination of their children.[30–32] Many parents follow novel vaccine schedules proposed by individual physicians (rather than those developed by expert committees with members representing multiple disciplines).[32,33] Most novel schedules involve administering vaccines over a longer period than that recommended by the Advisory Committee on Immunization Practices and the American Academy of Pediatrics or skipping the administration of some vaccines.

Individual Risk and Vaccine Refusal

Children with nonmedical exemptions are at increased risk for acquiring and transmitting vaccine-preventable diseases.[34,35] In a retrospective cohort study based on nationwide surveillance data from 1985 through 1992, children with exemptions were 35 times as likely to contract measles as nonexempt children (relative risk, 35; 95% confidence interval [CI], 34 to 37).[34] In a retrospective cohort study in Colorado based on data for the years 1987 through 1998, children with exemptions, as compared with unvaccinated children, were 22 times as likely to have had measles (relative risk, 22.2; 95% CI, 15.9 to 31.1) and almost six times as likely to have had pertussis (relative risk, 5.9; 95% CI, 4.2 to 8.2).[35] Earlier data showed that lower incidences of measles and mumps were associated with the existence and enforcement of immunization requirements for school entry.[12,36–38]

The consequences of delayed vaccination, as compared with vaccine refusal, have not been studied in detail. However, it is known that the risk of vaccine-preventable diseases and the risk of sequelae from vaccine-preventable diseases are not constant throughout childhood. Young children are often at increased risk for illness and death related to infectious diseases, and vaccine delays may leave them vulnerable at ages with a high risk of contracting several vaccine-preventable diseases. Moreover, novel vaccine schedules that recommend administering vaccines over a longer period may exacerbate health inequities, since parents with high socioeconomic status are more likely to make the extra visits required under the alternative schedules than parents with low socioeconomic status.[39]

Clustering of Vaccine Refusals and Community Risk

Multiple studies have shown an increase in the local risk of vaccine-preventable diseases when there is a geographic aggregation of persons refusing vaccination. In Michigan, significant overlap between geographic clusters of nonmedical exemptions and pertussis clusters was documented.[26] The odds ratio for the likelihood that a census tract included in a pertussis cluster would also be included in an exemptions cluster was 2.7 (95% CI, 2.5 to 3.6) after adjustment for demographic factors.

In Colorado, the county-level incidence of measles and pertussis in vaccinated children from 1987 through 1998 was associated with the frequency of exemptions in that county.[35] At least 11% of the nonexempt children who acquired measles were infected through contact with an exempt child.[35] Moreover, school-based outbreaks in Colorado have been associated with increased exemption rates; the mean exemption rate among schools with outbreaks was 4.3%, as compared with 1.5% for the schools that did not have an outbreak (P = 0.001).[35]

High vaccine coverage, particularly at the community level, is extremely important for children who cannot be vaccinated, including children who have medical contraindications to vaccination and those who are too young to be vaccinated. These groups are often more susceptible to the complications of infectious diseases than the general population of children and depend on the protection provided by the vaccination of children in their environs.[40–42]

Vaccine Refusal and the Recent Increase in Measles Cases

Measles vaccination has been extremely successful in controlling a disease that previously contributed to considerable morbidity and mortality. In the United States, the reported number of cases dropped from an average of 500,000 annually in the era before vaccination (with reported cases considered to be a fraction of the estimated total, which was more than 2 million) to a mean of 62 cases per year from 2000 through 2007.[43–45] Between January 1, 2008, and April 25, 2008, there were five measles outbreaks and a total of 64 cases reported.[45] All but one of the persons with measles were either unvaccinated or did not have evidence of immunization. Of the 21 cases among children and adolescents in the vaccine-eligible age group (16 months to 19 years) with a known reason for nonvaccination, 14, or 67%, had obtained a nonmedical exemption and all of the 10 school-age children had obtained a nonmedical exemption.[45] Thirteen cases occurred in children too young to be vaccinated, and in more than a third of the cases (18 of 44) occurring in a known transmission setting the disease was acquired in a health care facility.[45]

Outbreaks of vaccine-preventable disease often start among persons who refused vaccination, spread rapidly within unvaccinated populations, and also spread to other subpopulations. For example, of the four outbreaks with discrete index cases (one outbreak occurred by means of multiple importations) reported January through April 2008, three out of four index cases occurred in people who had refused vaccination due to personal beliefs; vaccination status could not be verified for the remaining cases.[45,46] In Washington State, a recent outbreak of measles occurred between April 12, 2008, and May 30, 2008, involving 19 cases. All of the persons with measles were unimmunized with the exception of the last case, a person who had been vaccinated. Of the other 18 cases, 1 was an infant who was

too young to be vaccinated, 2 were younger than 4 years of age, and the remaining 15 were of school age (unpublished data).

Who Refuses Vaccines and Why

Using data from the National Immunization Survey for the period from 1995 through 2001, Smith et al. compared the characteristics of children between the ages of 19 and 35 months who did not receive any vaccine (unvaccinated) with the characteristics of those who were partially vaccinated (undervaccinated).[47] As compared with the undervaccinated children, the unvaccinated children were more likely to be male, to be white, to belong to households with higher income, to have a married mother with a college education, and to live with four or more children.[47] Other studies have shown that children who are unvaccinated are likely to belong to families that intentionally refuse vaccines, whereas children who are undervaccinated are likely to have missed some vaccinations because of factors related to the health care system or sociodemographic characteristics.[48–51]

In a case–control study of the knowledge, attitudes, and beliefs of parents of exempt children as compared with parents of vaccinated children, respondents rated their views of their children's vulnerability to specific diseases, the severity of these diseases, and the efficacy and safety of the specific vaccines available for them. Composite scores were created on the basis of these vaccine-specific responses. As compared with parents of vaccinated children, significantly more parents of exempt children thought their children had a low susceptibility to the diseases (58% vs. 15%, P < 0.05), that the severity of the diseases was low (51% vs. 18%, P < 0.05), and that the efficacy and safety of the vaccines was low (54% vs. 17% for efficacy and 60% vs. 15% for safety, P < 0.05 for both comparisons).[52] Moreover, parents of exempt children were more likely than parents of vaccinated children both to have providers who offered complementary or alternative health care and to obtain information from the Internet and groups opposed to aspects of immunization.[52] The most frequent reason for nonvaccination, stated by 69% of the parents, was concern that the vaccine might cause harm.[52]

Other studies have also reported the importance of parents' concerns about vaccine safety when they decide against vaccination.[53–56] A national survey of parents from 2001 through 2002 showed that although only 1% of respondents thought vaccines were unsafe, the children of these parents were almost three times as likely to not be up to date on recommended vaccinations as the children of parents who thought that vaccines were safe.[54] In a separate case–control study with a national sample, underimmunization was associated with negative perceptions of vaccine safety (odds ratio, 2.0; 95% CI, 1.2 to 3.4).[55] And in another case–control study, Bardenheier et al. found that although concerns regarding general vaccine safety did not differ between the parents of vaccinated children and the parents of undervaccinated or unvaccinated children, more than half of the case and control parents did express concerns about vaccine safety to their child's health care provider.[57] Moreover, parents of undervaccinated or unvaccinated children were more likely to believe that children receive too many vaccines.[57]

The Role of Health Care Providers

Clinicians and other health care providers play a crucial role in parental decision making with regard to immunization. Health care providers are cited by parents, including parents of unvaccinated children, as the most frequent source of information about vaccination.[52]

In a study of the knowledge, attitudes, and practices of primary care providers, a high proportion of those providing care for children whose parents have refused vaccination and those providing care for appropriately vaccinated children were both found to have favorable opinions of vaccines.[58] However, those providing care for unvaccinated children were less likely to have confidence in vaccine safety (odds ratio, 0.37; 95% CI, 0.19 to 0.72) and less likely to perceive vaccines as benefitting individuals and communities.[58] Moreover, there was overlap between clinicians' unfavorable opinions of vaccines and the likelihood that they had unvaccinated children in their practice.[58]

There is evidence that health care providers have a positive overall effect on parents' decision making with regard to vaccination of their children. In a study by Smith et al., parents who reported that their immunization decisions were influenced by their child's health care provider were almost twice as likely to consider vaccines safe as parents who said their decisions were not influenced by the provider.[59]

In focus-group discussions, several parents who were not certain about vaccinating their child were willing to discuss their immunization concerns with a health care provider and wanted the provider to offer information relevant to their specific concerns.[56] These findings highlight the critical role that clinicians can play in explaining the benefits of immunization and addressing parental concerns about its risks.

Clinicians' Response to Vaccine Refusal

Some clinicians have discontinued or have considered discontinuing their provider relationship with families that refuse vaccines.[60,61] In a national survey of members of the American Academy of Pediatrics, almost 40% of respondents said they would not provide care to a family that refused all vaccines, and 28% said they would not provide care to a family that refused some vaccines.[61]

The academy's Committee on Bioethics advises against discontinuing care for families that decline vaccines and has recommended that pediatricians "share honestly what is and is not known about the risks and benefits of the vaccine in question."[62] The committee also recommends that clinicians address vaccine refusal by respectfully listening to parental concerns, explaining the risk of nonimmunization, and discussing the specific vaccines that are of most concern to parents.[62] The committee advises against more serious action in a majority of cases: "Continued refusal after adequate discussion should be respected unless the child is put at significant risk of serious harm (e.g., as might be the case during an epidemic). Only then should state agencies be involved to override parental discretion on the basis of medical neglect."[62]

Policy-Level Determinants of Vaccine Refusal

Immunization requirements and the policies that ensure compliance with the requirements vary considerably among the states; these variations have been associated with state-level exemption rates.[11,63] For example, the complexity of procedures for obtaining exemption has been shown to be inversely associated with rates of exemption.[63] Moreover, between 1991 and 2004, the mean annual incidence of pertussis was almost twice as high in states with administrative procedures that made it easy to obtain exemptions as in states that made it difficult.[11]

One possible way to balance individual rights and the greater public good with respect to vaccination would be to institute and broaden administrative controls. For example, a model law proposed for Arkansas suggested that parents seeking nonmedical exemptions be provided with counseling on the hazards of refusing vaccination.[64]

States also differ in terms of meeting the recommendations for age-appropriate coverage for children younger than 2 years of age.[65] School immunization requirements ensure completion by the time of school entry, but they do not directly influence the timeliness of vaccination among preschoolers. However, there is some evidence that school immunization laws have an indirect effect on preschool vaccine coverage. For example, varicella vaccine was introduced in the United States in 1995 and has played an important role in reducing the incidence of chickenpox.[66] In 2000, states that had implemented mandatory immunization for varicella by the time of school entry had coverage among children 19 to 35 months old that was higher than the average for all states. Having an immunization requirement could be an indicator of the effectiveness of a state's immunization program, but the effect of school-based requirements on coverage among preschoolers cannot be completely discounted.

Conclusions

Vaccine refusal not only increases the individual risk of disease but also increases the risk for the whole community. As a result of substantial gains in reducing vaccine-preventable diseases, the memory of several infectious diseases has faded from the public consciousness and the risk–benefit calculus seems to have shifted in favor of the perceived risks of vaccination in some parents' minds. Major reasons for vaccine refusal in the United States are parental perceptions and concerns about vaccine safety and a low level of concern about the risk of many vaccine-preventable diseases. If the enormous benefits to society from vaccination are to be maintained, increased efforts will be needed to educate the public about those benefits and to increase public confidence in the systems we use to monitor and ensure vaccine safety. Since clinicians have an influence on parental decision making, it is important that they understand the benefits and risks of vaccines and anticipate questions that parents may have about safety. There are a number of sources of information on vaccines that should be useful to both clinicians and parents (e.g., Appendix 1 in the fifth edition of *Vaccines,* edited by Plotkin et al.; the list of Web sites on vaccine safety posted on the World Health Organization's Web site; and the Web site of the National Center for Immunization and Respiratory Diseases).[67–69]

References

1. Chen RT, Hibbs B. Vaccine safety: current and future challenges. *Pediatr Ann* 1998;27:445–55.

2. Chen RT, DeStefano F. Vaccine adverse events: causal or coincidental? *Lancet* 1998;351:611–2.

3. DeStefano F. Vaccines and autism: evidence does not support a causal association. *Clin Pharmacol Ther* 2007;82:756–9.

4. Doja A, Roberts W. Immunizations and autism: a review of the literature. *Can J Neurol Sci* 2006;33:341–6.

5. Fombonne E, Cook EH. MMR and autistic enterocolitis: consistent epidemiological failure to find an association. *Mol Psychiatry* 2003;8:133–4.

6. Fombonne E. Thimerosal disappears but autism remains. *Arch Gen Psychiatry* 2008;65:15–6.

7. Schechter R, Grether JK. Continuing increases in autism reported to California's developmental services system: mercury in retrograde. *Arch Gen Psychiatry* 2008;65:19–24.

8. Thompson WW, Price C, Goodson B, et al. Early thimerosal exposure and neuropsychological outcomes at 7 to 10 years. *N Engl J Med* 2007;357:1281–92.

9. Offit PA. Vaccines and autism revisited—the Hannah Poling case. *N Engl J Med* 2008;358:2089–91.

10. Smith MJ, Ellenberg SS, Bell LM, Rubin DM. Media coverage of the measles-mumps-rubella vaccine and autism controversy and its relationship to MMR immunization rates in the United States. *Pediatrics* 2008;121(4):e836–e843.

11. Omer SB, Pan WK, Halsey NA, et al. Nonmedical exemptions to school immunization requirements: secular trends and association of state policies with pertussis incidence. *JAMA* 2006;296:1757–63.

12. Orenstein WA, Hinman AR. The immunization system in the United States—the role of school immunization laws. *Vaccine* 1999;17:Suppl 3:S19–S24.

13. Jackson CL. State laws on compulsory immunization in the United States. *Public Health Rep* 1969;84:787–95.

14. Colgrove J, Bayer R. Could it happen here? Vaccine risk controversies and the specter of derailment. *Health Aff* (Millwood) 2005;24:729–39.

15. Kaufman M. The American anti-vaccinationists and their arguments. *Bull Hist Med* 1967;41:463–78.

16. Stern BJ. Should we be vaccinated? A survey of the controversy in its historical and scientific aspects. New York: Harper & Brothers, 1927:93–109.

17. Jacobson v. Massachusetts, 197 U.S. 11 (1905).

18. Zucht v. King, 260 U.S. 174 (Nov. 13, 1922).

19. Middaugh JP, Zyla LD. Enforcement of school immunization law in Alaska. *JAMA* 1978;239:2128–30.

20. Lovejoy GS, Giandelia JW, Hicks M. Successful enforcement of an immunization law. *Public Health Rep* 1974;89:456–8.

21. Fowinkle EW, Barid S, Bass CM. A compulsory school immunization program in Tennessee. *Public Health Rep* 1981;96:61–6.

22. Measles—Florida, 1981. MMWR Morb Mortal Wkly Rep 1981;30:593–6.

23. Vaccine Exemptions. Johns Hopkins Bloomberg School of Public Health—Institute for Vaccine Safety, 2008. (Accessed April 16, 2009, at www.vaccinesafety.edu/ccexem.htm.)

24. National Center for Immunization and Respiratory Diseases. School and childcare vaccination surveys. May 2007. (Accessed April 13, 2009, at www.cdc.gov/vaccines/stats-surv/schoolsurv/default.htm.)

25. School Status Data Reports. Washington State Department of Health, 2009. (Accessed April 16, 2009, at //www.doh.wa.gov/cfh/Immunize/schools/schooldatarprts.htm.)

26. Omer SB, Enger KS, Moulton LH, Halsey NA, Stokley S, Salmon DA. Geographic clustering of nonmedical exemptions to school immunization requirements and associations with geographic clustering of pertussis. *Am J Epidemiol* 2008;168:1389–96.

27. Attitudes, networking and immunizations in a community with a high rate of religious exemptions. Presented at the 37th National Immunization Conference, Chicago, March 17–20, 2003. abstract.

28. Salmon DA, Omer SB, Moulton LH, et al. Exemptions to school immunization requirements: the role of school-level requirements, policies, and procedures. *Am J Public Health* 2005;95:436–40. [Erratum, Am J Public Health 2005;95:551.]

29. Salmon DA, Moulton LH, Omer SB, et al. Knowledge, attitudes, and beliefs of school nurses and personnel and associations with nonmedical immunization exemptions. *Pediatrics* 2004;113(6):e552–e559.

30. Luman ET, Barker LE, Shaw KM, McCauley MM, Buehler JW, Pickering LK. Timeliness of childhood vaccinations in the United States: days undervaccinated and number of vaccines delayed. *JAMA* 2005;293:1204–11.

31. Luman ET, Shaw KM, Stokley SK. Compliance with vaccination recommendations for U.S. children. *Am J Prev Med* 2008;34:463–70. [Erratum, Am J Prev Med 2008:35:319.]

32. Cohen E. Should I vaccinate my baby? Cable News Network. 2008. (Accessed April 13, 2009, at www.cnn.com/2008/HEALTH/family/06/19/ep.vaccines/index.html.)

33. Sears R. Dr. Bob's blog categories: alternative vaccine schedule. (Accessed April 13, 2009, at http://askdrsears.com/thevaccinebook/labels/Alternative%20Vaccine%20Schedule.asp.)

34. Salmon DA, Haber M, Gangarosa EJ, Phillips L, Smith NJ, Chen RT. Health consequences of religious and philosophical exemptions from immunization laws: individual and societal risk of measles. *JAMA* 1999;282:47–53. [Erratum, JAMA 2000;283:2241.]

35. Feikin DR, Lezotte DC, Hamman RF, Salmon DA, Chen RT, Hoffman RE. Individual and community risks of measles and

pertussis associated with personal exemptions to immunization. *JAMA* 2000;284:3145–50.

36. Measles—Unites States. MMWR Morb Mortal Wkly Rep 1977;26:109–11.

37. Robbins KB, Brandling-Bennett D, Hinman AR. Low measles incidence: association with enforcement of school immunization laws. *Am J Public Health* 1981;71:270–4.

38. van Loon FP, Holmes SJ, Sirotkin BI, et al. Mumps surveillance—United States, 1988–1993. *MMWR CDC Surveill* 1995;44:1–14.

39. Williams IT, Milton JD, Farrell JB, Graham NM. Interaction of socioeconomic status and provider practices as predictors of immunization coverage in Virginia children. *Pediatrics* 1995;96:439–46.

40. Bisgard KM, Pascual FB, Ehresmann KR, et al. Infant pertussis: who was the source? *Pediatr Infect Dis J* 2004;23:985–9.

41. Deen JL, Mink CA, Cherry JD, et al. Household contact study of Bordetella pertussis infections. *Clin Infect Dis* 1995;21:1211–9.

42. Poehling KA, Talbot TR, Griffin MR, et al. Invasive pneumococcal disease among infants before and after introduction of pneumococcal conjugate vaccine. *JAMA* 2006;295:1668–74.

43. Bloch AB, Orenstein WA, Stetler HC, et al. Health impact of measles vaccination in the United States. *Pediatrics* 1985;76:524–32.

44. Orenstein WA, Papania MJ, Wharton ME. Measles elimination in the United States. *J Infect Dis* 2004;189:Suppl 1:S1–S3.

45. Measles—United States, January 1–April 25, 2008. MMWR Morb Mortal Wkly Rep 2008;57:494–8.

46. Update: measles—United States, January–July 2008. MMWR Morb Mortal Wkly Rep 2008;57:893–6.

47. Smith PJ, Chu SY, Barker LE. Children who have received no vaccines: who are they and where do they live? *Pediatrics* 2004;114:187–95.

48. Allred NJ, Wooten KG, Kong Y. The association of health insurance and continuous primary care in the medical home on vaccination coverage for 19- to 35-month-old children. *Pediatrics* 2007;119:Suppl 1:S4–S11.

49. Daniels D, Jiles RB, Klevens RM, Herrera GA. Undervaccinated African-American preschoolers: a case of missed opportunities. *Am J Prev Med* 2001;20:Suppl:61–68.

50. Luman ET, McCauley MM, Shefer A, Chu SY. Maternal characteristics associated with vaccination of young children. *Pediatrics* 2003;111:1215–8.

51. Smith PJ, Santoli JM, Chu SY, Ochoa DQ, Rodewald LE. The association between having a medical home and vaccination coverage among children eligible for the Vaccines for Children program. *Pediatrics* 2005;116:130–9.

52. Salmon DA, Moulton LH, Omer SB, Dehart MP, Stokley S, Halsey NA. Factors associated with refusal of childhood vaccines among parents of school-aged children: a case-control study. *Arch Pediatr Adolesc Med* 2005;159:470–6.

53. Humiston SG, Lerner EB, Hepworth E, Blythe T, Goepp JG. Parent opinions about universal influenza vaccination for infants and toddlers. *Arch Pediatr Adolesc Med* 2005;159:108–12.

54. Allred NJ, Shaw KM, Santibanez TA, Rickert DL, Santoli JM. Parental vaccine safety concerns: results from the National Immunization Survey, 2001–2002. *Am J Prev Med* 2005;28:221–4.

55. Gust DA, Strine TW, Maurice E, et al. Underimmunization among children: effects of vaccine safety concerns on immunization status. *Pediatrics* 2004;114(1):e16–e22.

56. Fredrickson DD, Davis TC, Arnould CL, et al. Childhood immunization refusal: provider and parent perceptions. *Fam Med* 2004;36:431–9.

57. Bardenheier B, Yusuf H, Schwartz B, Gust D, Barker L, Rodewald L. Are parental vaccine safety concerns associated with receipt of measles-mumps-rubella, diphtheria and tetanus toxoids with acellular pertussis, or hepatitis B vaccines by children? *Arch Pediatr Adolesc Med* 2004;158:569–75.

58. Salmon DA, Pan WK, Omer SB, et al. Vaccine knowledge and practices of primary care providers of exempt vs. vaccinated children. *Hum Vaccin* 2008;4:286–91.

59. Smith PJ, Kennedy AM, Wooten K, Gust DA, Pickering LK. Association between health care providers' influence on parents who have concerns about vaccine safety and vaccination coverage. *Pediatrics* 2006;118(5):e1287–e1292.

60. Freed GL, Clark SJ, Hibbs BF, Santoli JM. Parental vaccine safety concerns: the experiences of pediatricians and family physicians. *Am J Prev Med* 2004;26:11–4.

61. Flanagan-Klygis EA, Sharp L, Frader JE. Dismissing the family who refuses vaccines: a study of pediatrician attitudes. *Arch Pediatr Adolesc Med* 2005;159:929–34.

62. Diekema DS. Responding to parental refusals of immunization of children. *Pediatrics* 2005;115:1428–31.

63. Rota JS, Salmon DA, Rodewald LE, Chen RT, Hibbs BF, Gangarosa EJ. Processes for obtaining nonmedical exemptions to state immunization laws. *Am J Public Health* 2001;91:645–8.

64. Salmon DA, Siegel AW. Religious and philosophical exemptions from vaccination requirements and lessons learned from conscientious objectors from conscription. *Public Health Rep* 2001;116:289–95.

65. Luman ET, Barker LE, McCauley MM, Drews-Botsch C. Timeliness of childhood immunizations: a state-specific analysis. *Am J Public Health* 2005;95:1367–74.

66. Seward JF, Watson BM, Peterson CL, et al. Varicella disease after introduction of varicella vaccine in the United States, 1995–2000. *JAMA* 2002;287:606–11.

67. Wexler DL, Anderson TA. Websites that contain information about immunization. In: Plotkin S, Orenstein WA, Offit PA, eds. Vaccines. 5th ed. Philadelphia: Saunders, 2008:1685–90.

68. Vaccine safety websites meeting credibility and content good information practices criteria. Geneva: World Health Organization, September 2008.

69. National Center for Immunization and Respiratory Diseases. Centers for Disease Control and Prevention, 2009. (Accessed April 16, 2009, at www.cdc.gov/ncird/.)

Assess Your Progress

1. Is vaccination more dangerous than getting the disease prevented by the vaccine?

2. Why do some parents refuse to have their children vaccinated? Are their reasons valid?

From the Hubert Department of Global Health, Rollins School of Public Health (S.B.O.), and the Emory Vaccine Center (S.B.O., W.A.O.), Emory University, Atlanta; the Department of International Health (S.B.O., D.A.S., N.H.) and the Institute for Vaccine Safety (N.H.), Johns Hopkins Bloomberg School of Public Health, Baltimore; the National Vaccine Program Office, Department of Health and Human Services, Washington, DC (D.A.S.); and Maternal and Child Health Assessment, Washington State Department of Health, Olympia (M.P.D.). Address reprint requests to Dr. Omer at the Hubert Department of Global Health, Rollins School of Public Health, Emory University, 1518 Clifton Rd. NE, Atlanta, GA 30322, or at somer@emory.edu.

Dr. Salmon reports serving on the Merck Vaccine Policy Advisory Board; Dr. Orenstein, receiving research funds from Novartis, Merck, and Sanofi Pasteur and a training grant from the Merck Foundation and serving on data and safety monitoring boards associated with GlaxoSmithKline and Encorium; and Dr. Halsey, receiving research funds from Wyeth and Berna, lecture fees from Sanofi, and payments for testimony to the Department of Justice regarding several vaccine compensation cases and serving on data and safety monitoring committees associated with Novartis and Merck. No other potential conflict of interest relevant to this article was reported.

We thank Tina Proveaux of the Johns Hopkins Bloomberg School of Public Health for reviewing an earlier version of the manuscript and Dr. Jane Seward of the Centers for Disease Control and Prevention for providing input on new measles cases.

Medical Tourism: What You Should Know

From international outsourcing to in-home visits, doctors and patients are reinventing the way medicine is viewed and practiced at home and around the world.

LORENE BURKHART AND LORNA GENTRY

In 2006, West Virginia lawmaker Ray Canterbury made headlines across the country when he introduced House Bill 4359, which would allow enrollees in the state government's health plan to travel to foreign countries for surgery and other medical services. In fact, not only would the bill allow for such a choice, it encourages it; those choosing to go to an approved foreign clinic for a procedure covered by the plan would have all of their medical and travel expenses (including those of one companion) paid, plus be given 20 percent of the savings they racked up by having the procedure done overseas, rather than here at home.

Canterbury's bill drew attention to a growing international boom in medical tourism—an industry with special appeal for many of America's 61 million uninsured or underinsured citizens. At prices as much as 80 to 90 percent lower than those here, hospitals in countries such as Costa Rica, Thailand, India, and the Philippines offer a wide range of healthcare procedures in accommodations equal to or even better than their American counterparts. Some estimate that 500,000 Americans went overseas for medical treatment in 2006 alone, and that medical tourism could become a $40 billion industry by 2010.

Overseas Surgery? What You Should Know

According to Canterbury and other proponents of medical service outsourcing, the idea is all about competition. Proponents believe the rate of healthcare inflation in this country, at almost four times the rate of overall inflation, has placed an unsustainable burden on the American economy.

"The best way to solve this problem is to rely on market forces," Canterbury writes. "My bills are designed to force domestic healthcare companies to compete for our business."

It's hard to argue with the economics of medical outsourcing. According to MedicalTourism.com, the cost of typical heart bypass surgery in the United States is $130,000. The same operation is estimated to cost approximately $10,000 in India, $11,000 in Thailand, and $18,500 in Singapore. A $43,000 hip replacement in an American hospital could be performed for $9,000 in India, or for $12,000 in either Thailand or Singapore. Even adding the costs of travel and lodging, consumers stand to save real money by traveling overseas for these and many other types of routine surgery, including angioplasties, knee replacements, and hysterectomies.

Of course, many people have serious concerns about the idea of shopping overseas for invasive medical procedures. What about the quality of the service? Follow up care? And what happens if something goes terribly wrong?. Those backing the business—including employers and lawmakers desperately seeking ways to cut the cost of employer-sponsored medical care—are quick to answer these concerns.

Most of the foreign medical facilities courting Western tourists are state-of-the-art facilities that offer luxurious accommodations and individual around-the-clock nursing attention. Thailand's Bumrungrad Hospital, for example, offers five-star hotel quality rooms, a lobby that includes Starbucks and other restaurants, valet parking, an international staff and interpreters, a travel agent, visa desk, and a meet-and-greet service at Bangkok's Suvarnabhumi Airport. In a 2007 report broadcast on NPR, an American woman told how when her doctor in Alaska announced that she needed double knee replacements at a cost of $100,000, she replied that she couldn't afford the treatment. Her doctor recommended that she wait four years, when she would be eligible for Medicare. Instead, the woman opted for treatment at Bumrungrad, where the two knee replacements cost $20,000 (including the services of two physicians, an anesthesiologist, and physical therapy), and she was able to recover in the hospital's luxurious surroundings with her husband at her side. Her husband, who underwent surgery in the United States the previous year, couldn't believe the amount of attention his wife received from her doctors and nurses, whom he said were in almost constant attendance.

Why is all of this lavish treatment and high-quality care so much cheaper abroad than here? We only need to look at all of the other services the United States has outsourced in the past decade to find the first part of the answer to that question: In places like Thailand and India—two popular destinations for cardiac, orthopedic, and cosmetic surgery—salaries are much lower than in the United States. Further, most services are provided under one roof, and patients select and pay for their medical services up front—no insurance billing. Medical malpractice liability insurance and claims caps in some foreign countries also help keep costs down.

But how safe are foreign medical facilities? Bumrungrad Hospital is accredited by the Joint Commission International (the same organization that accredits U.S. hospitals) and has over 200 U.S. board-certified physicians. And that hospital isn't unique in the world of international medicine. Increasing numbers of medical tourism facilities are staffed by American- and European-trained physicians and backed by well-funded research facilities. Dubai, already a luxury travel destination, is preparing to enter the business of international medical practice and research in a very serious way. Its 4.1 million square-foot Dubai Healthcare City is slated to open in 2010 and will offer academic medical research facilities, disease treatment, and wellness services backed by the oversight of a number of international partners, including a new department of the Harvard School of Medicine.

Good News for Patients Might Be Bad News for U.S. Hospitals

Most baby boomers love to travel, and many are only too happy to combine foreign travel experiences with low-cost and high-value medical procedures. And many insurance companies are eyeing medical outsourcing, too, as a way to cut costs for both enrollees and their employers. Blue Cross/Blue Shield of South Carolina, for example, has begun working with Bumrungrad to provide overseas alternatives for healthcare to its members.

Of course, one or two horrific medical mishaps alone could seriously damage the medical tourism industry. Most foreign countries don't support malpractice litigation to the extent that we do in the United States, and fears of the "what ifs" are keeping many private individuals and organizations from plunging in until they have a few more years to observe the medical outsourcing industry in action. For now, however, foreign medical facilities are eager to maintain standards high enough to avoid any claims of malpractice. And many Americans with our fondness for bargains and luxury are more than willing to give those facilities an opportunity to prove their worth.

Medical tourism is good news for patients, but it could pose consequences for America's already-ailing hospital system. If patients travel to foreign lands to avoid pricey surgeries at home, what kind of financial "hit" will American hospitals face? At 2007's International Medical Tourism Conference in Las Vegas, hospital physicians and administrators from around the globe gathered to discuss the issues surrounding medical tourism and its impact on the healthcare industry. In an interview about the conference, Sparrow Mahoney, chief executive officer of MedicalTourism.com and conference co-chair, admitted that American medical facilities are now in direct competition with their foreign competitors. "Hospitals will feel a pinch," she said.

Yes, We Make House Calls

All of us have experienced the frustrating and sometimes frightening wait for medical care that we desperately need. We have a raging fever and are told that the doctor can see us in three days. If we choose instead to go to the emergency room of a nearby hospital, we may wait for hours in a roomful of equally ill and distressed people with their impatient spouses, parents, or screaming children, and the constant chiming of cell phones. If our doctor agrees to "work us in," we're faced with an only slightly less daunting process, requiring what might be an hour or so wait. When we finally see a doctor, we're rushed through a few minutes of evaluation, given a prescription, and sent on our way—typically worn out and much worse for the wear of the experience.

But many Americans are opting out of this tribal experience and choosing instead to pay an annual fee (typically, $3,000 to $30,000 above insurance costs) to retain the personalized, private care of a family physician. The "boutique" healthcare movement began in the early 1990s in Seattle, Washington, and has since spread to urban areas around the nation. Instead of waiting days, weeks, or even months for an appointment that fits the doctor's schedule, members of these plans schedule medical visits at their convenience.

Need a house call? Not a problem with most boutique or "concierge" plans. Members have their doctor's cell phone number and can simply call to arrange for the doctor to come to their home. If a plan member needs to see a specialist or go to the emergency room, he or she is accompanied by a plan physician—and no rushing through appointments.

Although many primary care physicians have caseloads of as many as 3,000 to 5,000 patients, doctors in boutique plans might have no more than a few hundred patients under their care; Seattle retainer medicine pioneer MD^2 (pronounced "MD Squared") limits its doctor loads to no greater than 50 patients.

Some retainer plans require that members also carry insurance, while others refuse to process insurance payments at all. In a 2005 report on boutique medicine by CBS5 News in California, one doctor complained that he had lost patience with insurance companies that require reams of tedious paperwork and billing regulations, then reimburse at 20 percent of his billing rate. "I went to medical school to be a doctor and take care of patients," says Dr. Jordan Shlain of the San Francisco group On Call. "I didn't take one class on billings, on insurance company shenanigans and the HMO grip."

Although some concierge medical services charge fees aimed squarely at the middle class, most admit that their fees put them out of the range of many people. FirstLine Personal Health Care, in Indianapolis, charges members an annual retainer of a few thousand dollars in return for 24-hour access to one of the plan's doctors, unlimited office visits, and a small keychain hard drive loaded with their medical records. Even though their fees are modest in comparison with some concierge medical services, FirstLine doctors Kevin McCallum and Timothy Story know that many patients they saw prior to forming the service won't be able to afford membership.

Like other doctors around the country, however, McCallum and Story believe that retainer medicine offers the only option for family medicine doctors trying to escape the grinding demands of escalating practice costs and patient caseloads. With many family physicians around the country retiring early and medical students avoiding the low pay and high demands of a typical family practice, retainer-fee medical groups might be the most viable way to keep the "good old family doctor" in business.

We have yet to see what will happen when the average American is financially excluded from most family medicine clinics and groups—a fate that may occur in the not-so-distant future. Dr. Kevin Grumbach of the University of California at San Francisco was in family practice for more than 20 years and now worries that the rush to boutique medical services is threatening our nation's system of medical care.

"I have grave concerns," he told the CBS5 news reporter, "that . . . we are as a profession abandoning the need of the vast majority of Americans . . . . It's the middle class people that are increasingly left behind in an increasingly inequitable system."

Assess Your Progress

1. What is medical tourism?
2. Distinguish between the risks and benefits of medical tourism.

Caution: Killing Germs May Be Hazardous to Your Health

Our war on microbes has toughened them. Now, new science tells us we should embrace bacteria.

JERRY ADLER AND JENEEN INTERLANDI

Behold yourself, for a moment, as an organism. A trillion cells stuck together, arrayed into tissues and organs and harnessed by your DNA to the elemental goals of survival and propagation. But is that all? An electron microscope would reveal that you are teeming with other life-forms. Any part of your body that comes into contact with the outside world—your skin, mouth, nose and (especially) digestive tract—is home to bacteria, fungi and protozoa that outnumber the cells you call your own by 10, or perhaps a hundred, to one.

Their ancestors began colonizing you the moment you came into the world, inches from the least sanitary part of your mother's body, and their descendants will have their final feast on your corpse, and join you in death. There are thousands of different species, found in combinations "as unique as our DNA or our fingerprints," says Stanford biologist David Relman, who is investigating the complex web of interactions microbes maintain with our digestive, immune and nervous systems. Where do you leave off, and they begin? Microbes, Relman holds, are "a part of who we are."

Relman is a leader in rethinking our relationship to bacteria, which for most of the last century was dominated by the paradigm of Total Warfare. "It's awful the way we treat our microbes," he says, not intending a joke; "people still think the only good microbe is a dead one." We try to kill them off with antibiotics and hand sanitizers. But bacteria never surrender; if there were one salmonella left in the world, doubling every 30 minutes, it would take less than a week to give everyone alive diarrhea. In the early years of antibiotics, doctors dreamed of eliminating infectious disease. Instead, a new paper in The Journal of the American Medical Association reports on the prevalence of Methicillin-resistant Staphylococcus aureus (MRSA), which was responsible for almost 19,000 deaths in the United States in 2005—about twice as many as previously thought, and more than AIDS. Elizabeth Bancroft, a leading epidemiologist, called this finding "astounding."

As antibiotics lose their effectiveness, researchers are returning to an idea that dates back to Pasteur, that the body's natural microbial flora aren't just an incidental fact of our biology, but crucial components of our health, intimate companions on an evolutionary journey that began millions of years ago. The science writer Jessica Snyder Sachs summarizes this view in four words in the title of her ground-breaking new book: "Good Germs, Bad Germs." Our microbes do us the favor of synthesizing vitamins right in our guts; they regulate our immune systems and even our serotonin levels: germs, it seems, can make us happy. They influence how we digest our food, how much we eat and even what we crave. The genetic factors in weight control might reside partly in their genes, not ours. Regrettably, it turns out that bacteria exhibit a strong preference for making us fat.

Our well-meaning war on microbes has, by the relentless process of selection, toughened them instead. When penicillin began to lose its effectiveness against staph, doctors turned to methicillin, but then MRSA appeared—first as an opportunistic infection among people already hospitalized, now increasingly a wide-ranging threat that can strike almost anyone. The strain most commonly contracted outside hospitals, dubbed USA300, comes armed with the alarming ability to attack immune-system cells. Football players seem to be especially vulnerable: they get scraped and bruised and share equipment while engaging in prolonged exercise, which some researchers believe temporarily lowers immunity. In the last five years outbreaks have plagued the Cleveland Browns, the University of Texas and the University of Southern California, where trainers now disinfect equipment almost hourly. The JAMA article was a boon to makers of antimicrobial products, of which about 200 have been introduced in the United States so far this year. Press releases began deluging newsrooms, touting the benefits of antibacterial miracle compounds ranging from silver to honey. Charles Gerba, a professor of environmental microbiology at the University of Arizona, issued an ominous warning that teenagers were catching MRSA by sharing cell phones. Gerba is a consultant to the makers of Purell hand sanitizer, Clorox bleach and the Oreck antibacterial vacuum cleaner, which uses ultraviolet light to kill germs on your rug.

To be sure, MRSA is a scary infection, fast-moving and tricky to diagnose. Hunter Spence, a 12-year-old cheerleader from Victoria, Texas, woke up one Sunday in May with pain in her left leg. "I think I pulled a calf muscle," she told her mother, Peyton. By the next day, the pain was much worse and she was running a low-grade fever, but there was no other sign of infection. A doctor thought she might have the flu. By Wednesday her fever was 103 and the leg pain was unbearable. But doctors at two different community hospitals couldn't figure out what was wrong until Friday, when a blood culture came up positive for MRSA. By the time she arrived at Driscoll Children's Hospital in Corpus Christi—by helicopter—her temperature was 107 and her pulse 220. Doctors put her chance of survival at 20 percent.

Hunter needed eight operations over the next week to drain her infections, and an intravenous drip of two powerful new antibiotics, Zyvox and Cubicin. She did survive, and is home now, but her lung capacity is at 35 percent of normal. "We are seeing more infections, and more severe infections" with the USA300 strain, says Dr. Jaime Fergie, who treated her at Driscoll. In many cases, there's no clue as to how the infection was contracted, but a study Fergie did in 2005 of 350 children who were seen at Driscoll for unrelated conditions found that 21 percent of them were carrying MRSA, mostly in their noses. Then all it may take is a cut . . . and an unwashed hand.

And there are plenty of unwashed hands out there; Gerba claims that only one in five of us does the job properly, getting in all the spaces between the fingers and under the nails and rubbing for at least 20 seconds. Americans have been obsessed with eradicating germs ever since their role in disease was discovered in the 19th century, but they've been partial to technological fixes like antibiotics or sanitizers rather than the dirty work of cleanliness. Nancy Tomes, author of "The Gospel of Germs," believes the obsession waxes and wanes in response to social anxiety—about diseases such as anthrax, SARS or avian flu, naturally, but also about issues like terrorism or immigration that bear a metaphoric relationship to infection. "I can't protect myself from bin Laden, but I can rid myself of germs," she says. "Guarding against microbes is something Americans turn to when they're stressed." The plastic squeeze bottle of alcohol gel, which was introduced by Purell in 1997, is a powerful talisman of security. Sharon Morrison, a Dallas real-estate broker with three young daughters, estimates she has as many as 10 going at any time, in her house, her car, her purse, her office and her kids' backpacks. She swabs her grocery cart with sanitizing wipes and, when her children were younger, she would bring her own baby-seat cover from home and her own place mats to restaurants. Sales of Purell last year were $90 million, so she's clearly not alone. There's no question it kills germs, although it's not a substitute for washing; the Centers for Disease Control website notes that alcohol can't reach germs through a layer of dirt. Alcohol gels, which kill germs by drying them out, don't cause the kind of resistance that gives rise to superbugs like

Bacteria's Base

By the time you turn 2, microbes have colonized every inch of your body. Some regions are more densely populated than others.

Sharing Intelligence

How resistant bacteria spreads:

1. **Armed:** Some bacteria—but not all—carry extra genes that make them resistant to certain antibiotics.
2. **Dangerous Liaisons:** They can pass on these resistant genes by connecting to their nonresistant neighbors through a protein tube.
3. **Building Ranks:** As antibiotics kill off the vulnerable bacteria, the resistant ones thrive, and continue to pass their genes along.

The Hiding Places

The Mouth is made up of dozens of distinct microbial neighborhoods. Each tooth has its own species and strains.

The Appendix is now thought to be stockpiling gut microbes to replenish your intestine in the event of an illness.

The Gut houses more microbes than all other body parts combined. These bugs aid digestion and produce nutrients.

The Groin supplies most people with their first microbial residents, acquired as you pass through the birth canal.

The Skin is covered in different species of friendly staphylococcus that may help keep infectious strains from getting in.

Hospitalized by Staph

Methicillin-resistant Staphylococcus aureus hospital stays, 1993–2005

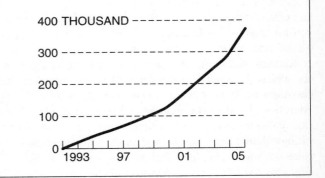

MRSA. But they're part of the culture of cleanliness that's led to a different set of problems.

In terms of infectious disease, the environment of the American suburb is unquestionably a far healthier place than most of the rest of the world. But we've made a Faustian bargain with our antibiotics, because most researchers now believe that our supersanitized world exacts a unique price in allergies, asthma and autoimmune diseases, most of which were unknown to our ancestors. Sachs warns that many people drew precisely the wrong conclusion from this, that contracting a lot of diseases in childhood is somehow beneficial. What we need is more exposure to the good microbes, and the job of medicine in the years to come will be sorting out the good microbes from the bad.

That's the goal of the Human Microbiome Project, a five-year multinational study that its advocates say could tell us almost as much about life as the recently completed work of sequencing the human genome. One puzzling result of the Human Genome Project was the paltry number of genes it found—about 20,000, which is only as many as it takes to make a fruit fly. Now some researchers think some of the "missing" genes may be found in the teeming populations of microbes we host.

And the microbe project—which as a first step requires sampling every crevice and orifice of 100 people of varying ages from a variety of climates and cultures—is "infinitely more complex and problematic than the genome," laments (or boasts) one of its lead researchers, Martin Blaser of NYU Medical School. Each part of the body is a separate ecosystem, and even two teeth in the same mouth can be colonized by different bacteria. In general, researchers know what they'll find— *Escherechia* (including the ubiquitous microbial Everyman, *E. coli*) in the bowel, lactobacilli in the vagina and staphylococcus on the skin. But the mix of particular species and strains will probably turn out to be unique to each individual, a product of chance, gender (men and women have different microbes on their skin but are similar in their intestines) and socioeconomic status and culture. (Race seems not to matter much.) Once the microbes establish themselves they stay for life and fight off newcomers; a broad-spectrum antibiotic may kill most of them but the same kinds usually come back after a few weeks. The most intriguing question is how microbes interact with each other and with our own cells. "There is a three-way conversation going on throughout our bodies," says Jane Peterson of the National Human Genome Research Institute. "We want to listen in because we think it will fill in a lot of blanks about human health—and human disease."

The vast majority of human microbes live in the digestive tract; they get there by way of the mouth in the first few months of life, before stomach acid builds to levels that are intended to kill most invaders. The roiling, fetid and apparently useless contents of the large intestine were a moral affront to doctors in the early years of modern medicine, who sought to cleanse them from the body with high-powered enemas. But to microbiologists, the intestinal bacteria are a marvel, a virtual organ of the body which just happens to have its own DNA. Researchers at Duke University claim it explains the persistence of the human appendix. It serves, they say, as a reservoir of beneficial microbes which can recolonize the gut after it's emptied by diseases such as cholera or dysentery.

Microbes play an important role in digestion, especially of polysaccharides, starch molecules found in foods such as potatoes or rice that may be hundreds or thousands of atoms long. The stomach and intestines secrete 99 different enzymes for breaking these down into usable 6-carbon sugars, but the humble gut-dwelling *Bacterioides theta* produces almost 250, substantially increasing the energy we can extract from a given meal.

Of course, "energy" is another way of saying "calories." Jeffrey Gordon of the University of Washington raised a colony of mice in sterile conditions, with no gut microbes at all, and although they ate 30 percent more food than normal mice they had less than half the body fat. When they were later inoculated with normal bacteria, they quickly gained back up to normal weight. "We are finding that the nutritional value of food is pretty individualized," Gordon says. "And a big part of what determines it is our microbial composition."

We can't raise humans in sterile labs, of course, but there's evidence that variations between people in their intestinal microbes correspond to differences in body composition. And other factors appear to be at work besides the ability to extract calories from starch. Bacteria seem able to adjust levels of the hormones ghrelin and leptin, which regulate appetite and metabolism. Certain microbes even seem to be associated with a desire for chocolate, according to research by the Nestlé Research Center. And a tiny study suggests that severe emotional stress in some people triggers an explosion in the population of *B. theta,* the starch-digesting bacteria associated with weight gain. That corresponds to folk wisdom about "stress eating," but it is also a profoundly disturbing and counterintuitive observation that something as intimate as our choice between a carrot and a candy bar is somehow mediated by creatures that are not us.

But these are the closest of aliens, so familiar that the immune system, which ordinarily attacks any outside organism, tolerates them by the trillions—a seeming paradox with profound implications for health. The microbes we have all our lives are the ones that colonize us in the first weeks and months after birth, while our immune system is still undeveloped; in effect, they become part of the landscape. "Dendritic" (treelike) immune cells send branches into the respiratory and digestive tracts, where they sample all the microbes we inhale or swallow. When they see the same ones over and over, they secrete an anti-inflammatory substance called interleukin-10, which signals the microbe-killing T-cells: stand down.

And that's an essential step in the development of a healthy immune system. The immune reaction relies on a network of positive and negative feedback loops, poised on a knife edge between the dangers of ignoring a deadly invader and overreacting to a harmless stimulus. But to develop properly it must be exposed to a wide range of harmless microbes early in life. This was the normal condition of most human infants until a few generations ago. Cover the dirt on the floor of the hut, banish the farm animals to a distant feedlot, treat an ear infection with penicillin, and the inflammation-calming interleukin-10 reaction may fail to develop properly. "Modern sanitation is a good thing, and pavement is a good thing," says Sachs, "but they keep kids at a distance from microbes." The effect is to tip the immune system in the direction of overreaction, either to outside stimuli or even to the body's own cells. If the former, the result is allergies or asthma. Sachs writes that "children who receive antibiotics in the first year of life have more than double the rate of allergies and asthma in later childhood." But if the immune system turns on the body itself, you see irritable bowel syndrome, lupus or multiple sclerosis, among the many autoimmune diseases that were virtually unknown to our ancestors but are increasingly common in the developed world.

That is the modern understanding of the "Hygiene Hypothesis," first formulated by David Strachan in 1989. In Strachan's original version, which has unfortunately lodged in the minds of many parents, actual childhood illness was believed to exert a protective effect. There was a brief vogue for intentionally exposing youngsters to disease. But researchers now believe the key is exposure to a wide range of harmless germs, such as might be found in a playground or a park.

Microbes synthesize vitamins, and regulate immune systems and even serotonin levels. Germs, it seems, can make you happy.

The task is complicated, in part because some bacteria seem to be both good and bad. The best-known is *Helicobacter pylori*, a microbe that has evolved to live in the acid environment of the stomach. It survives by burrowing into the stomach's mucous lining and secreting enzymes that reduce acidity. Nobel laureates Barry Marshall and Robin Warren showed it could cause gastric ulcers and stomach cancer. But then further studies discovered that infection with *H. pylori* was protective against esophageal reflux and cancer of the esophagus, and may also reduce the incidence of asthma. *H. pylori*, which is spread in drinking water and direct contact among family members, was virtually universal a few generations ago but is now on the verge of extinction in the developed world. The result is fewer ulcers and stomach cancer, but more cancer of the esophagus—which is increasing faster than any other form of cancer in America—more asthma, and . . . what else? We don't know. "H. pylori has colonized our guts since before humans migrated out of Africa," says Blaser. "You can't get rid of it and not expect consequences."

Blaser questions whether eliminating H. pylori is a good idea. Someday, conceivably, we might intentionally inoculate children with a bioengineered version of H. pylori that keeps its benefits without running the risk of stomach cancer. There is already a burgeoning market for "probiotics," bacteria with supposed health benefits, either in pill form or as food. Consumers last year slurped down more than $100 million worth of Dannon's Activia, a yogurt containing what the website impressively calls "billions" of beneficial microbes in every container. The microbes are a strain of *Bifidobacterium animalis*, which helps improve what advertisers delicately call "regularity," a fact Dannon has underscored by rechristening the species with its trademarked name "*Bifidus regularis*." Other products contain *Lactobacillus casei*, which is supposed to stimulate production of infection-fighting lymphocytes. Many others on the market are untested and of dubious value. Labels that claim antibiotic resistant ought to be considered a warning, not a boast. Bacteria swap genetic material among themselves, and the last thing you want to do is introduce a resistant strain, even of a beneficial microbe, into your body.

And there's one more thing that microbes can do, perhaps the most remarkable of all. *Mycobacterium vaccae*, a soil microbe found in East Africa that has powerful effects on the immune system, was tested at the University of Bristol as a cancer therapy. The results were equivocal, but researchers made the startling observation that patients receiving it felt better regardless of whether their cancer was actually improving. Neuroscientist Chris Lowry injected mice with it, and found, to his amazement, that it activated the serotonin receptors in the prefrontal cortex—in other words, it worked like an antidepressant, only without the side effects of insomnia and anxiety. Researchers believe *M. vaccae* works through the interleukin-10 pathway, although the precise mechanism is uncertain. But there is at least the tantalizing, if disconcerting, suggestion that microbes may be able to manipulate our happiness. Could the hygiene hypothesis help explain the rise in, of all things, depression? We're a long way from being able to say that, much less use that insight to treat people. But at least we are asking the right questions: not how to kill bacteria, but how to live with them.

Assess Your Progress

1. Why is it risky to try and kill all germs?
2. Why might the use of sanitizers cause health issues?

With Matthew Philips, Raina Kelley and Karen Springen.

Tattoos: Leaving Their Mark

Getting one is pretty safe these days, but what if you have second thoughts and want a tattoo removed? Even today's pinpoint lasers may not get rid of it entirely.

People have been getting tattoos for millennia, but only recently has tattooing entered the American mainstream. In a 2004 telephone survey of Americans ages 18 to 50, a quarter of those interviewed said they had a tattoo. Now it's probably more.

With acceptance has come safety, although there's still a chance of infection, so it's important that equipment be sterilized and that tattooists wash their hands and wear gloves. In 2004 and 2005, 44 people were infected with methicillin-resistant *Staphylococcus aureus* (MRSA) by unlicensed tattooists, some of whom fashioned guitar string into needles and used ink from printer cartridges for dye.

The flip side to the popularity of tattoos is increased demand for removal. Laser treatments work, but they're expensive, time-consuming, and may not erase the tattoo completely.

Bad Reactions

Tattoos are more or less permanent because the ink is injected into the dermis, the relatively stable level of skin beneath the epidermis, the outermost layer that's continually flaking off. They've been described as tiny, ink-filled puncture wounds; indeed, tattoos used to be created manually by jabbing a needle into the skin, and they are still done that way illicitly in prisons and elsewhere. But legal tattooists now depend on machines to rapidly inject the ink to just the right depth, about half a millimeter below the surface of the skin. Even with these machines, getting a tattoo may hurt.

Because there's usually some bleeding, the possibility of getting a blood-borne disease exists for both the tattoo artists and their customers. In the 1950s, New York City banned tattooing after a dramatic increase in tattoo-related hepatitis cases. An Australian study published last year found a link between hepatitis C infections and getting a tattoo in prison, but American health officials have said that there are no data so far in this country linking tattoos to transmission of hepatitis C.

A bigger problem than infections may be the allergic reactions and skin growths.

Some people get henna tattoos, especially while on vacation, because they fade in a couple of weeks. By itself, henna isn't a problem, but a chemical called paraphenylenediamine is sometimes added to intensify the color. Several case reports describe people having an allergic reaction to henna tattoos because of this darkening agent. Henna-based hair dyes have caused red and itchy scalps for the same reason.

The permanent inks can also be trouble. The mercury in red pigments made with mercuric sulfide (cinnabar) has caused allergic reactions.

Some people have developed strange skin growths—none full-fledged cancers—from permanent tattoos. Earlier this year, University of Maryland researchers described the case of a 38-year-old man who had a keratoacanthoma, a benign squamous cell growth, sprout from his month-old tattoo. Last year, doctors in Kansas City reported a case involving a 59-year-old woman who developed a different type of growth, called a pseudoepitheliomatous hyperplasia, in a two-year-old tattoo.

Lasering It Away

The permanence of tattoos is part of the attraction, but more than a few people have had regrets. Sometimes it's not a frivolous situation: cancer patients may get small tattoos to mark the spot where radiation is to be delivered. After their treatments are over, they want the marks removed.

In the past, dermatologists physically removed skin tissue to get rid of a tattoo, cutting or abrading it away. Now they depend on lasers to target and break apart the pigment particles so they get carried away by the lymphatic system. The lasers work in bursts that are nanoseconds long, so damage to nearby tissue is limited. Different wavelengths are used, depending on the color of the ink. Some colors— black, blue—are much easier to remove than others—yellow, orange. Local anesthesia is often needed, and there may be some bleeding.

Laser treatment is a big advance, but it's far from perfect. Many tattoos can't be completely removed: a realistic goal is 75% "clearing." Sometimes the tattoo may turn darker, rather than disappear, because the ink contains titanium dioxide or ferric oxide. The pigments used in tattoos to outline the eyes and lips (sometimes called permanent makeup) can be especially hard to remove. Up to 20 treatments may be needed. In people with dark skin, there's a danger of the skin turning white, so only lasers with a certain wavelength should be used. Allergic reactions may occur as the pigment particles get liberated from the dermis. Meanwhile, demand is growing for bigger, more complex and vibrantly colored tattoos that will be even harder to remove.

For these and other reasons, there's interest in tattoo inks that will stay sharp but can be removed more easily. The inks developed by Freedom-2, a New Jersey company, are a possibility.

They come encapsulated in tiny polymer spheres and leave the skin quickly after a laser beam bursts open the sphere. Results from animal experiments are impressive. Whether they will work as well in humans and be accepted by tattoo artists and their customers has yet to be determined.

Assess Your Progress

1. What are the risks associated with getting a tattoo?
2. Why is it so difficult to have a tattoo removed?

Excerpted from *Harvard Health Letter,* March 2008. Copyright © 2008 by the President and Fellow of Harvard College. Reprinted with permission. www.health.harvard.edu/health

Hazardous Health Plans

Coverage gaps can leave you in big trouble.

Many people who believe they have adequate health insurance actually have coverage so riddled with loopholes, limits, exclusions, and gotchas that it won't come close to covering their expenses if they fall seriously ill, a *Consumer Reports* investigation has found.

At issue are so-called individual plans that consumers get on their own when, say, they've been laid off from a job but are too young for Medicare or too "affluent" for Medicaid. An estimated 14,000 Americans a day lose their job-based coverage, and many might be considering individual insurance for the first time in their lives.

But increasingly, individual insurance is a nightmare for consumers: more costly than the equivalent job-based coverage, and for those in less-than-perfect health, unaffordable at best and unavailable at worst. Moreover, the lack of effective consumer protections in most states allows insurers to sell plans with "affordable" premiums whose skimpy coverage can leave people who get very sick with the added burden of ruinous medical debt.

Just ask Janice and Gary Clausen of Audubon, Iowa. They told us they purchased a United Healthcare limited benefit plan sold through AARP that cost about $500 a month after Janice lost her accountant job and her work-based coverage when the auto dealership that employed her closed in 2004.

"I didn't think it sounded bad," Janice said. "I knew it would only cover $50,000 a year, but I didn't realize how much everything would cost." The plan proved hopelessly inadequate after Gary received a diagnosis of colon cancer. His 14-month treatment, including surgery and chemo-therapy, cost well over $200,000. Janice, 64, and Gary, 65, expect to be paying off medical debt for the rest of their lives.

For our investigation, we hired a national expert to help us evaluate a range of real policies from many states and interviewed Americans who bought those policies. We talked to insurance experts and regulators to learn more. Here is what we found:

- Heath insurance policies with gaping holes are offered by insurers ranging from small companies to brand-name carriers such as Aetna and United Healthcare. And in most states, regulators are not tasked with evaluating overall coverage.
- Disclosure requirements about coverage gaps are weak or nonexistent. So it's difficult for consumers to figure

out in advance what a policy does or doesn't cover, compare plans, or estimate their out-of-pocket liability for a medical catastrophe. It doesn't help that many people who have never been seriously ill might have no idea how expensive medical care can be.

- People of modest means in many states might have no good options for individual coverage. Plans with affordable premiums can leave them with crushing medical debt if they fall seriously ill, and plans with adequate coverage may have huge premiums.
- There are some clues to a bad policy that consumers can spot. We tell you what they are, and how to avoid them if possible.
- Even as policymakers debate a major overhaul of the health-care system, government officials can take steps now to improve the current market.

Good Plans vs. Bad Plans

We think a good health-care plan should pay for necessary care without leaving you with lots of debt or high out-of-pocket costs. That includes hospital, ambulance, emergency-room, and physician fees; prescription drugs; outpatient treatments; diagnostic and imaging tests; chemotherapy, radiation, rehabilitation and physical therapy; mental-health treatment; and durable medical equipment, such as wheelchairs. Remember, health insurance is supposed to protect you in case of a catastrophically expensive illness, not simply cover your routine costs as a generally healthy person. And many individual plans do nowhere near the job.

For decades, individual insurance has been what economists call a "residual" market—something to buy only when you have run out of other options. The problem, according to insurance experts we consulted, is that the high cost of treatment in the U.S., which has the world's most expensive health-care system, puts truly affordable, comprehensive coverage out of the reach of people who don't have either deep pockets or a generous employer. Insurers tend to provide this choice: comprehensive coverage with a high monthly premium or skimpy coverage at a low monthly premium within the reach of middle- and low-income consumers.

More consumers are having to choose the latter as they become unemployed or their workplace drops coverage. (COBRA, the federal program that allows former employees to continue with the insurance from their old job by paying the full monthly premium, often costs $1,000 or more each month for family coverage. The federal government is temporarily subsidizing 65 percent of those premiums for some, but only for a maximum of nine months.) *Consumer Reports* and others label as "junk insurance" those so-called affordable individual plans with huge coverage gaps. Many such plans are sold throughout the nation, including policies from well-known companies.

Decent insurance covers more than just routine care.

Aetna's Affordable Health Choices plans, for example, offer limited benefits to part-time and hourly workers. We found one such policy that covered only $1,000 of hospital costs and $2,000 of out-patient expenses annually.

The Clausens' AARP plan, underwritten by insurance giant United Health Group, the parent company of United Healthcare, was advertised as "the essential benefits you deserve. Now in one affordable plan." AARP spokesman Adam Sohn said, "AARP has been fighting for affordable, quality health care for nearly a half-century, and while a fixed-benefit indemnity plan is not perfect, it offers our members an option to help cover some portion of their medical expenses without paying a high premium."

Nevertheless, AARP suspended sales of such policies last year after Sen. Charles Grassley, R-Iowa, questioned the marketing practices. Some 53,400 AARP members still have policies similar to the Clausens' that were sold under the names Medical Advantage Plan, Essential Health Insurance Plan, and Essential Plus Health Insurance Plan. In addition, at least 1 million members are enrolled in the AARP Hospital Indemnity Insurance Plan, Sohn said, an even more bare-bones policy. Members who have questions should first call 800-523-5800; for more help, call 888-687-2277. (Consumers Union, the nonprofit publisher of *Consumer Reports,* is working with AARP on a variety of health-care reforms.)

United American Insurance Co. promotes its supplemental health insurance as "an affordable solution to America's health-care crisis!" When Jeffrey E. Miller, 56, of Sarasota, Fla., received a diagnosis of prostate cancer a few months after buying one of the company's limited-benefit plans, he learned that it would not cover tens of thousands of dollars' worth of drug and radiation treatments he needed. As this article went to press, five months after his diagnosis, Miller had just begun treatment after qualifying for Florida Medicaid. A representative of United American declined to comment on its products.

Even governments are getting into the act. In 2008, Florida created the Cover Florida Health Care Access Program, which Gov. Charlie Crist said would make "affordable health coverage available to 3.8 million uninsured Floridians." But many of the basic "preventive" policies do not cover inpatient hospital treatments, emergency-room care, or physical therapy, and they severely limit coverage of everything else.

7 Signs a Health Plan Might Be Junk

Do Everything in Your Power to Avoid Plans with the Following Features:

Limited benefits. Never buy a product that is labeled "limited benefit" or "not major medical" insurance. In most states those phrases might be your only clue to an inadequate policy.

Low overall coverage limits. Health care is more costly than you might imagine if you've never experienced a serious illness. The cost of cancer or a heart attack can easily hit six figures. Policies with coverage limits of $25,000 or even $100,000 are not adequate.

"Affordable" premiums. There's no free lunch when it comes to insurance. To lower premiums, insurers trim benefits and do what they can to avoid insuring less healthy people. So if your insurance was a bargain, chances are good it doesn't cover very much. To check how much a comprehensive plan would cost you, go to *ehealthinsurance.com,* enter your location, gender, and age as prompted, and look for the most costly of the plans that pop up. It is probably the most comprehensive.

No coverage for important things. If you don't see a medical service specifically mentioned in the policy, assume it's not covered. We reviewed policies that didn't cover prescription drugs or outpatient chemotherapy but didn't say so anywhere in the policy document—not even in the section labeled "What is not covered."

Ceilings on categories of care. A $900-a-day maximum benefit for hospital expenses will hardly make a dent in a $45,000 bill for heart bypass surgery. If you have to accept limits on some services, be sure your plan covers hospital and outpatient medical treatment, doctor visits, drugs, and diagnostic and imaging tests without a dollar limit. Limits on mental-health costs, rehabilitation, and durable medical equipment should be the most generous you can afford.

Limitless out-of-pocket costs. Avoid policies that fail to specify a maximum amount that you'll have to pay before the insurer will begin covering 100 percent of expenses. And be alert for loopholes. Some policies, for instance, don't count co-payments for doctor visits or prescription drugs toward the maximum. That can be a catastrophe for seriously ill people who rack up dozens of doctor's appointments and prescriptions a year.

Random gotchas. The AARP policy that the Clausens bought began covering hospital care on the second day. That seems benign enough, except that the first day is almost always the most expensive, because it usually includes charges for surgery and emergency-room diagnostic tests and treatments.

The Wild West of Insurance

Compounding the problem of limited policies is the fact that policyholders are often unaware of those limits—until it's too late.

"I think people don't understand insurance, period," said Stephen Finan, associate director of policy at the American Cancer Society Cancer Action Network. "They know they need it. They look at the price, and that's it. They don't understand the language, and insurance companies go to great lengths to make it incomprehensible. Even lawyers don't always understand what it means."

Case in point: Jim Stacey of Fayetteville, N.C. In 2000, Stacey and his wife, Imelda, were pleased to buy a plan at what they considered an "incredible" price from the Mid-West National Life Insurance Co. of Tennessee. The policy's list of benefits included a lifetime maximum payout of up to $1 million per person. But after Stacey learned he had prostate cancer in 2005, the policy paid only $1,480 of the $17,453 it cost for the implanted radioactive pellets he chose to treat the disease.

"To this day, I don't know what went wrong," Stacey said about the bill.

We sent the policy, along with the accompanying Explanation of Benefit forms detailing what it did and didn't pay, to Karen Pollitz, research professor at the Georgetown University Health Policy Institute. We asked Pollitz, an expert on individual health insurance, to see whether she could figure out why the policy covered so little.

"The short answer is, 'Beats the heck out of me,'" she e-mailed back to us. The Explanation of Benefit forms were missing information that she would expect to see, such as specific billing codes that explain what treatments were given. And there didn't seem to be any connection between the benefits listed in the policy and the actual amounts paid.

Contacted for comment, a spokeswoman for HealthMarkets, the parent company of Mid-West National, referred us to the company website. It stated that the company "pays claims according to the insurance contract issued to each customer" and that its policies "satisfy a need in the marketplace for a product that balances the cost with the available benefit options." The spokeswoman declined to answer specific questions about Stacey's case, citing patient privacy laws.

One reason confusion abounds, Pollitz said, is that health insurance is regulated by the states, not by the federal government, and most states (Massachusetts and New York are prominent exceptions) do not have a standard definition of what constitutes health insurance.

"Rice is rice and gasoline is gasoline. When you buy it, you know what it is," Pollitz said. "Health insurance—who knows what it is? It is some product that's sold by an insurance company. It could be a little bit or a lot of protection. You don't know what is and isn't covered. Nothing can be taken for granted."

How to Protect Yourself

Seek out comprehensive coverage. A good plan will cover your legitimate health care without burdening you with oversized debt.

Want Better Coverage? Try Running for Congress

President Barack Obama says Americans should have access to the kind of health benefits Congress gets. We detail them below. Members of Congress and other U.S. government employees can receive care through the Federal Employees Health Benefits Program. Employees choose from hundreds of plans, but the most popular is a national Blue Cross and Blue Shield Preferred Provider Organization plan. Employee contributions for that plan are $152 per person, or $357 per family, per month.

Plan Features

- No annual or lifetime limits for major services
- Deductible of $300 per person and $600 per family
- Out-of-pocket limit of $5,000 per year with preferred providers, which includes most deductibles, co-insurance, and co-payments

Covered Services

- Inpatient and outpatient hospital care
- Inpatient and outpatient doctor visits
- Prescription drugs
- Diagnostic tests
- Preventive care, including routine immunizations
- Chemotherapy and radiation therapy
- Maternity care
- Family planning
- Durable medical equipment, orthopedic devices, and artificial limbs
- Organ and tissue transplants
- Inpatient and outpatient surgery
- Physical, occupational, and speech therapy
- Outpatient and inpatient mental-health care

"The idea of 'Cadillac' coverage vs. basic coverage isn't an appropriate way to think about health insurance," said Mila Kofman, Maine's superintendent of insurance. "It has to give you the care you need, when you need it, and some financial security so you don't end up out on the street."

What you want is a plan that has no caps on specific coverages. But if you have to choose, pick a plan offering unlimited coverage for hospital and outpatient treatment, doctor visits, drugs, and diagnostic and imaging tests. When it comes to lifetime coverage maximums, unlimited is best and $2 million should be the minimum. Ideally, there should be a single deductible for everything or, at most, one deductible for drugs and one for everything else. And the policy should pay for 100 percent of all expenses once your out-of-pocket payments hit a certain amount, such as $5,000 or $10,000.

If you are healthy now, do not buy a plan based on the assumption that you will stay that way. Don't think you can safely

The Real Cost of Illness Can Be Staggering . . .

Few Americans realize how much care costs. Coverage gaps can leave you in debt.

Condition	Treatment	Total Cost
Late-stage colon cancer	124 weeks of treatment, including two surgeries, three types of chemotherapy, imaging, prescription drugs, hospice care.	$285,946
Heart attack	56 weeks of treatment, including ambulance, ER workup, angioplasty with stent, bypass surgery, cardiac rehabilitation, counseling for depression, prescription drugs.	$110,405
Breast cancer	87 weeks of treatment, including lumpectomy, drugs, lab and imaging tests, chemotherapy and radiation therapy, mental-health counseling, and prosthesis.	$104,535
Type 2 diabetes	One year of maintenance care, including insulin and other prescription drugs, glucose test strips, syringes and other supplies, quarterly physician visits and lab, annual eye exam.	$5,949

. . . and Out-of-Pocket Expenses Can Vary Widely

With its lower premium and deductible, the California plan at right would seem the better deal. But because California, unlike Massachusetts, allows the sale of plans with large coverage gaps, a patient there will pay far more than a Massachusetts patient for the same breast cancer treatments, as the breakdown below shows.

Massachusetts Plan	California Plan
Monthly premium for any 55-year-old: $399	**Monthly premium for a healthy 55-year-old:** $246
Annual deductible: $2,200	**Annual deductible:** $1,000
Co-pays: $25 office visit, $250 outpatient surgery after deductible, $10 for generic drugs, $25 for nonpreferred generic and brand name, $45 for nonpreferred brand name	**Co-pays:** $25 preventive care office visits
	Co-insurance: 20% for most covered services
Co-insurance: 20% for some services	**Out-of-pocket maximum:** $2,500, includes hospital and surgical co-insurance only.
Out-of-pocket maximum: $5,000, includes deductible, co-insurance, and all co-payments	**Exclusions and limits:** Prescription drugs, most mental-health care, and wigs for chemotherapy patients not covered. Outpatient care not covered until out-of-pocket maximum satisfied from hospital/surgical co-insurance.
Exclusions and limits: Cap of 24 mental-health visits, $3,000 cap on equipment	
Lifetime benefits: Unlimited	**Lifetime benefits:** $5 million

Service and Total Cost	Patient Pays	Patient Pays
Hospital	$0	$705
Surgery	$981	$1,136
Office visits and procedures	$1,833	$2,010
Prescription drugs	$1,108	$5,985
Laboratory and imaging tests	$808	$3,772
Chemotherapy and radiation therapy	$1,987	$21,113
Mental-health care	$950	$2,700
Prosthesis	$0	$350
Total $104,535	$7,668	$37,767

Source: Karen Pollitz, Georgetown University Health Policy Institute, using real claims data and policies. Columns of figures do not add up exactly because all numbers are rounded.

go without drug coverage, for example, because you don't take any prescriptions regularly today. "You can't know in advance if you're going to be among the .01 percent of people who needs the $20,000-a-month biologic drug," said Gary Claxton, a vice president of the nonprofit Kaiser Family Foundation, a health-policy research organization. "What's important is if you get really sick, are you going to lose everything?"

Consider trade-offs carefully. If you have to make a trade-off to lower your premium, Claxton and Pollitz suggest opting for a higher deductible and a higher out-of-pocket limit rather than fixed dollar limits on services. Better to use up part of your retirement savings paying $10,000 up front than to lose your whole nest egg paying a $90,000 medical bill after your policy's limits are exhausted.

What Lawmakers Need to Do Next

Consumers Union, the nonprofit publisher of *Consumer Reports,* has long supported national health-care reform that makes affordable health coverage available to all Americans. The coverage should include a basic set of required, comprehensive health-care benefits, like those in the federal plan that members of Congress enjoy. Insurers should compete for customers based on price and the quality of their services, not by limiting their risk through confusing options, incomplete information, or greatly restricted benefits.

As reform is developed and debated, Consumers Union supports these changes in the way health insurance is presented and sold:

Clear terms. All key terms in policies, such as "out-of-pocket" and "annual deductible," should be defined by law and insurers should be required to use them that way in their policies.

Standard benefits. Ideally, all plans should have a uniform set of benefits covering all medically necessary care, but consumers should be able to opt for varying levels of cost-sharing. Failing that, states should establish a menu of standardized plans, as Medicare does for Medigap plans. Consumers would then have a basis for comparing costs of plans.

Transparency. Policies that insurers currently sell should be posted in full online or available by mail upon request for anyone who wants to examine them. They should be the full, legally binding policy documents, not just a summary or marketing brochure. In many states now, consumers can't see the policy document until after they have joined the plan. At that point, they're legally entitled to a "free look" period in which to examine the policy and ask for a refund if they don't like what they see. But if they turn the policy back in, they face the prospect of being uninsured until they can find another plan.

Disclosure of costs. Every plan must provide a standard "Plan Coverage" summary that clearly displays what is—and more important, is not—covered. The summary should include independently verified estimates of total out-of-pocket costs for a standard range of serious problems, such as breast cancer treatment or heart bypass surgery.

Moreover, reliable information should be available to consumers about the costs in their area of treating various medical conditions, so that they have a better understanding of the bills they could face without adequate health coverage.

With such a high deductible, in years when you are relatively healthy you might never collect anything from your health insurance. To economize on routine care, take advantage of free community health screenings, low-cost or free community health clinics, immediate-care clinics offered in some drugstores, and low-priced generic prescriptions sold at Target, Walmart, and elsewhere.

Look for a plan that doesn't cap your coverage.

If your financial situation is such that you can afford neither the higher premiums of a more comprehensive policy nor high deductibles, you really have no good choices, Pollitz said, adding, "It's why we need to fix our health-care system."

Check out the policy and company. You can, at least, take some steps to choose the best plan you can afford. First, see "7 signs a health plan might be junk" to learn to spot the most dangerous pitfalls and the preferred alternatives.

Use the Web to research insurers you're considering. The National Association of Insurance Commissioners posts complaint information online at www.naic.org.

Entering the name of the company and policy in a search engine can't hurt either. Consumers who did that recently would have discovered that Mid-West National was a subsidiary of HealthMarkets, whose disclosure and claims handling drew many customers' ire. Last year, HealthMarkets was fined $20 million after a multi state investigation of its sales practices and claims handling.

Don't rely on the salesperson's word. Jeffrey E. Miller, the Florida man whose policy failed to cover much of his cancer treatment, recalls being bombarded with e-mail and calls when he began shopping for insurance. "The salesman for the policy I bought told me it was great, and I was going to be covered, and it paid up to $100,000 for a hospital stay," he said. "But the insurance has turned out to pay very little."

Pollitz advises anyone with questions about their policy to ask the agent and get answers in writing. "Then if it turns out not to be true," she said, "you can complain."

Assess Your Progress

1. What should consumers look for when choosing health insurance?
2. What constitutes inadequate health care coverage?

The Rough Road to *Dreamland*

Sleep needs and patterns might be unique to each individual, but the typical thieves of restful slumber are not.

MICHAEL J. BREUS

Sleep affects how we work, relate to other people, and make decisions, as well as how we feel. The idea that we need to "sleep on it" when faced with a big decision is scientifically proven. A Dutch study shows that people make "better" decisions by letting the "unconscious" mind during sleep chum through the options presented. We know that sleep helps us think better and stronger, as well as prepare our minds for optimal functionality, but getting a good night's rest is difficult for many.

Sleep as a topic has gotten a lot of attention recently—and for good reason. Inadequate amounts have been shown to create poorer health, obesity, lower productivity on the job (including the occupation of being a full-time parent), more danger on the roads, a less vibrant sex life, and a lower quality of existence.

Research is not the only thing alerting us to the dangers of sleep deprivation, as the results of a series of polls taken by the National Sleep Foundation demonstrate the extent of the issue. About 75 percent of Americans frequently have a sleep problem symptom, including repeated waking during the night or snoring, and 25 percent maintain that their daily activities are affected by this lack of sleep, and that includes sexual relationships in which respondents say they have been having less sex or have lost interest in sex entirely. Sixty percent have driven while drowsy in the past year, and about four percent have had an accident or close call because of drowsiness or actually falling asleep at the wheel.

On average, adults are sleeping 6.8 hours a night on weekdays and 7.4 hours on weekends. Twenty-six percent of adults say they have "a good night's sleep" only a few nights a month or less. On average, people maintain they need a minimum of 6.5 hours of sleep a night to function at their best during the day. In general, men report needing less (6.2 hours) than women (6.8 hours). On average, it takes about 23 minutes to fall asleep on most nights.

When an individual is suffering from a lack of sleep, reaction time and the ability to think clearly and quickly slow down. A person is more likely to make poor decisions, become irritable and moody, be low on stamina, and have a compromised ability to fight off disease and weight gain. A chronic lack of sleep may put individuals at greater risk for type 2 diabetes.

When you consider how much of your life depends on others making good decisions—physicians, industrial workers, pilots, air-traffic controllers, drivers, train conductors, presidents, world leaders, and so on—you soon realize that sleep deprivation is not just about you, but everybody.

Scientists only are beginning to understand disordered sleep and how to treat it. We sleep less today than ever before. In the last 100 years, Americans have cut their sleep time by about 20%. How we sleep has had a few major changes over the centuries based on some interesting historical developments. The introduction of the light bulb in 1879 suddenly altered how long people could work. Another issue was the mainstreaming of caffeine (in consumable drinks) as an alerting agent, which prevents sleep, or at least replaces it for a short while. The concept of overtime also has molded sleep habits. Our lifestyles leave little time for sleep, and our society motivates people to work and play more while sleeping less. As humans in a modern society, we endure a great deal of stress, and that morphs into psychological problems such as anxiety, nervousness, depression, and, ultimately, lost sleep.

Measuring sleep deprivation is difficult without knowing exactly how many hours you need daily. Not everyone is created equal. Some people require seven hours to feel refreshed and alert all day long, whereas others might need nine hours, or only 6.5. Sleep needs might vary depending on what is going on in your life. You may require more sleep during times of acute stress, grief, hard work, physical training, illness, or depression. Your sleep habits also can change with age.

Is it possible to sleep too much? If you sleep more than nine hours a night, for instance, should you aim to cut back on your sleep time? Some studies have documented that there are health risks of sleeping too long. One found long sleepers had a 50% greater risk of stroke than did those who slept six to eight hours a night. They also may have higher rates of cardiovascular disease and possibly an increased risk for diabetes. A large Japanese study found that those who sleep more than 7.5 hours a day have a greater risk of death than those who get less than 6.5 hours—but do not be alarmed. These studies cannot make any definitive conclusions yet because the explanations behind the results are not clear, and there are just as many other studies to complicate some of this new evidence. For instance, research suggests that women who are, in fact, longer sleepers may have a lower risk of breast cancer.

There is no magical number for sleep that covers everybody's needs. Sleep requirements are individual. If you are a long sleeper who feels lethargic much of the day, you might benefit from restricting your time in bed. The point is to find which number of hours makes you feel the best and then aim to sleep that number every night. Thus, if you know you need eight hours a night and you only get seven hours for eight straight days, then you have lost one full night's sleep during that span. You probably know if you are chronically sleep deprived without having to take a test. It is not rocket science. Much like being thirsty, your body tells you when you are missing something it wants.

Who needs more sleep, men or women? From a clinical perspective, women tend to confess more about sleep issues than men. As a gender, women appear to bear more stresses seeking balance in their multiple roles as moms, wives, employees, chauffeurs, cooks, cleaners, entrepreneurs, family managers, caretakers, etc. One would think that, since women and men are physiologically different, they would have different sleep needs, but women from adolescence to post-menopause are underrepresented in studies of sleep and its disorders even though sleep complaints are twice as prevalent in females. Some studies show that women may be at greater risk for insomnia, or have a predisposition due to their sex, but explaining this from a purely scientific standpoint is not entirely possible at present.

Compounding this question is the fact that age can have more to do with sleep needs and experiences than gender. For instance, younger women may build up sleep debt more easily than older women, allowing the latter to function better with fewer hours of sleep. Whether or not this is true, however, is up for debate. In fact, plenty of sleep studies result in controversial and inconclusive data.

What we do know about sleep and aging is that the older you get, the more likely you are to suffer from interrupted sleep. Older individuals still need roughly the same number of sleep hours as they got when they were younger (it may deviate by 30 minutes to an hour over a lifetime), but the architecture of their sleep shifts. They do not get as much deep (delta) sleep, so they easily are awakened by noise, light, or even their own pain from a chronic medical condition. Sleep becomes more fragmented and inefficient, so the actual time spent sleeping is less than the time spent in bed.

Another influential aspect to aging that can affect sleep is circadian rhythm, the patterns of repeated activity associated with the environmental cycles of day and night. Our internal rhythms repeat roughly every 24 hours. A lot of people's sleep dilemmas can be attributed to an internal clock that has become out of sync or mismatched with the day-night cycle. Everyone's circadian pacemaker ticks at a different rate but, as you age, your pacemaker speeds up or slows down, thus altering how the body responds to that 24-hour cycle. Later on in life, our clocks speed up so the body does not match so well with the 24-hour day. It wants to go to bed early and get up super-early.

What is more important: the amount of minutes an individual gets or the quality of those minutes? If you wake up after seven to eight hours of sleep and still feel unrefreshed, your problem may not be about quantity, but quality. The quality of sleep is as vitally important to health and well-being as the quantity. Our sleep has a complex pattern, or architecture, which consists of five stages that run through various cycles during the night. During certain stages and times of the sleep cycles, we secrete hormones and other substances that help regulate our metabolism and support our general health. What happens in our brains during REM sleep is how we retain information, organize our memories, and prepare to learn something new or perform a special task. If our sleep patterns are altered, it may leave us feeling unrefreshed, tired, and sleepy, as well as put us at risk for a host of minor or even serious medical conditions.

Disturbed or Disordered?

Could a person have disordered sleep and not a sleep disorder? Wake up to this simple fact: you are not supposed to be sleepy, with your feet dragging and lids lagging during the day. If you literally are asleep before your head hits the pillow, it probably is not a good sign. Do not let the notion that "I have always been this way" fool you into thinking it is okay. You should awaken feeling relatively refreshed and remain alert throughout the day—every day. If you do not, it could be the result of one of two problems: a sleep disorder or simply disordered sleep. What is the difference? The distinction is important. Think of sleep disorders as formal syndromes with definitive criteria, which repeat time after time. They can be primary sleep disorders, which are not attributed to other conditions, or secondary sleep disorders, which arise due to an underlying physical or mental condition.

The criteria that define disorders are developed and agreed upon by national researchers and societies to help the medical field understand how to identify a particular set of circumstances. Once a disorder has been identified, the goal is to develop systematically a therapy to avert the symptoms associated with it, or cure the underlying situation. There are more than 85 recognized sleep disorders, with the most diagnosed being insomnia, apnea, narcolepsy, and restless leg syndrome. These and others may manifest themselves in various ways.

Disordered sleep refers to everything else that relates to sleep but does not qualify as a disorder. One's symptoms might not quite meet the disorder criteria based on severity or frequency, or there might be an external behavioral factor that is affecting sleep, such as a cat in the bed or too much heat in the room. Disordered sleep also can reflect the value we place on sleep, or the quality of sleep we get.

For the vast majority of people, disordered sleep is the biggest culprit. In fact, sleep problems often occur as the result of poor "sleep hygiene"—bad habits that do not support a good sleep experience. These entail a range of practices and environmental factors, many of which are under your control. They include things such as smoking; alcohol and caffeine intake; exercise; eating large amounts before bed; jet lag; and psychological stressors (deadlines, exams, marital conflict, job crises, etc.) that intrude on one's ability to fall or stay asleep. Designing and sticking with a good sleep hygiene program should alleviate these types of difficulties, or at least give you a disciplined way to handle them so that they affect your sleep minimally.

The most common type of disordered sleep I see in my practice is nonrefreshing. Patients will come in and say they have been waking up after enough sleep, but feels as if they have slept poorly. This can be caused by several things: poor diet, stress, environment, genetics. My job is to figure out which of these, if not a combination, is the culprit and take action. The most common treatments include behavioral and relaxation techniques, environmental tips, and suggestions for medications or supplements.

Sleep needs and patterns might be unique to each individual, but the typical thieves of restful slumber are not. Clinicians hear time and time again the same complaints and discover that the roots of the problems—of disordered sleep—typically fall under one of six categories: anxiety, stress, and nervousness; caffeine consumption; parenting; bed partners; hormonal fluctuations (culprits or either the X or Y chromosome); and traveling, especially business travel.

Of course, you might have issues with more than one of these culprits. For instance, you might be a working mother who uses caffeine to stay alert through the day, struggles to juggle work and home life, has a husband whose sleep habits do not jibe with your own, and experiences severe hormonal fluctuations through the month that impact your sleep-wake cycle. The surprising part is that most people, when asked what they would do if they thought they had a sleep problem, would not speak with a physician about it—and about two in 10 would just assume the problem will go away, so they would opt to do nothing. Maybe it will go away, but chances are it will not.

Assess Your Progress

1. Why are humans getting less sleep these days?
2. What are the health implications of sleep deprivation?

MICHAEL J. BREUS is a clinical psychologist, dipolomate of the American Board of Sleep Medicine, and the author of *Good Night: The Sleep Doctor's 4 Week Program to Better Sleep and Better Health.*

The *Surprising Reason* Why Heavy Isn't Healthy

It's not just because fat ups your risk of disease. How much you weigh can keep you from getting the same health care everyone else gets. Our *special report* looks at a growing problem in women's health.

GINNY GRAVES

It's shocking, but it's true: Being a woman who's more than 20 pounds overweight may actually hike your risk of getting poor medical treatment. In fact, weighing too much can have surprising—and devastating—health repercussions beyond the usual diabetes and heart-health concerns you've heard about for years. A startling new *Health* magazine investigation reveals that if you're an overweight woman you:

- may have a harder time getting health insurance or have to pay higher premiums;
- are at higher risk of being misdiagnosed or receiving inaccurate dosages of drugs;
- are less likely to find a fertility doctor who will help you get pregnant;
- are less likely to have cancer detected early and get effective treatment for it.

What's going on here? Fat discrimination is part of the problem. A recent Yale study suggested that weight bias can start when a woman is as little as 13 pounds over her highest healthy weight. "Our culture has enormous negativity toward overweight people, and doctors aren't immune," says Harvard Medical School professor Jerome Groopman, MD, author of *How Doctors Think*. "If doctors have negative feelings toward patients, they're more dismissive, they're less patient, and it can cloud their judgment, making them prone to diagnostic errors." With nearly 70 million American women who are considered overweight, the implications of this new information is disturbing, to say the least. Here, what you need to know to get the top-quality health care you deserve—no matter what you weigh.

How Weight Gets in the Way

When Jen Seelaus, from Danbury, Connecticut, went to her doc's office because she was wheezing, she expected to get her asthma medication tweaked. Instead, she was told she'd feel better if she'd just lose some weight. "I didn't go to be lectured about my weight. I was there because I couldn't breathe," says the 5-foot-3, 195-pound woman. "Asthma can be dangerous if it gets out of control, and the nurse practitioner totally ignored that because of my weight."

Seelaus's nurse made a classic diagnostic error, according to Dr. Groopman. "It's called attribution, because your thinking is colored by a stereotype and you attribute the entire clinical picture to that stereotype. Because obesity can cause so many health problems, it's very easy to blame a variety of complaints, from knee pain to breathing troubles, on a patient's weight. That's why doctors—and patients—need to constantly ask, 'What else could this be?'"

There aren't statistics on how many diagnostic errors are due to weight, but the data for the general population is disturbing enough. "Doctors make mistakes in diagnosing 10 to 15 percent of all patients, and in half of those cases it causes real harm," Dr. Groopman says. Based on anecdotal evidence—patients who've told her that their doctors are often too quick to blame symptoms on weight—Rebecca Puhl, PhD, director of Research and Weight Stigma Initiatives at the Rudd Center for Food Policy and Obesity at Yale University, suspects that being heavy could further increase the odds of being misdiagnosed.

Even if doctors are aware of the potential traps they can fall into when diagnosing an overweight patient, extra body fat can literally obscure some illnesses, including heart disease and different types of cancer. "It's more difficult to hear heart and lung sounds in heavy people," says Mary Margaret Huizinga, MD, MPH, director of the Johns Hopkins Digestive Weight Loss Center. "I use an electronic stethoscope, which works well, but I'm very aware of the issues that can crop up in overweight patients. Not all doctors have these stethoscopes—or are aware they need one."

Jeffrey C. King, MD, professor and director of maternal-and-fetal medicine at the University of Louisville School of Medicine, says that "the more tissue between the palpating hand and what you're trying to feel, the harder it is to detect a mass." That may be what happened to Karen Tang [not her real name], a 5-foot-8, 280-pound woman who went to the doctor for pelvic pain. Her doc palpated her uterus but didn't feel anything. "By the time I was referred to a gynecologist, I had a fibroid the size of a melon—so large it was putting pressure on my bladder," she recalls.

Even a routine pelvic exam can be tricky, especially if you've had children. "The vaginal walls become lax and collapse into the middle, obscuring the cervix," Dr. King says. Larger or modified speculums can help, but not all docs have them and they can make the exam more uncomfortable, says Lynda Wolf, MD, a reproductive endocrinologist at Reproductive Medicine Associates of Michigan.

That may explain the disturbing finding that obese women are less likely to get Pap smears than normal-weight women. But doctors may be partly to blame for the screening lapse, too. A University of Connecticut study of more than 1,300 physicians found that 17 percent were reluctant to do pelvic exams on obese women and that 83 percent were hesitant if the patient herself seemed reluctant.

Physical exams aren't the only things hampered by obesity. Large patients may not fit into diagnostic scanning machines—computed tomography (CT) and magnetic resonance imaging (MRI), for instance—and X-rays and ultrasounds may not be as effective, says Raul N. Uppot, MD, a radiologist in the Division of Abdominal Imaging and Intervention at Massachusetts General Hospital in Boston. "Ultrasound is the approach that's the most limited by body fat, because the beams can't penetrate the tissue if you have more than 8 centimeters of subcutaneous fat," he says.

This affects women, in particular, because ultrasound is used to diagnose uterine tumors and ovarian cysts and to evaluate the mother's and baby's health during pregnancy. Just last May, researchers at the University of Texas Southwestern Medical Center at Dallas reported a 20 percent decrease in the ability to detect problems in fetuses of obese women with ultrasound. In another study, obese women were 20 percent more likely to have false-positive results from mammograms—readings that can lead to unnecessary biopsies and anxiety.

Too much body fat can *obscure organs on scans,* giving doctors fuzzy results.

While CT scans are less affected by body fat, getting clear images in heavy patients typically requires a lot more radiation than with normal-weight patients, making it riskier, especially if numerous CT scans are required. But trying to diagnose a health problem without proper imaging is like driving blindfolded. Doctors are sometimes left with little to go on except symptoms and intuition, especially in the emergency room, where physicians make life-and-death decisions in minutes. "If we can't get the imaging because of a patient's weight, and we are concerned about a pulmonary embolism or appendicitis, for example, we have to go ahead and treat based on our clinical impression," says Archana Reddy, MD, a Chicago-area ER physician.

A Big, Eat Health Insurance Problem

Need to lose weight? That's not going to make your insurance company happy. If ou're overweight or obese it probably costs them more. Even if you're in an employer's health insurance plan, you may all have to pay higher premiums if there are overweight people in the office filing more health claims.

But the real challenge is for those women who are trying to get private insurance—finding affordable health coverage can be difficult, if not impossible, if you're overweight. Rules vary by insurance company. But, in general, heavier women are likely to take a financial hit. For instance, a woman who is 5 feet 4 inches tall and has no other health problems will likely need a medical exam and pay higher premiums if she weighs more than around 180 or 190 pounds says John Barrett of Health Insurance Brokers in Pasadena, California. Rates may range from 20 to 100 percent higher, depending on the carrier. And if that 5 foot 4 woman weighs more than around 220? She could be automatically declined coverage.

Women who try to lose weight don't get much help, either. "Weight counseling and early preventive treatment of obesity aren't covered by many plans," says John Wilder Baker, MD, president of the American Society for Metabolic and Bariatric Surgery. And insurance plans often won't cover bariatric surgery or other obesity treatments.

Being overweight can get in the way of effective cancer treatment, too, experts say. The problem: underdosing. "Oncologists usually base chemo on patients' ideal weight rather than their true weight, partly because chemo is so toxic and partly because drug trials typically include only average women, so we don't know the correct dose for bigger women," says Kellie Schneider, MD, a gynecologic oncologist at the University of Alabama at Birmingham. "But underdosing can mean the difference between life and death."

Doctors have long known that obese women are more likely to die of ovarian and breast cancers, but when Dr. Schneider and her colleagues recently gave a group of overweight ovarian cancer patients chemotherapy based on their *actual* weights, they found that the women were as likely to survive the illness as thinner patients. "Doctors aren't intentionally under-treating overweight women," Dr. Schneider says. "We're just working with limited information."

Why Heavy Patients Can't Find Help

There are no studies on how often doctors refuse to treat patients because of their weight. But Sondra Solovay, an Oakland, California, attorney and author of *Tipping the Scales of*

Justice: Fighting Weight-Based Discrimination, says she hears enough anecdotes to believe it's commonplace.

Because of recent studies about various complications, A.J. Yates Jr., MD, associate professor in the Department of Orthopaedic Surgery at the University of Pittsburgh Medical Center, says there are legitimate concerns about operating on patients with a very high body mass index (BMI). But Dr. Yates also notes that some surgeons are reluctant to offer surgery to very overweight patients because the operations are more difficult and time-consuming.

And because data on surgical-complication rates is often calculated without accounting for the higher risk of an obese patient, even a few patients with complications can make the surgeon or hospital look bad to insurance companies. "If hospitals feel they're not looking good they could put subtle pressure on surgeons to avoid risky patients," Dr. Yates says. His concern is that overweight people could be increasingly discriminated against because of this.

Suzy Smith, a 5-foot-3, 400-pound woman from Colonial Beach, Virginia, believes she was one of those people. When her doctor found a large tumor on her kidney, she struggled to find a surgeon who would treat her. Her urologist said that the hospital where he practiced didn't have a table sturdy enough to hold her, and he referred her to a surgeon several hours away. "As soon as that doctor walked in the room, I could tell something was wrong by the look on his face," she says. "He told me he wouldn't operate. He wouldn't risk it," she says. Instead, he offered her cryoablation—a technique that freezes and removes tissue but is less effective than surgery for large tumors.

"I was so shocked," Smith says. "He was basically telling me he wouldn't do the thing that was the most likely to save my life." Finally, in early-December 2008, a doctor removed the tumor. The surgery, after all the preceding drama, was anticlimactic. "It went fantastically well," Smith says. "My doctors were really pleased." But the overall experience, she says, was degrading and disheartening. "Here I was trying to deal with a diagnosis of cancer, worrying that the cancer might spread with every day that went by, and the medical field was closing doors on me left and right."

Infertile couples who are told they can't have in vitro fertilization (IVF) because of the woman's weight also feel doors shutting. Most fertility clinics have stringent rules. "I'd say 95 percent won't do IVF on a woman with a BMI higher than 39 [5-foot-4, weighing 228 pounds, for example], and they usually require an electrocardiogram (EKG) and blood tests if it's higher than 34, because being overweight reduces your chance of getting pregnant and having a healthy pregnancy," says Laurence Jacobs, MD, of Fertility Centers of Illinois. In most cases, he can't accept a patient with a BMI of 40, even if she has no other health issues, because IVF typically takes place in an outpatient setting that's not set up for the higher anesthesia risks associated with obese patients. "No anesthesiologist is going to take that risk for someone who's not willing to make the effort to lose weight," Dr. Jacobs says.

Even more worrisome, a study from Duke University found that obese patients were less likely to receive procedures like cardiac catheterization that can help diagnose and treat heart

How to Get the Care You Deserve

Here, ways women can speak out for better care and more respectful treatment—and get the help they need to reach a healthier weight:

- **Find a physician who isn't fatphobic.** Ask for referrals from heavier friends. Doctors who have struggled with their own weight may be more understanding.
- **Take a friend with you.** "A clinician is much less likely to treat someone badly when there's a witness," says Pat Lyons, RN, co-developer of *A Big Woman's Passport to Best Health,* a guide to overcoming barriers to health care.
- **Be your own advocate.** Have your doc run your numbers so you have all of your measures of health, from body mass index (BMI) to cholesterol and blood sugar. Ask for an assessment of your health based on the big picture.
- **Ask for tools.** Tell your doctor you're interested in sustainable health habits, like walking and eating right. Request a reasonable healthy weight and BMI range so you have goal.
- **Dig deeper.** If you've tried and tried and still can't lose weight, insist that your doc give you more help. For some people there's a medical reason for weight gain that goes beyond lifestyle choices, including medications or conditions that might cause weight gain. "We're trying to educate doctors so they provide obese women with more sensitive and in-depth care," says Keith Bachman, MD, a weight-management expert with Kaiser Permanente's Care Management Institute. The goal: to help doctors see the whole patient and look for all the possible causes of weight gain.
- **Stick to your symptoms.** During your visit say, "Here are the symptoms I'm concerned about. I know some health problems can be caused by weight, but I'd like you to focus on the symptoms I'm here to see you about."
- **Get the doctor you deserve.** If you feel your doctor isn't giving you the kind of care you deserve, find a new one. "When I asked physicians what they would do if they perceived a negative attitude from their doctor, each one said he or she would find another doctor," says Harvard's Jerome Groopman, MD. It's your right to do the same.

disease, perhaps because doctors are concerned about potential complications, says lead author William Yancy Jr., MD, an associate professor at Duke and a staff physician at the VA Medical Center in Durham, North Carolina. Because of the high risk of heart disease in obese patients, the benefits of catheterization may outweigh the risks, he says. "But if the tests aren't performed, heavy patients may not receive appropriate therapy."

Even organ transplants may be withheld because of weight. Patients with BMIs higher than 35—if you're, say, 5 feet

4 inches tall and weigh 205 pounds—are typically less likely to be given a kidney or liver transplant because of the increased risk of postsurgery complications, including infections, blood clots, and pneumonia.

"It's a very difficult issue," says Shawn Pelletier, MD, surgical director of liver transplants at the University of Michigan Health System in Ann Arbor. "We have an obligation to use donor organs in a responsible way. But this is lifesaving surgery, and we don't want to turn people away. Obese kidney-transplant patients may not survive as long as thinner patients, but they live an average of three times longer than if they didn't get the transplant. That's a big benefit, even if there are risks."

Many experts believe the issue goes beyond the strictly medical and into the arena of ethics. "Doctors need to ask themselves, 'Is this obese person less deserving of medical care than the same person would be after weight-loss surgery?'" says Barbara Thompson, vice-chair of the Obesity Action Coalition, a nonprofit advocacy group. "How do we determine whether a person's weight somehow justifies withholding needed medical care or whether bias by providers is the reason treatment is denied?" Yale's Rebecca Puhl asks. "It's an extremely important question with significant implications."

Fat People Get No Respect

When Celina Reeder, a 5-foot-5, 185-pound woman with a torn ligament in her right knee, was told by her surgeon she needed to stop eating so much fast food before he would schedule surgery, the Woodacre, California, woman was astounded. "I left his office feeling ashamed," she recalls. "And I don't even eat fast food! The more I thought about it, the madder I got. So I switched surgeons. Anybody who thinks doctors treat heavy women the same as thin women has obviously never had a weight problem. I really felt like my doctor didn't respect me."

She may have been right. University of Pennsylvania researchers found that more than 50 percent of primary care physicians viewed obese patients as awkward, unattractive, and noncompliant; one third said they were weak-willed, sloppy, and lazy. In addition, researchers at Rice University and the University of Texas School of Public Health in Houston found that as patient BMI increased doctors reported liking their jobs less and having less patience and desire to help the patient.

Whether they know it or not, doctors' attitudes may actually encourage unhealthy behavior. Feeling dissed about their weight can make some women turn to food for comfort. "Stigma is a form of stress, and many obese women cope by eating or refusing to diet," Puhl says. "So weight bias could actually fuel obesity."

Studies have also found that overweight women are more likely to delay doctors' appointments and preventive care, including screenings for cancer, because they don't want to face criticism. "It can be frustrating to treat obese patients,"

admits Lee Green, MD, MPH, a professor of family medicine at the University of Michigan in Ann Arbor. "I spend most of my time treating the consequences of unhealthy lifestyles instead of actual illnesses. People come in complaining of foot or knee pain, and I'm thinking, *Do you not see that you're in pain because you're 60 pounds overweight?* I don't say that, of course. I try to encourage them to lose weight."

Seeing heavy patients was *a waste of time*, doctors admitted in one survey.

Dr. Green seems to be in the minority when it comes to focusing on weight-loss solutions. One study found that just 11 percent of overweight patients received weight-loss counseling when they visited a family-practice doctor.

A Healthy-Weight Wakeup Call

Without a doubt, the medical community needs to take a hard look at the secret biases that may be coloring how they care for overweight women. But some progress is being made. The National Institutes of Health has been encouraging researchers to start identifying and fixing the barriers heavy people face when trying to get health care, says Susan Yanovski, MD, co-director of the Office of Obesity Research at the National Institute of Diabetes and Digestive and Kidney Diseases. And some hospitals are adding larger surgical instruments, wheelchairs, and other equipment.

There's an even bigger problem, though: when heavy women are ignored, the obesity epidemic is ignored, too—and that has to stop, experts say. "Being mistreated or dismissed by your doctor because of your weight is unacceptable. But what's just as important is that doctors are missing an opportunity to help their patients lose weight and improve their health," says Dr. Huizinga of Johns Hopkins. "Doctors and patients need to be able to speak openly about weight-related issues, whether it's the diseases caused by excess weight or the reasons why a patient overeats. That level of conversation requires a certain degree of comfort, and the basis for that is mutual respect, plain and simple," she says. "That's how we can help *all* women get healthier."

Assess Your Progress

1. Why are overweight women less likely to receive quality health care?
2. How can being overweight affect your health insurance?
3. How can a doctor's attitude encourage unhealthy behavior?

UNIT 10

Contemporary Health Hazards

Unit Selections

Learning Outcomes

After reading this unit, you should be able to:

- Describe the government's efforts to reduce the risk of food poison.

- Explain the risks associated with the 'choking game.'

- Explain the health impact of chemicals in plastic water bottles.

- Explain why manufacturers continue to use bisphenol A (BPA) despite the potential health concerns.

- Contrast chronic and acute AIDS.

- Discuss reasons why some people continue to engage in high risk behaviors that increase their susceptibility to contracting HIV.

- Explain the risks associated with contracting MRSA.

- Discuss who is most likely to contract MRSA.

- Describe the diseases that are most likely to have an environmental link.

- Discuss the health risks which typically occur after an earthquake.

- Describe the health challenges Haitians faced after the 2010 earthquake.

Student Website

www.mhhe.com/cls

Internet References

Centers for Disease Control: Flu
www.cdc.gov/flu
Environmental Protection Agency
www.epa.gov
World Health Organization
www.who.org

This unit examines a variety of health hazards that Americans face on a daily basis and includes topics ranging from environmental health issues to newly emerging or, rather, reemerging infectious illnesses. During the 1970s and 1980s, Americans became deeply concerned about environmental changes that affected the air, water, and food we take in. While some improvements have been observed in these areas, much remains to be done, as new areas of concern continue to emerge.

Global warming is responsible for climatic changes, including an increase in the number of weather disasters such as hurricanes and other natural disasters. In "Post-Earthquake Public Health in Haiti," author Stan Deresinski addresses the serious health concerns that remain in that country following a deadly earthquake in early 2010.

We face newly recognized diseases such as methicillin-resistant *Staphlococcus aureus,* Avian Flu, Severe Acute Respiratory Syndrome (SARS), AIDS, West Nile virus, and mad cow disease. Some diseases may have their causes rooted in environmental factors. Author Zach Patton discusses the changes in the way AIDS is treated and perceived in "HIV Apathy." In "Methicillin-Resistant *Staphlococcus aureus,*" author Priya Sampathkumar takes a look at the growing health problem related to this drug-resistant bacterial infection. It is a particular concern among the institutionalized elderly and in any place where many people are in close contact with each other. A more common infection is treated by Glenn Davidson, who describes a recent outbreak of salmonella infections linked to peanut butter in "When Government Makes Us Sick."

Pauline Chen describes a rising, but less well-known health concern in "Discovering Teenagers' Risky 'Game' Too Late." Kids playing "the choking game" in order to get high strangle themselves until just before they lose consciousness, typically using a noose. Programs have been started to educate doctors about the warning signs associated with this activity and its sometimes lethal consequences.

Another area of concern has to do with the potential health danger of bisphenol A, an issue addressed by Valerie Jablow in "Chemical in Plastic Bottles Fuels Science, Concern-and Litigation."

While this unit focuses on exogenous factors that influence our state of health, it is important to remember that health is a dynamic state representing the degree of harmony or balance that exists between endogenous and exogenous factors. This

© Thinkstock/PunchStock

concept of balance applies to the environment as well. Due to the intimate relationship that exists between people, animals, and their environment, it is impossible to promote the concept of wellness without also safeguarding the quality of our environment, both the physical and the social.

When Government Makes Us Sick

GLENN DAVIDSON

Like many Americans, I pick up an energy bar from time to time without giving a moment's thought to my safety before eating it. Earlier this year, that choice hit me with a case of **salmonella** poisoning. Across the country, the outbreak caused by tainted **peanuts** plunged hundreds of young and elderly people into medical trauma and tragically led to nine deaths.

I confidently consume processed food products—as do millions of other Americans—because I assume that regulators, especially the Food and Drug Administration, are on the case ensuring our safety.

Yet FDA failed miserably to protect the public in the case of **salmonella**-laced peanut products, and it wasn't the first or only instance. The public has a right to know what FDA knew about the Georgia peanut plant that was responsible, how far back the agency knew it, and why officials didn't take immediate action to shut down the entire chain of contaminated products that went to market from the plant at the first warning sign.

FDA is making the case that the manufacturer is to blame, and there's no doubt that the company is primarily at fault. But can we accept FDA's conclusion that food safety in the United States is a matter of industry self-policing? If private industry had a strong track record of compliance and FDA had a record of challenging internal tests or punishing companies that abuse the system, maybe then such a system could be defended.

But FDA's recent record on food and consumer product safety is dismal:

A peer-reviewed report (www.ehjournal.net/content/8/1/2) in the journal *Environmental Health* found that high fructose corn syrup is commonly tainted with trace levels of mercury. The lead author of the study, Renee Dufault, was an FDA researcher who was aware of the results in 2005, then went public after retiring from the agency in 2008.

Researchers at the University of Rochester in New York say in a study (www.ehponline.org/members/2009/0800376/0800376 .pdf) released in January that bisphenol A, which is used to make plastic and suspected of causing cancer, stays in the body much longer than previously thought. In 2008, FDA declared the chemical safe for all use in an assessment that contained language from reports written on behalf of chemical-makers or others with a financial stake in BPA.

According to a Jan. 23 article (www.govexec.com/dailyfed/ 0109/012309cdam2.htm) by Government Executive.com's sister publication *CongressDaily,* "Earlier this month, a group of FDA scientists wrote to President Obama's transition team a letter similar to one they sent Rep. John Dingell, D-Mich., in October claiming FDA brass interferes with the medical-device review process to push through approvals based on faulty and unethical evidence."

It's no wonder the Government Accountability Office recently put FDA on its high-risk list, noting the agency's regulatory scope has expanded while resources to conduct that mission have not kept pace. There's no question FDA's mission should be reviewed and, when appropriate, get more funding to fulfill it.

But there are other important questions that go beyond agency funding levels. Why weren't food safety experts empowered to act on reports of problems at the Georgia peanut factories in real time? Why were the reports of respected scientists ignored in the instance of high fructose corn syrup? Why were industry groups allowed to write public safety reports on BPA? And why were political appointees interfering with a scientific review process about medical devices?

All these examples support a chilling similarity of failure—every one of them resulting from the federal government's broken human capital management system, which isn't merely wasting taxpayer dollars, but also is putting the health and safety of Americans at risk every day.

If only these problems were confined to FDA, we could sweep out its system and replace it with that of a better performing agency. Unfortunately, there are no examples of better performing government agencies, only more examples of failure—from the Federal Emergency Management Agency's tragic incompetence in New Orleans to NASA's ignored red flags before the space shuttle Columbia disaster to collapsed bridges, poorly explained prescription drug programs and financial systems run amok. The list goes on in today's newspapers.

The Bush administration's command-and-control approach to governance is largely responsible for the sad state of federal management. The White House persistently pushed its agenda down to departments and agencies rather than involving people in the decision-making process or creating market forces that help drive decisions. All management improvement initiatives were led centrally, resulting in a backlash among the rank and file.

This is the federal government President Obama has inherited. New marching orders and higher morale are good things, and a larger federal workforce probably is a necessity. But if the president doesn't act quickly to overhaul the way people are managed in all agencies, change the culture and change it fast, everything he tries to do—from health care reform to energy independence projects—could be imperiled.

Only the Office of Personnel Management has the governmentwide scope to deal with these issues in a comprehensive and continuous manner. OPM must become, at all levels and in all ways, part of the larger human resources community. While public sector HR management poses distinct challenges, it overlaps far more with the broader world of HR management than many in the public sector acknowledge or practice. OPM should stop being insular and isolated and come to understand what's going on in the public and private sectors.

By focusing on getting the most out of its workforce, the federal government would make major, long-overdue investments in effective government. Good, cost-effective government starts with staying out of the news and making what Americans expect to be routine, routine again.

All Americans ask is that the next time we pick up a piece of peanut butter candy or drink from a plastic container, please, no surprises.

Assess Your Progress

1. What has the government done to reduce the risks of food poisoning?
2. What steps need to be taken to ensure the safety of our food? Explain.

GLENN DAVIDSON is managing director of EquaTerra's public sector practice, serving federal, state and local government clients. In the public sector he was chief of staff for former Virginia Gov. L. Douglas Wilder and legislative director for former Ohio Congressman Ron Mottl.

Discovering Teenagers' Risky 'Game' Too Late

Pauline W. Chen, MD

The patient was tall, with legs that extended to the very end of the operating table, a chest barely wider than his 16-year-old hips and a chin covered with pimples and peach fuzz.

He looked like any number of boys I knew in high school, I reflected. And then the other transplant surgeons and I began the operation to remove the dead boy's liver, kidneys, pancreas, lungs and heart.

We knew the organs would be perfect. He had been a healthy teenager, and the cause of death was not a terrible, mutilating car or motorcycle crash.

The boy had hanged himself. He had been discovered early, though not early enough to have survived.

While I had operated on more than a few suicide victims, I had never come across someone so young who had chosen to die in this way. I asked one of the nurses who had spent time with the family about the circumstances. Was he depressed? Had anyone ever suspected? Who found him?

"He was playing the choking game," she said quietly.

I stopped what I was doing and, not believing I had heard correctly, turned to look straight at her.

"You know that game where kids try to get high," she explained. "They strangle themselves until just before they lose consciousness." She put her hand on the boy's arm and continued: "Problem was that this poor kid couldn't wiggle out of the noose he had made for himself. His parents found him hanging by his belt on his bedroom doorknob."

That image comes rushing back whenever I meet another victim or read about the grim mortality statistics associated with this "game." But one thing has haunted me even more in the years since that night. As a doctor who counts adolescents among her patients, I knew nothing about the choking game before I cared for a child who had died playing it.

Some try strangulation in the hopes of attaining a legal high.

Until recently, there has been little attention among health care professionals to this particular form of youthful thrill-seeking. What has been known, however, is that those ages 7 to 21 participate in such activities alone or in groups, holding their breath, strangling one another or dangling in a noose in the hopes of attaining a legal high.

Two years ago the Centers for Disease Control and Prevention reported 82 deaths attributable to the choking game and related activities. This year the C.D.C. released the results of the first statewide survey and found that 1 in 3 eighth graders in Oregon had heard of the game, while more than 1 in 20 had participated.

The popularity of the choking game may be due in part to the misguided belief that it is safe. In one recent study, almost half of the youths surveyed believed there was no risk associated with the game. And unlike other risk-taking behaviors like alcohol or drug abuse, where doctors and parents can counsel teenagers on the dangers involved, no one is countering this gross misperception regarding the safety of near strangulation.

Why? Because like me that night in the operating room, many of my colleagues have no clue that such a game even exists.

This month in the journal Pediatrics, researchers from the Rainbow Babies and Children's Hospital in Cleveland reported that almost a third of physicians surveyed were unaware of the choking game. These physicians could not describe any of the 11 warning signs, which include bloodshot eyes and frequent and often severe headaches. And they failed to identify any of the 10 alternative names for the choking game, startlingly benign monikers like "Rush," "Space Monkey," "Purple Dragon" and "Funky Chicken."

"Doctors have a unique opportunity to see and prevent this," the senior author of the study, Dr. Nancy E. Bass, an associate professor of pediatrics and neurology at Case Western Reserve University, said in an interview. "But how are they going to educate parents and patients if they don't know about it?"

In situations where a patient may be contemplating or already participating in choking activities, frank discussions about the warning signs can be particularly powerful. "The sad thing about these cases," Dr. Bass observed, "is that every parent says, 'If we had known what to look for, we probably could have prevented this.'" One set of parents told Dr. Bass that they had noticed knotted scarves and ties on a closet rod in their son's room weeks before his death.

"They had the telltale signs," Dr. Bass said, "but they never knew what to look for."

Broaching the topic can be difficult for parents and doctors alike. Some parents worry that talking about such activities will paradoxically encourage adolescents to participate. "But that's kind of a naïve thought," Dr. Bass countered. "Children can go to the Internet and YouTube to learn about the choking game." In another study published last year, for example, Canadian researchers found 65 videos of the choking game on YouTube over an 11-day period. The videos showed various techniques of strangulation and were viewed almost 175,000 times. But, added Dr. Bass, "these videos don't say that kids can die from doing this."

Few doctors discuss these types of activities with their adolescent patients. Only two doctors in Dr. Bass's study reported ever having tackled the topic because of a lack of time. "Talking about difficult topics is really hard to do," Dr. Bass noted, "when you just have 15 minutes to follow up."

But it is even harder when neither doctor nor patient has any idea of what the activity is or of its lethal consequences.

Based on the results of their study, Dr. Bass and her co-investigators have started programs that educate doctors, particularly those in training, about the warning signs and dangers of strangulation activities. "The choking game may not be as prominent as some of the other topics we cover when we talk with patients," Dr. Bass said, "but it results in death.

"If we don't talk to doctors about this issue, they won't know about the choking game until one of their patients dies."

Assess Your Progress

1. Describe the risks associated with the 'choking game.'
2. What are some of the warning signs of strangulation activities, and what can be done to prevent adolescents from participating in them?

Chemical in Plastic Bottles Fuels Science, Concern—and Litigation

VALERIE JABLOW

A common chemical denominator in the stuff of modern life—helmets, CDs, baby bottles, sunglasses, cell phones, can coatings, and dental sealants—is the focus of increasing scientific and legislative scrutiny, as well as lawsuits. More than 20 cases have been filed, mostly since April, against manufacturers and sellers of baby and water bottles containing bisphenol A (BPA).

BPA, studied in the 1930s as an estrogen mimic, came into commercial use in the 1950s after scientists discovered that it could make clear, hard, yet not easily breakable plastic compounds called polycarbonates. These plastics, along with epoxy resin can linings containing BPA, have become ubiquitous in food uses, where they are prized for their durability. Today, more than 6 billion pounds of BPA is produced each year; the United States alone accounts for more than a third of worldwide production.

But BPA's association with food has attracted controversy. Although the FDA had maintained that the chemical did not leach out of containers made with it, in 1999 scientists began using more sensitive testing techniques, allowing them to measure very low levels of BPA.

Studies since then have measured the chemical in a variety of human tissues, including placenta, cord blood, fetal blood, and urine. The Centers for Disease Control and Prevention (CDC) found that nearly 93 percent of people tested had measurable levels of BPA in their urine, with children having the highest levels.

The Centers for Disease Control and Prevention found that nearly 93 percent of people tested had measurable levels of BPA in their urine, with children having the highest levels.

Scientists believe that most human exposure comes from diet, through the leaching of BPA from can linings and polycarbonate water bottles and baby bottles. Researchers have shown that leaching occurs at a higher rate when the bottles are heated, such as for warming milk or formula or for hot-water washing or sterilizing of baby bottles.

All of which may be cause for concern—depending on who you talk to.

In testimony before the House Subcommittee on Commerce, Trade, and Consumer Protection on June 10, Marian Stanley, senior director of the American Chemistry Council, a trade group for the plastics industry, concluded a presentation of BPA studies by noting that "no restriction on [BPA's] uses in current applications is warranted at this time." Stanley said studies showing low-dose effects of BPA in animals were "unvalidated."

But in April, a draft report on BPA by the National Toxicology Program (NTP) noted that such low doses produce in fetal and young animals changes in "behavior and the brain, prostate gland, mammary gland, and the age at which females attain puberty." Because those low doses are similar to human exposure levels, the report raised "some concern for neural and behavioral effects in fetuses, infants, and children at current human exposures" and "some concern" about how BPA exposure in young children might affect their prostate and mammary glands and the onset of puberty in females.

The NTP—a joint program of agencies within the FDA, CDC, and National Institutes of Health—concluded that "the possibility that bisphenol A may alter human development cannot be dismissed."

The NTP draft came in the wake of more than 150 low-dose BPA studies in animals showing harmful effects ranging from cancer to genital malformations to early puberty. Other studies found high levels of the chemical in human amniotic fluid and showed that fetuses cannot metabolize BPA.

After the NTP issued the draft report, Sen. Charles Schumer (D-N.Y.) proposed legislation banning BPA in children's products, and Reps. John Dingell (D-Mich.) and Bart Stupak (D-Mich.) asked four infant formula makers to stop using the chemical in their packaging. In June, Rep. Edward Markey (D-Mass.) proposed legislation to prohibit the use of BPA in all food and beverage containers.

Several polycarbonate bottle manufacturers, including Playtex and Nalgene, have said they will use alternatives to BPA, and Wal-Mart and Toys "R" Us are in the process of pulling BPA-containing items for babies from store shelves. The California senate in May passed a bill to ban BPA from food or beverage containers for children younger than three.

The FDA, which regulates containers that come into contact with food, is not yet raising alarm bells. Norris Alderson, an associate commissioner for science at the agency, testified at the June congressional hearing that the FDA is reviewing the use of BPA in food containers, but that currently it is satisfied that "exposure levels to BPA from these materials . . . are below those that may cause health effects."

The FDA has been criticized for relying on two studies, both funded by the chemical industry, to arrive at this conclusion. Dingell and Stupak are investigating that connection.

Class Actions

Lawsuits against the makers of polycarbonate baby bottles and covered "sippy" cups for toddlers (including Gerber, Avent, and Playtex) have been filed in several states, including Arkansas, California, Connecticut, Illinois, Kansas, Missouri, and Washington. Most have been filed in federal court and claim that the sale of products containing BPA violates various state consumer protection acts. None of the claims allege personal injury.

Other claims include breach of express and implied warranties, defective design, failure to warn, false and misleading advertising, fraudulent concealment, intentional and negligent misrepresentation, unfair and deceptive business practices, and unjust enrichment. The cases seek reimbursement to consumers who bought the products, in addition to punitive and actual damages.

Although most of the BPA lawsuits emerged earlier this year, the first—a California class action against makers and retailers of plastic baby bottles and cups—was filed in 2007. (*Ganjei v. Ralphs*, No. 367732 (Cal., Los Angeles Co. Super. filed Mar. 12, 2007).) The lead plaintiffs are five children with varying disorders—including congenital genital injury, attention deficit hyperactivity disorder, premature puberty, and Down syndrome—who used polycarbonate baby bottles and cups. Although the complaint does not say that BPA caused the children's disabilities, it alleges that most of their conditions are associated with exposure to BPA.

Stephen Murakami, a Jericho, New York, lawyer who is handling the class action, said proving specific causation is not yet possible. But, he noted, "the primary suspect group are infants and children, who are most susceptible to the dose of estrogen-like chemical [BPA] during critical times during their development. It changes them permanently. They're not equipped to handle that level of estrogen that affects their brain and sexual development."

The first class action concerning the use of BPA in water bottles was filed in April, also in California. The lead plaintiff, a mother of two daughters who also used the bottles, claims that the company violated the California Business and Professions Code by "omitting, suppressing, and withholding material information regarding the bottles' BPA-related risks," according to the complaint. (*Felix-Lozano v. Nalge Nunc Intl. Corp.*, No. 08-cv-854 (E.D. Cal. filed Apr. 22, 2008).)

The defendant, Nalge Nunc International, notes on its website that it believes that its water bottles containing BPA "are safe for their intended use." Meanwhile, the company is phasing out the use of the chemical in its bottles because of consumer requests for alternative materials, it says.

In May, a group of plaintiff attorneys asked the district court in the Northern District of Illinois to consolidate 13 similar class actions filed in seven federal districts. One of the lawyers, Scott Poynter of Little Rock, Arkansas, noted that the classes would be hard to certify if they included personal injury claims.

Cause and Effect

Causation—and BPA's effects in humans—is a point of frequent debate. In 1987, the EPA said a BPA exposure level of 50 micrograms per kilogram per day (micrograms/kg/day) was safe in humans, based on animal experiments then available showing that 1,000 times that amount in rodents caused weight loss.

Today, the BPA level known to cause birth defects in pregnant mice is 2.4 micrograms/kg/day. But the level in humans that is harmful remains uncertain and contentious, in large part because few human studies have been conducted.

And some studies have reached different conclusions about human and animal harm from BPA. Why the disparity? A 2005 review of many studies found that one factor may be the researchers' funding source. In 94 of 104 published studies on BPA funded by the government, researchers found that doses of less than 50 milligrams/kg/day had significant effects. But none of 11 industry-funded studies found significant effects at those doses.

Almost everyone involved in the issue agrees that further study of BPA in humans is needed. Meanwhile, the chemical's ubiquity will likely continue to cause powerful clashes. For instance, attempts to pass or enact legislation banning BPA in Maryland, Minnesota, and San Francisco have failed. The plastics industry even sued San Francisco when it attempted to enact its ban.

Some BPA critics say the industry's reach affects official government statements on the chemical as well. In 2007, the Center for the Evaluation of Risks to Human Reproduction, part of NTP, assembled a nonexpert panel to look at 500 BPA studies. But the company hired to compile the data was also doing work for Dow Chemical, a BPA maker.

Although the company was fired from the project, the panel concluded that most people were safe because exposure levels were below those set by the government. (It did note some concern for BPA in young children and fetuses.)

Then, in June, the NTP draft report on BPA underwent peer review by the program's Board of Scientific Counselors, made up of 19 researchers from academia, pharmaceutical companies, and biological research firms. One board member works for Dow Chemical, and all are appointed by the secretary of the Department of Health and Human Services.

The board voted to lower the concern expressed in the NTP draft—from "some concern" to "minimal concern"—for BPA's effects on young children's mammary glands and puberty onset in females. The NTP's final report is due at the end of the summer.

Assess Your Progress

1. What are the risks associated with exposure to bisphenol A in plastic water bottles?

2. Why do water bottle manufacturers continue to use bisphenol A in their products?

HIV Apathy

New drugs have changed HIV from a terminal to a chronic illness. To counter complacency, health officials are pushing to make testing more widespread.

Zach Patton

On a rainy day last June, local officials in Washington, D.C., gathered under tents erected on a public plaza to be tested for HIV. The District of Columbia's health department was kicking off a sweeping new effort to encourage city residents to take action against the disease. With banners, music and mobile-testing units, officials hoped the launch event and the campaign would help raise local awareness about HIV—and help the city address its most pressing health concern.

Washington has the nation's highest rate of new AIDS cases, and the city's goal—HIV testing for every resident between the ages of 14 and 84, totaling over 400,000 people—was unprecedented in its scope. City officials said the campaign, which also included distributing an initial 80,000 HIV tests to doctors' offices, hospitals and health clinics, would enable them to get a better idea of how many residents are infected with HIV. And making such screenings routine, they hoped, would help erase the stigma against getting tested for the disease.

Six months later, though, the effort was faltering. Fewer than 20,000 people had been tested. Many of the HIV test kits expired before they were distributed, forcing the city to throw them away. Others were donated to the Maryland health department to use before they went bad. And the city still lacked a comprehensive plan for ensuring effective treatment for those residents who test positive for the disease.

It's not all bad news. The District nearly tripled the number of sites offering free HIV screenings, and the Department of Corrections began screening all inmates for HIV. And the city improved its disease-surveillance technique, recording information on behaviors and lifestyles, in addition to counting the number of new HIV cases.

But D.C.'s struggle to meet its goals underscores a challenge common to local health officials across the country. More than a million U.S. residents are infected with HIV, and one-quarter of them don't know it, experts estimate. Diagnosis rates of HIV have stabilized in recent years, but large cities continue to grapple with much higher rates. They're dealing with higher incidents of the risky behaviors—drug use and unprotected sex, particularly gay sex—that tend to spread the disease. But they're also trying to battle something less tangible: complacency. Antiretroviral drugs have largely changed HIV from a terminal illness into a chronic one. And the fears associated with AIDS have faded over the past

20 years. As health officials work to combat HIV, they're finding that their hardest fight is the one against apathy.

Testing Laws

The first test for the human immunodeficiency virus was licensed by the FDA in March 1985. It was quickly put into use by blood banks, health departments and clinics across the country. But HIV testing at that time faced some major obstacles, which would continue to thwart HIV policies for much of the following two decades. For one, it usually took two weeks to obtain lab results, requiring multiple visits for patients waiting to see if they had HIV. Many patients—in some places, as many as half—never returned for the second visit. Another barrier was that, at the time, a diagnosis of the disease was a death sentence. With no reliable drugs to slow the progression of HIV into AIDS, and with an attendant stigma that could decimate a person's life, many people just didn't want to know if they were HIV-positive. "The impact of disclosure of someone's HIV-positive status could cost them their job, their apartment and their social circle," says Dr. Adam Karpati, assistant commissioner for HIV/AIDS Prevention & Control for the New York City health department. "In a basic calculus, the value to the patient was questionable. Knowing their status could only maybe help them, but it could definitely hurt them."

Because of that stigma and the seriousness of a positive diagnosis, many cities and states developed rigorous measures to ensure that testing was voluntary and confidential, and that it included a full discussion of the risks associated with the disease. That meant requiring written consent in order to perform tests, and mandatory pre- and post-test counseling. "A lot of the laws were, appropriately, concerned with confidentiality and protecting people's rights," Karpati says.

Two major developments have since changed the method—and the purpose—of HIV testing. First, the development of antiretroviral drugs in the mid-1990s has lessened the impact of HIV as a fatal disease. And in the past two or three years, advancements in testing technology have effectively eliminated the wait time for receiving results. Rapid tests using a finger-prick or an oral swab can be completed in 20 minutes, meaning nearly everyone can receive results within a single visit.

Those changes, along with aggressive counseling and education about risk-prevention measures, helped stabilize the rate of HIV diagnosis. After peaking in 1992, rates of AIDS cases leveled off by 1998. Today, about 40,000 AIDS cases are diagnosed every year. Data on non-AIDS HIV infection rates are much harder to come by, but they seem to have stabilized as well.

The problem, however, remains especially acute in urban areas. While health experts take pains to stress that HIV/AIDS is no longer just a "big city" problem, the fact is that 85 percent of the nation's HIV infections have been in metropolitan areas with more than half a million people. "Urban areas have always been the most heavily impacted by the HIV epidemic, and they continue to be," says Jennifer Ruth of the Centers for Disease Control and Prevention. Intravenous drug use, risky sexual behavior and homosexual sex all contribute to higher HIV rates, and they are all more prevalent in urban areas. But cities face other complicating factors as well, including high poverty rates and residents with a lack of access to medical care, which exacerbate the challenges of HIV care.

Prevention Fatigue

Nowhere is that more evident than in Washington, D.C., where an estimated one in every 20 residents is HIV-positive. That's 10 times the national average. But that figure is only a rough guess. The truth is that health officials don't even know what the city's HIV rate is. Last year's campaign was supposed to change that. By setting a goal to test nearly all city residents, District health officials hoped to make HIV screening a routine part of medical care. In the process, the health department hoped it could finally get a handle on just how bad the crisis was. "We've had problems in the past, I'll be the first to say," says D.C. health department director Dr. Gregg A. Pane. "But we have galvanized interest and action, and we've highlighted the problem in a way it hasn't been before."

The effort stumbled, though. The Appleseed Center for Law and Justice, a local public advocacy group, has issued periodic report cards grading the District's progress on HIV. The most recent assessment, published six months into last year's testing push, found mismanagement and a lack of coordination with the medical community. The District was testing substantially more people than it had been, but the number was still falling far short of officials' goal. "D.C. took a great step forward, but it takes more than just a report announcing it," says Walter Smith, executive director for the Appleseed Center. "You have to make sure there's a plan."

What D.C. did achieve, however, was a fundamental shift in the way health officials perceive the HIV epidemic. "This is a disease that affects everyone," says Pane. "It's our No. 1 public health threat, and treating it like a public health threat is the exact right thing to do."

That paradigm change has been happening in health departments across the country. Last year, the CDC made waves when it announced new recommendations for treating HIV as an issue of public health. That means testing as many people as possible, making HIV testing a routine part of medical care, and removing the barriers to getting tested. Washington was the first city to adopt the CDC's recommendations for comprehensive testing, but other cities have also moved to make testing more routine. San Francisco health officials dropped their written-consent and mandatory-counseling requirements for those about to be tested. New York City has been moving in a similar direction, although removing the written-consent rule there will require changing state law. Many health officials think that since testing has become so easy and social attitudes about the disease have shifted, the strict testing regulations adopted in the 1980s are now cumbersome. The protections have become barriers.

Officials also are moving away from "risk-assessment testing," in which doctors first try to identify whether a patient falls into a predetermined high-risk category. "What has evolved is that, with an epidemic, risk-based testing is not sufficient," says New York City's Karpati. "Now there's a general move toward comprehensive testing." Privacy advocates and many AIDS activists oppose the shift away from individual protections. Yes, the stigma isn't what it used to be, they say, but it still exists. HIV isn't like tuberculosis or the measles, so they believe health officials shouldn't treat it like it is.

But even if officials could strike the perfect balance between public health and private protection, there's another factor that everyone agrees is thwarting cities' efforts to combat HIV. Call it burnout or complacency or "prevention fatigue." In an age when testing consists of an oral swab and a 20-minute wait, and an HIV-positive diagnosis means taking a few pills a day, health officials are battling a growing sense of apathy toward the disease. "The very successes we've made in the past 20 years have hurt us, in a sense," Karpati says. "We don't have hospital wards full of HIV patients. We don't have people dying as much. There's a whole new generation of folks growing up who don't remember the fear of the crisis in the 1980s."

That casual attitude toward the disease can lead to riskier behavior and, in turn, more infections. With HIV and AIDS disproportionately affecting low-income residents, any increase in infections places an additional burden on governments. And while prescription drugs have made the disease more manageable, the fact is that 40 percent of the new HIV diagnoses in the nation are still made within a year of the infection's progressing to AIDS—which is usually too late for medicine to do much good. As cities try to fight HIV complacency through refined testing policies and a focus on comprehensive testing, residents will have increasingly widespread access to tests for the disease. But for health officials, the greatest challenge will be getting the right people to care.

Assess Your Progress

1. Distinguish between chronic and acute AIDS.
2. Why do some individuals continue to engage in risky behaviors that increase their chance of contracting HIV?

ZACH PATTON can be reached at zpatton@governing.com.

Methicillin-Resistant *Staphylococcus aureus*

The Latest Health Scare

PRIYA SAMPATHKUMAR

For decades, methicillin-resistant *Staphylococcus aureus* (MRSA) has been the most commonly identified multidrug-resistant pathogen in many parts of the world, including the United States. Recently, it has become the focus of intense media attention. Some of this attention stems from a recent article in the *Journal of the American Medical Association* that provided estimates of MRSA infections annually in the United States.[1] (The occurrence of the word "staph" increased by 10-fold in the 2 weeks after this report.[2]) In addition, both health care safety initiatives (eg, Joint Commission National Patient Safety Goals, Institute for Healthcare Improvement) and consumer groups (eg, American Association of Retired Persons, StopHospitalInfection.org) have begun calling for hospitals to do more to reduce MRSA infections. Legislation related to hospital infections, including measures targeting MRSA control and public reporting of MRSA infections, is being introduced in many states and at the federal level.[3-5] Finally, increasing reports of MRSA occurring in community settings, eg, day care centers, schools, and sports teams, along with several reports of deaths in previously healthy children and young adults, have also prompted fears that we are now facing a new "superbug."

Historical Background

Staphylococcus aureus is one of the most successful and adaptable human pathogens. Its remarkable ability to acquire antibiotic resistance has contributed to its emergence as an important pathogen in a variety of settings. In the preantibiotic era, *S aureus* infections were associated with very high mortality. When penicillin was first introduced in the early 1940s, much of its success was in the treatment of *S aureus* bloodstream infections. However, as early as 1942 the first strains of penicillin-resistant *S aureus* were detected in hospitals (Table 1). These subsequently spread into the community; by 1960, most *S aureus* strains both in hospitals and in the community were resistant to penicillin. Shortly after the introduction in 1959 of methicillin, a semisynthetic penicillin, resistance to it emerged; the first hospital outbreak of MRSA was reported in 1963.[6] Initially spreading widely in Europe, India, and Australia, MRSA strains were detected in the United States in the late 1960s.[7] By the 1980s, MRSA had become firmly established in US hospitals, and rates of MRSA infection have since continued to increase. In large US hospitals, MRSA rates (the proportion of all *S aureus* isolates that are MRSA) increased from 4% in the 1980s to 50% in the late 1990s. According to National Nosocomial Infections Surveillance data, the increase in MRSA rates in intensive care units was even greater, reaching 60% in 2003.[8]

Nosocomial MRSA is remarkable for its clonal pattern of spread. Currently, 5 major MRSA clones account for approximately 70% of MRSA isolates in hospitals in the United States, South America, and Europe. The major cause of this clonal spread is infection control lapses by health care professionals. The traditional risk factors for MRSA acquisition include previous hospitalization, antibiotic use, residence in long-term care facilities, and long-term hemodialysis. Increasing use of vancomycin to treat MRSA led to the emergence of *S aureus* with intermediate resistance to vancomycin (VISA) and then vancomycin-resistant *S aureus* (VRSA) in the 1990s.[9, 10] Fortunately, VISA and VRSA infections have been sporadic, and intense infection control measures have ensured that they did not circulate widely in health care settings.

In the early 1980s, several instances of community-onset MRSA were reported in the upper Midwest. Because many of these early cases involved intravenous drug users or people with serious underlying disease, it was thought that the infections were acquired during contact with health care personnel. However, in the 1990s serious MRSA infections were reported in patients with no prior contact with the health care system, heralding the onset of community-acquired MRSA (CA-MRSA) outbreaks. The seriousness of CA-MRSA was highlighted by a report in 1999 of 4 deaths in children infected with CA-MRSA in Minnesota and South Dakota.[11] Since then, many reports have described CA-MRSA infections, particularly in children, and CA-MRSA is a growing problem worldwide. Clusters of CA-MRSA have been reported in correctional facilities,[12] professional sports teams,[13] high school athletes,[14] day care centers,[15] healthy newborns,[16] military personnel,[17, 18] and tattoo recipients.[19] The term "health care-acquired MRSA" (HA-MRSA) has been used to differentiate the earlier hospital strains of MRSA from these newer CA-MRSA strains.

Differences between HA-MRSA and CA-MRSA

A review article by Kowalski et al[20] contrasted the features of CA-MRSA and HA-MRSA. To summarize, HA-MRSA and CA-MRSA strains carry different types of the gene complex known as staphylococcal chromosome cassette mec (SCC mec), which contains the mecA gene that confers methicillin resistance. Health care-acquired MRSA strains carry SCC mec types I, II, and III and tend to be multidrug resistant. They typically cause bloodstream and postoperative wound infections along with nosocomial pneumonia in hospitalized patients.

In contrast, CA-MRSA strains carry SCC mec types IV and V and usually cause skin and soft tissue infections in community-dwelling children and adults. The most common clinical presentations are furuncles, superficial abscesses, and boils that are often mistakenly attributed

Table 1 Timeline of *Staphylococcus aureus* Infection and Resistance

Year	Event
1940	Penicillin introduced
1942	Penicillin-resistant *Staphylococcus aureus* appears
1959	Methicillin introduced; most *S aureus* strains in both hospital and community settings are penicillin resistant
1961	Methicillin-resistant *S aureus* appears
1963	First hospital outbreak of methicillin-resistant *S aureus* (MRSA)
1968	First MRSA strain in US hospitals
1970s	Clonal spread of MRSA globally, very high MRSA rates in Europe
1982	4% MRSA rate in the United States
1980s, early 1990s	Dramatic decreases in MRSA rates due to search-and-destroy programs in Northern Europe
	By 1999, <1% MRSA rate in the Netherlands; that rate has been sustained to date despite increasing MRSA rates in other parts of the world
1996	Vancomycin-resistant *S aureus* (VRSA) reported in Japan
1997	Approximately 25% MRSA rate in US hospitals; vancomycin use increases; vancomycin-intermediate *S aureus* (VISA) appears; serious community-acquired MRSA (CA-MRSA) infections reported; pediatric deaths reported
2002	First clinical infection with VRSA in the United States
2003	MRSA rates continue to increase; approximately 60% MRSA rate in intensive care units; outbreaks of CA-MRSA (predominantly USA 300 clone) reported in numerous community settings and also implicated in hospital outbreaks
2006	>50% of staphylococcal skin infections seen in emergency departments caused by CA-MRSA
	HA-MRSA rate continues to increase
	Distinction between HA-MRSA and CA-MRSA on epidemiological basis becomes increasingly difficult
2007	"The Year of MRSA?"
	Report of active, population-based surveillance for invasive MRSA done in 2004–2005 estimates 95,000 invasive MRSA infections and 19,000 deaths from MRSA per year
	Continued reports in the medical literature and the lay press about severe CA-MRSA infections
	Several states pass or are considering legislation regarding control of MRSA and public reporting of MRSA rates
	Strategies to control MRSA, including public reporting of MRSA infections, are hotly debated; "staph" and MRSA become household words

to spider bites. Like HA-MRSA, CA-MRSA also spreads clonally, and the USA 300 clone is the predominant strain circulating in the United States.[21] Although resistant to methicillin and other β-lactam antibiotics (eg, penicillin, cephalosporins, carbapenems), CA-MRSA often remains sensitive to many other classes of antibiotics, including trimethoprim-sulfamethoxazole and tetracyclines. Resistance to macrolides, clindamycin, and fluoroquinolones varies by region. In addition to skin infections, cases of severe necrotizing pneumonia (including postinfluenza pneumonia) and necrotizing fasciitis caused by CA-MRSA have been described.[22, 23] Many cases of necrotizing pneumonia and some soft tissue infections have been characterized by rapid progression to septic shock and death. Most CA-MRSA strains carry the Panton-Valentine leukocidin gene. This gene could play a role in the pathogenesis of more severe infection, especially pneumonia.[24] Community-acquired MRSA strains are also associated with production of other toxins, such as staphylococcal enterotoxin A, B, C, and H, which are capable of causing illness resembling toxic shock syndrome in animal models[25,26] and could play a role in severe human infections.

The epidemiological differences between these strains are becoming increasingly blurred. Community-acquired MRSA strains are making their way into health care settings, and several outbreaks of nosocomial infections with these strains have been reported.[27–30] They are also becoming increasingly drug resistant[31] and are spreading rapidly within defined populations and in select geographical regions, particularly in large urban centers. In some metro-politan areas, CA-MRSA accounts for as high as 80% of all *S aureus* infections seen in emergency departments.[21]

Prevalence of *S aureus* and MRSA

Staphylococcus aureus is a common colonizer of the skin and the nose. A 2001–2002 population-based study in the United States showed that the prevalence of nasal colonization with *S aureus* and with MRSA was 31.6% and 0.84%, respectively,[32] meaning that there are approximately 2.3 million MRSA-colonized people in the United States. Women, people older than 65 years, those with diabetes mellitus, or those who have been in long-term care in the preceding year are more likely to be colonized with MRSA. Two nasal *S aureus* carriage patterns can be distinguished: persistent and intermittent. The density of *S aureus* in the nose is highest in persistent carriers, as is its colonization of other body sites, including the hands, axillae, and perineal regions.

Although the relationship between colonization and infection is not completely understood, both are associated with intrinsic host factors, as well as the strain of *S aureus*. Nasal colonization with *S aureus* is a risk factor for subsequent infection. Both higher rates of *S aureus* nasal carriage and subsequent higher rates of infection have been associated with many underlying diseases or conditions, including insulin-dependent diabetes mellitus, long-term dialysis, intravenous drug abuse, repeated injections for allergies, liver cirrhosis, liver transplant, human immuno-deficiency virus infection, and hospitalization. Also correlated with higher *S aureus* infection rates are activities leading to skin lesions such as contact sports. The common factor between these conditions seems to be the repeated violation of the skin or mucosa as anatomical barriers.

Impact of MRSA

Patients colonized with MRSA are more likely to develop infections than patients colonized with methicillin-sensitive *S aureus* (MSSA).[33] Methicillin-resistant *S aureus* infections lengthen hospital stays (by an average of 10 days) and are associated with a 2.5-fold higher mortality rate and increased health care costs.[34, 35] A diagnosis of *S aureus* infection accounts for an estimated 292,000 hospitalizations per year in the United States.[36] In 2005, approximately 94,000 persons were diagnosed as having invasive (ie, serious) MRSA infections, an estimated 19,000 of whom died. Of these MRSA infections, 86% were health care acquired and 14% were community acquired.[1] The annual cost of treating MRSA in hospitalized patients in the United States has been estimated to be between $3.2 and $4.2 billion.[37]

Transmission and Control of MRSA

In health care settings, MRSA is transmitted from patient to patient primarily via health care professionals' hands. It can survive on surfaces for days to weeks; hence, contaminated patient care equipment can play a role in transmission.[38] The factors that promote transmission of MRSA in community settings have been called the *5 Cs* and are summarized in Table 2. Although the strategies to control HA-MRSA and true CA-MRSA share many features, they differ in some respects. Rates of infection with both these organisms can be reduced by good antibiotic stewardship, which will prevent the selection of MRSA from among a population of *S aureus*. Good hand hygiene practices will limit person-to-person transmission and decrease the pool of persons who are colonized. In health care settings, active surveillance cultures to identify patients with MRSA, contact precautions (use of gown and gloves while caring for these patients), and good environmental cleaning have been proposed as additional strategies to limit MRSA transmission[39, 40] In selected patients, decolonization could help reduce infection. However, widespread use of decolonization is not recommended because it is expensive, its benefit is usually short lived (most patients become recolonized during the next few months), and it carries the risk of promoting resistance to agents, such as mupirocin, that are used in decolonizing regimens.

Table 2 Factors Associated with Community-Acquired Methicillin-Resistant *Staphylococcus aureus* Transmission (The *5 Cs*)

- Crowded living conditions
- Frequent skin-to-skin Contact
- Compromised skin
- Sharing Contaminated personal items such as towels and razors
- Lack of Cleanliness

In July 2004, Mayo Clinic Rochester expanded its MRSA control program. In addition to isolating patients known to be carriers of MRSA and electronically flagging their records so that isolation procedures could be reinstituted on readmission, staff members began to screen high-risk patients for MRSA and preemptively isolated them until negative culture results were obtained. In the 36 months after institution of this program, rates of MRSA rates decreased by 25% (ie, from 42% to 29% of *S aureus* isolates) (unpublished data). Several Scandinavian countries have reduced MRSA infection rates to less than 2% through intensive infection control programs and have successfully maintained these low rates over the past several years.[41, 42]

Physicians can help control the spread of CA-MRSA in communities by encouraging hand hygiene, maintaining a high degree of suspicion for MRSA as an etiologic agent when treating skin and soft tissue infections, knowing local rates of CA-MRSA (public health departments might be able to provide these data), emphasizing the importance of hygiene to patients with MRSA, and discouraging the sharing of personal items such as towels and razors. Draining lesions should be kept covered, and return to team sports should be limited until the lesion has healed or can be adequately covered. Flu shots (especially in children) could be helpful in reducing the risk of postinfluenza bacterial pneumonia with MRSA.

Treatment Options

Selection of initial antibiotic regimens should be guided by the local prevalence of MRSA, the presence of health care-associated risk factors, and the severity and type of clinical presentation. For severe infections, intravenous vancomycin should be included in initial empiric therapy. Microbiological data and antibiotic susceptibility testing should be used to guide subsequent therapy. First approved in 1958, vancomycin became standard therapy for MRSA in the 1960s. Its advantages include its good safety profile, the long experience with its use, and its relatively infrequent dosing regimen. Disadvantages include the need for intravenous administration and monitoring of levels in critically ill patients and in those with changing renal function. In addition, the molecule is large, limiting its penetration into tissues. Recently, there have been reports of vancomycin failure due to either relative vancomycin resistance or MRSA infections in sites that have poor vancomycin penetration.[43, 44]

Overall, vancomycin remains standard treatment for MRSA; however, some alternatives have recently received Food and Drug Administration approval and could be good options in selected patients, including linezolid (a synthetic oxazolidinone), tigecycline (a derivative of minocycline), and daptomycin (a cyclic lipopeptide). Daptomycin should be avoided in the treatment of MRSA-associated pneumonia because it is inactivated by pulmonary surfactant. Additional agents that appear promising include dalbavancin, a semisynthetic lipoglycopeptide that can be dosed once a week, and ceftobiprole, an investigational cephalosporin.

For soft tissue CA-MRSA infections, surgical drainage is crucial, with antibiotics serving as adjunctive therapy. Severe infections should be managed with intravenous antibiotics as aforementioned. Oral antibiotics can be used for less severe infections in the outpatient setting. For initial empiric therapy, oral trimethoprim-sulfamethoxazole is a good choice. Other alternatives include minocycline, clindamycin, or a macrolide antibiotic, depending on local susceptibility patterns.

In summary, MRSA is a growing public health problem. Initially, it was feared that HA-MRSA, long a cause of health care-associated infections, would escape into community settings. Instead, in the past few years, CA-MRSA strains that are genetically different from HA-MRSA have appeared, are now circulating widely in many communities, and are causing a wide variety of infections, ranging from minor skin infections to rapidly progressive, life-threatening ones. Ironically, these more virulent CA-MRSA strains have been imported from the community into health care settings and have been responsible for outbreaks of infections in hospitals. Infection control measures have been successful in limiting the spread of MRSA in many parts of the world, and most hospitals in the United States are increasing MRSA control activities to improve patient safety and quality of care.

Currently, the health care industry is under increasing scrutiny by both the public and governmental agencies. Medicare and other groups have threatened not to reimburse for hospital-acquired infections. Legislation is being considered or has already been passed in some states mandating the reporting of health care-acquired infection rates and separate reporting of MRSA rates. The spread of MRSA and other drug-resistant organisms can be limited by infection control measures. It is time that we, as health care professionals, incorporate proven infection control measures such as hand hygiene and the use of appropriate personal protective equipment (gowns and gloves) into our daily patient care routines. The next influenza pandemic might or might not happen in our lifetime. The MRSA pandemic is here.

Notes

1. Klevens RM, Morrison MA, Nadle J, et al, Active Bacterial Core surveillance (ABCs) MRSA Investigators. Invasive methicillin-resistant *Staphylococcus aureus* infections in the United States. *JAMA.* 2007;298(15): 1763–1771.

2. Pitts L Jr. Media fall victim to the journalism of fear. LJWorld. com. November 5, 2007. Available at: http://www2.ljworld. com/news/2007/nov/05/media_fall_victim_journalism_fear/. Accessed November 7, 2007.

3. Staph outbreak prompts legislation. *Chicago Tribune.* October 29, 2007. Available at: www.chicagotribune.com/news/local/ chi-durbinoct29,0,6847984.story?coll=chi_tab01_ layout. Accessed November 7, 2007.

4. Hester T. NJ law requires hospitals to report infections. *The Philadelphia Inquirer.* November 1, 2007. Available at: www. philly.com/inquirer/health_science/daily/20071101_N_J__ law_requires_hospitals_to_report_infections.html. Accessed November 7, 2007.

5. Gormley M. States consider new laws to fight spread of staph infections. *Press and Sun Bulletin*, Greater Binghampton, NY. October 27, 2007. Available at: http://forums.pressconnects.com/ viewtopic.php?t=11922. Accessed November 7, 2007.

6. Stewart GT, Holt RJ. Evolution of natural resistance to the newer penicillins. *Br Med J.* 1963; 1(5326):308–311.

7. Barrett FF, McGehee RFJr, Finland M. Methicillin-resistant *Staphylococcus aureus* at Boston City Hospital: bacteriologic and epidemiologic observations. *N Engl J Med.* 1968;279(9):441–448.

8. National Nosocomial Infections Surveillance (NNIS) System Report, data summary from January 1992 through June 2004, issued October 2004. *Am J Infect Control.* 2004;32(8):470–485.

9. Centers for Disease Control and Prevention (CDC). Update: *Staphylococcus aureus* with reduced susceptibility to vancomycin—United States, 1997 [published correction appears in *MMWR Morb Mortal Wkly Rep.* 1997;46(35):851]. *MMWR Morb Mortal Wkly Rep.* 1997;46(35):813–815.

10. Centers for Disease Control and Prevention (CDC). *Staphylococcus aureus* resistant to vancomycin—United States, 2002. *MMWR Morb Mortal Wkly Rep.* 2002;51(26):565–567.

11. Centers for Disease Control and Prevention (CDC). Four pediatric deaths from community-acquired methicillin-resistant *Staphylococcus aureus*—Minnesota and North Dakota, 1997–1999. *JAMA.* 1999;282(12):1123–1125.

12. Centers for Disease Control and Prevention (CDC). Methicillin-resistant *Staphylococcus aureus* infections in correctional facilities—Georgia, California, and Texas, 2001–2003. *MMWR Morb Mortal Wkly Rep.* 2003;52(41):992–996.

13. Kazakova SV, Hageman JC, Matava M, et al. A clone of methicillin-resistant *Staphylococcus aureus* among professional football players. *N Engl J Med.* 2005;352(5):468–475.

14. Lindenmayer JM, Schoenfeld S, O'Grady R, Carney JK. Methicillin-resistant *Staphylococcus aureus* in a high school wrestling team and the surrounding community. *Arch Intern Med.* 1998;158(8):895–899.

15. Jensen JU, Jensen ET, Larsen AR, et al. Control of a methicillin-resistant *Staphylococcus aureus* (MRSA) outbreak in a day-care institution. *J Hosp Infect.* 2006 May;63(1):84–92. Epub 2006 Mar 15.

16. Centers for Disease Control and Prevention (CDC). Community-associated methicillin-resistant *Staphylococcus aureus* infection among healthy newborns—Chicago and Los Angeles County, 2004. *MMWR Morb Mortal Wkly Rep.* 2006;55(12):329–332.

17. Beilman GJ, Sandifer G, Skarda D, et al. Emerging infections with community-associated methicillin-resistant *Staphylococcus aureus* in outpatients at an Army Community Hospital. *Surg Infect (Larchmt).* 2005 Spring;6(1):87–92.

18. Pagac BB, Reiland RW, Bolesh DT, Swanson DL. Skin lesions in barracks: consider community-acquired methicillin-resistant *Staphylococcus aureus* infection instead of spider bites. *Mil Med.* 2006;171(9):830–832.

19. Centers for Disease Control and Prevention (CDC). Methicillin-resistant *Staphylococcus aureus* skin infections among tattoo recipients—Ohio, Kentucky, and Vermont, 2004–2005. *MMWR Morb Mortal Wkly Rep.* 2006;55(24):677–679.

20. Kowalski TJ, Berbari EF, Osmon Dr. Epidemiology, treatment, and prevention of community-acquired methicillin-resistant *Staphylococcus aureus* infections. *Mayo Clin Proc.* 2005;80(9):1201–1208.

21. King MD, Humphrey BJ, Wang YF, Kourbatova EV, Ray SM, Blumberg HM. Emergence of community-acquired methicillin-resistant *Staphylococcus aureus* USA 300 clone as the predominant cause of skin and soft-tissue infections. *Ann Intern Med.* 2006;144(5):309–317.

22. Centers for Disease Control and Prevention (CDC). Severe methicillin-resistant *Staphylococcus aureus* community-acquired pneumonia associated with influenza—Louisiana and Georgia, December 2006—January 2007. *MMWR Morb Mortal Wkly Rep.* 2007;56(14):325–329.

23. Miller LG, Perdreau-Remington F, Rieg G, et al. Necrotizing fasciitis caused by community-associated methicillin-resistant *Staphylococcus aureus* in Los Angeles. *N Engl J Med.* 2005;352(14):1445–1453.

24. Labandeira-Rey M, Couzon F, Boisset S, et al. *Staphylococcus aureus* Panton-Valentine leukocidin causes necrotizing pneumonia. *Science.* 2007 Feb 23;315(5815): 1130–1133. Epub 2007 Jan 18.

25. McCollister BD, Kreiswirth BN, Novick RP, Schlievert PM. Production of toxic shock syndrome-like illness in rabbits by *Staphylococcus aureus* D4508: association with enterotoxin A. *Infect Immun.* 1990;58(7):2067–2070.

26. Omoe K, Ishikawa M, Shimoda Y, Hu DL, Ueda S, Shinagawa K. Detection of *seg, seh*, and *sei* genes in *Staphylococcus aureus* isolates and determination of the enterotoxin productivities of *S. aureus* isolates harboring *seg, seh,* or *sei* genes. *J Clin Microbiol.* 2002;40(3):857–862.

27. David MD, Kearns AM, Gossain S, Ganner M, Holmes A. Community-associated methicillin-resistant *Staphylococcus aureus*: nosocomial transmission in a neonatal unit. *J Hosp Infect.* 2006 Nov;64(3):244–250. Epub 2006 Aug 22.

28. Davis SL, Rybak MJ, Amjad M, Kaatz GW, McKinnon PS. Characteristics of patients with healthcare-associated infection due to SCCmec type IV methicillin-resistant *Staphylococcus aureus*. *Infect Control Hosp Epidemiol.* 2006 Oct;27(10): 1025–1031. Epub 2006 Sep 19.

29. Schramm GE, Johnson JA, Doherty JA, Micek ST, Kollef MH. Increasing incidence of sterile-site infections due to non-multidrug-resistant, oxacillin-resistant *Staphylococcus aureus* among hospitalized patients. *Infect Control Hosp Epidemiol.* 2007 Jan;28(1):95–97. Epub 2006 Dec 20.

30. Seybold U, Kourbatova EV, Johnson JG, et al. Emergence of community-associated methicillin-resistant *Staphylococcus aureus* USA300 genotype as a major cause of health care-associated blood stream infections. *Clin Infect Dis.* 2006 Mar 1; 42(5):647–656. Epub 2006 Jan 25.

31. Han LL, McDougal LK, Gorwitz RJ, et al. High frequencies of clindamycin and tetracycline resistance in methicillin-resistant *Staphylococcus aureus* pulsed-field type USA300 isolates collected at a Boston ambulatory health center. *J Clin Microbiol.* 2007 Apr;45(4):1350–1352. Epub 2007 Feb 7.

32. Graham PL III, Lin SX, Larson EL. A US population-based survey of *Staphylococcus aureus* colonization. *Ann Intern Med.* 2006;144(5):318–325.

33. Huang SS, Platt R. Risk of methicillin-resistant *Staphylococcus aureus* infection after previous infection or colonization. *Clin Infect Dis.* 2003 Feb 1;36(3):281–285. Epub 2003 Jan 17.

34. Shurland S, Zhan M, Bradham DD, Roghmann MC. Comparison of mortality risk associated with bacteremia due to methicillin-resistant and methicillin-susceptible *Staphylococcus aureus*. *Infect Control Hosp Epidemiol.* 2007 Mar;28(3): 273–279. Epub 2007 Feb 15.

35. Selvey LA, Whitby M, Johnson B. Nosocomial methicillin-resistant *Staphylococcus aureus* bacteremia: is it any worse than nosocomial methicillin-sensitive *Staphylococcus aureus* bacteremia? *Infect Control Hosp Epidemiol.* 2000;21(10): 645–648.

36. Kuehnert MJ, Hill HA, Kupronis BA, Tokars JI, Solomon SL, Jernigan DB. Methicillin-resistant-*Staphylococcus aureus* hospitalizations, United States [published correction appears in *Emerg Infect Dis.* 2006;12(9):1472]. *Emerg Infect Dis.* 2005;11(6):868–872.

37. Association for Professionals in Infection Control and Epidemiology, Inc (APIC). Guide to the elimination of methicillin-resistant *Staphylococcus aureus* (MRSA) transmission in hospital settings, March 2007. Available at: www.apic.org/Content/NavigationMenu/GovernmentAdvocacy/MethicillinResistantStaphylococcusAureusMRSA/Resources/MRSAguide.pdf. Accessed November 8, 2007.

38. Huang SS, Datta R, Platt R. Risk of acquiring antibiotic-resistant bacteria from prior room occupants. *Arch Intern Med.* 2006;166(18):1945–1951.

39. Siegel JD, Rhinehart E, Jackson M, Chiarello L, Healthcare Infection Control Practices Advisory Committee. Guideline for isolation precautions: preventing transmission of infectious agents in healthcare settings 2007. Available at: www.cdc.gov/ncidod/dhqp/gl_isolation.html. Accessed November 8, 2007.

40. Siegel JD, Rhinehart E, Jackson M, Chiarello L, Healthcare Infection Control Practices Advisory Committee. Management of multidrug-resistant organisms in healthcare settings, 2006. Available at: http://0-www.cdc.gov.mill1.sjlibrary.org/ncidod/dhqp/pdf/ar/mdroGuideline2006.pdf. Accessed November 8, 2007.

41. Van Trijp MJ, Melies DC, Hendriks WD, Parlevliet GA, Gommans M, Ott A. Successful control of widespread methicillin-resistant *Staphylococcus aureus* colonization and infection in a large teaching hospital in the Netherlands. *Infect Control Hosp Epidemiol.* 2007 Aug;28(8):970–975. Epub 2007 Jun 19.

42. Vos MC, Ott A, Verbrugh HA. Successful search-and-destroy policy for methicillin-resistant *Staphylococcus aureus* in The Netherlands [letter]. *J Clin Microbiol.* 2005;43(4):2034.

43. Jones RN. Microbiological features of vancomycin in the 21st century: minimum inhibitory concentration creep, bactericidal/static activity, and applied breakpoints to predict clinical outcomes or detect resistant strains. *Clin Infect Dis.* 2006;42(suppl 1):S13–S24.

44. Wang G, Hindler JF, Ward KW, Bruckner DA. Increased vancomycin MICs for *Staphylococcus aureus* clinical isolates from a university hospital during a 5-year period. *J Clin Microbiol.* 2006 Nov;44(11):3883–3886. Epub 2006 Sep 6.

Assess Your Progress

1. What are the risks associated with contracting MRSA?

2. Who is most at risk of contracting MRSA?

Address correspondence to Priya Sampathkumar, MD, Division of Infectious Diseases, Mayo Clinic, 200 First St SW, Rochester, MN 55905 (sampathkumar.priya@mayo.edu).

Post-Earthquake Public Health in Haiti

At a depth of 13 km, and just 25 km from Port-Au-Prince, Haiti, a fault system along the boundary separating the North American and Caribbean plates abruptly experienced a rapid acceleration of its usual super-slow motion lateral strike slip faulting. On January 12, 2009, at 16:53 local time, the result was the devastation of portions of the western third of the island of Hispaniola by an earthquake of magnitude 7.0 on the Richter scale. This was not the first earthquake to strike Haiti—Port-Au-Prince was largely destroyed by one in 1770—but it appears to be the strongest recorded. It has been estimated that the number of deaths directly resulting from the event exceeds 50,000, perhaps by many tens of thousands. The injured must be dealt with and the population provided water and food. The conditions created by the devastation, particularly in a country that some considered a disaster before the earthquake, will produce a colossal public health challenge. WHO has posted a preliminary statement aimed at facilitating the response to the challenges presented by this calamity.

STAN DERESINSKI

Haiti, with a 2007 population of 9.7 million, is the poorest country in the Western Hemisphere, with 55% of households earning less than one U.S. dollar a day. Before the earthquake, 45% of the population lacked access to safe water and 83% lacked access to adequate sanitation. Most health care is provided by traditional healers. Malnutrition is commonplace, and multiple infectious diseases, including HIV and tuberculosis, are endemic. Vaccination rates are inadequate (see Table 1).

Traumatic injuries, including crushes and burns, are common after earthquakes. These obviously necessitate the availability of surgical facilities and intensive care—which will require evacuation to medical facilities in other countries. These will also result in infections, including gangrenous ones. The limited vaccination coverage of the population makes tetanus an important risk, as was seen in Aceh after its tsunami. The injuries and infections, as well as the lack of drinking water in a hot tropical climate, will lead to many cases of acute renal failure, necessitating dialysis.

The lack of safe drinking water is not likely to be solved by rain since, during the winter dry season, there are only an average of three days with measurable rainfall, yielding a total of 32 mm in the month of January. Water that is available is often not safe, putting the population at risk of water-borne diseases, such as typhoid, hepatitis A, and hepatitis E. Leptospirosis is endemic in Haiti but, fortunately, cholera is not. Polio has been eliminated from Haiti.

Resettlement of displaced individuals to camps often results in crowding (although crowding in urban Haiti existed already), with resultant transmission of a number of respiratory infections, including measles, diphtheria, pertussis, and a variety of

Table 1 Vaccine Coverage at One Year of Age, 2007

Antigen	Coverage
BCG	75%
DPT, 3rd dose	53%
Measles	58%
Polio, 3rd dose	52%

respiratory viral infections. Of note, is that pandemic influenza A (H1N1) 2009 is currently circulating in Haiti. Meningococcal disease also may spread under these conditions. Of great concern in conditions of crowding is tuberculosis, which, in 2007, had an incidence of 147 cases per 100,000 population. Approximately 4,000 patients were receiving treatment for tuberculosis in Port-Au-Prince at the time of the earthquake. Many with tuberculosis are coinfected with HIV.

Vector-borne diseases also may pose a risk, especially with the population abandoning their homes for fear of aftershocks and living in the streets. West Nile virus has been detected in Haiti. All four dengue types are endemic in Haiti, where transmission mainly occurs during April through November. Malaria, however, is transmitted year round throughout the country. Only *Plasmodium falciparum* is present; it has been considered to always be susceptible to chloroquine, and failures of treatment with this drug have not been reported. However, mutations in the *pfcrt* gene associated with chloroquine resistance were recently identified in some isolates obtained in the

Artibonite Valley.[1] Lymphatic filariasis is common. Zoonoses of concern include leptospirosis and rabies. A program of mass rabies vaccination of dogs was in progress at the time of the earthquake.

WHO has enunciated a set of priority interventions for immediate implementation (see Table 2).

An element to consider with regard to essential emergent medical and surgical care is appropriate triage. Contaminated or infected wounds or those present for more than six hours should not be closed. Patients with wounds should be given tetanus prophylaxis. Standard infection control precautions should be maintained. Post-exposure prophylaxis should be available for health care, rescue, and other workers. Protection of the blood supply must be maintained. Measures must be taken to prevent interruption of treatment of patients with tuberculosis, HIV, and chronic non-infectious diseases, such as diabetes mellitus. Provisions for mental health and psychosocial support must be made available.

Measles vaccination is an immediate priority for children aged 6 months to 14 years living in crowded or camp settings, regardless of previous vaccination or disease history. Supplementation with vitamin A should be administered to children six months through 59 months of age. Mass tetanus vaccination is not indicated. Hepatitis A vaccination can be considered, and typhoid vaccination may be useful for control of outbreaks.

Large numbers of medical and other workers are entering Haiti to provide relief services. Guidance regarding personal measures for individuals planning on volunteering are addressed in this WHO document, but a more extensive set of recommendations has been posted by CDC.[2]

A medical correspondent on CNN warned of the danger of unburied corpses. As it has indicated before, WHO states, "It is important to convey to all parties that corpses do not represent

Table 2 Immediate Priorities

- Ensuring access to surgical, medical and emergency obstetric care and proper case management, particularly trauma, wound, and burn care
- Shelter and site planning
- Provision of sufficient and safe water and sanitation
- Priority immunizations, including for measles
- Communicable disease surveillance and response, including outbreak

a public health threat. When death is due to the initial impact of the event and not because of disease, dead bodies have not been associated with outbreaks. Standard infection control precautions are recommended for those managing corpses."

References

1. Londono BL, et al. Chloroquine-resistant haplotype *Plasmodium falciparum* parasites, Haiti. *Emerg Infect Dis.* 2009;15:735–740.

2. CDC. Guidance for Relief Workers and Others Traveling to Haiti for Earthquake Response. http://wwwnc.cdc.gov/travel/content/news-announcements/relief-workers-haiti.aspx

Assess Your Progress

1. What are the diseases that are most likely to have an environmental link?
2. What health risks typically occur after a natural disaster?
3. What challenges did the Haitian people face after the 2010 earthquake?

Test-Your-Knowledge Form

We encourage you to photocopy and use this page as a tool to assess how the articles in *Annual Editions* expand on the information in your textbook. By reflecting on the articles you will gain enhanced text information. You can also access this useful form on a product's book support website at www.mhhe.com/cls

NAME: DATE:

_____

TITLE AND NUMBER OF ARTICLE:

_____

BRIEFLY STATE THE MAIN IDEA OF THIS ARTICLE:

_____

LIST THREE IMPORTANT FACTS THAT THE AUTHOR USES TO SUPPORT THE MAIN IDEA:

_____

WHAT INFORMATION OR IDEAS DISCUSSED IN THIS ARTICLE ARE ALSO DISCUSSED IN YOUR TEXTBOOK OR OTHER READINGS THAT YOU HAVE DONE? LIST THE TEXTBOOK CHAPTERS AND PAGE NUMBERS:

_____

LIST ANY EXAMPLES OF BIAS OR FAULTY REASONING THAT YOU FOUND IN THE ARTICLE:

_____

LIST ANY NEW TERMS/CONCEPTS THAT WERE DISCUSSED IN THE ARTICLE, AND WRITE A SHORT DEFINITION:

We Want Your Advice

ANNUAL EDITIONS revisions depend on two major opinion sources: one is our Advisory Board, listed in the front of this volume, which works with us in scanning the thousands of articles published in the public press each year; the other is you—the person actually using the book. Please help us and the users of the next edition by completing the prepaid article rating form on this page and returning it to us. Thank you for your help!

ANNUAL EDITIONS: Health 11/12

ARTICLE RATING FORM

Here is an opportunity for you to have direct input into the next revision of this volume.
We would like you to rate each of the articles listed below, using the following scale:

1. **Excellent: should definitely be retained**
2. **Above average: should probably be retained**
3. **Below average: should probably be deleted**
4. **Poor: should definitely be deleted**

Your ratings will play a vital part in the next revision.
Please mail this prepaid form to us as soon as possible.
Thanks for your help!

RATING	ARTICLE
	1. Are Bad Times Healthy?
	2. The Perils of Higher Education
	3. Mars vs. Venus: The Gender Gap in Health
	4. Carrots and Sticks, and Health Care Reform—Problems with Wellness Incentives
	5. Redefining Depression as Mere Sadness
	6. "I Can't Let Anything Go:" A Case Study with Psychological Testing of a Patient with Pathologic Hoarding
	7. Seasonal Affective Disorder
	8. Dealing with the Stressed
	9. Eating Well on a Downsized Food Budget
	10. Breastfeeding is Not Obscene
	11. An Oldie Vies for Nutrient of the Decade
	12. What Good is Breakfast?: The New Science of the Loneliest Meal
	13. A Big-Time Injury Striking Little Players' Knees
	14. The Skinny Sweepstakes
	15. Dieting on a Budget
	16. In Obesity Epidemic, What's One Cookie?
	17. Great Drug, but Does It Prolong Life?
	18. Vital Signs
	19. Drinking Too Much, Too Young
	20. A Pill Problem
	21. Helping Workers Kick the Habit
	22. Scents and Sensibility
	23. The Expectations Trap
	24. Girl or Boy?: As Fertility Technology Advances, So Does an Ethical Debate
	25. Is Pornography Adultery?

RATING	ARTICLE
	26. 'Diabesity,' a Crisis in an Expanding Country
	27. Sex, Drugs, Prisons, and HIV
	28. New Mammogram Guidelines Raise Questions
	29. Who Still Dies of AIDS and Why
	30. A Mandate in Texas: The Story of a Compulsory Vaccination and What It Means
	31. Pharmacist Refusals: A Threat to Women's Health
	32. Curbing Medical Costs
	33. Myth Diagnosis
	34. The *Case for* Killing Granny
	35. Incapacitated, Alone and Treated to Death
	36. Docs and Doctorates
	37. Vaccine Refusal, Mandatory Immunization, and the Risks of Vaccine-Preventable Diseases
	38. Medical Tourism: What You Should Know
	39. Caution: Killing Germs May Be Hazardous to Your Health
	40. Tattoos: Leaving Their Mark
	41. Hazardous Health Plans
	42. The Rough Road to *Dreamland*
	43. The *Surprising Reason* Why Heavy Isn't Healthy
	44. When Government Makes Us Sick
	45. Discovering Teenagers' Risky 'Game' Too Late
	46. Chemical in Plastic Bottles Fuels Science, Concern—and Litigation
	47. HIV Apathy
	48. Methicillin-Resistant *Staphylococcus Aureus*: The Latest Health Scare
	49. Post-Earthquake Public Health in Haiti

||||

BUSINESS REPLY MAIL
FIRST CLASS MAIL PERMIT NO. 551 DUBUQUE IA

POSTAGE WILL BE PAID BY ADDRESSEE

McGraw-Hill Contemporary Learning Series
501 BELL STREET
DUBUQUE, IA 52001

ABOUT YOU

Name _____   Date _____

Are you a teacher? ❏ A student? ❏
Your school's name _____

Department _____

Address _____ City _____ State _____ Zip _____

School telephone # _____

YOUR COMMENTS ARE IMPORTANT TO US!

Please fill in the following information:
For which course did you use this book?
_____

Did you use a text with this ANNUAL EDITION? ❏ yes ❏ no
What was the title of the text?
_____

What are your general reactions to the Annual Editions concept?
_____

Have you read any pertinent articles recently that you think should be included in the next edition? Explain.
_____

Are there any articles that you feel should be replaced in the next edition? Why?
_____

Are there any World Wide Websites that you feel should be included in the next edition? Please annotate.
_____

May we contact you for editorial input? ❏ yes ❏ no
May we quote your comments? ❏ yes ❏ no

NOTES

NOTES

NOTES

NOTES